W9-AZD-452

Expanded Edition

How People Learn

Brain, Mind, Experience, and School

Committee on Developments in the Science of Learning

John D. Bransford, Ann L. Brown, and Rodney R. Cocking, *editors*

with additional material from the

Committee on Learning Research and Educational Practice

M. Suzanne Donovan, John D. Bransford, and James W. Pellegrino, *editors*

Commission on Behavioral and Social Sciences and Education

National Research Council

NATIONAL ACADEMY PRESS
Washington, D.C.

NATIONAL ACADEMY PRESS • 2101 Constitution Avenue N.W. • Washington, D.C. 20418

NOTICE: The project that is the subject of this report was approved by the Governing Board of the National Research Council, whose members are drawn from the councils of the National Academy of Sciences, the National Academy of Engineering, and the Institute of Medicine. The members of the committee responsible for the report were chosen for their special competences and with regard for appropriate balance.

This study was supported by Grant No. R117U40001-94A between the National Academy of Sciences and the U.S. Department of Education. Any opinions, findings, conclusions, or recommendations expressed in this publication are those of the author(s) and do not necessarily reflect the view of the organizations or agencies that provided support for this project.

Library of Congress Cataloging-in-Publication Data

How people learn : brain, mind, experience, and school / John D.
Bransford ... [et al.], editors ; Committee on Developments in the
Science of Learning and Committee on Learning Research and Educational
Practice, Commission on Behavioral and Social Sciences and Education,
National Research Council.— Expanded ed.
        p. cm.
Includes bibliographical references and index.
    ISBN 0-309-07036-8 (pbk.)
    1. Learning, Psychology of. 2. Learning—Social aspects. I.
Bransford, John. II. National Research Council (U.S.). Committee on
Developments in the Science of Learning. III. National Research Council
(U.S.). Committee on Learning Research and Educational Practice. IV.
Title.
    LB1060 .H672 2000
    370.15'23—dc21
                                        00-010144

Additional copies of this report are available from:

National Academy Press
2101 Constitution Avenue, N.W.
Washington, D.C. 20418
Call 800-624-6242 or 202-334-3313 (in the Washington Metropolitan Area).

This volume is also available on line at **http://www.nap.edu**

Printed in the United States of America

THE NATIONAL ACADEMIES

National Academy of Sciences
National Academy of Engineering
Institute of Medicine
National Research Council

The **National Academy of Sciences** is a private, nonprofit, self-perpetuating society of distinguished scholars engaged in scientific and engineering research, dedicated to the furtherance of science and technology and to their use for the general welfare. Upon the authority of the charter granted to it by the Congress in 1863, the Academy has a mandate that requires it to advise the federal government on scientific and technical matters. Dr. Bruce M. Alberts is president of the National Academy of Sciences.

The **National Academy of Engineering** was established in 1964, under the charter of the National Academy of Sciences, as a parallel organization of outstanding engineers. It is autonomous in its administration and in the selection of its members, sharing with the National Academy of Sciences the responsibility for advising the federal government. The National Academy of Engineering also sponsors engineering programs aimed at meeting national needs, encourages education and research, and recognizes the superior achievements of engineers. Dr. William A. Wulf is president of the National Academy of Engineering.

The **Institute of Medicine** was established in 1970 by the National Academy of Sciences to secure the services of eminent members of appropriate professions in the examination of policy matters pertaining to the health of the public. The Institute acts under the responsibility given to the National Academy of Sciences by its congressional charter to be an adviser to the federal government and, upon its own initiative, to identify issues of medical care, research, and education. Dr. Kenneth I. Shine is president of the Institute of Medicine.

The **National Research Council** was organized by the National Academy of Sciences in 1916 to associate the broad community of science and technology with the Academy's purposes of furthering knowledge and advising the federal government. Functioning in accordance with general policies determined by the Academy, the Council has become the principal operating agency of both the National Academy of Sciences and the National Academy of Engineering in providing services to the government, the public, and the scientific and engineering communities. The Council is administered jointly by both Academies and the Institute of Medicine. Dr. Bruce M. Alberts and Dr. William A. Wulf are chairman and vice chairman, respectively, of the National Research Council.

In Memory of
Ann L. Brown
(1943-1999)
Scholar and Scientist
Champion of Children and Those Who Teach Them
Whose Vision It Was to
Bring Learning Research
into the Classroom

COMMITTEE ON DEVELOPMENTS IN THE SCIENCE OF LEARNING

JOHN D. BRANSFORD (*Cochair*), Learning Technology Center, Vanderbilt University

ANN L. BROWN *(Cochair)*, Graduate School of Education, University of California, Berkeley

JOHN R. ANDERSON, Department of Psychology, Carnegie Mellon University

ROCHEL GELMAN, Department of Psychology, University of California, Los Angeles

ROBERT GLASER, Learning Research and Development Center, University of Pittsburgh

WILLIAM T. GREENOUGH, Department of Psychology and Beckman Institute, University of Illinois, Urbana

GLORIA LADSON-BILLINGS, Department of Curriculum and Instruction, University of Wisconsin, Madison

BARBARA M. MEANS, Education and Health Division, SRI International, Menlo Park, California

JOSÉ P. MESTRE, Department of Physics and Astronomy, University of Massachusetts, Amherst

LINDA NATHAN, Boston Arts Academy, Boston, Massachusetts

ROY D. PEA, Center for Technology in Learning, SRI International, Menlo Park, California

PENELOPE L. PETERSON, School of Education and Social Policy, Northwestern University

BARBARA ROGOFF, Department of Psychology, University of California, Santa Cruz

THOMAS A. ROMBERG, National Center for Research in Mathematical Sciences Education, University of Wisconsin, Madison

SAMUEL S. WINEBURG, College of Education, University of Washington, Seattle

RODNEY R. COCKING, *Study Director*
M. JANE PHILLIPS, *Senior Project Assistant*

COMMITTEE ON LEARNING RESEARCH AND EDUCATIONAL PRACTICE

JOHN D. BRANSFORD *(Cochair),* Peabody College of Education and Human Development, Vanderbilt University

JAMES W. PELLEGRINO *(Cochair),* Peabody College of Education and Human Development, Vanderbilt University

DAVID BERLINER, Department of Education, Arizona State University, Tempe

MYRNA S. COONEY, Taft Middle School, Cedar Rapids, IA

ARTHUR EISENKRAFT, Bedford Public Schools, Bedford, NY

HERBERT P. GINSBURG, Department of Human Development, Teachers College, Columbia University

PAUL D. GOREN, John D. and Catherine T. MacArthur Foundation, Chicago

JOSÉ P. MESTRE, Department of Physics and Astronomy, University of Massachusetts, Amherst

ANNEMARIE S. PALINCSAR, School of Education, University of Michigan, Ann Arbor

ROY PEA, SRI International, Menlo Park, CA

M. SUZANNE DONOVAN, *Study Director*

WENDELL GRANT, *Senior Project Assistant*

Preface

This expanded edition of *How People Learn* is the result of the work of two committees of the Commission on Behavioral and Social Sciences and Education of the National Research Council (NRC). The original volume, published in April 1999, was the product of a 2-year study conducted by the Committee on Developments in the Science of Learning. Following its publication, a second NRC committee, the Committee on Learning Research and Educational Practice, was formed to carry that volume an essential step further by exploring the critical issue of how better to link the findings of research on the science of learning to actual practice in the classroom. The results of that effort were captured in *How People Learn: Bridging Research and Practice*, published in June 1999. The present volume draws on that report to expand on the findings, conclusions, and research agenda presented in the original volume.

During the course of these efforts, a key contributor and one of the most eloquent voices on the importance of applying the science of learning to classroom practice was lost. The educational community mourns the death of Ann L. Brown, Graduate School of Education, University of California at Berkeley, cochair of the Committee on Developments in the Science of Learning and an editor of *How People Learn*. Her insight and dedication to improving education through science will be sorely missed.

John D. Bransford, *Cochair*
Committee on Developments in the Science of Learning
Committee on Learning Research and Educational Practice

Contents

Part I
Introduction

1 Learning: From Speculation to Science   3

Part II
Learners and Learning

2 How Experts Differ from Novices   31
3 Learning and Transfer   51
4 How Children Learn   79
5 Mind and Brain   114

Part III
Teachers and Teaching

6 The Design of Learning Environments   131
7 Effective Teaching: Examples in History, Mathematics,
   and Science   155
8 Teacher Learning   190
9 Technology to Support Learning   206

Part IV
Future Directions for the
Science of Learning

10 Conclusions   233
11 Next Steps for Research   248

References   285

Biographical Sketches of Committees' Members and Staff   349

Acknowledgments   358

Index   363

I

INTRODUCTION

1

Learning:
From Speculation to Science

The essence of matter, the origins of the universe, the nature of the human mind—these are the profound questions that have engaged thinkers through the centuries. Until quite recently, understanding the mind—and the thinking and learning that the mind makes possible—has remained an elusive quest, in part because of a lack of powerful research tools. Today, the world is in the midst of an extraordinary outpouring of scientific work on the mind and brain, on the processes of thinking and learning, on the neural processes that occur during thought and learning, and on the development of competence.

The revolution in the study of the mind that has occurred in the last three or four decades has important implications for education. As we illustrate, a new theory of learning is coming into focus that leads to very different approaches to the design of curriculum, teaching, and assessment than those often found in schools today. Equally important, the growth of interdisciplinary inquiries and new kinds of scientific collaborations have begun to make the path from basic research to educational practice somewhat more visible, if not yet easy to travel. Thirty years ago, educators paid little attention to the work of cognitive scientists, and researchers in the nascent field of cognitive science worked far removed from classrooms. Today, cognitive researchers are spending more time working with teachers, testing and refining their theories in real classrooms where they can see how different settings and classroom interactions influence applications of their theories.

What is perhaps currently most striking is the variety of research approaches and techniques that have been developed and ways in which evidence from many different branches of science are beginning to converge. The story we can now tell about learning is far richer than ever before, and it promises to evolve dramatically in the next generation. For example:

- Research from cognitive psychology has increased understanding of the nature of competent performance and the principles of knowledge organization that underlie people's abilities to solve problems in a wide variety of areas, including mathematics, science, literature, social studies, and history.

- Developmental researchers have shown that young children understand a great deal about basic principles of biology and physical causality, about number, narrative, and personal intent, and that these capabilities make it possible to create innovative curricula that introduce important concepts for advanced reasoning at early ages.

- Research on learning and transfer has uncovered important principles for structuring learning experiences that enable people to use what they have learned in new settings.

- Work in social psychology, cognitive psychology, and anthropology is making clear that all learning takes place in settings that have particular sets of cultural and social norms and expectations and that these settings influence learning and transfer in powerful ways.

- Neuroscience is beginning to provide evidence for many principles of learning that have emerged from laboratory research, and it is showing how learning changes the physical structure of the brain and, with it, the functional organization of the brain.

- Collaborative studies of the design and evaluation of learning environments, among cognitive and developmental psychologists and educators, are yielding new knowledge about the nature of learning and teaching as it takes place in a variety of settings. In addition, researchers are discovering ways to learn from the "wisdom of practice" that comes from successful teachers who can share their expertise.

- Emerging technologies are leading to the development of many new opportunities to guide and enhance learning that were unimagined even a few years ago.

All of these developments in the study of learning have led to an era of new relevance of science to practice. In short, investment in basic research is paying off in practical applications. These developments in understanding of how humans learn have particular significance in light of changes in what is expected of the nation's educational systems.

In the early part of the twentieth century, education focused on the acquisition of literacy skills: simple reading, writing, and calculating. It was not the general rule for educational systems to train people to think and read critically, to express themselves clearly and persuasively, to solve complex problems in science and mathematics. Now, at the end of the century, these aspects of high literacy are required of almost everyone in order to successfully negotiate the complexities of contemporary life. The skill demands for work have increased dramatically, as has the need for organizations and workers to change in response to competitive workplace pressures. Thoughtful participation in the democratic process has also become increasingly complicated as the locus of attention has shifted from local to national and global concerns.

Above all, information and knowledge are growing at a far more rapid rate than ever before in the history of humankind. As Nobel laureate Herbert Simon wisely stated, the meaning of "knowing" has shifted from being able to remember and repeat information to being able to find and use it (Simon, 1996). More than ever, the sheer magnitude of human knowledge renders its coverage by education an impossibility; rather, the goal of education is better conceived as helping students develop the intellectual tools and learning strategies needed to acquire the knowledge that allows people to think productively about history, science and technology, social phenomena, mathematics, and the arts. Fundamental understanding about subjects, including how to frame and ask meaningful questions about various subject areas, contributes to individuals' more basic understanding of principles of learning that can assist them in becoming self-sustaining, lifelong learners.

FOCUS: PEOPLE, SCHOOLS, AND THE POTENTIAL TO LEARN

The scientific literatures on cognition, learning, development, culture, and brain are voluminous. Three organizing decisions, made fairly early in the work of the committee, provided the framework for our study and are reflected in the contents of this book.

• First, we focus primarily on research on human learning (though the study of animal learning provides important collateral information), including new developments from neuroscience.
• Second, we focus especially on learning research that has implications for the design of formal instructional environments, primarily preschools, kindergarten through high schools (K-12), and colleges.
• Third, and related to the second point, we focus on research that helps explore the possibility of helping all individuals achieve their fullest potential.

New ideas about ways to facilitate learning—and about who is most capable of learning—can powerfully affect the quality of people's lives. At different points in history, scholars have worried that formal educational environments have been better at selecting talent than developing it (see, e.g., Bloom, 1964). Many people who had difficulty in school might have prospered if the new ideas about effective instructional practices had been available. Furthermore, given new instructional practices, even those who did well in traditional educational environments might have developed skills, knowledge, and attitudes that would have significantly enhanced their achievements.

Learning research suggests that there are new ways to introduce students to traditional subjects, such as mathematics, science, history and literature, and that these new approaches make it possible for the majority of individuals to develop a deep understanding of important subject matter. This committee is especially interested in theories and data that are relevant to the development of new ways to introduce students to such traditional subjects as mathematics, science, history, and literature. There is hope that new approaches can make it possible for a majority of individuals to develop a moderate to deep understanding of important subjects.

DEVELOPMENT OF THE SCIENCE OF LEARNING

This report builds on research that began in the latter part of the nineteenth century—the time in history at which systematic attempts were made to study the human mind through scientific methods. Before then, such study was the province of philosophy and theology. Some of the most influential early work was done in Leipzig in the laboratory of Wilhelm Wundt, who with his colleagues tried to subject human consciousness to precise analysis—mainly by asking subjects to reflect on their thought processes through introspection.

By the turn of the century, a new school of behaviorism was emerging. In reaction to the subjectivity inherent in introspection, behaviorists held that the scientific study of psychology must restrict itself to the study of observable behaviors and the stimulus conditions that control them. An extremely influential article, published by John B. Watson in 1913, provides a glimpse of the behaviorist credo:

> . . . all schools of psychology except that of behaviorism claim that "consciousness" is the subject-matter of psychology. Behaviorism, on the contrary, holds that the subject matter of human psychology is the behavior or activities of the human being. Behaviorism claims that "consciousness" is neither a definable nor a useable concept; that it is merely another word for the "soul" of more ancient times. The old psychology is thus dominated by a kind of subtle religious philosophy (p. 1).

Drawing on the empiricist tradition, behaviorists conceptualized learning as a process of forming connections between stimuli and responses. Motivation to learn was assumed to be driven primarily by drives, such as hunger, and the availability of external forces, such as rewards and punishments (e.g., Thorndike, 1913; Skinner, 1950).

In a classic behaviorist study by Edward L. Thorndike (1913), hungry cats had to learn to pull a string hanging in a "puzzle box" in order for a door to open that let them escape and get food. What was involved in learning to escape in this manner? Thorndike concluded that the cats did not think about how to escape and then do it; instead, they engaged in trial-and-error behavior; see Box 1.1. Sometimes a cat in the puzzle box accidentally pulled the strings while playing and the door opened, allowing the cat to escape. But this event did not appear to produce an insight on the part of

BOX 1.1   A Cat's Learning

"When put into the box, the cat would show evident signs of discomfort and impulse to escape from confinement. It tries to squeeze through any opening; it claws and bites at the wire; it thrusts its paws out through any opening and claws at everything it reaches. . . . It does not pay very much attention to the food outside but seems simply to strive instinctively to escape from confinement. . . . The cat that is clawing all over the box in her impulsive struggle will probably claw the string or loop or button so as to open the door. And gradually all the other unsuccessful impulses will be stamped out and the particular impulse leading to the successful act will be stamped in by the resulting pleasure, until, after many trials, the cat will, when put in the box, immediately claw the button or loop in a definite way" (Thorndike, 1913:13).

the cat because, when placed in the puzzle box again, the cat did not immediately pull the string to escape. Instead, it took a number of trials for the cats to learn through trial and error. Thorndike argued that rewards (e.g., food) increased the strength of connections between stimuli and responses. The explanation of what appeared to be complex problem-solving phenomena as escaping from a complicated puzzle box could thus be explained without recourse to unobservable mental events, such as thinking.

A limitation of early behaviorism stemmed from its focus on observable stimulus conditions and the behaviors associated with those conditions. This orientation made it difficult to study such phenomena as understanding, reasoning, and thinking—phenomena that are of paramount importance for education. Over time, radical behaviorism (often called "Behaviorism with a Capital B") gave way to a more moderate form of behaviorism ("behaviorism with a small b") that preserved the scientific rigor of using behavior as data, but also allowed hypotheses about internal "mental" states when these became necessary to explain various phenomena (e.g., Hull, 1943; Spence, 1942).

In the late 1950s, the complexity of understanding humans and their environments became increasingly apparent, and a new field emerged— cognitive science. From its inception, cognitive science approached learning from a multidisciplinary perspective that included anthropology, linguistics, philosophy, developmental psychology, computer science, neuroscience, and several branches of psychology (Norman, 1980,1993; Newell and Simon, 1972). New experimental tools, methodologies, and ways of postulating theories made it possible for scientists to begin serious study of mental functioning: to test their theories rather than simply speculate about thinking and learning (see, e.g., Anderson, 1982, 1987; deGroot, 1965,1969; Newell and Simon, 1972; Ericsson and Charness, 1994), and, in recent years, to develop insights into the importance of the social and cultural contexts of learning (e.g., Cole, 1996; Lave, 1988; Lave and Wenger, 1991; Rogoff, 1990; Rogoff et al., 1993). The introduction of rigorous qualitative research methodologies have provided perspectives on learning that complement and enrich the experimental research traditions (Erickson, 1986; Hammersly and Atkinson, 1983; Heath, 1982; Lincoln and Guba, 1985; Marshall and Rossman, 1955; Miles and Huberman, 1984; Spradley, 1979).

Learning with Understanding

One of the hallmarks of the new science of learning is its emphasis on learning with understanding. Intuitively, understanding is good, but it has been difficult to study from a scientific perspective. At the same time, students often have limited opportunities to understand or make sense of topics because many curricula have emphasized memory rather than understanding. Textbooks are filled with facts that students are expected to memorize, and most tests assess students' abilities to remember the facts. When studying about veins and arteries, for example, students may be expected to remember that arteries are thicker than veins, more elastic, and carry blood from the heart; veins carry blood back to the heart. A test item for this information may look like the following:

1. Arteries
   a. Are more elastic than veins
   b. Carry blood that is pumped from the heart
   c. Are less elastic than veins
   d. Both a and b
   e. Both b and c

The new science of learning does not deny that facts are important for thinking and problem solving. Research on expertise in areas such as chess, history, science, and mathematics demonstrate that experts' abilities to think and solve problems depend strongly on a rich body of knowledge about subject matter (e.g., Chase and Simon, 1973; Chi et al., 1981; deGroot, 1965). However, the research also shows clearly that "usable knowledge" is not the same as a mere list of disconnected facts. Experts' knowledge is connected and organized around important concepts (e.g., Newton's second law of motion); it is "conditionalized" to specify the contexts in which it is applicable; it supports understanding and transfer (to other contexts) rather than only the ability to remember.

For example, people who are knowledgeable about veins and arteries know more than the facts noted above: they also understand why veins and arteries have particular properties. They know that blood pumped from the heart exits in spurts and that the elasticity of the arteries helps accommodate pressure changes. They know that blood from the heart needs to move upward (to the brain) as well as downward and that the elasticity of an artery permits it to function as a one-way valve that closes at the end of each spurt and prevents the blood from flowing backward. Because they understand relationships between the structure and function of veins and arteries, knowledgeable individuals are more likely to be able to use what they have learned to solve novel problems—to show evidence of transfer. For example, imagine being asked to design an artificial artery—would it have to be elastic? Why or why not? An understanding of reasons for the properties of arteries suggests that elasticity may not be necessary—perhaps the problem can be solved by creating a conduit that is strong enough to handle the pressure of spurts from the heart and also function as a one-way valve. An understanding of veins and arteries does not guarantee an answer to this design question, but it does support thinking about alternatives that are not readily available if one only memorizes facts (Bransford and Stein, 1993).

Pre-Existing Knowledge

An emphasis on understanding leads to one of the primary characteristics of the new science of learning: its focus on the processes of knowing (e.g., Piaget, 1978; Vygotsky, 1978). Humans are viewed as goal-directed agents who actively seek information. They come to formal education with a range of prior knowledge, skills, beliefs, and concepts that significantly influence what they notice about the environment and how they organize and interpret it. This, in turn, affects their abilities to remember, reason, solve problems, and acquire new knowledge.

Even young infants are active learners who bring a point of view to the learning setting. The world they enter is not a "booming, buzzing confusion" (James, 1890), where every stimulus is equally salient. Instead, an infant's brain gives precedence to certain kinds of information: language, basic concepts of number, physical properties, and the movement of animate and inanimate objects. In the most general sense, the contemporary view of learning is that people construct new knowledge and understandings based on what they already know and believe (e.g., Cobb, 1994; Piaget, 1952, 1973a,b, 1977, 1978; Vygotsky, 1962, 1978). A classic children's book illustrates this point; see Box 1.2.

A logical extension of the view that new knowledge must be constructed from existing knowledge is that teachers need to pay attention to the incomplete understandings, the false beliefs, and the naive renditions of concepts that learners bring with them to a given subject. Teachers then need to build on these ideas in ways that help each student achieve a more mature understanding. If students' initial ideas and beliefs are ignored, the understandings that they develop can be very different from what the teacher intends.

Consider the challenge of working with children who believe that the earth is flat and attempting to help them understand that it is spherical. When told it is round, children picture the earth as a pancake rather than as a sphere (Vosniadou and Brewer, 1989). If they are then told that it is round like a sphere, they interpret the new information about a spherical earth within their flat-earth view by picturing a pancake-like flat surface inside or on top of a sphere, with humans standing on top of the pancake. The children's construction of their new understandings has been guided by a model of the earth that helped them explain how they could stand or walk upon its surface, and a spherical earth did not fit their mental model. Like *Fish Is Fish*, everything the children heard was incorporated into that pre-existing view.

Fish Is Fish is relevant not only for young children, but for learners of all ages. For example, college students often have developed beliefs about physical and biological phenomena that fit their experiences but do not fit scientific accounts of these phenomena. These preconceptions must be

BOX 1.2   *Fish Is Fish*

Fish Is Fish (Lionni, 1970) describes a fish who is keenly interested in learning about what happens on land, but the fish cannot explore land because it can only breathe in water. It befriends a tadpole who grows into a frog and eventually goes out onto the land. The frog returns to the pond a few weeks later and reports on what he has seen. The frog describes all kinds of things like birds, cows, and people. The book shows pictures of the fish's representations of each of these descriptions: each is a fish-like form that is slightly adapted to accommodate the frog's descriptions—people are imagined to be fish who walk on their tailfins, birds are fish with wings, cows are fish with udders. This tale illustrates both the creative opportunities and dangers inherent in the fact that people construct new knowledge based on their current knowledge.

addressed in order for them to change their beliefs (e.g., Confrey, 1990; Mestre, 1994; Minstrell, 1989; Redish, 1996).

A common misconception regarding "constructivist" theories of knowing (that existing knowledge is used to build new knowledge) is that teachers should never tell students anything directly but, instead, should always allow them to construct knowledge for themselves. This perspective confuses a theory of pedagogy (teaching) with a theory of knowing. Constructivists assume that all knowledge is constructed from previous knowledge, irrespective of how one is taught (e.g., Cobb, 1994)—even listening to a lecture involves active attempts to construct new knowledge. *Fish Is Fish* (Lionni, 1970) and attempts to teach children that the earth is round (Vosniadou and Brewer, 1989) show why simply providing lectures frequently does not work. Nevertheless, there are times, usually after people have first grappled with issues on their own, that "teaching by telling" can work extremely well (e.g., Schwartz and Bransford, 1998). However, teachers still need to pay attention to students' interpretations and provide guidance when necessary.

There is a good deal of evidence that learning is enhanced when teachers pay attention to the knowledge and beliefs that learners bring to a learning task, use this knowledge as a starting point for new instruction, and monitor students' changing conceptions as instruction proceeds. For example, sixth graders in a suburban school who were given inquiry-based physics instruction were shown to do better on conceptual physics problems than eleventh and twelfth grade physics students taught by conventional methods in the same school system. A second study comparing seventh-ninth grade urban students with the eleventh and twelfth grade suburban physics students again showed that the younger students, taught by the inquiry-based approach, had a better grasp of the fundamental principles of physics (White and Frederickson, 1997, 1998). New curricula for young children have also demonstrated results that are extremely promising: for example, a new approach to teaching geometry helped second-grade children learn to represent and visualize three-dimensional forms in ways that exceeded the skills of a comparison group of undergraduate students at a leading university (Lehrer and Chazan, 1998). Similarly, young children have been taught to demonstrate powerful forms of early geometry generalizations (Lehrer and Chazan, 1998) and generalizations about science (Schauble et al., 1995; Warren and Rosebery, 1996).

Active Learning

New developments in the science of learning also emphasize the importance of helping people take control of their own learning. Since understanding is viewed as important, people must learn to recognize when they understand and when they need more information. What strategies might they use to assess whether they understand someone else's meaning? What kinds of evidence do they need in order to believe particular claims? How can they build their own theories of phenomena and test them effectively?

Many important activities that support active learning have been studied under the heading of "metacognition," a topic discussed in more detail in Chapters 2 and 3. Metacognition refers to people's abilities to predict their performances on various tasks (e.g., how well they will be able to remember various stimuli) and to monitor their current levels of mastery and understanding (e.g., Brown, 1975; Flavell, 1973). Teaching practices congruent with a metacognitive approach to learning include those that focus on sense-making, self-assessment, and reflection on what worked and what needs improving. These practices have been shown to increase the degree to which students transfer their learning to new settings and events (e.g., Palincsar and Brown, 1984; Scardamalia et al., 1984; Schoenfeld, 1983, 1985, 1991).

Imagine three teachers whose practices affect whether students learn to take control of their own learning (Scardamalia and Bereiter, 1991). Teacher A's goal is to get the students to produce work; this is accomplished by supervising and overseeing the quantity and quality of the work done by the students. The focus is on activities, which could be anything from old-style workbook activities to the trendiest of space-age projects. Teacher B assumes responsibility for what the students are learning as they carry out their activities. Teacher C does this as well, but with the added objective of continually turning more of the learning process over to the students. Walking into a classroom, you cannot immediately tell these three kinds of teachers apart. One of the things you might see is the students working in groups to produce videos or multimedia presentations. The teacher is likely to be found going from group to group, checking how things are going and responding to requests. Over the course of a few days, however, differences between Teacher A and Teacher B would become evident. Teacher A's focus is entirely on the production process and its products—whether the students are engaged, whether everyone is getting fair treatment, and whether they are turning out good pieces of work. Teacher B attends to all of this as well, but Teacher B is also attending to what the students are learning from the experience and is taking steps to ensure that the students are processing content and not just dealing with show. To see a difference between Teachers B and C, however, you might need to go back into the history of the media production project. What brought it about in the first place? Was it conceived from the start as a learning activity, or did it emerge from the students' own knowledge building efforts? In one striking example of a Teacher C classroom, the students had been studying cockroaches and had learned so much from their reading and observation that they wanted to share it with the rest of the school; the production of a video came about to achieve that purpose (Lamon et al., 1997).

The differences in what might seem to be the same learning activity are thus quite profound. In Teacher A's classroom, the students are learning something of media production, but the media production may very well be getting in the way of learning anything else. In Teacher B's classroom, the teacher is working to ensure that the original educational purposes of the activity are met, that it does not deteriorate into a mere media production exercise. In Teacher C's classroom, the media production is continuous with and a direct outgrowth of the learning that is embodied in the media production. The greater part of Teacher C's work has been done before the idea of a media production even comes up, and it remains only to help the students keep sight of their purposes as they carry out the project.

These hypothetical teachers—A, B, and C—are abstract models that of course fit real teachers only partly, and more on some days than others. Nevertheless, they provide important glimpses of connections between goals for learning and teaching practices that can affect students' abilities to accomplish these goals.

Implications for Education

Overall, the new science of learning is beginning to provide knowledge to improve significantly people's abilities to become active learners who seek to understand complex subject matter and are better prepared to transfer what they have learned to new problems and settings. Making this happen is a major challenge (e.g., Elmore et al., 1996), but it is not impossible. The emerging science of learning underscores the importance of rethinking what is taught, how it is taught, and how learning is assessed. These ideas are developed throughout this volume.

An Evolving Science

This volume synthesizes the scientific basis of learning. The scientific achievements include a fuller understanding of: (1) memory and the structure of knowledge; (2) problem solving and reasoning; (3) the early foundations of learning; (4) regulatory processes that govern learning, including metacognition; and (5) how symbolic thinking emerges from the culture and community of the learner.

These key characteristics of learned proficiency by no means plumb the depths of human cognition and learning. What has been learned about the principles that guide some aspects of learning do not constitute a complete picture of the principles that govern all domains of learning. The scientific bases, while not superficial in themselves, do represent only a surface level of a complete understanding of the subject. Only a few domains of learning have been examined in depth, as reflected in this book, and new, emergent areas, such as interactive technologies (Greenfield and Cocking, 1996) are challenging generalizations from older research studies.

As scientists continue to study learning, new research procedures and methodologies are emerging that are likely to alter current theoretical conceptions of learning, such as computational modeling research. The scientific work encompasses a broad range of cognitive and neuroscience issues in learning, memory, language, and cognitive development. Studies of parallel distributed processing, for example (McClelland et al., 1995; Plaut et al., 1996; Munakata et al., 1997; McClelland and Chappell, 1998) look at learning as occurring through the adaptation of connections among participating neurons. The research is designed to develop explicit computational models to refine and extend basic principles, as well as to apply the models to substantive research questions through behavioral experiments, computer simulations, functional brain imaging, and mathematical analyses. These studies are thus contributing to modification of both theory and practice. New models also encompass learning in adulthood to add an important dimension to the scientific knowledge base.

Key Findings

This volume provides a broad overview of research on learners and learning and on teachers and teaching. Three findings are highlighted here because they have both a solid research base to support them and strong implications for how we teach.

1. Students come to the classroom with preconceptions about how the world works. If their initial understanding is not engaged, they may fail to grasp the new concepts and information that are

taught, or they may learn them for purposes of a test but revert to their preconceptions outside the classroom.

Research on early learning suggests that the process of making sense of the world begins at a very young age. Children begin in preschool years to develop sophisticated understandings (whether accurate or not) of the phenomena around them (Wellman, 1990). Those initial understandings can have a powerful effect on the integration of new concepts and information. Sometimes those understandings are accurate, providing a foundation for building new knowledge. But sometimes they are inaccurate (Carey and Gelman, 1991). In science, students often have misconceptions of physical properties that cannot be easily observed. In humanities, their preconceptions often include stereotypes or simplifications, as when history is understood as a struggle between good guys and bad guys (Gardner, 1991). A critical feature of effective teaching is that it elicits from students their preexisting understanding of the subject matter to be taught and provides opportunities to build on—or challenge—the initial understanding. James Minstrell, a high school physics teacher, describes the process as follows (Minstrell, 1989: 130-131):

> Students' initial ideas about mechanics are like strands of yarn, some unconnected, some loosely interwoven. The act of instruction can be viewed as helping the students unravel individual strands of belief, label them, and then weave them into a fabric of more complete understanding. Rather than denying the relevancy of a belief, teachers might do better by helping students differentiate their present ideas from and integrate them into conceptual beliefs more like those of scientists.

The understandings that children bring to the classroom can already be quite powerful in the early grades. For example, some children have been found to hold onto their preconception of a flat earth by imagining a round earth to be shaped like a pancake (Vosniadou and Brewer, 1989). This construction of a new understanding is guided by a model of the earth that helps the child explain how people can stand or walk on its surface. Many young children have trouble giving up the notion that one-eighth is greater than one-fourth, because 8 is more than 4 (Gelman and Gallistel, 1978). If children were blank slates, telling them that the earth is round or that one-fourth is greater than one-eighth would be adequate. But since they already have ideas about the earth and about numbers, those ideas must be directly addressed in order to transform or expand them.

Drawing out and working with existing understandings is important for learners of all ages. Numerous research experiments demonstrate the persistence of preexisting understandings among older students even after a new model has been taught that contradicts the naïve understanding. For example, in a study of physics students from elite, technologically oriented colleges, Andrea DiSessa (1982) instructed them to play a computerized game that required them to direct a computer-simulated object called a dynaturtle so that it would hit a target and do so with minimum speed at impact. Participants were introduced to the game and given a hands-on trial that allowed them to apply a few taps with a small wooden mallet to a tennis ball on a table before beginning the game. The same game was also played by elementary schoolchildren. DiSessa found that both groups of students failed dismally. Success would have required demonstrating an understanding of Newton's laws of motion. Despite their training, college physics students, like the elementary schoolchildren, aimed the moving dynaturtle directly at the target, failing to take momentum into account. Further investigation of one college student who participated in the study revealed that she knew the relevant physical properties and formulas, yet, in the context of the game, she fell back on her untrained conception of how the physical world works.

Students at a variety of ages persist in their beliefs that seasons are caused by the earth's distance from the sun rather than by the tilt of the earth (Harvard-Smithsonian Center for Astrophysics, 1987), or that an object that had been tossed in the air has both the force of gravity and the force of the hand that tossed it acting on it, despite training to the contrary (Clement, 1982). For the scientific understanding to replace the naïve understanding, students must reveal the latter and have the opportunity to see where it falls short.

2. To develop competence in an area of inquiry, students must: (a) have a deep foundation of factual knowledge, (b) understand facts and ideas in the context of a conceptual framework, and (c) organize knowledge in ways that facilitate retrieval and application.

This principle emerges from research that compares the performance of experts and novices and from research on learning and transfer. Experts, regardless of the field, always draw on a richly structured information base; they are not just "good thinkers" or "smart people." The ability to plan a task, to notice patterns, to generate reasonable arguments and explanations, and to draw analogies to other problems are all more closely intertwined with factual knowledge than was once believed.

But knowledge of a large set of disconnected facts is not sufficient. To develop competence in an area of inquiry, students must have opportunities to learn with understanding. Deep understanding of subject matter transforms factual information into usable knowledge. A pronounced difference between experts and novices is that experts' command of concepts shapes their understanding of new information: it allows them to see patterns, relationships, or discrepancies that are not apparent to novices. They do not necessarily have better overall memories than other people. But their conceptual understanding allows them to extract a level of meaning from information that is not apparent to novices, and this helps them select and remember relevant information. Experts are also able to fluently access relevant knowledge because their understanding of subject matter allows them to quickly identify what is relevant. Hence, their attention is not overtaxed by complex events.

In most areas of study in K-12 education, students will begin as novices; they will have informal ideas about the subject of study, and will vary in the amount of information they have acquired. The enterprise of education can be viewed as moving students in the direction of more formal understanding (or greater expertise). This will require both a deepening of the information base and the development of a conceptual framework for that subject matter.

Geography can be used to illustrate the manner in which expertise is organized around principles that support understanding. A student can learn to fill in a map by memorizing states, cities, countries, etc., and can complete the task with a high level of accuracy. But if the boundaries are removed, the problem becomes much more difficult. There are no concepts supporting the student's information. An expert who understands that borders often developed because natural phenomena (like mountains or water bodies) separated people, and that large cities often arose in locations that allowed for trade (along rivers, large lakes, and at coastal ports) will easily outperform the novice. The more developed the conceptual understanding of the needs of cities and the resource base that drew people to them, the more meaningful the map becomes. Students can become more expert if the geographical information they are taught is placed in the appropriate conceptual framework.

A key finding in the learning and transfer literature is that organizing information into a conceptual framework allows for greater "transfer"; that is, it allows the student to apply what was learned in new situations and to learn related information more quickly (see Box 1.3). The student who has learned geographical information for the Americas in a conceptual framework approaches the task of learning the geography of another part of the globe with questions, ideas, and expectations that help guide acquisition of the new information. Understanding the geographical importance of the Mississippi River sets the stage for the student's understanding of the geographical importance of the Nile. And as concepts are reinforced, the student will transfer learning beyond the classroom, observing and inquiring, for example, about the geographic features of a visited city that help explain its location and size (Holyoak, 1984; Novick and Holyoak, 1991).

3. A "metacognitive" approach to instruction can help students learn to take control of their own learning by defining learning goals and monitoring their progress in achieving them.

In research with experts who were asked to verbalize their thinking as they worked, it was revealed that they monitored their own understanding carefully, making note of when additional information was required for understanding, whether new information was consistent with what they already knew, and what analogies could be drawn that would advance their understanding. These meta-cognitive monitoring activities are an important component of what is called adaptive expertise (Hatano and Inagaki, 1986).

Because metacognition often takes the form of an internal conversation, it can easily be assumed that individuals will develop the internal dialogue on their own. Yet many of the strategies we use for thinking reflect cultural norms and methods of inquiry (Hutchins, 1995; Brice-Heath, 1981, 1983; Suina and Smolkin, 1994). Research has demonstrated that children can be taught these strategies, including the ability to predict outcomes, explain to oneself in order to improve understanding, note failures to comprehend, activate background knowledge, plan ahead, and apportion time and memory. Reciprocal teaching, for example, is a technique designed to improve students' reading comprehension by helping them explicate, elaborate, and monitor their understanding as they read (Palincsar and Brown, 1984). The model for using the meta-cognitive strategies is provided initially by the

BOX 1.3   Throwing Darts Under Water

In one of the most famous early studies comparing the effects of learning a procedure with learning with understanding, two groups of children practiced throwing darts at a target under water (described in Judd, 1908; see a conceptual replication by Hendrickson and Schroeder, 1941). One group received an explanation of the refraction of light, which causes the apparent location of the target to be deceptive. The other group only practiced dart throwing, without the explanation. Both groups did equally well on the practice task, which involved a target 12 inches under water. But the group that had been instructed about the abstract principle did much better when they had to transfer to a situation in which the target was under only 4 inches of water. Because they understood what they were doing, the group that had received instruction about the refraction of light could adjust their behavior to the new task.

teacher, and students practice and discuss the strategies as they learn to use them. Ultimately, students are able to prompt themselves and monitor their own comprehension without teacher support.

The teaching of metacognitive activities must be incorporated into the subject matter that students are learning (White and Frederickson, 1998). These strategies are not generic across subjects, and attempts to teach them as generic can lead to failure to transfer. Teaching metacognitive strategies in context has been shown to improve understanding in physics (White and Frederickson, 1998), written composition (Scardamalia et al., 1984), and heuristic methods for mathematical problem solving (Schoenfeld, 1983, 1984, 1991). And metacognitive practices have been shown to increase the degree to which students transfer to new settings and events (Lin and Lehman, in press; Palincsar and Brown, 1984; Scardamalia et al., 1984; Schoenfeld, 1983, 1984, 1991).

Each of these techniques shares a strategy of teaching and modeling the process of generating alternative approaches (to developing an idea in writing or a strategy for problem solving in mathematics), evaluating their merits in helping to attain a goal, and monitoring progress toward that goal. Class discussions are used to support skill development, with a goal of independence and self-regulation.

Implications for Teaching

The three core learning principles described above, simple though they seem, have profound implications for the enterprise of teaching and teacher preparation.

1. *Teachers must draw out and work with the preexisting understandings that their students bring with them.* This requires that:

- The model of the child as an empty vessel to be filled with knowledge provided by the teacher must be replaced. Instead, the teacher must actively inquire into students' thinking, creating classroom tasks and conditions under which student thinking can be revealed. Students' initial conceptions then provide the foundation on which the more formal understanding of the subject matter is built.
- The roles for assessment must be expanded beyond the traditional concept of testing. The use of frequent formative assessment helps make students' thinking visible to themselves, their peers, and their teacher. This provides feedback that can guide modification and refinement in thinking. Given the goal of learning with understanding, assessments must tap understanding rather than merely the ability to repeat facts or perform isolated skills.

- Schools of education must provide beginning teachers with opportunities to learn: (a) to recognize predictable preconceptions of students that make the mastery of particular subject matter challenging, (b) to draw out preconceptions that are not predictable, and (c) to work with preconceptions so that children build on them, challenge them and, when appropriate, replace them.

2. Teachers must teach some subject matter in depth, providing many examples in which the same concept is at work and providing a firm foundation of factual knowledge. This requires that:

- Superficial coverage of all topics in a subject area must be replaced with in-depth coverage of fewer topics that allows key concepts in that discipline to be understood. The goal of coverage need not be abandoned entirely, of course. But there must be a sufficient number of cases of in-depth study to allow students to grasp the defining concepts in specific domains within a discipline. Moreover, in-depth study in a domain often requires that ideas be carried beyond a single school year before students can make the transition from informal to formal ideas. This will require active coordination of the curriculum across school years.
- Teachers must come to teaching with the experience of in-depth study of the subject area themselves. Before a teacher can develop powerful pedagogical tools, he or she must be familiar with the progress of inquiry and the terms of discourse in the discipline, as well as understand the relationship between information and the concepts that help organize that information in the discipline. But equally important, the teacher must have a grasp of the growth and development of students' thinking about these concepts. The latter will be essential to developing teaching expertise, but not expertise in the discipline. It may therefore require courses, or course supplements, that are designed specifically for teachers.
- Assessment for purposes of accountability (e.g., statewide assessments) must test deep understanding rather than surface knowledge. Assessment tools are often the standard by which teachers are held accountable. A teacher is put in a bind if she or he is asked to teach for deep conceptual understanding, but in doing so produces students who perform more poorly on standardized tests. Unless new assessment tools are aligned with new approaches to teaching, the latter are unlikely to muster support among the schools and their constituent parents. This goal is as important as it is difficult to achieve. The format of standardized tests can encourage measurement of factual knowledge rather than conceptual understanding, but it also facilitates objective scoring. Measuring depth of understanding can pose challenges for objectivity. Much work needs to be done to minimize the trade-off between assessing depth and assessing objectively.

3. *The teaching of metacognitive skills should be integrated into the curriculum in a variety of subject areas.* Because metacognition often takes the form of an internal dialogue, many students may be unaware of its importance unless the processes are explicitly emphasized by teachers. An emphasis on metacognition needs to accompany instruction in each of the disciplines, because the type of monitoring required will vary. In history, for example, the student might be asking himself, "who wrote this document, and how does that affect the interpretation of events," whereas in physics the student might be monitoring her understanding of the underlying physical principle at work.

- Integration of metacognitive instruction with discipline-based learning can enhance student achievement and develop in students the ability to learn independently. It should be consciously incorporated into curricula across disciplines and age levels.
- Developing strong metacognitive strategies and learning to teach those strategies in a classroom environment should be standard features of the curriculum in schools of education.

Evidence from research indicates that when these three principles are incorporated into teaching, student achievement improves. For example, the Thinker Tools Curriculum for teaching physics in an interactive computer environment focuses on fundamental physical concepts and properties, allowing students to test their preconceptions in model building and experimentation activities. The program includes an "inquiry cycle" that helps students monitor where they are in the inquiry process. The program asks for students' reflective assessments and allows them to review the assessments of their fellow students. In one study, sixth graders in a suburban school who were taught physics using Thinker Tools performed better at solving conceptual physics problems than did eleventh and twelfth grade physics students in the same school system taught by conventional methods. A second study comparing urban students in grades 7 to 9 with suburban students in grades 11 and 12 again showed that the younger students taught by the inquiry-based approach had a superior grasp of the fundamental principles of physics (White and Frederickson, 1997, 1998).

Bringing Order to Chaos

A benefit of focusing on how people learn is that it helps bring order to a seeming cacophony of choices. Consider the many possible teaching strategies that are debated in education circles and the media. Figure 1.1 depicts them in diagram format: lecture-based teaching, text-based teaching, inquiry-based teaching, technology-enhanced teaching, teaching organized

FIGURE 1.1 *With knowledge of how people learn, teachers can choose more purposefully among techniques to accomplish specific goals.*

around individuals versus cooperative groups, and so forth. Are some of these teaching techniques better than others? Is lecturing a poor way to teach, as many seem to claim? Is cooperative learning effective? Do attempts to use computers (technology-enhanced teaching) help achievement or hurt it?

This volume suggests that these are the wrong questions. Asking which teaching technique is best is analogous to asking which tool is best—a hammer, a screwdriver, a knife, or pliers. In teaching as in carpentry, the selection of tools depends on the task at hand and the materials one is working with. Books and lectures *can* be wonderfully efficient modes of transmitting new information for learning, exciting the imagination, and honing students' critical faculties—but one would choose other kinds of activities to elicit from students their preconceptions and level of understanding, or to help them see the power of using meta-cognitive strategies to monitor their learning. Hands-on experiments *can* be a powerful way to ground emergent knowledge, but they do not alone evoke the underlying conceptual understandings that aid generalization. There is no universal best teaching practice.

If, instead, the point of departure is a core set of learning principles, then the selection of teaching strategies (mediated, of course, by subject matter, grade level, and desired outcome) can be purposeful. The many possibilities then become a rich set of opportunities from which a teacher constructs an instructional program rather than a chaos of competing alternatives.

Focusing on how people learn also will help teachers move beyond either-or dichotomies that have plagued the field of education. One such issue is whether schools should emphasize "the basics" or teach thinking and problem-solving skills. This volume shows that both are necessary. Students' abilities to acquire organized sets of facts and skills are actually enhanced when they are connected to meaningful problem-solving activities, and when students are helped to understand why, when, and how those facts and skills are relevant. And attempts to teach thinking skills without a strong base of factual knowledge do not promote problem-solving ability or support transfer to new situations.

Designing Classroom Environments

Chapter 6 of this volume proposes a framework to help guide the design and evaluation of environments that can optimize learning. Drawing heavily on the three principles discussed above, it posits four interrelated attributes of learning environments that need cultivation.

1. *Schools and classrooms must be learner centered.* Teachers must pay close attention to the knowledge, skills, and attitudes that learners bring into the classroom. This incorporates the preconceptions regarding subject matter already discussed, but it also includes a broader understanding of the learner. For example:

• Cultural differences can affect students' comfort level in working collaboratively versus individually, and they are reflected in the background knowledge students bring to a new learning situation (Moll et al., 1993).

• Students' theories of what it means to be intelligent can affect their performance. Research shows that students who think that intelligence is a fixed entity are more likely to be performance oriented than learning oriented—they want to look good rather than risk making mistakes while learning. These students are especially likely to bail out when tasks become difficult. In contrast, students who think that intelligence is malleable are more willing to struggle with challenging tasks; they are more comfortable with risk (Dweck, 1989; Dweck and Legget, 1988).

Teachers in learner-centered classrooms also pay close attention to the individual progress of each student and devise tasks that are appropriate.

Learner-centered teachers present students with "just manageable difficul-ties"—that is, challenging enough to maintain engagement, but not so difficult as to lead to discouragement. They must therefore have an understanding of their students' knowledge, skill levels, and interests (Duckworth, 1987).

2. *To provide a knowledge-centered classroom environment, attention must be given to what is taught (information, subject matter), why it is taught (understanding), and what competence or mastery looks like*. As mentioned above, research discussed in the following chap-ters shows clearly that expertise involves well-organized knowledge that supports understanding, and that learning with understanding is important for the development of expertise because it makes new learning easier (i.e., supports transfer).

Learning with understanding is often harder to accomplish than simply memorizing, and it takes more time. Many curricula fail to support learning with understanding because they present too many disconnected facts in too short a time—the "mile wide, inch deep" problem. Tests often reinforce memorizing rather than understanding. The knowledge-centered environ-ment provides the necessary depth of study, assessing student understanding rather than factual memory. It incorporates the teaching of meta-cognitive strategies that further facilitate future learning.

Knowledge-centered environments also look beyond engagement as the primary index of successful teaching (Prawaf et al., 1992). Students' interest or engagement in a task is clearly important. Nevertheless, it does not guarantee that students will acquire the kinds of knowledge that will support new learning. There are important differences between tasks and projects that encourage hands-on doing and those that encourage doing with understanding; the knowledge-centered environment emphasizes the latter (Greeno, 1991).

3. *Formative assessments—ongoing assessments designed to make students' thinking visible to both teachers and students—are essential. They permit the teacher to grasp the students' preconcep-tions, understand where the students are in the "developmental cor-ridor" from informal to formal thinking, and design instruction accordingly. In the assessment-centered classroom environment, for-mative assessments help both teachers and students monitor progress.*

An important feature of assessments in these classrooms is that they be learner-friendly: they are not the Friday quiz for which information is memo-rized the night before, and for which the student is given a grade that ranks him or her with respect to classmates. Rather, these assessments should provide students with opportunities to revise and improve their thinking (Vye et al., 1998b), help students see their own progress over the course of weeks or months, and help teachers identify problems that need to be remedied (problems that may not be visible without the assessments). For example, a high school class studying the principles of democracy might be given a scenario in which a colony of people have just settled on the moon and must establish a government. Proposals from students of the defining features of such a government, as well as discussion of the problems they foresee in its establishment, can reveal to both teachers and students areas in which student thinking is more and less advanced. The exercise is less a test than an indicator of where inquiry and instruction should focus.

4. *Learning is influenced in fundamental ways by the context in which it takes place. A community-centered approach requires the development of norms for the classroom and school, as well as connections to the outside world, that support core learning values.*

The norms established in the classroom have strong effects on students' achievement. In some schools, the norms could be expressed as "don't get caught not knowing something." Others encourage academic risk-taking and opportunities to make mistakes, obtain feedback, and revise. Clearly, if students are to reveal their preconceptions about a subject matter, their questions, and their progress toward understanding, the norms of the school must support their doing so.

Teachers must attend to designing classroom activities and helping students organize their work in ways that promote the kind of intellectual camaraderie and the attitudes toward learning that build a sense of community. In such a community, students might help one another solve problems by building on each other's knowledge, asking questions to clarify explanations, and suggesting avenues that would move the group toward its goal (Brown and Campione, 1994). Both cooperation in problem solving (Evans, 1989; Newstead and Evans, 1995) and argumentation (Goldman, 1994; Habermas, 1990; Kuhn, 1991; Moshman, 1995a, 1995b; Salmon and Zeitz, 1995; Youniss and Damon, 1992) among students in such an intellectual community enhance cognitive development.

Teachers must be enabled and encouraged to establish a community of learners among themselves (Lave and Wegner, 1991). These communities can build a sense of comfort with questioning rather than knowing the answer and can develop a model of creating new ideas that build on the contributions of individual members. They can engender a sense of the excitement of learning that is then transferred to the classroom, conferring a sense of ownership of new ideas as they apply to theory and practice.

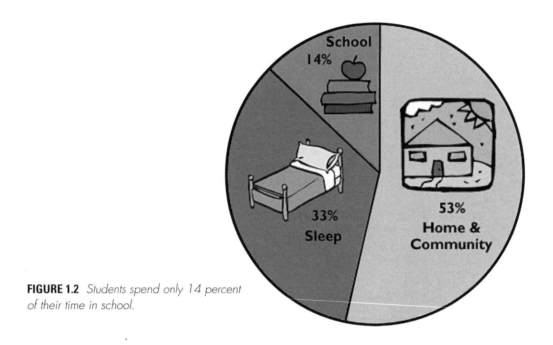

FIGURE 1.2 *Students spend only 14 percent of their time in school.*

Not least, schools need to develop ways to link classroom learning to other aspects of students' lives. Engendering parent support for the core learning principles and parent involvement in the learning process is of utmost importance (Moll, 1990; 1986a, 1986b). Figure 1.2 shows the percentage of time, during a calendar year, that students in a large school district spent in school. If one-third of their time outside school (not counting sleeping) is spent watching television, then students apparently spend more hours per year watching television than attending school. A focus only on the hours that students currently spend in school overlooks the many opportunities for guided learning in other settings.

Applying the Design Framework to Adult Learning

The design framework summarized above assumes that the learners are children, but the principles apply to adult learning as well. This point is particularly important because incorporating the principles in this volume into educational practice will require a good deal of adult learning. Many approaches to teaching adults consistently violate principles for optimizing learning. Professional development programs for teachers, for example, frequently:

- *Are not learner centered.* Rather than ask teachers where they need help, they are simply expected to attend prearranged workshops.
- *Are not knowledge centered.* Teachers may simply be introduced to a new technique (like cooperative learning) without being given the opportunity to understand why, when, where, and how it might be valuable to them. Especially important is the need to integrate the structure of activities with the content of the curriculum that is taught.
- *Are not assessment centered.* In order for teachers to change their practices, they need opportunities to try things out in their classrooms and then receive feedback. Most professional development opportunities do not provide such feedback. Moreover, they tend to focus on change in teaching practice as the goal, but they neglect to develop in teachers the capacity to judge successful transfer of the technique to the classroom or its effects on student achievement.
- *Are not community centered.* Many professional development opportunities are conducted in isolation. Opportunities for continued contact and support as teachers incorporate new ideas into their teaching are limited, yet the rapid spread of Internet access provides a ready means of maintaining such contact if appropriately designed tools and services are available.

The principles of learning and their implications for designing learning environments apply equally to child and adult learning. They provide a lens through which current practice can be viewed with respect to K-12 teaching *and* with respect to preparation of teachers in the research and development agenda. The principles are relevant as well when we consider other groups, such as policy makers and the public, whose learning is also required for educational practice to change.

II

LEARNERS

AND LEARNING

2

How Experts Differ from Novices

People who have developed expertise in particular areas are, by definition, able to think effectively about problems in those areas. Understanding expertise is important because it provides insights into the nature of thinking and problem solving. Research shows that it is not simply general abilities, such as memory or intelligence, nor the use of general strategies that differentiate experts from novices. Instead, experts have acquired extensive knowledge that affects what they notice and how they organize, represent, and interpret information in their environment. This, in turn, affects their abilities to remember, reason, and solve problems.

This chapter illustrates key scientific findings that have come from the study of people who have developed expertise in areas such as chess, physics, mathematics, electronics, and history. We discuss these examples *not* because all school children are expected to become experts in these or any other areas, but because the study of expertise shows what the results of successful learning look like. In later chapters we explore what is known about processes of learning that can eventually lead to the development of expertise.

We consider several key principles of experts' knowledge and their potential implications for learning and instruction:

1. Experts notice features and meaningful patterns of information that are not noticed by novices.

2. Experts have acquired a great deal of content knowledge that is organized in ways that reflect a deep understanding of their subject matter.

3. Experts' knowledge cannot be reduced to sets of isolated facts or propositions but, instead, reflects contexts of applicability: that is, the knowledge is "conditionalized" on a set of circumstances.

4. Experts are able to flexibly retrieve important aspects of their knowledge with little attentional effort.

5. Though experts know their disciplines thoroughly, this does not guarantee that they are able to teach others.

6. Experts have varying levels of flexibility in their approach to new situations.

MEANINGFUL PATTERNS OF INFORMATION

One of the earliest studies of expertise demonstrated that the same stimulus is perceived and understood differently, depending on the knowledge that a person brings to the situation. DeGroot (1965) was interested in understanding how world-class chess masters are consistently able to out-think their opponents. Chess masters and less experienced but still extremely good players were shown examples of chess games and asked to think aloud as they decided on the move they would make if they were one of the players; see Box 2.1. DeGroot's hypothesis was that the chess masters would be more likely than the nonmasters to (a) think through all the possibilities before making a move (greater breadth of search) and (b) think through all the possible countermoves of the opponent for every move considered (greater depth of search). In this pioneering research, the chess masters did exhibit considerable breadth and depth to their searches, but so did the lesser ranked chess players. And none of them conducted searches that covered all the possibilities. Somehow, the chess masters considered possibilities for moves that were of higher quality than those considered by the lesser experienced players. Something other than differences in general strategies seemed to be responsible for differences in expertise.

DeGroot concluded that the knowledge acquired over tens of thousands of hours of chess playing enabled chess masters to out-play their opponents. Specifically, masters were more likely to recognize meaningful chess configurations and realize the strategic implications of these situations; this recognition allowed them to consider sets of possible moves that were superior to others. The meaningful patterns seemed readily apparent to the masters, leading deGroot (1965:33-34) to note:

> We know that increasing experience and knowledge in a specific field (chess, for instance) has the effect that things (properties, etc.) which, at earlier stages, had to be abstracted, or even inferred are apt to be immediately perceived at later stages. To a rather large extent, abstraction is replaced by perception, but we do not know much about how this works, nor where the borderline lies. As an effect of this replacement, a so-called 'given' problem situation is not really given since it is seen differently by an expert than it is perceived by an inexperienced person. . . .

DeGroot's think-aloud method provided for a very careful analysis of the conditions of specialized learning and the kinds of conclusions one can draw from them (see Ericsson and Simon, 1993). Hypotheses generated from think-aloud protocols are usually cross-validated through the use of other methodologies.

The superior recall ability of experts, illustrated in the example in the box, has been explained in terms of how they "chunk" various elements of a configuration that are related by an underlying function or strategy. Since there are limits on the amount of information that people can hold in short-term memory, short-term memory is enhanced when people are able to chunk information into familiar patterns (Miller, 1956). Chess masters perceive chunks of meaningful information, which affects their memory for what they see. Chess masters are able to chunk together several chess pieces in a configuration that is governed by some strategic component of the game. Lacking a hierarchical, highly organized structure for the domain, novices cannot use this chunking strategy. It is noteworthy that people do not have to be world-class experts to benefit from their abilities to encode meaningful chunks of information: 10- and 11-year-olds who are experienced in chess are able to remember more chess pieces than college students who are not chess players. In contrast, when the college students were presented with other stimuli, such as strings of numbers, they were able to remember more (Chi, 1978; Schneider et al., 1993); see Figure 2.3.

Skills similar to those of master chess players have been demonstrated for experts in other domains, including electronic circuitry (Egan and Schwartz, 1979), radiology (Lesgold, 1988), and computer programming (Ehrlich and Soloway, 1984). In each case, expertise in a domain helps people develop a sensitivity to patterns of meaningful information that are not available to novices. For example, electronics technicians were able to reproduce large portions of complex circuit diagrams after only a few seconds of viewing; novices could not. The expert circuit technicians chunked several individual circuit elements (e.g., resistors and capacitors) that performed the function of an amplifier. By remembering the structure and function of a typical amplifier, experts were able to recall the arrangement of many of the individual circuit elements comprising the "amplifier chunk."

Mathematics experts are also able to quickly recognize patterns of information, such as particular problem types that involve specific classes of mathematical solutions (Hinsley et al., 1977; Robinson and Hayes, 1978). For example, physicists recognize problems of river currents and problems of headwinds and tailwinds in airplanes as involving similar mathematical principles, such as relative velocities. The expert knowledge that underlies the ability to recognize problem types has been characterized as involving the development of organized conceptual structures, or schemas, that guide how problems are represented and understood (e.g., Glaser and Chi, 1988).

Expert teachers, too, have been shown to have schemas similar to those found in chess and mathematics. Expert and novice teachers were shown a videotaped classroom lesson (Sabers et al., 1991). The experimental set-up involved three screens that showed simultaneous events occurring throughout the classroom (the left, center, and right). During part of the session, the expert and novice teachers were asked to talk aloud about what they were seeing. Later, they were asked questions about classroom events. Overall,

BOX 2.1 **What Experts See**

FIGURE 2.1 *Chess board positions used in memory experiments. SOURCE: Adapted from Chase and Simon (1973).*

In one study, a chess master, a Class A player (good but not a master), and a novice were given 5 seconds to view a chess board position from the middle of a chess game; see Figure 2.1. After 5 seconds the board was covered, and each participant attempted to reconstruct the board position on another board. This procedure was repeated for multiple trials until everyone received a perfect score. On the first trial, the master player correctly placed many more pieces than the Class A player, who in turn placed more than the novice: 16, 8, and 4, respectively.

However, these results occurred only when the chess pieces were arranged in configurations that conformed to meaningful games of chess. When chess pieces were randomized and presented for 5 seconds, the recall of the chess master and Class A player were the same as the novice—they placed from 2 to 3 positions correctly. Data over trials for valid and random middle games are shown in Figure 2.2.

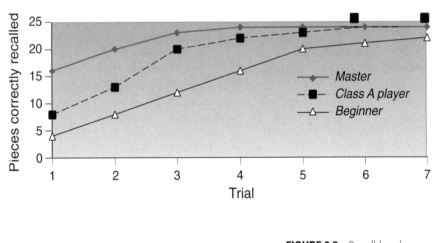

FIGURE 2.2 *Recall by chess players by level of expertise.*

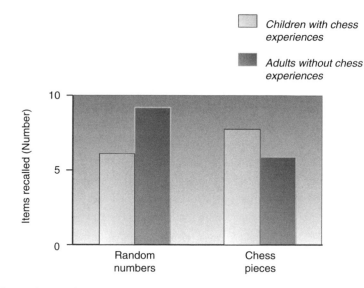

FIGURE 2.3 *Recall for numbers and chess pieces. SOURCE: Adapted from Chi (1978).*

the expert teachers had very different understandings of the events they were watching than did the novice teachers; see examples in Box 2.2.

The idea that experts recognize features and patterns that are not noticed by novices is potentially important for improving instruction. When viewing instructional texts, slides, and videotapes, for example, the information noticed by novices can be quite different from what is noticed by experts (e.g., Sabers et al., 1991; Bransford et al., 1988). One dimension of acquiring greater competence appears to be the increased ability to segment the perceptual field (learning how to see). Research on expertise suggests the importance of providing students with learning experiences that specifically enhance their abilities to recognize meaningful patterns of information (e.g., Simon, 1980; Bransford et al., 1989).

ORGANIZATION OF KNOWLEDGE

We turn now to the question of how experts' knowledge is organized and how this affects their abilities to understand and represent problems. Their knowledge is not simply a list of facts and formulas that are relevant to their domain; instead, their knowledge is organized around core concepts or "big ideas" that guide their thinking about their domains.

BOX 2.2 **What Expert and Novice Teachers Notice**

Expert and novice teachers notice very different things when viewing a videotape of a classroom lesson.

Expert 6: On the left monitor, the students' note taking indicates that they have seen sheets like this and have had presentations like this before; it's fairly efficient at this point because they're used to the format they are using.

Expert 7: I don't understand why the students can't be finding out this information on their own rather than listening to someone tell them because if you watch the faces of most of them, they start out for about the first 2 or 3 minutes sort of paying attention to what's going on and then just drift off.

Expert 2: . . . I haven't heard a bell, but the students are already at their desks and seem to be doing purposeful activity, and this is about the time that I decide they must be an accelerated group because they came into the room and started something rather than just sitting down and socializing.

Novice 1: . . . I can't tell what they are doing. They're getting ready for class, but I can't tell what they're doing.

Novice 3: She's trying to communicate with them here about something, but I sure couldn't tell what it was.

Another novice: It's a lot to watch.

In an example from physics, experts and competent beginners (college students) were asked to describe verbally the approach they would use to solve physics problems. Experts usually mentioned the major principle(s) or law(s) that were applicable to the problem, together with a rationale for why those laws applied to the problem and how one could apply them (Chi et al., 1981). In contrast, competent beginners rarely referred to major principles and laws in physics; instead, they typically described which equations they would use and how those equations would be manipulated (Larkin, 1981, 1983).

Experts' thinking seems to be organized around big ideas in physics, such as Newton's second law and how it would apply, while novices tend to perceive problem solving in physics as memorizing, recalling, and manipulating equations to get answers. When solving problems, experts in physics often pause to draw a simple qualitative diagram—they do not simply attempt to plug numbers into a formula. The diagram is often elaborated as the expert seeks to find a workable solution path (e.g., see Larkin et al., 1980; Larkin and Simon, 1987; Simon and Simon, 1978).

Differences in how physics experts and novices approach problems can also be seen when they are asked to sort problems, written on index cards, according to the approach that could be used to solve them (Chi et al., 1981). Experts' problem piles are arranged on the basis of the principles that can be applied to solve the problems; novices' piles are arranged on the basis of the problems' surface attributes. For example, in the physics subfield of mechanics, an expert's pile might consist of problems that can be solved by conservation of energy, while a novice's pile might consist of problems that contain inclined planes; see Figure 2.4. Responding to the surface characteristics of problems is not very useful, since two problems that share the same objects and look very similar may actually be solved by entirely different approaches.

Some studies of experts and novices in physics have explored the organization of the knowledge structures that are available to these different groups of individuals (Chi et al., 1982); see Figure 2.5. In representing a schema for an incline plane, the novice's schema contains primarily surface features of the incline plane. In contrast, the expert's schema immediately connects the notion of an incline plane with the laws of physics and the conditions under which laws are applicable.

Pause times have also been used to infer the structure of expert knowledge in domains such as chess and physics. Physics experts appear to evoke sets of related equations, with the recall of one equation activating related equations that are retrieved rapidly (Larkin, 1979). Novices, in contrast, retrieve equations more equally spaced in time, suggesting a sequential search in memory. Experts appear to possess an efficient organization of knowledge with meaningful relations among related elements clustered into related units that are governed by underlying concepts and principles; see Box 2.3. Within this picture of expertise, "knowing more" means having more conceptual chunks in memory, more relations or features defining each chunk, more interrelations among the chunks, and efficient methods for retrieving related chunks and procedures for applying these informational units in problem-solving contexts (Chi et al., 1981).

Differences between how experts and nonexperts organize knowledge has also been demonstrated in such fields as history (Wineburg, 1991). A group of history experts and a group of gifted, high-achieving high school seniors enrolled in an advanced placement course in history were first given a test of facts about the American Revolution. The historians with back-

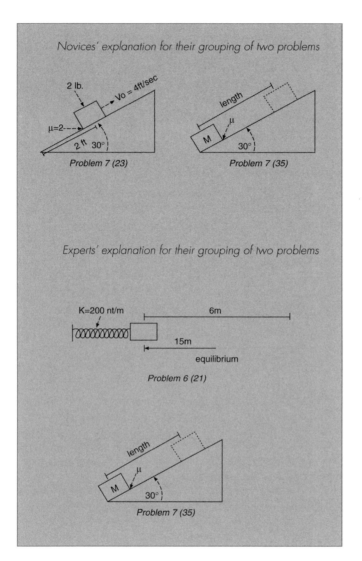

FIGURE 2.4 *An example of sortings of physics problems made by novices and experts. Each picture above represents a diagram that can be drawn from the storyline of a physics problem taken from an introductory physics textbook. The novices and experts in this study were asked to categorize many such problems based on similarity of solution. The two pairs show a marked contrast in the experts' and novices' categorization schemes. Novices tend to categorize physics problems as being solved similarly if they "look the same" (that is, share the same surface features), whereas experts categorize according to the major principle that could be applied to solve the problems.*
SOURCE: Adapted from Chi et al. (1981).

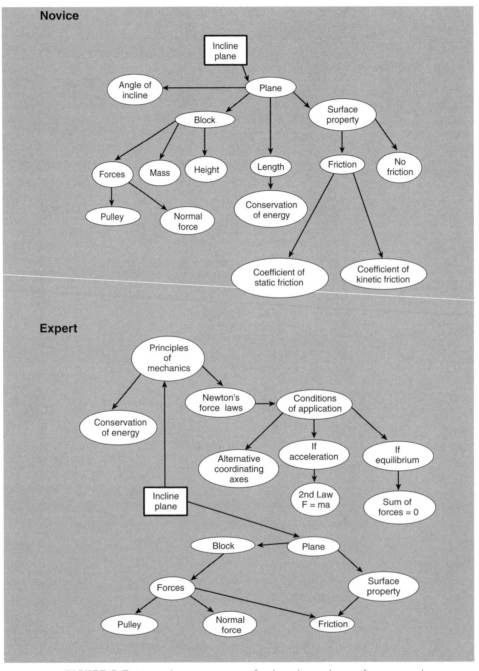

FIGURE 2.5 *Network representations of incline plane schema of novices and experts.*
SOURCE: Chi et al. (1982:58). Used with permission of Lawrence Erlbaum Associates.

BOX 2.3 Understanding and Problem Solving

In mathematics, experts are more likely than novices to first try to understand problems, rather than simply attempt to plug numbers into formulas. Experts and students in one study (Paige and Simon, 1966) were asked to solve algebra word problems, such as:

> A board was sawed into two pieces. One piece was two-thirds as long as the whole board and was exceeded in length by the second piece by four feet. How long was the board before it was cut?

The experts quickly realize that the problem as stated is logically impossible. Although some students also come to this realization, others simply apply equations, which results in the answer of a negative length.

A similar example comes from a study of adults and children (Reusser, 1993), who were asked:

> There are 26 sheep and 10 goats on a ship. How old is the captain?

Most adults have enough expertise to realize that this problem is unsolvable, but many school children didn't realize this at all. More than three-quarters of the children in one study attempted to provide a numerical answer to the problems. They asked themselves whether to add, subtract, multiply, or divide, rather than whether the problem made sense. As one fifth-grade child explained, after giving the answer of 36: "Well, you need to add or subtract or multiply in problems like this, and this one seemed to work best if I add" (Bransford and Stein, 1993:196).

grounds in American history knew most of the items. However, many of the historians had specialties that lay elsewhere and they knew only one-third of the facts on the tests. Several of the students outscored several of the historians on the factual test. The study then compared how the historians and students made sense of historical documents; the result revealed dramatic differences on virtually any criterion. The historians excelled in the elaborateness of understandings they developed in their ability to pose alternative explanations for events and in their use of corroborating evidence. This depth of understanding was as true for the Asian specialists and the medievalists as it was for the Americanists.

When the two groups were asked to select one of three pictures that best reflect their understanding of the battle of Lexington, historians and students displayed the greatest differences. Historians carefully navigated back and forth between the corpus of written documents and the three images of the battlefield. For them, the picture selection task was the quintessential epistemological exercise, a task that explored the limits of historical knowledge. They knew that no single document or picture could tell the story of history; hence, they thought very hard about their choices. In contrast, the students generally just looked at the pictures and made a selection without regard or qualification. For students, the process was similar to finding the correct answer on a multiple choice test.

In sum, although the students scored very well on facts about history, they were largely unacquainted with modes of inquiry with real historical thinking. They had no systematic way of making sense of contradictory claims. Thrust into a set of historical documents that demanded that they sort out competing claims and formulate a reasoned interpretation, the students, on the whole, were stymied. They lacked the experts' deep understanding of how to formulate reasoned interpretations of sets of historical documents. Experts in other social sciences also organize their problem solving around big ideas (see, e.g., Voss et al., 1984).

The fact that experts' knowledge is organized around important ideas or concepts suggests that curricula should also be organized in ways that lead to conceptual understanding. Many approaches to curriculum design make it difficult for students to organize knowledge meaningfully. Often there is only superficial coverage of facts before moving on to the next topic; there is little time to develop important, organizing ideas. History texts sometimes emphasize facts without providing support for understanding (e.g., Beck et al., 1989, 1991). Many ways of teaching science also overemphasize facts (American Association for the Advancement of Science, 1989; National Research Council, 1996).

The Third International Mathematics and Science Survey (TIMSS) (Schmidt et al., 1997) criticized curricula that were "a mile wide and an inch deep" and argued that this is much more of a problem in America than in most other countries. Research on expertise suggests that a superficial coverage of many topics in the domain may be a poor way to help students develop the competencies that will prepare them for future learning and work. The idea of helping students organize their knowledge also suggests that novices might benefit from models of how experts approach problem solving—especially if they then receive coaching in using similar strategies (e.g., Brown et al., 1989; we discuss this more fully in Chapters 3 and 7).

CONTEXT AND ACCESS TO KNOWLEDGE

Experts have a vast repertoire of knowledge that is relevant to their domain or discipline, but only a subset of that knowledge is relevant to any particular problem. Experts do not have to search through everything they know in order to find what is relevant; such an approach would overwhelm their working memory (Miller, 1956). For example, the chess masters described above considered only a subset of possible chess moves, but those moves were generally superior to the ones considered by the lesser ranked players. Experts have not only acquired knowledge, but are also good at retrieving the knowledge that is relevant to a particular task. In the language of cognitive scientists, experts' knowledge is "conditionalized"—it includes a specification of the contexts in which it is useful (Simon, 1980; Glaser, 1992). Knowledge that is not conditionalized is often "inert" because it is not activated, even though it is relevant (Whitehead, 1929).

The concept of conditionalized knowledge has implications for the design of curriculum, instruction, and assessment practices that promote effective learning. Many forms of curricula and instruction do not help students conditionalize their knowledge: "Textbooks are much more explicit in enunciating the laws of mathematics or of nature than in saying anything about when these laws may be useful in solving problems" (Simon, 1980:92). It is left largely to students to generate the condition-action pairs required for solving novel problems.

One way to help students learn about conditions of applicability is to assign word problems that require students to use appropriate concepts and formulas (Lesgold, 1984, 1988; Simon, 1980). If well designed, these problems can help students learn when, where, and why to use the knowledge they are learning. Sometimes, however, students can solve sets of practice problems but fail to conditionalize their knowledge because they know which chapter the problems came from and so automatically use this information to decide which concepts and formulas are relevant. Practice problems that are organized into very structured worksheets can also cause this problem. Sometimes students who have done well on such assignments—and believe that they are learning—are unpleasantly surprised when they take tests in which problems from the entire course are randomly presented so there are no clues about where they appeared in a text (Bransford, 1979).

The concept of conditionalized knowledge also has important implications for assessment practices that provide feedback about learning. Many types of tests fail to help teachers and students assess the degree to which the students' knowledge is conditionalized. For example, students might be asked whether the formula that quantifies the relationship between mass and energy is $E = MC$, $E = MC^2$, or $E = MC^3$. A correct answer requires no knowledge of the conditions under which it is appropriate to use the formula. Similarly, students in a literature class might be asked to explain the meaning of familiar proverbs, such as "he who hesitates is lost" or "too many cooks spoil the broth." The ability to explain the meaning of each proverb provides no guarantee that students will know the conditions under which either proverb is useful. Such knowledge is important because, when viewed solely as propositions, proverbs often contradict one another. To use them effectively, people need to know when and why it is appropriate to apply the maxim "too many cooks spoil the broth" versus "many hands make light work" or "he who hesitates is lost" versus "haste makes waste" (see Bransford and Stein, 1993).

FLUENT RETRIEVAL

People's abilities to retrieve relevant knowledge can vary from being "effortful" to "relatively effortless" (fluent) to "automatic" (Schneider and Shiffrin, 1977). Automatic and fluent retrieval are important characteristics of expertise.

Fluent retrieval does not mean that experts always perform a task faster than novices. Because experts attempt to understand problems rather than to jump immediately to solution strategies, they sometimes take more time than novices (e.g., Getzels and Csikszentmihalyi, 1976). But within the overall process of problem solving there are a number of subprocesses that, for experts, vary from fluent to automatic. Fluency is important because effortless processing places fewer demands on conscious attention. Since the amount of information a person can attend to at any one time is limited (Miller, 1956), ease of processing some aspects of a task gives a person more capacity to attend to other aspects of the task (LaBerge and Samuels, 1974; Schneider and Shiffrin, 1985; Anderson, 1981, 1982; Lesgold et al., 1988).

Learning to drive a car provides a good example of fluency and automaticity. When first learning, novices cannot drive and simultaneously carry on a conversation. With experience, it becomes easy to do so. Similarly, novice readers whose ability to decode words is not yet fluent are unable to devote attention to the task of understanding what they are reading (LaBerge and Samuels, 1974). Issues of fluency are very important for understanding learning and instruction. Many instructional environments stop short of helping all students develop the fluency needed to successfully perform cognitive tasks (Beck et al., 1989; Case, 1978; Hasselbring et al., 1987; LaBerge and Samuels, 1974).

An important aspect of learning is to become fluent at recognizing problem types in particular domains—such as problems involving Newton's second law or concepts of rate and functions—so that appropriate solutions can be easily retrieved from memory. The use of instructional procedures that speed pattern recognition are promising in this regard (e.g., Simon, 1980).

EXPERTS AND TEACHING

Expertise in a particular domain does not guarantee that one is good at helping others learn it. In fact, expertise can sometimes hurt teaching because many experts forget what is easy and what is difficult for students.

Recognizing this fact, some groups who design educational materials pair content area experts with "accomplished novices" whose area of expertise lies elsewhere: their task is to continually challenge the experts until the experts' ideas for instruction begin to make sense to them (Cognition and Technology Group at Vanderbilt, 1997).

The content knowledge necessary for expertise in a discipline needs to be differentiated from the pedagogical content knowledge that underlies effective teaching (Redish, 1996; Shulman, 1986, 1987). The latter includes information about typical difficulties that students encounter as they attempt to learn about a set of topics; typical paths students must traverse in order to achieve understanding; and sets of potential strategies for helping students overcome the difficulties that they encounter. Shulman (1986, 1987) argues that pedagogical content knowledge is not equivalent to knowledge of a content domain plus a generic set of teaching strategies; instead, teaching strategies differ across disciplines. Expert teachers know the kinds of difficulties that students are likely to face; they know how to tap into students' existing knowledge in order to make new information meaningful; and they know how to assess their students' progress. Expert teachers have acquired pedagogical content knowledge as well as content knowledge; see Box 2.4. In the absence of pedagogical content knowledge, teachers often rely on textbook publishers for decisions about how to best organize subjects for students. They are therefore forced to rely on the "prescriptions of absentee curriculum developers" (Brophy, 1983), who know nothing about the particular students in each teacher's classroom. Pedagogical content knowledge is an extremely important part of what teachers need to learn to be more effective. (This topic is discussed more fully in Chapter 7.)

ADAPTIVE EXPERTISE

An important question for educators is whether some ways of organizing knowledge are better at helping people remain flexible and adaptive to new situations than others. For example, contrast two types of Japanese sushi experts (Hatano and Inagaki, 1986): one excels at following a fixed recipe; the other has "adaptive expertise" and is able to prepare sushi quite creatively. These appear to be examples of two very different types of expertise, one that is relatively routinized and one that is flexible and more adaptable to external demands: experts have been characterized as being "merely skilled" versus "highly competent" or more colorfully as "artisans" versus "virtuosos" (Miller, 1978). These differences apparently exist across a wide range of jobs.

One analysis looked at these differences in terms of information systems design (Miller, 1978). Information systems designers typically work with clients who specify what they want. The goal of the designer is to construct systems that allow people to efficiently store and access relevant informa-

BOX 2.4 Teaching *Hamlet*

Two new English teachers, Jake and Steven, with similar subject-matter backgrounds from elite private universities, set out to teach *Hamlet* in high school (Grossman, 1990).

In his teaching, Jake spent 7 weeks leading his students through a word-by-word *explication du texte*, focusing on notions of "linguistic reflexivity," and issues of modernism. His assignments included in-depth analyses of soliloquies, memorization of long passages, and a final paper on the importance of language in *Hamlet*. Jake's model for this instruction was his own undergraduate coursework; there was little transformation of his knowledge, except to parcel it out in chunks that fit into the 50-minute containers of the school day. Jake's image for how students would respond was his own responses as a student who loved Shakespeare and delighted in close textual analysis. Consequently, when students responded in less than enthusiastic ways, Jake was ill-equipped to understand their confusion: "The biggest problem I have with teaching by far is trying to get into the mind-set of a ninth grader . . . "

Steven began his unit on *Hamlet* without ever mentioning the name of the play. To help his students grasp the initial outline of the themes and issues of the play, he asked them to imagine that their parents had recently divorced and that their mothers had taken up with a new man. This new man had replaced their father at work, and "there's some talk that he had something to do with the ousting of your dad" (Grossman, 1990:24). Steven then asked students to think about the circumstances that might drive them so mad that they would contemplate murdering another human being. Only then, after students had contemplated these issues and done some writing on them, did Steven introduce the play they would be reading.

tion (usually through computers). Artisan experts seek to identify the functions that their clients want automated; they tend to accept the problem and its limits as stated by the clients. They approach new problems as opportunities to use their existing expertise to do familiar tasks more efficiently. It is important to emphasize that artisans' skills are often extensive and should not be underestimated. In contrast, however, the virtuoso experts treat the client's statement of the problem with respect, but consider it "a point for departure and exploration" (Miller, 1978). They view assignments as opportunities to explore and expand their current levels of expertise. Miller also observes that, in his experience, virtuosos exhibit their positive characteristics *despite* their training, which is usually restricted solely to technical skills.

The concept of adaptive expertise has also been explored in a study of history experts (Wineburg, 1998). Two history experts and a group of future teachers were asked to read and interpret a set of documents about Abraham Lincoln and his view of slavery. This is a complex issue that, for Lincoln, involved conflicts between enacted law (the Constitution), natural law (as encoded in the Declaration of Independence), and divine law (assumptions about basic rights). One of the historians was an expert on Lincoln; the second historian's expertise lay elsewhere. The Lincoln expert brought detailed content knowledge to the documents and easily interpreted them; the other historian was familiar with some of the broad themes in the documents but quickly became confused in the details. In fact, at the beginning of the task, the second historian reacted no differently than a group of future high school teachers who were faced with the same task (Wineburg and Fournier, 1994): attempting to harmonize discrepant information about Lincoln's position, they both appealed to an array of present social forms and institutions—such as speech writers, press conferences, and "spin doctors"—to explain why things seemed discrepant. Unlike the future teachers, however, the second historian did not stop with his initial analysis. He instead adopted a working hypothesis that assumed that the apparent contradictions might be rooted less in Lincoln's duplicity than in his own ignorance of the nineteenth century. The expert stepped back from his own initial interpretation and searched for a deeper understanding of the issues. As he read texts from this perspective, his understanding deepened, and he learned from the experience. After considerable work, the second historian was able to piece together an interpretive structure that brought him by the task's end to where his more knowledgeable colleague had begun. The future history teachers, in contrast, never moved beyond their initial interpretations of events.

An important characteristic exhibited by the history expert involves what is known as "metacognition"—the ability to monitor one's current level of understanding and decide when it is not adequate. The concept of metacognition was originally introduced in the context of studying young children (e.g., Brown, 1980; Flavell, 1985, 1991). For example, young children often erroneously believe that they can remember information and hence fail to use effective strategies, such as rehearsal. The ability to recognize the limits of one's current knowledge, then take steps to remedy the situation, is extremely important for learners at all ages. The history expert who was not a specialist in Lincoln was metacognitive in the sense that he successfully recognized the insufficiency of his initial attempts to explain Lincoln's position. As a consequence, he adopted the working hypothesis that he needed to learn more about the context of Lincoln's times before coming to a reasoned conclusion.

Beliefs about what it means to be an expert can affect the degree to which people explicitly search for what they don't know and take steps to improve the situation. In a study of researchers and veteran teachers, a common assumption was that "an expert is someone who knows all the answers" (Cognition and Technology Group at Vanderbilt, 1997). This assumption had been implicit rather than explicit and had never been questioned and discussed. But when the researchers and teachers discussed this concept, they discovered that it placed severe constraints on new learning because the tendency was to worry about looking competent rather than publicly acknowledging the need for help in certain areas (see Dweck, 1989, for similar findings with students). The researchers and the teachers found it useful to replace their previous model of "answer-filled experts" with the model of "accomplished novices." Accomplished novices are skilled in many areas and proud of their accomplishments, but they realize that what they know is minuscule compared to all that is potentially knowable. This model helps free people to continue to learn even though they may have spent 10 to 20 years as an "expert" in their field.

The concept of adaptive expertise (Hatano and Inagaki, 1986) provides an important model of successful learning. Adaptive experts are able to approach new situations flexibly and to learn throughout their lifetimes. They not only use what they have learned, they are metacognitive and continually question their current levels of expertise and attempt to move beyond them. They don't simply attempt to do the same things more efficiently; they attempt to do things better. A major challenge for theories of learning is to understand how particular kinds of learning experiences develop adaptive expertise or "virtuosos."

CONCLUSION

Experts' abilities to reason and solve problems depend on well-organized knowledge that affects what they notice and how they represent problems. Experts are not simply "general problem solvers" who have learned a set of strategies that operate across all domains. The fact that experts are more likely than novices to recognize meaningful patterns of information applies in all domains, whether chess, electronics, mathematics, or classroom teaching. In deGroot's (1965) words, a "given" problem situation is not really a given. Because of their ability to see patterns of meaningful information, experts begin problem solving at "a higher place" (deGroot, 1965). An emphasis on the patterns perceived by experts suggests that pattern recognition is an important strategy for helping students develop confidence and competence. These patterns provide triggering conditions for accessing knowledge that is relevant to a task.

Studies in areas such as physics, mathematics, and history also demonstrate that experts first seek to develop an understanding of problems, and this often involves thinking in terms of core concepts or big ideas, such as Newton's second law in physics. Novices' knowledge is much less likely to be organized around big ideas; they are more likely to approach problems by searching for correct formulas and pat answers that fit their everyday intuitions.

Curricula that emphasize breadth of knowledge may prevent effective organization of knowledge because there is not enough time to learn anything in depth. Instruction that enables students to see models of how experts organize and solve problems may be helpful. However, as discussed in more detail in later chapters, the level of complexity of the models must be tailored to the learners' current levels of knowledge and skills.

While experts possess a vast repertoire of knowledge, only a subset of it is relevant to any particular problem. Experts do not conduct an exhaustive search of everything they know; this would overwhelm their working memory (Miller, 1956). Instead, information that is relevant to a task tends to be selectively retrieved (e.g., Ericsson and Staszewski, 1989; deGroot, 1965).

The issue of retrieving relevant information provides clues about the nature of usable knowledge. Knowledge must be "conditionalized" in order to be retrieved when it is needed; otherwise, it remains inert (Whitehead, 1929). Many designs for curriculum instruction and assessment practices fail to emphasize the importance of conditionalized knowledge. For example, texts often present facts and formulas with little attention to helping students learn the conditions under which they are most useful. Many assessments measure only propositional (factual) knowledge and never ask whether students know when, where, and why to use that knowledge.

Another important characteristic of expertise is the ability to retrieve relevant knowledge in a manner that is relatively "effortless." This fluent retrieval does not mean that experts always accomplish tasks in less time than novices; often they take more time in order to fully understand a problem. But their ability to retrieve information effortlessly is extremely important because fluency places fewer demands on conscious attention, which is limited in capacity (Schneider and Shiffrin, 1977, 1985). Effortful retrieval, by contrast, places many demands on a learner's attention: attentional effort is being expended on remembering instead of learning. Instruction that focuses solely on accuracy does not necessarily help students develop fluency (e.g., Beck et al., 1989; Hasselbring et al., 1987; LaBerge and Samuels, 1974).

Expertise in an area does not guarantee that one can effectively teach others about that area. Expert teachers know the kinds of difficulties that students are likely to face, and they know how to tap into their students' existing knowledge in order to make new information meaningful plus assess their students' progress. In Shulman's (1986, 1987) terms, expert teachers have acquired pedagogical content knowledge and not just content knowledge. (This concept is explored more fully in Chapter 7.)

The concept of adaptive expertise raises the question of whether some ways of organizing knowledge lead to greater flexibility in problem solving than others (Hatano and Inagaki, 1986; Spiro et al., 1991). Differences between the "merely skilled" (artisans) and the "highly competent" (virtuosos) can be seen in fields as disparate as sushi making and information design. Virtuosos not only apply expertise to a given problem, they also consider whether the problem as presented is the best way to begin.

The ability to monitor one's approach to problem solving—to be metacognitive—is an important aspect of the expert's competence. Experts step back from their first, oversimplistic interpretation of a problem or situation and question their own knowledge that is relevant. People's mental models of what it means to be an expert can affect the degree to which they learn throughout their lifetimes. A model that assumes that experts know all the answers is very different from a model of the accomplished novice, who is proud of his or her achievements and yet also realizes that there is much more to learn.

We close this chapter with two important cautionary notes. First, the six principles of expertise need to be considered simultaneously, as parts of an overall system. We divided our discussion into six points in order to facilitate explanation, but each point interacts with the others; this interrelationship has important educational implications. For example, the idea of promoting fluent access to knowledge (principle 4) must be approached with an eye toward helping students develop an understanding of the subject matter (principle 2), learn when, where and why to use information (principle 3), and learn to recognize meaningful patterns of information (principle 1). Furthermore, all these need to be approached from the perspective of helping students develop adaptive expertise (principle 6), which includes helping them become metacognitive about their learning so that they can assess their own progress and continually identify and pursue new learning goals. An example in mathematics is getting students to recognize when a proof is needed. Metacognition can help students develop personally relevant pedagogical content knowledge, analogous to the pedagogical content knowledge available to effective teachers (principle 5). In short, students need to develop the ability to teach themselves.

The second cautionary note is that although the study of experts provides important information about learning and instruction, it can be misleading if applied inappropriately. For example, it would be a mistake simply to expose novices to expert models and assume that the novices will learn effectively; what they will learn depends on how much they know already. Discussions in the next chapters (3 and 4) show that effective instruction begins with the knowledge and skills that learners bring to the learning task.

3

Learning and Transfer

Processes of learning and the transfer of learning are central to understanding how people develop important competencies. Learning is important because no one is born with the ability to function competently as an adult in society. It is especially important to understand the kinds of learning experiences that lead to transfer, defined as the ability to extend what has been learned in one context to new contexts (e.g., Byrnes, 1996:74). Educators hope that students will transfer learning from one problem to another within a course, from one year in school to another, between school and home, and from school to workplace. Assumptions about transfer accompany the belief that it is better to broadly "educate" people than simply "train" them to perform particular tasks (e.g., Broudy, 1977).

Measures of transfer play an important role in assessing the quality of people's learning experiences. Different kinds of learning experiences can look equivalent when tests of learning focus solely on remembering (e.g., on the ability to repeat previously taught facts or procedures), but they can look quite different when tests of transfer are used. Some kinds of learning experiences result in effective memory but poor transfer; others produce effective memory plus positive transfer.

Thorndike and his colleagues were among the first to use transfer tests to examine assumptions about learning (e.g., Thorndike and Woodworth, 1901). One of their goals was to test the doctrine of "formal discipline" that was prevalent at the turn of the century. According to this doctrine, practice by learning Latin and other difficult subjects had broad-based effects, such as developing general skills of learning and attention. But these studies raised serious questions about the fruitfulness of designing educational experiences based on the assumption of formal discipline. Rather than developing some kind of "general skill" or "mental muscle" that affected a wide range of performances, people seemed to learn things that were more specific; see Box 3.1.

Early research on the transfer of learning was guided by theories that emphasized the similarity between conditions of learning and conditions of transfer. Thorndike (1913), for example, hypothesized that the degree of transfer between initial and later learning depends upon the match between

BOX 3.1 **What People Learn**

Ericsson et al. (1980) worked extensively with a college student for well over a year, increasing his capacity to remember digit strings (e.g., 982761093 . . .). As expected, at the outset he could remember only about seven numbers. After practice, he could remember 70 or more; see Figure 3.1. How? Did he develop a general skill analogous to strengthening a "mental muscle?" No, what happened was that he learned to use his specific background knowledge to "chunk" information into meaningful groups. The student had extensive knowledge about winning times for famous track races, including the times of national and world records. For example 941003591992100 could be chunked into 94100 (9.41 seconds for 100 yards). 3591 (3 minutes, 59.1 seconds for a mile), etc. But it took the student a huge amount of practice before he could perform at his final level, and when he was tested with *letter* strings, he was back to remembering about seven items.

SOURCE: Ericsson et al. (1980:1181-1182). Reprinted by permission.

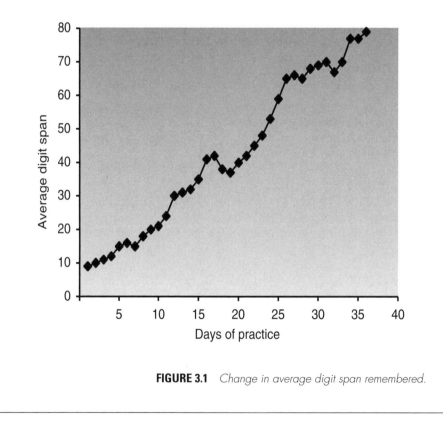

FIGURE 3.1 *Change in average digit span remembered.*

elements across the two events. The essential elements were presumed to be specific facts and skills. By such an account, skills of writing letters of the alphabet are useful to writing words (vertical transfer). The theory posited that transfer from one school task and a highly similar task (near transfer), and from school subjects to nonschool settings (far transfer), could be facilitated by teaching knowledge and skills in school subjects that have elements *identical* to activities encountered in the transfer context (Klausmeier, 1985). Transfer could also be negative in the sense that experience with one set of events could hurt performance on related tasks (Luchins and Luchins, 1970); see Box 3.2.

The emphasis on identical elements of tasks excluded consideration of any learner characteristics, including when attention was directed, whether relevant principles were extrapolated, problem solving, or creativity and motivation. The primary emphasis was on drill and practice. Modern theories of learning and transfer retain the emphasis on practice, but they specify the kinds of practice that are important and take learner characteristics (e.g., existing knowledge and strategies) into account (e.g., Singley and Anderson, 1989).

In the discussion below we explore key characteristics of learning and transfer that have important implications for education:

- Initial learning is necessary for transfer, and a considerable amount is known about the kinds of learning experiences that support transfer.
- Knowledge that is overly contextualized can reduce transfer; abstract representations of knowledge can help promote transfer.
- Transfer is best viewed as an active, dynamic process rather than a passive end-product of a particular set of learning experiences.
- All new learning involves transfer based on previous learning, and this fact has important implications for the design of instruction that helps students learn.

ELEMENTS THAT PROMOTE INITIAL LEARNING

The first factor that influences successful transfer is degree of mastery of the original subject. Without an adequate level of initial learning, transfer cannot be expected. This point seems obvious, but it is often overlooked.

The importance of initial learning is illustrated by a series of studies designed to assess the effects of learning to program in the computer language LOGO. The hypothesis was that students who learned LOGO would transfer this knowledge to other areas that required thinking and problem solving (Papert, 1980). Yet in many cases, the studies found no differences on transfer tests between students who had been taught LOGO and those who had not (see Cognition and Technology Group at Vanderbilt, 1996;

BOX 3.2 **An Example of Negative Transfer**

Luchins and Luchins (1970) studied how prior experience can limit people's abilities to function efficiently in new settings. They used water jar problems where participants had three jars of varying sizes and an unlimited water supply and were asked to obtain a required amount of water. Everyone received a practice problem. People in the experimental group then received five problems (problems 2-6) prior to critical test problems (7, 8, 10, and 11). People in the control group went straight from the practice problems to problems 7-11. Problems 2-6 were designed to establish a "set" (Einstellung) for solving the problems in a particular manner (using containers b-a-2c as a solution). People in the experimental group were highly likely to use the Einstellung Solution on the critical problems even though more efficient procedures were available. In contrast, people in the control group used solutions that were much more direct.

Problem	Given Jars of the Following Sizes			Obtain the Amount
	A	B	C	
1	29	3		20
2 Einstellung 1	21	127	3	100
3 Einstellung 2	14	163	25	99
4 Einstellung 3	18	43	10	5
5 Einstellung 4	9	42	6	21
6 Einstellung 5	20	59	4	31
7 Critical 1	23	49	3	20
8 Critical 2	15	39	3	18
9	28	76	3	25
10 Critical 3	18	48	4	22
11 Critical 4	14	36	8	6

BOX 3.2 **An Example of Negative Transfer (*continued*)**

Possible Answers for Critical Problems (7, 8, 10, 11)

Problem	Einstellung Solution	Direct Solution
7	$49 - 23 - 3 - 3 = 20$	$23 - 3 = 20$
8	$39 - 15 - 3 - 3 = 18$	$15 + 3 = 18$
10	$48 - 18 - 4 - 4 = 22$	$18 + 4 = 22$
11	$36 - 14 - 8 - 8 = 6$	$14 - 8 = 6$

Performance of Typical Subjects on Critical Problems

Group	Einstellung Solution (percent)	Direct Solution (percent)	No Solution (percent)
Control (Children)	1	89	10
Experimental (Children)	72	24	4
Control (Adults)	0	100	0
Experimental (Adults)	74	26	0

SOURCE: Adapted from Luchins and Luchins (1970).

Mayer, 1988). However, many of these studies failed to assess the degree to which LOGO was learned in the first place (see Klahr and Carver, 1988; Littlefield et al., 1988). When initial learning was assessed, it was found that students often had not learned enough about LOGO to provide a basis for transfer. Subsequent studies began to pay more attention to student learning, and they did find transfer to related tasks (Klahr and Carver, 1988; Littlefield et al., 1988). Other research studies have shown that additional qualities of initial learning affect transfer and are reviewed next.

Understanding Versus Memorizing

Transfer is affected by the degree to which people learn with understanding rather than merely memorize sets of facts or follow a fixed set of procedures; see Boxes 3.3 and 3.4.

In Chapter 1, the advantages of learning with understanding were illus-

BOX 3.3 Throwing Darts

In one of the most famous early studies comparing the effects of "learning a procedure" with "learning with understanding," two groups of children practiced throwing darts at a target underwater (Scholckow and Judd, described in Judd, 1908; see a conceptual replication by Hendrickson and Schroeder, 1941). One group received an explanation of refraction of light, which causes the apparent location of the target to be deceptive. The other group only practiced dart throwing, without the explanation. Both groups did equally well on the practice task, which involved a target 12 inches under water. But the group that had been instructed about the abstract principle did much better when they had to transfer to a situation in which the target was under only 4 inches of water. Because they understood what they were doing, the group that had received instruction about the refraction of light could adjust their behavior to the new task.

trated with an example from biology that involved learning about the physical properties of veins and arteries. We noted that the ability to remember properties of veins and arteries (e.g., that arteries are thicker than veins, more elastic, and carry blood from the heart) is not the same as understanding why they have particular properties. The ability to understand becomes important for transfer problems, such as: "Imagine trying to design an artificial artery. Would it have to be elastic? Why or why not?" Students who only memorize facts have little basis for approaching this kind of problem-solving task (Bransford and Stein, 1993; Bransford et al., 1983). The act of organizing facts about veins and arteries around more general principles such as "how structure is related to function" is consistent with the knowledge organization of experts discussed in Chapter 2.

Time to Learn

It is important to be realistic about the amount of time it takes to learn complex subject matter. It has been estimated that world-class chess masters require from 50,000 to 100,000 hours of practice to reach that level of expertise; they rely on a knowledge base containing some 50,000 familiar chess patterns to guide their selection of moves (Chase and Simon, 1973; Simon and Chase, 1973). Much of this time involves the development of pattern recognition skills that support the fluent identification of meaningful patterns of information plus knowledge of their implications for future outcomes (see Chapter 2). In all domains of learning, the development of

BOX 3.4   **Finding the Area of a Figure**

Understanding Method

The understanding method encouraged students to see the structural relations in the parallelogram, for example, that the parallelogram could be rearranged into a rectangle by moving a triangle from one side to the other. Since the students knew how to find the area of a rectangle, finding the area of a parallelogram was easy once they discovered the appropriate structural relations.

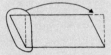

Rote Method

In the rote method, students were taught to drop a perpendicular and then apply the memorized solution formula.

Area = $n \times b$

Transfer

Both groups performed well on typical problems asking for the area of parallelograms; however, only the understanding group could transfer to novel problems, such as finding the area of the figures below.

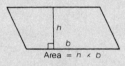

or distinguishing between solvable and unsolvable problems such as

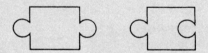

The response of the "rote" group to novel problems was, "We haven't had that yet."

SOURCE: Based on Wertheimer (1959).

BOX 3.5 Learning Algebra

> Students taking regular algebra in a major school system received an average of 65 hours of instruction and homework during the year. In contrast, those taking honors algebra received approximately 250 hours of instruction and homework (John Anderson, personal communication). Clearly, it was recognized that significant learning takes major investments of time.

expertise occurs only with major investments of time, and the amount of time it takes to learn material is roughly proportional to the amount of material being learned (Singley and Anderson, 1989); see Box 3.5. Although many people believe that "talent" plays a role in who becomes an expert in a particular area, even seemingly talented individuals require a great deal of practice in order to develop their expertise (Ericsson et al., 1993).

Learners, especially in school settings, are often faced with tasks that do not have apparent meaning or logic (Klausmeier, 1985). It can be difficult for them to learn with understanding at the start; they may need to take time to explore underlying concepts and to generate connections to other information they possess. Attempts to cover too many topics too quickly may hinder learning and subsequent transfer because students (a) learn only isolated sets of facts that are not organized and connected or (b) are introduced to organizing principles that they cannot grasp because they lack enough specific knowledge to make them meaningful. Providing students with opportunities to first grapple with specific information relevant to a topic has been shown to create a "time for telling" that enables them to learn much more from an organizing lecture (as measured by subsequent abilities to transfer) than students who did not first have these specific opportunities; see Box 3.6.

Providing students with time to learn also includes providing enough time for them to process information. Pezdek and Miceli (1982) found that on one particular task, it took 3rd graders 15 seconds to integrate pictorial and verbal information; when given only 8 seconds, they couldn't mentally integrate the information, probably due to short-term memory limitations. The implication is that learning cannot be rushed; the complex cognitive activity of information integration requires time.

Beyond "Time on Task"

It is clear that different ways of using one's time have different effects on learning and transfer. A considerable amount is known about variables that affect learning. For example, learning is most effective when people engage

BOX 3.6 Preparation for Learning with Understanding

Three different groups of college students received different kinds of instruction about schema theory and memory and then completed a transfer task where they were asked to make detailed predictions about the results of a new memory study. Students in Group 1 read and summarized a text on the topic of schema theory and then listened to a lecture designed to help them organize their knowledge and learn with understanding. Group 2 did not read the text but, instead, actively compared simplified data sets from schema experiments on memory and then heard the same lecture as Group 1. Group 3 spent twice as much time as Group 2 working with the data sets but did not receive the organizing lecture. On the transfer test, students in Group 2 performed much better than those in Groups 1 and 3. Their work with the data sets set the stage for them to learn from the lecture. The lecture was necessary, as indicated by the poor performance of Group 3.

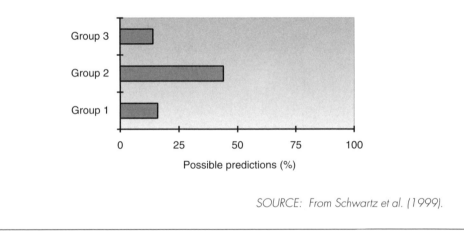

SOURCE: From Schwartz et al. (1999).

in "deliberate practice" that includes active monitoring of one's learning experiences (Ericsson et al., 1993). Monitoring involves attempts to seek and use feedback about one's progress. Feedback has long been identified as important for successful learning (see, e.g., Thorndike, 1913), but it should not be regarded as a unidimensional concept. For example, feedback that signals progress in memorizing facts and formulas is different from feedback that signals the state of the students' understanding (Chi et al., 1989, 1994). In addition, as noted in Chapter 2, students need feedback about the degree to which they know when, where, and how to use the knowledge they are learning. By inadvertently relying on clues—such as which chapter in a text the practice problems came from—students can erroneously think they have conditionalized their knowledge when, in fact, they have not (Bransford, 1979).

Understanding when, where, and why to use new knowledge can be enhanced through the use of "contrasting cases," a concept from the field of perceptual learning (see, e.g., Gagné and Gibson, 1947; Garner, 1974; Gibson and Gibson, 1955). Appropriately arranged contrasts can help people notice new features that previously escaped their attention and learn which features are relevant or irrelevant to a particular concept. The benefits of appropriately arranged contrasting cases apply not only to perceptual learning, but also to conceptual learning (Bransford et al., 1989; Schwartz et al., 1999). For example, the concept of linear function becomes clearer when contrasted with nonlinear functions; the concept of recognition memory becomes clearer when contrasted with measures such as free recall and cued recall.

A number of studies converge on the conclusion that transfer is enhanced by helping students see potential transfer implications of what they are learning (Anderson et al., 1996). In one of the studies on learning LOGO programming (Klahr and Carver, 1988), the goal was to help students learn to generate "bug-free" instructions for others to follow. The researchers first conducted a careful task analysis of the important skills underlying the ability to program in LOGO and focused especially on LOGO debugging skills—the process by which children find and correct errors in their programs. Part of the researchers' success in teaching LOGO depended on this task analysis. The researchers identified the four key aspects of debugging a program as identifying the buggy behavior, representing the program, locating the bug in the program, and then correcting the bug. They highlighted these key abstract steps and signaled to the students that the steps would be relevant to the transfer task of writing debugging directions. Students who had LOGO training increased from 33 percent correct instructions to 55 percent correct instructions. They could have approached this task by memorizing the procedures for programming LOGO routines to "make a house," "make a polygon," and so forth. Simply memorizing the procedures, however, would not be expected to help students accomplish the transfer task of generating clear, bug-free instructions.

Motivation to Learn

Motivation affects the amount of time that people are willing to devote to learning. Humans are motivated to develop competence and to solve problems; they have, as White (1959) put it, "competence motivation." Although extrinsic rewards and punishments clearly affect behavior (see Chapter 1), people work hard for intrinsic reasons, as well.

Challenges, however, must be at the proper level of difficulty in order to be and to remain motivating: tasks that are too easy become boring; tasks that are too difficult cause frustration. In addition, learners' tendencies to persist in the face of difficulty are strongly affected by whether they are "performance oriented" or "learning oriented" (Dweck, 1989). Students who are learning oriented like new challenges; those who are performance oriented are more worried about making errors than about learning. Being learning oriented is similar to the concept of adaptive expertise discussed in Chapter 2. It is probable, but needs to be verified experimentally, that being "learning oriented" or "performance oriented" is not a stable trait of an individual but, instead, varies across disciplines (e.g., a person may be performance oriented in mathematics but learning oriented in science and social studies or vice versa).

Social opportunities also affect motivation. Feeling that one is contributing something to others appears to be especially motivating (Schwartz et al., 1999). For example, young learners are highly motivated to write stories and draw pictures that they can share with others. First graders in an inner-city school were so highly motivated to write books to be shared with others that the teachers had to make a rule: "No leaving recess early to go back to class to work on your book" (Cognition and Technology Group at Vanderbilt, 1998).

Learners of all ages are more motivated when they can see the usefulness of what they are learning and when they can use that information to do something that has an impact on others—especially their local community (McCombs, 1996; Pintrich and Schunk, 1996). Sixth graders in an inner-city school were asked to explain the highlights of their previous year in fifth grade to an anonymous interviewer, who asked them to describe anything that made them feel proud, successful, or creative (Barron et al., 1998). Students frequently mentioned projects that had strong social consequences, such as tutoring younger children, learning to make presentations to outside audiences, designing blueprints for playhouses that were to be built by professionals and then donated to preschool programs, and learning to work effectively in groups. Many of the activities mentioned by the students had involved a great deal of hard work on their part: for example, they had had to learn about geometry and architecture in order to get the chance to create blueprints for the playhouses, and they had had to explain their blueprints to a group of outside experts who held them to very high standards. (For other examples and discussions of highly motivating activities, see Pintrich and Schunk, 1996.)

OTHER FACTORS THAT INFLUENCE TRANSFER

Context

Transfer is also affected by the context of original learning; people can learn in one context, yet fail to transfer to other contexts. For example, a group of Orange County homemakers did very well at making supermarket best-buy calculations despite doing poorly on equivalent school-like paper-and-pencil mathematics problems (Lave, 1988). Similarly, some Brazilian street children could perform mathematics when making sales in the street but were unable to answer similar problems presented in a school context (Carraher, 1986; Carraher et al., 1985).

How tightly learning is tied to contexts depends on how the knowledge is acquired (Eich, 1985). Research has indicated that transfer across contexts is especially difficult when a subject is taught only in a single context rather than in multiple contexts (Bjork and Richardson-Klavhen, 1989). One frequently used teaching technique is to get learners to elaborate on the examples used during learning in order to facilitate retrieval at a later time. The practice, however, has the potential of actually making it more difficult to retrieve the lesson material in other contexts, because knowledge tends to be especially context-bound when learners elaborate the new material with details of the context in which the material is learned (Eich, 1985). When a subject is taught in multiple contexts, however, and includes examples that demonstrate wide application of what is being taught, people are more likely to abstract the relevant features of concepts and to develop a flexible representation of knowledge (Gick and Holyoak, 1983).

The problem of overly contextualized knowledge has been studied in instructional programs that use case-based and problem-based learning. In these programs, information is presented in a context of attempting to solve complex, realistic problems (e.g., Barrows, 1985; Cognition and Technology Group at Vanderbilt, 1997; Gragg, 1940; Hmelo, 1995; Williams, 1992). For example, fifth- and sixth-grade students may learn mathematical concepts of distance-rate-time in the context of solving a complex case involving planning for a boat trip. The findings indicate that if students learn only in this context, they often fail to transfer flexibly to new situations (Cognition and Technology Group at Vanderbilt, 1997). The issue is how to promote wide transfer of the learning.

One way to deal with lack of flexibility is to ask learners to solve a specific case and then provide them with an additional, similar case; the goal is to help them abstract general principles that lead to more flexible transfer (Gick and Holyoak, 1983); see Box 3.7. A second way to improve flexibility is to let students learn in a specific context and then help them engage in "what-if" problem solving designed to increase the flexibility of their understanding. They might be asked: "What if this part of the problem were changed, or this part?" (Cognition and Technology Group at Vanderbilt, 1997). A third way is to generalize the case so that learners are asked to create a solution that applies not simply to a single problem, but to a whole class of related problems. For example, instead of planning a single boat trip, students might run a trip planning company that has to advise people on travel times for different regions of the country. Learners are asked to adopt the goal of learning to "work smart" by creating mathematical models that characterize a variety of travel problems and using these models to create tools, ranging from simple tables and graphs to computer programs. Under these conditions, transfer to novel problems is enhanced (e.g., Bransford et al., 1998).

Problem Representations

Transfer is also enhanced by instruction that helps students represent problems at higher levels of abstraction. For example, students who create a specific business plan for a complex problem may not initially realize that their plan works well for "fixed-cost" situations but not for others. Helping students represent their solution strategies at a more general level can help them increase the probability of positive transfer and decrease the degree to which a previous solution strategy is used inappropriately (negative transfer).

Advantages of abstract problem representations have been studied in the context of algebra word problems involving mixtures. Some students were trained with pictures of the mixtures and other students were trained with abstract tabular representations that highlighted the underlying mathematical relationships (Singley and Anderson, 1989). Students who were trained on specific task components without being provided with the principles underlying the problems could do the specific tasks well, but they could not apply their learning to new problems. By contrast, the students who received abstract training showed transfer to new problems that involved *analogous* mathematical relations. Research has also shown that developing a suite of representations enables learners to think flexibly about complex domains (Spiro et al., 1991).

Relationships Between Learning and Transfer Conditions

Transfer is always a function of relationships between what is learned and what is tested. Many theorists argue that the amount of transfer will be a function of the overlap between the original domain of learning and the novel one. Measuring overlap requires a theory of how knowledge is represented and conceptually mapped across domains. Examples of research

BOX 3.7   Flexible Transfer

College students were presented with the following passage about a general and a fortress (Gick and Holyoak, 1980:309).

> A general wishes to capture a fortress located in the center of a country. There are many roads radiating outward from the fortress. All have been mined so that while small groups of men can pass over the roads safely, a large force will detonate the mines. A full-scale direct attack is therefore impossible. The general's solution is to divide his army into small groups, send each group to the head of a different road, and have the groups converge simultaneously on the fortress.

Students memorized the information in the passage and were then asked to try another task, which was to solve the following problem (Gick and Holyoak, 1980:307-308).

> You are a doctor faced with a patient who has a malignant tumor in his stomach. It is impossible to operate on the patient, but unless the tumor is destroyed the patient will die. There is a kind of ray that may be used to destroy the tumor. If the rays reach the tumor all at once and with sufficiently high intensity, the tumor will be destroyed, but surrounding tissue may be damaged as well. At lower intensities the rays are harmless to healthy tissue, but they will not affect the tumor either. What type of procedure might be used to destroy the tumor with the rays, and at the same time avoid destroying the healthy tissue?

Few college students were able to solve this problem when left to their own devices. However, over 90 percent were able to solve the tumor problem when they were explicitly told to use information about the general and the fortress to help them. These students perceived the analogy between dividing the troops into small units and using a number of small-dose rays that each converge on the same point—the cancerous tissue. Each ray is too weak to harm tissue except at the point of convergence. Despite the relevance of the fortress problem to the tumor problem, the information was not used spontaneously—the connection between the two sets of information had to be explicitly pointed out.

studies on conceptual representation include Brown (1986), Bassok and Holyoak (1989a, b), and Singley and Anderson (1989). Whether students will transfer across domains—such as distance formulas from physics to formally equivalent biological growth problems, for example—depends on whether they conceive of the growth as occurring continuously (successful transfer) or in discrete steps (unsuccessful transfer) (Bassok and Olseth, 1995).

Singley and Anderson (1989) argue that transfer between tasks is a function of the degree to which the tasks share *cognitive* elements. This hypothesis was also put forth very early in the development of research on transfer of identical elements, mentioned previously (Thorndike and Woodworth, 1901; Woodworth, 1938), but it was hard to test experimentally until there was a way to identify task components. In addition, modern theorists include cognitive representations and strategies as "elements" that vary across tasks (Singley and Anderson, 1989).

Singley and Anderson taught students several text editors, one after another, and sought to predict transfer, defined as the savings in time of learning a new editor when it was not taught first. They found that students learned subsequent text editors more rapidly and that the number of procedural elements shared by two text editors predicted the amount of this transfer. In fact, there was large transfer across editors that were very different in surface structures but that had common abstract structures. Singley and Anderson also found that similar principles govern transfer of mathematical competence across multiple domains when they considered transfer of declarative as well as procedural knowledge.

A study by Biederman and Shiffrar (1987) is a striking example of the benefits of abstract instruction. They studied a task that is typically difficult to learn in apprentice-like roles: how to examine day-old chicks to determine their sex. Biederman and Shiffrar found that twenty minutes of instruction on abstract principles helped the novices improve considerably (see also Anderson et al., 1996). Research studies generally provide strong support for the benefits of helping students represent their experiences at levels of abstraction that transcend the specificity of particular contexts and examples (National Research Council, 1994). Examples include algebra (Singley and Anderson, 1989), computer language tasks (Klahr and Carver, 1988), motor skills (e.g., dart throwing, Judd, 1908), analogical reasoning (Gick and Holyoak, 1983), and visual learning (e.g., sexing chicks, Biederman and Shiffrar, 1987).

Studies show that abstracted representations do not remain as isolated instances of events but become components of larger, related events, schemata (Holyoak, 1984; Novick and Holyoak, 1991). Knowledge representations are built up through many opportunities for observing similarities and differences across diverse events. Schemata are posited as particularly important guides to complex thinking, including analogical reasoning: "Successful analogical transfer leads to the induction of a general schema for the solved problems that can be applied to subsequent problems" (National Research Council, 1994:43). Memory retrieval and transfer are promoted by schemata because they derive from a broader scope of related instances than single learning experiences.

Active Versus Passive Approaches to Transfer

It is important to view transfer as a dynamic process that requires learners to actively choose and evaluate strategies, consider resources, and receive feedback. This active view of transfer is different from more static views, which assume that transfer is adequately reflected by learners' abilities to solve a set of transfer problems right after they have engaged in an initial learning task. These "one-shot" tests often seriously underestimate the amount of transfer that students display from one domain to another (Bransford and Schwartz, 1999; Brown et al., 1983; Bruer, 1993).

Studies of transfer from learning one text editor to another illustrate the importance of viewing transfer from a dynamic rather than a static perspective. Researchers have found much greater transfer to a second text editor on the *second* day of transfer than the first (Singley and Anderson, 1989): this finding suggests that transfer should be viewed as increased speed in learning a new domain—not simply initial performance. Similarly, one educational goal for a course in calculus is how it facilitates learning of physics, but not necessarily its benefit on the first day of physics class.

Ideally, an individual spontaneously transfers appropriate knowledge without a need for prompting. Sometimes, however, prompting is necessary. With prompting, transfer can improve quite dramatically (e.g., Gick and Holyoak, 1980; Perfetto et al., 1983). "The amount of transfer depends on where attention is directed during learning or at transfer" (Anderson et al., 1996:8).

An especially sensitive way to assess the degree to which students' learning has prepared them for transfer is to use methods of dynamic assessment, such as "graduated prompting" (Campione and Brown, 1987; Newman et al., 1989). This method can be used to assess the amount of help needed for transfer by counting the number and types of prompts that are necessary before students are able to transfer. Some learners can transfer after receiving a general prompt such as "Can you think of something you did earlier that might be relevant?" Other learners need prompts that are much more specific. Tests of transfer that use graduated prompting provide more fine-grained analysis of learning and its effects on transfer than simple one-shot assessments of whether or not transfer occurs.

Transfer and Metacognition

Transfer can be improved by helping students become more aware of themselves as learners who actively monitor their learning strategies and resources and assess their readiness for particular tests and performances. We briefly discussed the concept of metacognition in Chapters 1 and 3 (see Brown, 1975; Flavell, 1973). Metacognitive approaches to instruction have been shown to increase the degree to which students will transfer to new situations without the need for explicit prompting. The following examples illustrate research on teaching metacognitive skills across domains of reading, writing, and mathematics.

Reciprocal teaching to increase reading comprehension (Palincsar and Brown, 1984) is designed to help students acquire specific knowledge and also to learn a set of strategies for explicating, elaborating, and monitoring the understanding necessary for independent learning. The three major components of reciprocal teaching are instruction and practice with strategies that enable students to monitor their understanding; provision, initially by a teacher, of an expert model of metacognitive processes; and a social setting that enables joint negotiation for understanding. The knowledge-acquisition strategies the students learn in working on a specific text are not acquired as abstract memorized procedures, but as skills instrumental in achieving subject-area knowledge and understanding. The instructional procedure is reciprocal in the sense that a teacher and a group of students take turns in leading the group to discuss and use strategies for comprehending and remembering text content.

A program of procedural facilitation for teaching written composition (Scardamalia et al., 1984) shares many features with reciprocal teaching. The method prompts learners to adopt the metacognitive activities embedded in sophisticated writing strategies. The prompts help learners think about and reflect on the activities by getting them to identify goals, generate new ideas, improve and elaborate existing ideas, and strive for idea cohesion. Students in the procedural facilitation program take turns presenting their ideas to the group and detailing how they use prompts in planning to write. The teacher also models these procedures. Thus, the program involves modeling, scaffolding, and taking turns which are designed to help students externalize mental events in a collaborative context.

Alan Schoenfeld (1983, 1985, 1991) teaches heuristic methods for mathematical problem solving to college students. The methods are derived, to some extent, from the problem-solving heuristics of Polya (1957). Schoenfeld's program adopts methods similar to reciprocal teaching and procedural facilitation. He teaches and demonstrates control or managerial strategies and makes explicit such processes as generating alternative courses of action, evaluating which course one will be able to carry out and whether it can be managed in the time available, and assessing one's progress. Again, elements of modeling, coaching, and scaffolding, as well as collective problem solving and whole-class and small group discussions, are used. Gradually, students come to ask self-regulatory questions themselves as the teacher fades out. At the end of each of the problem-solving sessions, students and teacher alternate in characterizing major themes by analyzing what they did and why. The recapitulations highlight the generalizable features of the critical decisions and actions and focus on strategic levels rather than on the specific solutions (see also White and Frederickson, 1998).

An emphasis on metacognition can enhance many programs that use new technologies to introduce students to the inquiry methods and other tools that are used by professionals in the workplace (see Chapter 8). The important role of metacognition for learning has been demonstrated in the context of a "thinker tools" program that lets students run simulations of physics experiments (White and Frederickson, 1998), as well as in adding a metacognitive component to a computer program designed to help college students learn biology. The value of using video to model important metacognitive learning procedures has also been shown to help learners analyze and reflect on models (Bielaczyc et al., 1995). All of these strategies engage learners as active participants in their learning by focusing their attention on critical elements, encouraging abstraction of common themes or procedures (principles), and evaluating their own progress toward understanding.

LEARNING AS TRANSFER FROM PREVIOUS EXPERIENCES

When people think about transfer, it is common to think first about learning something and then assessing the learner's abilities to apply it to something else. But even the initial learning phase involves transfer because it is based on the knowledge that people bring to any learning situation; see Box 3.8. The principle that people learn by using what they know to construct new understandings (see Chapter 1) can be paraphrased as "all learning involves transfer from previous experiences." This principle has a number of important implications for educational practice. First, students may have knowledge that is relevant to a learning situation that is not activated. By helping activate this knowledge, teachers can build on students' strengths. Second, students may misinterpret new information because of previous knowledge they use to construct new understandings. Third, students may have difficulty with particular school teaching practices that conflict with practices in their community. This section discusses these three implications.

BOX 3.8   **Everyday and Formal Math**

The importance of building on previous experiences is relevant for adults as well as children. A mathematics instructor describes his realization of his mother's knowledge (Fasheh, 1990:21-22):

> Math was necessary for my mother in a much more profound and real sense than it was for me. Unable to read or write, my mother routinely took rectangles of fabric and, with new measurements and no patterns, cut them and turned them into perfectly fitted clothing for people . . . I realized that the mathematics she was using was beyond my comprehension. Moreover, although mathematics was a subject matter that I studied and taught, for her it was basic to the operation of her understanding. What she was doing was math in the sense that it embodied order, pattern, relations, and measurement. It was math because she was breaking a whole into smaller parts and constructing a new whole out of most of the pieces, a new whole that had its own style, shape, size, and that had to fit a specific person. Mistakes in her math entailed practical consequences, unlike mistakes in my math.

Imagine Fasheh's mother enrolling in a course on formal mathematics. The structure of many courses would fail to provide the kinds of support that could help her make contact with her rich set of informal knowledge. Would the mother's learning of formal mathematics be enhanced if it were connected to this knowledge? The literature on learning and transfer suggests that this is an important question to pursue.

Building on Existing Knowledge

Children's early mathematics knowledge illustrates the benefits of helping students draw on relevant knowledge that can serve as a source of transfer. By the time children begin school, most have built a considerable knowledge store relevant to arithmetic. They have experiences of adding and subtracting numbers of items in their everyday play, although they lack the symbolic representations of addition and subtraction that are taught in school. If children's knowledge is tapped and built on as teachers attempt to teach them the formal operations of addition and subtraction, it is likely that children will acquire a more coherent and thorough understanding of these processes than if they taught them as isolated abstractions. Without specific guidance from teachers, students may fail to connect everyday knowledge to subjects taught in school.

Understanding Conceptual Change

Because learning involves transfer from previous experiences, one's existing knowledge can also make it difficult to learn new information. Sometimes new information will seem incomprehensible to students, but this feeling of confusion can at least let them identify the existence of a problem (see, e.g., Bransford and Johnson, 1972; Dooling and Lachman, 1971). A more problematic situation occurs when people construct a coherent (for them) representation of information while deeply misunderstanding the new information. Under these conditions, the learner doesn't realize that he or she is failing to understand. Two examples of this phenomenon are in Chapter 1: *Fish Is Fish* (Lionni, 1970), where the fish listens to the frog's descriptions of people and constructs its own idiosyncratic images, and attempts to help children learn that the earth is spherical (Vosniadou and Brewer, 1989). Children's interpretations of the new information are much different than what adults intend.

The *Fish Is Fish* scenario is relevant to many additional attempts to help students learn new information. For example, when high school or college physics students are asked to identify the forces being exerted on a ball that is thrown vertically up in the air after it leaves the hand, many mention the "force of the hand" (Clement, 1982a, b). This force is exerted only so long as the ball is in contact with the hand, but is not present when the ball is in flight. Students claim that this force diminishes as the ball ascends and is used up by the time the ball reaches the top of its trajectory. As the ball descends, these students claim, it "acquires" increasing amounts of the gravitational force, which results in the ball picking up speed as it falls back down. This "motion requires a force" misconception is quite common among students and is akin to the medieval theory of "impetus" (Hestenes et al., 1992). These explanations fail to take account of the fact that the only forces being exerted on the ball while it is traveling through the air are the gravitational force caused by the earth and the drag force due to air resistance. (For similar examples, see Mestre, 1994.)

In biology, people's knowledge of human and animal needs for food provides an example of how existing knowledge can make it difficult to understand new information. A study of how plants make food was conducted with students from elementary school through college. It probed understanding of the role of soil and photosynthesis in plant growth and of the primary source of food in green plants (Wandersee, 1983). Although students in the higher grades displayed a better understanding, students from all levels displayed several misconceptions: soil is the plants' food; plants get their food from the roots and store it in the leaves; and chlorophyll is the plants' blood. Many of the students in this study, especially those in the higher grades, had already studied photosynthesis. Yet formal instruction had done little to overcome their erroneous prior beliefs. Clearly, presenting a sophisticated explanation in science class, without also probing for students' preconceptions on the subject, will leave many students with incorrect understanding (for a review of studies, see Mestre, 1994).

For young children, early concepts in mathematics guide students' attention and thinking (Gelman, 1967; we discuss this more in Chapter 4). Most children bring to their school mathematics lessons the idea that numbers are grounded in the counting principles (and related rules of addition and subtraction). This knowledge works well during the early years of schooling. However, once students are introduced to rational numbers, their assumptions about mathematics can hurt their abilities to learn.

Consider learning about fractions. The mathematical principles underlying the numberhood of fractions are not consistent with the principles of counting and children's ideas that numbers are sets of things that are counted and addition involves "putting together" two sets. One cannot count things to generate a fraction. Formally, a fraction is defined as the division of one cardinal number by another: this definition solves the problem that there is a lack of closure of the integers under division. To complicate matters, some number-counting principles do not apply to fractions. Rational numbers do not have unique successors; there is an infinite number of numbers between any two rational numbers. One cannot use counting-based algorithms for sequencing fractions: for example, 1/4 is not more than 1/2. Neither the nonverbal nor the verbal counting principle maps to a tripartite symbolic representations of fractions—two cardinal numbers X and Y separated by a line. Related mapping problems have been noted by others (e.g., Behr et al., 1992; Fishbein et al., 1985; Silver et al., 1993). Overall, early knowledge of numbers has the potential to serve as a barrier to learning about fractions—and for many learners it does.

The fact that learners construct new understandings based on their current knowledge highlights some of the dangers in "teaching by telling." Lectures and other forms of direct instruction can sometimes be very useful, but only under the right conditions (Schwartz and Bransford, 1998). Often, students construct understandings like those noted above. To counteract these problems, teachers must strive to make students' thinking visible and find ways to help them reconceptualize faulty conceptions. (Strategies for such teaching are discussed in more detail in Chapters 6 and 7.)

Transfer and Cultural Practices

Prior knowledge is not simply the individual learning that students bring to the classroom, based on their personal and idiosyncratic experiences (e.g., some children will know many things because they have traveled widely or because their parents have particular kinds of jobs; some children may have suffered a traumatic experience). Prior knowledge is also not only a generic set of experiences attributable to developmental stages through which learners may have passed (i.e., believing that heaven is "up" or that milk comes from refrigerated cartons). Prior knowledge also includes the kind of knowledge that learners acquire because of their social roles, such as those connected with race, class, gender, and their culture and ethnic affiliations (Brice-Heath, 1981, 1983; Lave, 1988; Moll and Whitmore, 1993; Moll et al., 1993-1998; Rogoff, 1990, 1998; Saxe, 1990). This cultural knowledge can sometimes support and sometimes conflict with children's learning in schools (Greenfield and Suzuki, 1998); see Box 3.9.

School failure may be partly explained by the mismatch between what students have learned in their home cultures and what is required of them in school (see Allen and Boykin, 1992; Au and Jordan, 1981; Boykin and Tom, 1985; Erickson and Mohatt, 1982). Everyday family habits and rituals can either be reinforced or ignored in schools, and they can produce different responses from teachers (Heath, 1983). For example, if young learners are never asked questions at home that seem obvious to some families—such as "What color is the sky?" or "Where is your nose?"—teachers who ask such questions may find students reluctant or resistant to answer. How teachers interpret this reticence or resistance has consequences for how intelligent or academically capable they judge students and their instructional approaches toward them.

BOX 3.9 Eating Pie and Learning Fractions

Even small differences in cultural knowledge have the potential to affect students' learning. For example, a primary school teacher is helping students to understand fractional parts by using what she thinks is a commonplace reference. "Today, we're going to talk about cutting up a Thanksgiving holiday favorite—pumpkin pie." She continues with an explanation of parts. Well into her discourse, a young African American boy, looking puzzled, asks, "What is pumpkin pie?" (Tate, 1994).

Most African Americans are likely to serve sweet potato pie for holiday dinners. In fact, one of the ways that African American parents explain pumpkin pie to their children is to say that it is something like sweet potato pie. For them, sweet potato pie is the common referent. Even the slight difference of being unfamiliar with pumpkin pie can serve as a source of interference for the student. Rather than be engaged actively in the lesson, he may have been preoccupied with trying to imagine pumpkin pie: What does it taste like? How does it smell? Is its texture chunky like apple or cherry pie? In the mind of a child, all of these questions can become more of the focus than the subject of fractions that the teacher is attempting to teach.

These differences have their roots in early adult-infant interactions (Blake, 1994). Whereas middle-class Anglo mothers tend to have frequent language interactions that are focused on didactic naming and pointing with their infants around objects ("Look at that red truck!"), African American mothers show comparable frequency levels of language interactions with their infants, but focused on affective dimensions of language ("Isn't that a pretty toy? Doesn't it make you feel happy?"). The language that children bring with them to school involves a broad set of skills rooted in the early context of adult-child interactions. What happens when the adults, peers, and contexts change (Suina, 1988; Suina and Smolkin, 1994)? This is an important question that relates to the transfer of learning.

The meanings that are attached to cultural knowledge are important in promoting transfer—that is, in encouraging people to use what they have learned. For example, story-telling is a language skill. Topic-associative oral styles have been observed among African American children (Michaels, 1981a,b; 1986). In contrast, white children use a more linear narrative style that more closely approximates the linear expository style of writing and speaking that schools teach (see Gee, 1989; Taylor and Lee, 1987; Cazden et al., 1985; Lee and Slaughter-Defoe, 1995). Judgments may be made by white and black teachers as they listen to these two language styles: white teachers find the topic-associative stories hard to follow and are much more likely to infer that the narrator is a low-achieving student; black teachers are more likely to positively evaluate the topic-associative style (Cazden, 1988:17). African American children who come to school speaking in a topic-associative style may be seen by many teachers as having less potential for learning. Teachers can be helped to view different cultural backgrounds as strengths to be built on, rather than as signs of "deficits."

TRANSFER BETWEEN SCHOOL AND EVERYDAY LIFE

We began this chapter by stressing that the ultimate goal of learning is to have access to information for a wide set of purposes—that the learning will in some way transfer to other circumstances. In this sense, then, the ultimate goal of schooling is to help students transfer what they have learned in school to everyday settings of home, community, and workplace. Since transfer between tasks is a function of the similarity by transfer tasks and learning experiences, an important strategy for enhancing transfer from schools to other settings may be to better understand the nonschool environments in which students must function. Since these environments change rapidly, it is also important to explore ways to help students develop the characteristics of adaptive expertise (see Chapter 1).

The question of how people function in a number of practical settings has been examined by many scientists, including cognitive anthropologists, sociologists, and psychologists (e.g., Lave, 1988; Rogoff, 1990). One major contrast between everyday settings and school environments is that the latter place much more emphasis on individual work than most other environments (Resnick, 1987). A study of navigation on U.S. ships found that no individual can pilot the ship alone; people must work collaboratively and share their expertise. More recent studies of collaboration confirm its importance. For example, many scientific discoveries in several genetics laboratories involve in-depth collaboration (Dunbar, 1996). Similarly, decision making in hospital emergency rooms is distributed among many different members of the medical team (Patel et al., 1996).

A second major contrast between schools and everyday settings is the heavy use of tools to solve problems in everyday settings, compared with "mental work" in school settings (Resnick, 1987). The use of tools in practical environments helps people work almost error free (e.g., Cohen, 1983; Schliemann and Acioly, 1989; Simon, 1972; see also Norman, 1993). New technologies make it possible for students in schools to use tools very much like those used by professionals in workplaces (see Chapter 8). Proficiency with relevant tools may provide a way to enhance transfer across domains.

A third contrast between schools and everyday environments is that abstract reasoning is often emphasized in school, whereas contextualized reasoning is often used in everyday settings (Resnick, 1987). Reasoning can be improved when abstract logical arguments are embodied in concrete contexts (see Wason and Johnson-Laird, 1972). A well-known study of people in a Weight Watchers program provides similar insights into everyday problem solving (see Lave et al., 1984). One example is of a man who needed three-fourths of two-thirds of a cup of cottage cheese to create a dish he was cooking. He did not attempt to multiply the fractions as students would do in a school context. Instead, he measured two-thirds of a cup of cottage cheese, removed that amount from the measuring cup and then patted the cheese into a round shape, divided it into quarters, and used three of the quarters; see Box 3.10. Abstract arithmetic was never used. In similar examples of contextualized reasoning, dairy workers use knowledge, such as the size of milk cases, to make their computational work more efficient (Scribner, 1984); grocery store shoppers use nonschool mathematics under standard supermarket and simulated conditions (Lave, 1988); see Box 3.11.

There are potential problems with contextualized reasoning, which are similar to those associated with overly contextualized knowledge in general. The "pat it out" strategy used for cottage cheese works in only a narrow range of situations; the man would have difficulty if he were trying to measure molasses or other liquids rather than cottage cheese (Wineburg, 1989a, b; see also Bereiter, 1997). Could he generate a new strategy for molasses or other liquids? The answer to this question depends on the degree to which he can relate his procedure to more general sets of solution strategies.

BOX 3.10   The Cottage Cheese Problem

How can you get 3/4 of 2/3 cup of cottage cheese?

3/4 of

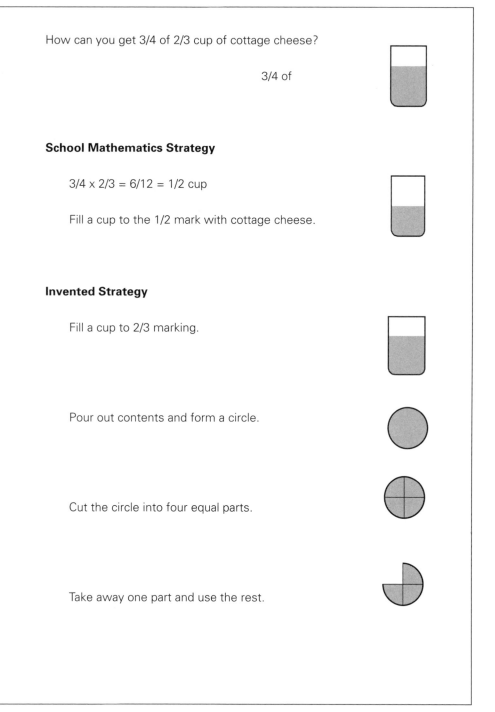

School Mathematics Strategy

3/4 x 2/3 = 6/12 = 1/2 cup

Fill a cup to the 1/2 mark with cottage cheese.

Invented Strategy

Fill a cup to 2/3 marking.

Pour out contents and form a circle.

Cut the circle into four equal parts.

Take away one part and use the rest.

BOX 3.11 Three Solutions to the Best-Buy Problem

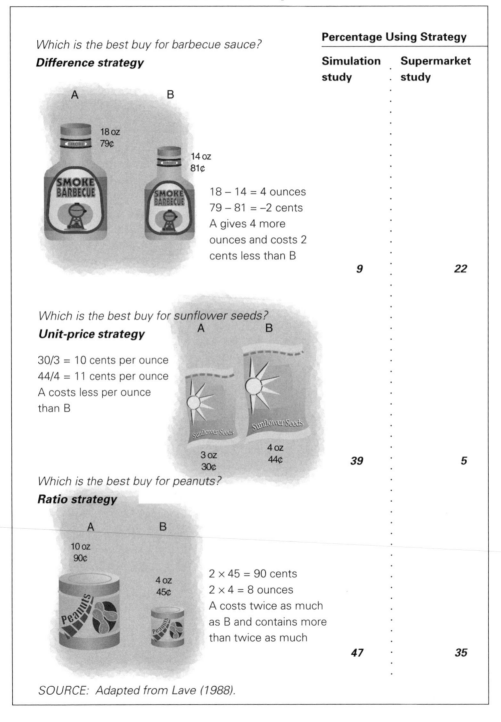

Which is the best buy for barbecue sauce?

Difference strategy

A   B

18 oz
79¢

14 oz
81¢

18 − 14 = 4 ounces
79 − 81 = −2 cents
A gives 4 more
ounces and costs 2
cents less than B

Which is the best buy for sunflower seeds?

Unit-price strategy

A   B

30/3 = 10 cents per ounce
44/4 = 11 cents per ounce
A costs less per ounce
than B

3 oz
30¢

4 oz
44¢

Which is the best buy for peanuts?

Ratio strategy

A   B

10 oz
90¢

4 oz
45¢

2 × 45 = 90 cents
2 × 4 = 8 ounces
A costs twice as much
as B and contains more
than twice as much

	Percentage Using Strategy	
	Simulation study	Supermarket study
Difference strategy	9	22
Unit-price strategy	39	5
Ratio strategy	47	35

SOURCE: Adapted from Lave (1988).

Analyses of everyday environments have potential implications for education that are intriguing but need to be thought through and researched carefully. There are many appealing strengths to the idea that learning should be organized around authentic problems and projects that are frequently encountered in nonschool settings: in John Dewey's vision, "School should be less about preparation for life and more like life itself." The use of problem-based learning in medical schools is an excellent example of the benefits of looking at what people need to do once they graduate and then crafting educational experiences that best prepare them for these competencies (Barrows, 1985). Opportunities to engage in problem-based learning during the first year of medical school lead to a greater ability to diagnose and understand medical problems than do opportunities to learn in typical lecture-based medical courses (Hmelo, 1995). Attempts to make schooling more relevant to the subsequent workplace have also guided the use of case-based learning in business schools, law schools, and schools that teach educational leadership (Hallinger et al., 1993; Williams, 1992).

The transfer literature also highlights some of the potential limitations of learning in particular contexts. Simply learning to perform procedures, and learning in only a single context, does not promote flexible transfer. The transfer literature suggests that the most effective transfer may come from a balance of specific examples and general principles, not from either one alone.

SUMMARY AND CONCLUSION

A major goal of schooling is to prepare students for flexible adaptation to new problems and settings. The ability of students to transfer provides an important index of learning that can help teachers evaluate and improve their instruction. Many approaches to instruction look equivalent when the only measure of learning is memory for information that was specifically presented. Instructional differences become more apparent when evaluated from the perspective of how well the learning transfers to new problems and settings.

Several critical features of learning affect people's abilities to transfer what they have learned. The amount and kind of initial learning is a key determinant of the development of expertise and the ability to transfer knowledge. Students are motivated to spend the time needed to learn complex subjects and to solve problems that they find interesting. Opportunities to use knowledge to create products and benefits for others are particularly motivating for students.

While time on task is necessary for learning, it is not sufficient for effective learning. Time spent learning for understanding has different consequences for transfer than time spent simply memorizing facts or procedures from textbooks or lectures. In order for learners to gain insight into their learning and their understanding, frequent feedback is critical: students need to monitor their learning and actively evaluate their strategies and their current levels of understanding.

The context in which one learns is also important for promoting transfer. Knowledge that is taught in only a single context is less likely to support flexible transfer than knowledge that is taught in multiple contexts. With multiple contexts, students are more likely to abstract the relevant features of concepts and develop a more flexible representation of knowledge. The use of well-chosen contrasting cases can help students learn the conditions under which new knowledge is applicable. Abstract representations of problems can also facilitate transfer. Transfer between tasks is related to the degree to which they share common elements, although the concept of elements must be defined cognitively. In assessing learning, the key is increased speed of learning the concepts underlying the new material, rather than early performance attempts in a new subject domain.

All new learning involves transfer. Previous knowledge can help or hinder the understanding of new information. For example, knowledge of everyday counting-based arithmetic can make it difficult to deal with rational numbers; assumptions based on everyday physical experiences (e.g., walking upright on a seemingly flat earth) can make it difficult for learners to understand concepts in astronomy and physics and so forth. Teachers can help students change their original conceptions by helping students make their thinking visible so that misconceptions can be corrected and so that students can be encouraged to think beyond the specific problem or to think about variations on the problem. One aspect of previous knowledge that is extremely important for understanding learning is cultural practices that support learners' prior knowledge. Effective teaching supports positive transfer by actively identifying the relevant knowledge and strengths that students bring to a learning situation and building on them.

Transfer from school to everyday environments is the ultimate purpose of school-based learning. An analysis of everyday environments provides opportunities to rethink school practices in order to bring them into alignment with the requirements of everyday environments. But it is important to avoid instruction that is overly dependent on context. Helping learners choose, adapt, and invent tools for solving problems is one way to facilitate transfer while also encouraging flexibility.

Finally, a metacognitive approach to teaching can increase transfer by helping students learn about themselves as learners in the context of acquiring content knowledge. One characteristic of experts is an ability to monitor and regulate their own understanding in ways that allows them to keep learning adaptive expertise: this is an important model for students to emulate.

4

How Children Learn

Children differ from adult learners in many ways, but there are also surprising commonalities across learners of all ages. In this chapter we provide some insights into children as learners. A study of young children fulfills two purposes: it illustrates the strengths and weaknesses of the learners who populate the nation's schools, and it offers a window into the development of learning that cannot be seen if one considers only well-established learning patterns and expertise. In studying the development of children, an observer gets a dynamic picture of learning unfolding over time. A fresh understanding of infant cognition and of how young children from 2 to 5 years old build on that early start also sheds new light on how to ease their transition into formal school settings.

INFANTS' CAPABILITIES

Theories

It was once commonly thought that infants lack the ability to form complex ideas. For much of this century, most psychologists accepted the traditional thesis that a newborn's mind is a blank slate (*tabula rasa*) on which the record of experience is gradually impressed. It was further thought that language is an obvious prerequisite for abstract thought and that, in its absence, a baby could not have knowledge. Since babies are born with a limited repertoire of behaviors and spend most of their early months asleep, they certainly appear passive and unknowing. Until recently, there was no obvious way for them to demonstrate otherwise.

But challenges to this view arose. It became clear that with carefully designed methods, one could find ways to pose rather complex questions about what infants and young children know and can do. Armed with new methodologies, psychologists began to accumulate a substantial body of data about the remarkable abilities that young children possess that stands in stark contrast to the older emphases on what they lacked. It is now known that very young children are competent, active agents of their own conceptual development. In short, the mind of the young child has come to life (Bruner, 1972, 1981a, b; Carey and Gelman, 1991; Gardner, 1991; Gelman and Brown, 1986; Wellman and Gelman, 1992).

A major move away from the *tabula rasa* view of the infant mind was taken by the Swiss psychologist Jean Piaget. Beginning in the 1920s, Piaget argued that the young human mind can best be described in terms of complex cognitive structures. From close observations of infants and careful questioning of children, he concluded that cognitive development proceeds through certain stages, each involving radically different cognitive schemes.

While Piaget observed that infants actually seek environmental stimulation that promotes their intellectual development, he thought that their initial representations of objects, space, time, causality, and self are constructed only gradually during the first 2 years. He concluded that the world of young infants is an egocentric fusion of the internal and external worlds and that the development of an accurate representation of physical reality depends on the gradual coordination of schemes of looking, listening, and touching.

After Piaget, others studied how newborns begin to integrate sight and sound and explore their perceptual worlds. For perceptual learning theorists, learning was considered to proceed rapidly due to the initial availability of exploration patterns that infants use to obtain information about the objects and events of their perceptual worlds (Gibson, 1969). As information processing theories began to emerge, the metaphor of mind as computer, information processor, and problem solver came into wide usage (Newell et al., 1958) and was quickly applied to the study of cognitive development.

Although these theories differed in important ways, they shared an emphasis on considering children as active learners who are able to set goals, plan, and revise. Children are seen as learners who assemble and organize material. As such, cognitive development involves the acquisition of organized knowledge structures including, for example, biological concepts, early number sense, and early understanding of basic physics. In addition, cognitive development involves the gradual acquisition of strategies for remembering, understanding, and solving problems.

The active role of learners was also emphasized by Vygotsky (1978), who pointed to other supports for learning. Vygotsky was deeply interested in the role of the social environment, included tools and cultural objects, as well as people, as agents in developing thinking. Perhaps the most powerful idea from Vygotsky to influence developmental psychology was that of a *zone of proximal development* (Vygotsky, 1978), described in Box 4.1. It refers to a bandwidth of competence (Brown and Reeve, 1987) that learners can navigate with aid from a supportive context, including the assistance of others. (For modern treatments of this concept, see Newman et al., 1989;

BOX 4.1   Zone of Proximal Development

The zone of proximal development is the distance between the actual developmental level as determined by independent problem solving and the level of potential development as determined through problem solving under adult guidance, or in collaboration with more capable peers (Vygotsky, 1978:86). What children can do with the assistance of others is even more indicative of their mental development than what they can do alone (Vygotsky, 1978:85).

The zone of proximal development embodies a concept of readiness to learn that emphasizes upper levels of competence. These upper boundaries are not immutable, however, but constantly changing with the learner's increasing independent competence. What a child can perform today with assistance she will be able to perform tomorrow independently, thus preparing her for entry into a new and more demanding collaboration. These functions could be called the "buds," rather than the fruits of development. The actual developmental level characterizes mental development retrospectively, while the zone of proximal development characterizes mental development prospectively (Vygotsky, 1978:86-87).

Moll and Whitmore, 1993; Rogoff and Wertsch, 1984; from a different theoretical perspective, see Bidell and Fischer, 1997.) This line of work has drawn attention to the roles of more capable peers, parents, and other partners in challenging and extending children's efforts to understand. It has also contributed to an understanding of the relationship between formal and informal teaching and learning situations (Lave and Wenger, 1991) and cognition distributed across people and tools (Salomon, 1993).

As a result of these theoretical and methodological developments, great strides have been made in studying young children's learning capacities. To summarize an enormous body of research, there have been dramatic increases in knowledge in four major areas of research, illustrated in this chapter:

1. *Early predisposition to learn about some things but not others* No evidence exists that infants come into the world as "blank slates" capable only of registering the ambient events that impinge on their senses in an undisciplined way. Young children show positive biases to learn types of information readily and early in life. These forms of knowledge, referred to as *privileged domains*, center on broadly defined categories, notably physi-

cal and biological concepts, causality, number, and language (Carey and Gelman, 1991).

2. *Strategies and metacognition* Outside of these privileged domains children, like all learners, must depend on will, ingenuity, and effort to enhance their learning. It was previously thought that young children lacked the strategic competence and knowledge about learning (metacognition) to learn intentionally, but the last 30 years have witnessed a great deal of research that reveals hitherto unrecognized strategic and metacognitive competence in the young (Brown and DeLoache, 1978; DeLoache et al., 1998).

3. *Theories of mind* As they mature, children develop theories of what it means to learn and understand that profoundly influence how they situate themselves in settings that demand effortful and intentional learning (Bereiter and Scardamalia, 1989). Children entertain various theories of mind and intelligence (Dweck and Legget, 1988). Indeed, not all learners in schools come ready to learn in exactly the same way. Some theorists argue that there is more than one way to learn, more than one way to be "intelligent." Understanding that there are multiple intelligences (Gardner, 1983) may suggest ways of helping children learn by supporting their strengths and working with their weakenesses.

4. *Children and community* Although a great deal of children's learning is self-motivated and self-directed, other people play major roles as guides in fostering the development of learning in children. Such guides include other children as well as adults (caretakers, parents, teachers, coaches, etc.). But not only people can serve as guides; so, too, can powerful tools and cultural artifacts, notably television, books, videos, and technological devices of many kinds (Wright and Huston, 1995). A great deal of research on such assisted learning has been influenced by Vygotsky's notion of zones of proximal development and the increasing popularity of the concept of "communities of learners," be they face-to-face or through electronic media and technologies (see Chapters 8 and 9).

Methodological Advances

The large increase in the number of studies that address early learning came about as a result of methodological advances in the field of developmental psychology. Much of what is now known about the human mind comes from the study of how infants learn. This work demonstrates that the human mind is a biologically prepared organism (Carey and Gelman, 1991). In order to study what babies know and can learn about readily, researchers needed to develop techniques of "asking" infants, who cannot speak, what they know. Because infants are so limited physically, experimenters interested in finding out how babies think had to find methods suitable to an infant's motor capabilities. New ways were developed for measuring what infants prefer to look at (Fantz, 1961) and detecting changes in events to which they are sensitive. Three such methods are non-nutritive sucking, habituation, and visual expectation.

Non-nutritive sucking is a way to use a physical capability that even the youngest infants have. In one experiment, the researchers (Kalnins and Bruner, 1973) showed 5- to 12-week-old infants a silent color film and gave the infants a pacifier to suck, the nipple of which was connected to a pressure switch that controlled the projector lens. The infants quickly learned to suck at a given rate to bring the movie into focus, showing not only that they were capable of and interested in learning how to control their own sensory environment, but also that they preferred a clear image to a blurry one.

The second method demonstrates an infant's thirst for novelty. The habituation paradigm involves presenting babies with an event (a stimulus)—a picture, sound, or series of sounds—to which the baby attends either by looking at it, turning to it, or doing something to keep the event continuing. Over a period of time infants stop responding to repeated presentations of the same event: that is, they *habituate*. They recover interest if a recognizably different event is presented. A combination of non-nutritive sucking and habituation was used in a study (Eimas et al., 1971) to show that 4-month-old infants will suck vigorously when first introduced to the phoneme (speech sound) "ba," then gradually lose interest and stop sucking. But when presented with a different phoneme, "pa," they resume sucking.

Because infants will look at things they find interesting, researchers developed the method of visual expectation to study infants' comprehension of events. It uses infants' gaze patterns to determine if they are comprehending patterns of visual events. For example, an experimenter establishes a pattern of flashing a picture two times on the left side of a screen and then three times on the right side. Once this alternating pattern has been established, the experimenter can watch an infant's gaze while the pictures continue to be flashed. If the baby continues to gaze at the left side of the screen after one flash, but then shifts its gaze to the right side after the second picture appears, then it is assumed that a distinction has been made between one, two, and three events. Using this procedure, infants as young as 5 months have shown that they can count up to three (Canfield and Smith, 1996).

Thus, using infants' capacities for looking, sucking, and interest in novelty, developmental psychologists devised methods for reliably studying early aspects of infant cognition. These studies have been refined for studying early infant memory development by using bodily actions, such as leg kicking and arm movements, for determining object recognition (Rovee-Collier, 1989).

Studies like these do more than simply show that infants actively select experiences; they also demonstrate what infants are capable of perceiving, knowing, and remembering. Recovery of interest in a novel speech sound could only occur if infants could recognize the rather subtle difference between "pa" and "ba." Discovering that very young infants can see, hear, smell, and be particular about what exactly they wish to explore led to an emboldened attitude about the kinds of experimental questions that could be asked. The answers about infant understanding of physical and biological causality, number, and language have been quite remarkable. These studies have profoundly altered scientific understanding of how and when humans begin to grasp the complexities of their worlds. In the next section, we present a few examples of infants' learning in these domains.

EARLY COMPETENCIES IN THE PRIVILEGED DOMAINS

Physical Concepts

How do infants learn about the physical world? Research studies have demonstrated that infants as early as 3-4 months of age have the beginnings of useful knowledge. Three examples from many: they understand that objects need support to prevent them from falling; that stationary objects are displaced when they come into contact with moving objects; and that inanimate objects need to be propelled into motion.

Consider the notion of support—that an object cannot be suspended in mid-air. In one study, infants are seated in front of a table that includes a platform. They see an experimenter's gloved hand reach out from a side window and put a box on top of the platform (possible event) and then withdraw her hand. Alternatively, when the experimenter reaches out from the side window, she places the box beyond the platform, leaving the impression that the box is suspended in mid-air when she withdraws her hand (impossible condition); see Figure 4.1.

Using the visual habituation methodology, studies have found that infants as young as 3 months old look reliably longer at the impossible events. This reaction indicates that infants *expect* that a box can be stable when a hand releases it onto a platform, but not when there is no supporting platform (Baillargeon et al., 1992; Needham and Baillargeon, 1993; Kolstad and Baillargeon, 1994); see Figure 4.2.

In a study of visual fixation on consistent and inconsistent events with light and heavy objects, Schilling and Clifton (1998) also showed that 9-month-old infants look longer at the physically inconsistent events than those that are consistent with their expectations; see Figure 4.3. Another well-documented example of infants' early understanding of physical causality is that stationary objects are displaced when hit by moving objects. Research studies have demonstrated that infants as young as 2-1/2 months understand

Possible
Event

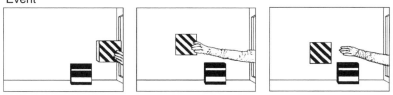

Impossible
Event

FIGURE 4.1 *Testing infants' understanding of possible and impossible physical events.*
SOURCE: Test events used in Needham and Baillargeon (1993).

this concept, though it is not until about 6-1/2 months of age that they relate the size of the moving object and the distance of displacement of the stationary objects. "When looking at collision events between a moving and a stationary object, infants first form an initial concept centered on an impact/no-impact decision. With further experience, infants begin to identify variables that influence this initial concept" (Baillargeon, 1995:193).

In the first year of life, infants can understand that inanimate objects need to be propelled into action, that the objects cannot move themselves. For example, Leslie (1994a,b) showed that 4- to 7-month-old infants expect a point of contact to be involved in physical displacement. In one study, the infant watches a film in which a hand approaches a stationary doll and either appears to pick it up (contact condition) and moves away or the doll moves in tandem but without physical contact (no-contact condition). Using the habituation methodology, Leslie demonstrated that infants are highly sensitive to spatiotemporal discontinuities: they see the hand as an agent to cause movement in an inanimate object, but the no-contact conditions are seen as anomalous events—violations of causal principles.

The early understandings just described are soon reflected in children's spontaneous actions. In studies of his own young children's exploratory play, Piaget found that by 12 months of age they clearly understood the

Habituation Events

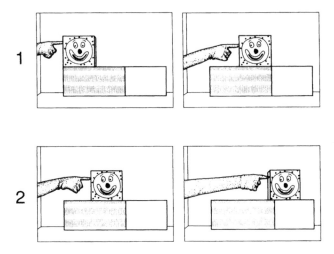

Test Events

Possible Event

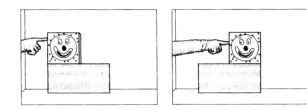

Impossible Event

FIGURE 4.2 *Habituation and test for physical concepts. SOURCE: Test events used in Baillargeon, Needham, and Devos (1992).*

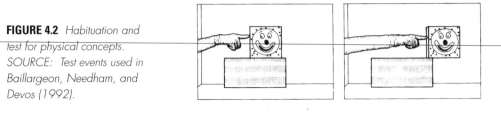

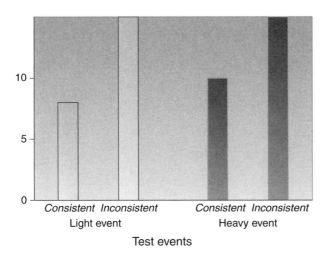

FIGURE 4.3 *Average visual fixation duration. SOURCE: Adapted from Schilling and Clifton (1998).*

need for a point of contact to bring inanimate objects into range. For example, Jacqueline (9 months) discovers that she can bring a toy within reach by pulling a blanket (support) on which it is placed. During the weeks that follow, she frequently uses this "schema" (Piaget, 1952:285). Lucienne (12 months), once having witnessed the action of the support, rapidly generalized the schema to sheets, handkerchiefs, table cloths, pillows, boxes, books, and so on. Once the baby understood the notion of the support, this knowledge transferred rapidly to a variety of potential supports. The same learning is true of stick-like things (push schema) and string-like objects (pull schema), as "means for bringing" (Piaget, 1952:295). Each new acquisition brings with it its own realm of generalization.

A series of laboratory studies has reaffirmed and extended Piaget's original naturalistic observations and provided a fairly detailed description of development of the push/pull schema from 4 to 24 months of age. As noted above, Leslie showed that 7-month-olds are sensitive to the need for point of contact in a pushing scenario. Bates et al. (1980) looked at infants' ability to reach a toy using various tools. And Brown and Slattery (described in Brown, 1990) looked at children's ability to choose the correct tool (with adequate length, rigidity, and pushing or pulling head) from an array of available tools. It was not until 24 months of age that children immediately selected the adequate tool, but by 14 months children could do so with some practice. Across the age range of 10-24 months, children first used tools effectively that were physically attached (unbreakable contact) in contrast to tools that could be unattached at the contact point (breakable contact) or when the point of contact needed to be imagined (no contact). Children showed distress or surprise at trick events—when a tool appeared to be attached but wasn't or vice versa, thus violating their pulling schema (Brown, 1990).

These studies, taken together, paint an interesting developmental scenario. Although children in habituation paradigms seem to understand the need for point of contact early (5-7 months), they cannot at 10 months apply that knowledge to tool use tasks *unless* the contact between the tool and the goal is provided in the physical layout of the task: the tool touches the object; the solution is physically situated in the environment itself. Several months later, infants can learn, with a demonstration, to envision the point of contact that is not specified in the visual array, but is invited by the pulling features of the tools. They can see that a hook would work in getting the tool if it is rigid and long enough. By 24 months, children readily note the pulling potential of unattached tools and can make a choice between available tools on the basis of their adequacy. The research shows that young children have the requisite knowledge in some sense very early on, but they need help in the form of demonstrations to prompt the application of what they know.

Biological Causality

During the past 30 years, a great deal has been learned about primitive concepts of biological causality. We concentrate here on the differences between animate and inanimate objects.

Infants learn rapidly about the differences between inanimate and animate: as we have seen, they know that inanimate objects need to be pushed or propelled into motion. Infants as young as 6 months can distinguish animate versus inanimate movements as patterns of lights attached to forces or people (Bertenthal, 1993). And Spelke (1990) has shown that if two people come close together and move away in tandem without touching, 7-months-olds show no surprise; but if two people-sized inanimate objects come together and move without a point of contact, they are perturbed (as measured by the habituation paradigm).

Young children show an early understanding that animate objects have the potential to move themselves because they are made of "biological stuff"—they obey what R. Gelman (1990) calls the "innards principle of mechanism." Inanimate objects, in contrast, obey the external-agent principle: they cannot move themselves, but must be propelled into action by an external force.

For example, Massey and Gelman (1988) reported that 3- and 4-year-old children correctly responded when asked if novel objects like an echidna and a statue can move themselves up and down a hill. Despite the fact that the echidna looked less like a familiar animal than did a statue, the children claimed that only the living object could move itself up and down a hill.

Similarly, young children in this age range can give sensible answers to questions about the difference between the insides and outsides of animals, machines, and natural inanimate objects; see Figure 4.4.

These are only a handful of findings from a large body of research that goes a long way to challenge the idea that young children are incapable of considering non-perceptual data in scientific areas. Given that there is a mounting body of evidence showing that youngsters are busy constructing coherent accounts of their physical and biological worlds, one needs to ask to what extent these early competencies serve as a bridge for further learning when they enter school.

Early Number Concepts

An ever-increasing body of evidence shows that the human mind is endowed with an implicit mental ability that facilitates attention to and use of representations of the number of items in a visual array, sequence of drumbeats, jumps of a toy bunny, numerical values represented in arrays, etc. For example, Starkey et al. (1990) showed 6- to 8-month-old infants a series of photographic slides of either 2- or 3-item displays. Each successive picture showed different household items, including combs, pipes, lemons, scissors, and corkscrews that varied in color, shape, size, and texture and spatial position. Half of the infants saw a series of two-item displays while the other half were shown a series of three-item displays. When they became bored, their looking times dropped by 50 percent (they habituated). At this point, they were then shown displays that alternated between two and three items, and if the displays showed a different number of items from what they had seen before, the infants began to show interest by looking again. The only common characteristic within the two-item and three-item displays was their numerical value, so one can say the infants habituated to the set of two or three things and then recovered interest when they were shown a different number of things. The infants could have focused on perceptual attributes of the items such as their shapes, motion, textural complexity, and so on, but they did not. This is an important clue that they are able to process information that represents number at a rather abstract level.

Other researchers have shown that infants pay attention to the number of times a toy rabbit jumps up and down, so long as the number of jumping events they have to keep track of is kept between two and four jumps (Wynn, 1996). An especially interesting demonstration of infants' ability to notice abstract number information in the environment was reported by Canfield and Smith (1996). They found that 5-month-old infants used visual expectation (see previous section) to show that infants are able to distinguish three pictures presented in one location from two pictures in another.

Young infants and toddlers also respond correctly to the effects of the

FIGURE 4.4 *Drawings used in studying preschoolers' reasoning about movement. SOURCE: Massey and Gelman (1988:309).*

arithmetic operations of adding and subtracting. Through their surprise or search reactions, young children are able to tell us when an item is added or subtracted from what they expected (Wynn, 1990, 1992a, b; Starkey, 1992). For example, 5-month-old infants first saw two objects repeatedly; then a screen covered the objects and they watched as an experimenter proceeded to add another object or remove one from the hidden display. The screen was then removed, revealing one more or one less item than before. In both the less and more conditions, infants looked longer at the numerically "incorrect" display—that is, the unexpected value that did not correspond to their initial training; if they saw one added, they expected three, not one, and vice versa (Wynn, 1992a, b).

Experimental evidence of this kind implies a psychological process that relates the effect of adding or removing items to a *numerical representation* of the initial display. A similar line of evidence with preschool children indicates that very young children are actively engaged in using their implicit knowledge of number to attend to and make sense of novel examples of numerical data in their environments; see Box 4.2.

There are many other demonstrations of young children's interpreting sets of objects in terms of number. Together, the findings indicate that even young children can actively participate in their own learning and problem solving about number. This ability is why children often deal with novel conditions rather well, as when they tell puppets who are "just learning to count" if they are correct and if they are wrong or even invent counting solutions (Groen and Resnick, 1977; Siegler and Robinson, 1982; Starkey and Gelman, 1982; Sophian, 1994).

But just because children have some knowledge of numbers before they enter school is not to say that there is little need for careful learning later. Early understanding of numbers can guide their entry into school-based learning about number concepts. Successful programs based on developmental psychology already exist, notably the Right Start Program (Griffin and Case, 1997). Although making the entry levels easier, these early number concepts can also be problematic when it comes to the transitions to higher-level mathematics. Rational numbers (fractions) do not behave like whole numbers, and attempting to treat them as such leads to serious problems. It is therefore noteworthy that many children experience just these sorts of problems in mathematics when they encounter "fractions": They believe the larger number always represents a bigger quantity or larger unit.

Early Attention to Language

We introduced the idea that children come equipped with the means necessary for understanding their worlds when considering physical and biological concepts. It should not be surprising that infants also possess

BOX 4.2 How Many?

How do 3- to 5-year old children react when they encounter unexpected changes in the number of items? Before the dialog below, children had been playing with five toy mice that were on a plate; the plate and mice were then covered and the experimenter surreptitiously took away two mice before uncovering the plate (Gelman and Gallistel, 1978:172). What follows is one child's attempts to reconcile the differences in the number of mice:

Child:	*Must have disappeared.*
Experimenter:	*What?*
Child:	*The other mousses?...*
Experimenter:	*How many now?*
Child:	*One, two, three.*
Experimenter:	*How many at the beginning of the game?*
Child:	*There was one there, one there, one there, one there, one there.*
Experimenter:	*How many?*
Child:	*Five—this one is three now but before it was five.*
Experimenter:	*What would you need to fix the game?*
Child:	*I'm not really sure because my brother is real big and he could tell.*
Experimenter:	*What do you think he would need?*
Child:	*Well I don't know...Some things have to come back.*
Experimenter:	[Hands the child some objects including four mice].
Child:	[Puts all four mice on the plate]. *There. Now there's one, two, three, four, five, six, seven! No...I'll take these* [points to two] *off and we'll see how many.*
Child:	[Removes one and counts]. *One, two, three, four, five; no—one, two, three, four. Uh...there were five, right?*
Experimenter:	*Right.*
Child:	*I'll take out this one here* [on the table] *and then we'll see how many there is now.*
Child:	[Takes one off and counts]. *One, two, three, four, five. Five! Five.*

such mechanisms for learning language. They begin at an early age to develop knowledge of their linguistic environments, using a set of specific mechanisms that guide language development.

Infants have to be able to distinguish linguistic information from nonlinguistic stimuli: they attribute meaning and linguistic function to words and not to dog barks or telephone rings (Mehler and Christophe, 1995). By 4 months of age, infants clearly show a preference for listening to words over other sounds (Colombo and Bundy, 1983). And they can distinguish changes in language. For example, after being habituated to English sentences, infants detected the shift to a different language, such as Spanish; they did not register shifts to different English utterances (Bahrick and Pickens, 1988), which indicates that they noticed the novel Spanish utterances. Figure 4.5 illustrates that American-born infants, at 2 months of age, start reacting to English utterances significantly faster than they do to French utterances. Young infants learn to pay attention to the features of speech, such as intonation and rhythm, that help them obtain critical information about language and meaning. As they get older, they concentrate on utterances that share a structure that corresponds to their maternal language, and they neglect utterances that do not.

By 6 months of age, infants distinguish some of the properties that characterize the language of their immediate environment (Kuhl et al., 1992). Around 8-10 months of age, infants stop treating speech as consisting of mere sounds and begin to represent only the linguistically *relevant* contrasts (Mehler and Christophe, 1995). For example, Kuhl et al. (1992) have shown that the contrasts "ra" and "la" can be learned by very young English and Japanese babies alike, but later on only the contrast relevant to the mother

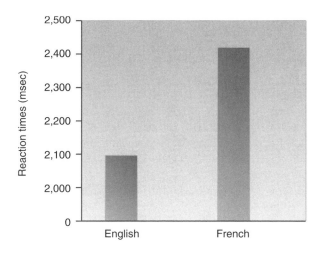

FIGURE 4.5 *Reaction time to French and English sentences for 2-month-old infants. Mean latencies of initiation of a visual saccade in the direction of the sound for American 2-month-olds listening to French and English sentences. SOURCE: Adapted from Mehler and Christophe (1995:947).*

language is retained as the other one drops out (e.g., "la" drops out for Japanese infants). Such studies illustrate that the learning environment is critical for determining what is learned even when the basic learning mechanisms do not vary.

Young infants are also predisposed to attend to the language spoken by others around them. They are attracted to human faces, and look especially often at the lips of the person speaking. They appear to expect certain types of coordination between mouth movements and speech. When shown videos of people talking, infants can detect the differences between lip movements that are synchronized with the sounds and those that are not.

Young children also actively attempt to understand the meaning of the language that is spoken around them. Roger Brown (1958) discussed "The Original Word Game" that children play with parents. Successful participation involves the child's making inferences about what someone must mean by paying attention to the surrounding context. Parents of 1-year-olds report that their children understand much of what is said to them, although there is obviously a great deal of information that children really do not understand (Chapman, 1978). For example, Lewis and Freedle (1973) analyzed the comprehension abilities of a 13-month-old child. When handed an apple while she was in her high chair and told "Eat the apple," the child bit it. When handed an apple while playing in her playpen and told "Throw the apple," the child threw it. Lewis and Freedle performed an experiment in order to test whether the child really understood words such as "eat" and "throw." They handed the child an apple while she was in her high chair and asked her to "throw the apple." The child bit it. Later, when the child was in her playpen she was handed an apple and told "eat the apple." She threw it. The child's strategy was basically to assume that she should "do what you usually do in this situation." This sound strategy is frequently correct.

In everyday settings, young children have rich opportunities for learning because they can use context to figure out what someone must mean by various sentence structures and words. Unless she was being tested by tricky experimenters, for example, the child discussed above could determine the general meanings of "apple," "eat," and "throw." Similarly, if a mother says "Get your shirt" while pointing to the only loose object (a shirt) on the rug, the child begins to understand the meaning of "get" and "shirt." Language acquisition cannot take place in the absence of shared social and situational contexts because the latter provide information about the meanings of words and sentence structures (Chapman, 1978). The child uses meaning as a clue to language rather than language as a clue to meaning (MacNamara, 1972). Parents and other caregivers take into account both context and children's emerging abilities as they help them extend their competencies. The extremely important guiding role that caregivers have in children's cognitive development is discussed further below.

Language development studies illustrate that children's biological capacities are set into motion by their environments. The biological underpinnings enable children to become fluent in language by about age three, but if they are not in a language-using environment, they will not develop this capacity. Experience is important; but the opportunity to use the skills—practice—is also important. Janellen Huttenlocher, for example, has shown that language has to be practiced as an ongoing and active process and not merely passively observed by watching television (Huttenlocher, cited in *Newsweek*, 1996).

STRATEGIES FOR LEARNING AND METACOGNITION

So far we have reviewed research that has tapped into infants' amazing competencies that biologically predispose them to learn. These predispositions help prepare human infants for the complex challenges of adaptive learning that come later in life. In order to thrive, children must still engage in self-directed and other-directed learning, even in areas of early competence. In this section we look at how children learn about things that they would not be predisposed to attend to, such as chess or the capital cities of countries. We discuss how children come to be able to learn almost anything through effort and will.

It has generally been assumed that in the arena of deliberate, intentional, mindful, and strategic learning, young children are woefully inadequate. But recent scientific studies have revealed hitherto unsuspected strategic competence and metacognitive knowledge in young children.

The Importance of Capacity, Strategies, Knowledge, and Metacognition

A traditional view of learning and development was that young children know and can do little, but with age (maturation) and experience (of any kind) they become increasingly competent. From this view, learning is development and development is learning. There is no need to postulate special forms of learning nor for learners to be particularly active (see Bijou and Baer, 1961; Skinner, 1950). Yet even in privileged domains, as described above, this passive view does not fully apply.

In addition, research in another major area began to show how learners process information, remember, and solve problems in nonprivileged domains. Known as information processing (Simon, 1972; Newell and Simon, 1972), this branch of psychology was quickly adopted to explain developments in children's learning. All human learners have limitations to their short-term memory for remembering and for solving problems. Simon (1972) and others (e.g., Chi, 1978; Siegler, 1978; Klahr and Wallace, 1973) argued that development means overcoming information-processing constraints, such as limited short-term memory capacity. The crucial argument for developmental psychologists is whether young learners are particularly hampered by memory limitations and whether, compared with adults, they are less able to overcome general limitations through the clever use of strategies or by lack of relevant knowledge factors.

One view of learning in children is that they have a less memory capacity than adults. While there is no doubt that, in general, children's learning and memory abilities increase with age, controversy surrounds the mechanisms that affect these changes. One view is that children's short-term memory capacity, or the amount of mental space they have (M-space), increases as children mature (Pascual-Leone, 1988). With more mental space, they can retain more information and perform more complex mental operations. A complementary view is that the mental operations of older children are more rapid, enabling them to make use of their limited capacity more effectively (Case, 1992). If one holds either of these positions, one would expect relatively uniform improvement in performance across domains of learning (Case, 1992; Piaget, 1970).

A second view is that children and adults have roughly the same mental capacity, but that with development children acquire knowledge and develop effective activities to use their minds well. Such activities are often called strategies. There are a variety of well-known strategies that increase remembering, such as rehearsal (repeating items over and over), which tends to improve rote recall (Belmont and Butterfield, 1971); elaboration (Reder and Anderson, 1980), which improves retention of more meaningful units such as sentences; and summarization (Brown and Day, 1984), which increases retention and comprehension. These are just three of many strategies.

Perhaps the most pervasive strategy used to improve memory performance is clustering: organizing disparate pieces of information into meaningful units. Clustering is a strategy that depends on organizing knowledge. In a classic paper, Miller (1956) described the persistence of a phenomenon he called the "magical number 7 ± 2" in human mental processing. Given a list of numbers to remember, sounds (phonemes) to distinguish from one another, or a set of unrelated facts to recall, there is a critical change in performance at around seven items. Up to seven items (between five and nine, actually, hence Miller's title), people can readily handle a variety of tasks; with more than seven, they simply cannot process them handily. People have developed ways around this memory constraint by organizing information, such as grouping together or "chunking" disparate elements into sets of letters, numbers, or pictures that make sense to them.

Known as the chunking effect, this memory strategy improves the performance of children, as well as adults. A prototype experiment would involve, for example, presenting 4- to 10-year-olds with long lists of pictures to remember, far more than they could if they simply tried to remember them individually. Such a list might consist of pictures of a cat, rose, train, hat, airplane, horse, tulip, boat, coat, etc. Given a 20-item list, older children remember more than younger children, but the factor responsible for better recall is not age per se, but whether the child notices that the list consists of four *categories* (animals, plants, means of transportation, and articles of clothing). If the categories are noticed, young children often recall the entire list. In the absence of category recognition, performance is poorer and shows the age effect. Younger children employ categorization strategies less often than older ones. However, the skill is knowledge related, not age related; the more complex the categories, the older the child is before noticing the structure. One has to know a structure before one can use it.

These varying views of children's learning have different implications for what one expects from children. If one believes that learning differences are determined by gradual increases in capacity or speed of processing, one would expect relatively uniform increases in learning across most domains. But if one believes that strategies and knowledge are important, one would expect different levels of learning, depending on the children's conceptual knowledge and their control over strategies that organize that knowledge for learning. For example, in a comparison of college students' and third graders' abilities to recall 30 items that included the names of Saturday morning television shows, children's cartoon characters, etc., the third graders clustered more and subsequently recalled more (Linberg, 1980). Similarly, a group of 8- to 12-year-old "slow learners" performed much better than "normal" adults on a task of recalling large numbers of pop stars because of a clustering strategy (Brown and Lawton, 1977). An outstanding example of the intertwining of capacity, knowledge, and strategies in children's chess performance is provided in Box 2.1 (see Chapter 2).

Metacognition is another important aspect of children's learning (see Brown, 1978; Flavell and Wellman, 1977). The importance of prior knowledge in determining performance, crucial to adults as well as children, includes knowledge about learning, knowledge of their own learning strengths and weaknesses, and the demands of the learning task at hand. Metacognition also includes self-regulation—the ability to orchestrate one's learning: to plan, monitor success, and correct errors when appropriate—all necessary for effective intentional learning (Bereiter and Scardamalia, 1989).

Metacognition also refers to the ability to reflect on one's own performance. Whereas self-regulation may appear quite early, reflection appears to be late developing. If children lack insight to their own learning abilities, they can hardly be expected to plan or self-regulate efficiently. But metacognition does not emerge full-blown in late childhood in some "now you have it, now you don't" manner. The evidence suggests that, like other forms of learning, metacognition develops gradually and is as dependent on knowledge as experience. It is difficult to engage in self-regulation and reflection in areas that one does not understand. However, on topics that children know, primitive forms of self-regulation and reflection appear early (Brown and DeLoache, 1978).

Attempts at deliberate remembering in preschool children provide glimpses of the early emergence of the ability to plan, orchestrate, and apply strategies. In a famous example, 3- and 4-year-old children were asked to watch while a small toy dog was hidden under one of three cups. The children were instructed to remember where the dog was. The children were anything but passive as they waited alone during a delay interval (Wellman et al., 1975). Some children displayed various behaviors that resemble well-known mnemonic strategies, including clear attempts at retrieval practice, such as looking at the target cup and nodding yes, looking at the non-target cups and nodding no, and retrieval cueing, such as marking the correct cup by resting a hand on it or moving it to a salient position. Both of these strategies are precursors to more mature rehearsal activities. These efforts were rewarded: children who prepared actively for retrieval in these ways more often remembered the location of the hidden dog. Box 4.3 shows a glimmer of even earlier emergence of "rehearsal."

These attempts to aid remembering involve a dawning awareness of metacognition—that without some effort, forgetting would occur. And the strategies involved resemble the more mature forms of strategic intervention, such as rehearsal, used by older school-aged children. Between 5 and 10 years of age, children's understanding of the need to use strategic effort in order to learn becomes increasingly sophisticated, and their ability to talk about and reflect on learning continues to grow throughout the school years (Brown et al., 1983). By recognizing this dawning understanding in children, one can begin to design learning activities in the early school years that build on and strengthen their understanding of what it means to learn and remember.

Multiple Strategies, Strategy Choices

The strategies that children use to memorize, conceptualize, reason, and solve problems grow increasingly effective and flexible, and are applied more broadly, with age and experience. But different strategies are not solely related to age. To demonstrate the variety, we consider the specific case of the addition of single-digit numbers, which has been the subject of a great deal of cognitive research.

Given a problem such as 3 + 5, it was initially believed that preschool children add up from 1 (i.e., 1,2,3 | 4,5,6,7,8), that 6- to 8-year-olds add by

BOX 4.3 Remembering Where Big Bird Is

For a group of 18- and 24-month-old children, an attractive toy, Big Bird, was hidden in a variety of locations in a playroom, such as behind a pillow, on a couch, or under a chair. The children were told that "Big Bird is going to hide, and when the bell rings, you can find him." While waiting to retrieve the toy, even though they were engaged by an adult in play and conversation, the children did not wait passively. Instead, they often interrupted their play with a variety of activities that showed they were still preoccupied with the memory task. They talked about the toy, saying, "Big Bird"; the fact that it was hidden, "Big Bird hiding"; where it was hidden, "Big Bird, chair"; or about their plan to retrieve it later, "Me find Big Bird." Other rehearsal-like behaviors included looking or pointing at the hiding place, hovering near it, and attempting to peek at the toy. Although less systematic and well formed than an older person's rehearsal strategies, the young children's activities similarly function to keep alive the information to be remembered, the hidden toy and its location (DeLoache et al., 1985a).

counting from the larger number ("5, then 6, 7, 8,"), and that from 9 years on, children retrieve answers from memory because they know the answer (Ashcraft, 1985; Resnick and Ford, 1981). More recently, however, a more complex and interesting picture has emerged (Siegler, 1996). On a problem-by-problem basis, children of the same age often use a wide variety of strategies. This finding has emerged in domains as diverse as arithmetic (Cooney et al., 1988; Geary and Burlingham-Dubree, 1989; Goldman et al., 1988; Siegler and Robinson, 1982), causal and scientific reasoning (Lehrer and Schauble, 1996; Kuhn, 1995; Schauble, 1990; Shultz, 1982), spatial reasoning (Ohlsson, 1991); referential communications (Kahan and Richards, 1986), recall from memory (Coyle and Bjorklund, 1997), reading and spelling (Jorm and Share, 1983), and judgments of plausibility (Kuhara-Kojima and Hatano, 1989). Even the same child presented the same problem on two successive days often uses different strategies (Siegler and McGilly, 1989). For example, when 5-year-olds add numbers, they sometimes count from 1, as noted above, but they also sometimes retrieve answers from memory, and sometimes they count from the larger number (Siegler, 1988).

The fact that children use diverse strategies is not a mere idiosyncrasy of human cognition. Good reasons exist for people to know and use multiple strategies. Strategies differ in their accuracy, in the amounts of time their execution requires, in their processing demands, and in the range of problems to which they apply. Strategy choices involve tradeoffs among these properties. The broader the range of strategies that children know and can appreciate where they apply, the more precisely they can shape their approaches to the demands of particular circumstances.

Even young children can capitalize on the strengths of different strategies and use each one for the problems for which its advantages are greatest. For example, for an easy addition problem such as 4+1, first graders are likely to retrieve the answer; for problems with large differences between the numbers, such as 2+9, they are likely to count from the larger number ("9,10,11"); for problems excluding both of these cases, such as 6+7, they are likely to count from one (Geary, 1994; Siegler, 1988). The adaptiveness of these strategy choices increases as children gain experience with the domain, though it is obvious even in early years (Lemaire and Siegler, 1995).

Once it is recognized that children know multiple strategies and choose among them, the question arises: How do they construct such strategies in the first place? This question is answered through studies in which individual children who do not yet know a strategy are given prolonged experiences (weeks or months) in the subject matter; in this way, researchers can study how children devise their various strategies (Kuhn, 1995; Siegler and Crowley, 1991; see also DeLoache et al., 1985a). These are referred to as "microgenetic" studies, meaning small-scale studies of the development of a concept. In this approach, one can identify when a new strategy is first used, which in turn allows examination of what the experience of discovery was like, what led to the discovery, and how the discovery was generalized beyond its initial use.

Three key findings have emerged from these studies: (1) discoveries are often made not in response to impasses or failures but rather in the context of successful performance; (2) short-lived transition strategies often precede more enduring approaches; and (3) generalization of new approaches often occurs very slowly, even when children can provide compelling rationales for their usefulness (Karmiloff-Smith, 1992; Kuhn, 1995; Siegler and Crowley, 1991). Children often generate useful new strategies without ever having generated conceptually flawed ones. They seem to seek conceptual understanding of the requisites of appropriate strategies in a domain. On such tasks as single-digit addition, multidigit subtraction, and the game of tic-tac-toe, children possess such understanding, which allows them to recognize the usefulness of new, more advanced strategies before they generate them spontaneously (Hatano and Inagaki, 1996; Siegler and Crowley, 1994).

The new understanding of children's strategic development has led to instructional initiatives. A common feature of such innovations as reciprocal teaching (Palincsar and Brown, 1984), communities of learners (Brown and Campione, 1994, 1996; Cognition and Technology Group at Vanderbilt, 1994), the ideal student (Pressley et al., 1992), and Project Rightstart (Griffin et al., 1992) is that they recognize the importance of students' knowing and using diverse strategies. These programs differ, but all are aimed at helping students to understand how strategies can help them solve problems, to recognize when each strategy is likely to be most useful, and to transfer strategies to novel situations. The considerable success that these instructional programs have enjoyed, with young as well as older children and with low-income as well as middle-income children, attests to the fact that the development of a repertoire of flexible strategies has practical significance for learning.

Multiple Intelligences

Just as the concept of multiple strategies has improved understanding of children's learning and influenced approaches to education, so, too, has the growing interest in multiple forms of intelligence. In his theory of multiple intelligences, Gardner (1983, 1991) proposed the existence of seven relatively autonomous intelligences: linguistic, logical, musical, spatial, bodily kinesthetic, interpersonal, and intrapersonal. Recently, Gardner (1997) proposed an eighth intelligence, "naturalistic." The first two intelligences are those typically tapped on tests and most valued in schools.

The theory of multiple intelligences was developed as a psychological theory, but it sparked a great deal of interest among educators, in this country and abroad, in its implications for teaching and learning. The experimental educational programs based on the theory have focused generally in two ways. Some educators believe that all children should have each intelligence nurtured; on this basis, they have devised curricula that address each intelligence directly. Others educators have focused on the development of specific intelligences, like the personal ones, because they believe these intelligences receive short shrift in American education. There are strengths and weaknesses to each approach.

The application of multiple intelligences to education is a grass roots movement among teachers that is only just beginning. An interesting development is the attempt to modify traditional curricula: whether one is teaching history, science, or the arts, the theory of multiple intelligences offers a teacher a number of different approaches to the topic, several modes of representing key concepts, and a variety of ways in which students can demonstrate their understandings (Gardner, 1997).

CHILDREN'S VIEWS OF INTELLIGENCE AND THEIR LEARNING: MOTIVATION TO LEARN AND UNDERSTAND

Children, like their elders, have their own conceptions about their minds and those of others and how humans learn and are "intelligent" (see Wellman, 1990; Wellman and Hickey, 1994; Gelman, 1988; Gopnik, 1990). Children are said to have one of two main classes of beliefs: entity theories and incremental theories (Dweck, 1989; Dweck and Elliot, 1983; Dweck and Leggett, 1988). Children with entity theories believe that intelligence is a fixed property of individuals; children with incremental theories believe that intelligence is malleable (see also Resnick and Nelson-LeGall, 1998). Children who are entity theorists tend to hold performance goals in learning situations: they strive to perform well or appear to perform well, attain positive judgments of their competence, and avoid assessments. They avoid challenges that will reflect them in poor light. They show little persistence in the face of failure. Their aim is to perform well. In contrast, children who are incremental theorists have learning goals: they believe that intelligence can be improved by effort and will. They regard their own increasing competence as their goal. They seek challenges and show high persistence. It is clear that children's theories about learning affect how they learn and how they think about learning. Although most children probably fall on the continuum between the two theories and may simultaneously be incremental theorists in mathematics and entity theorists in art, the motivational factors affect their persistence, learning goals, sense of failure, and striving for success. Teachers can guide children to a more healthy conceptualization of their learning potential if they understand the beliefs that children bring to school.

Self-Directed and Other-Directed Learning

Just as children are often self-directed learners in privileged domains, such as those of language and physical causality, young children exhibit a strong desire to apply themselves in intentional learning situations. They also learn in situations where there is no external pressure to improve and no feedback or reward other than pure satisfaction—sometimes called achievement or competence motivation (White, 1959; Yarrow and Messer, 1983; Dichter-Blancher et al., 1997). Children are both problem solvers and problem generators; they not only attempt to solve problems presented to them, but they also seek and create novel challenges. An adult struggling to solve a crossword puzzle has much in common with a young child trying to assemble a jigsaw puzzle. Why do they bother? It seems that humans have a need to solve problems; see Box 4.4. One of the challenges of schools is to build on children's motivation to explore, succeed, understand (Piaget, 1978) and harness it in the service of learning.

GUIDING CHILDREN'S LEARNING

Along with children's natural curiosity and their persistence as self-motivated learners, what they learn during their first 4 or 5 years is not learned

BOX 4.4   Solving a Problem

Children 18 to 36 months of age are given nesting cups to play with (DeLoache et al., 1985b; see also Karmiloff-Smith and Inhelder, 1974, on children balancing blocks). Five plastic cups are dumped on a table in front of a child, who is simply told, "These are for you to play with." Although the children have previously seen the cups nested together, there was no real need for them to attempt to nest the cups themselves; they could easily have stacked them, made an imaginary train, pretended to drink from them, etc. However, the children immediately started trying to fit the cups together, often working long and hard in the process.

Overall, in their spontaneous manipulations of a set of nesting cups, very young children progress from trying to correct their errors by exerting physical force without changing any of the relations among the elements, to making limited changes in a part of the problem set, to considering and operating on the problem as a whole. This "developmental" trend is observed not only across age, but also in the same children of the same age (30 months) given extensive time to play with the cups.

Most important, the children persist, not because they have to, or are guided to, or even because they are responding to failure; they persist because success and understanding are motivating in their own right.

in isolation. Infants' activities are complemented by adult-child relationships that encourage the gradual involvement of children in the skilled and valued activities of the society in which they live. Research has shown that learning is strongly influenced by these social interactions. In fact, studies of interactions of drug-abusing mothers and their infants show how the absence of these critical learning interactions depresses 3- and 6-month-old infants' learning (Mayes et al., 1998).

Parents and others who care for children arrange their activities and facilitate learning by regulating the difficulty of the tasks and by modeling mature performance during joint participation in activities. A substantial body of observational research has provided detailed accounts of the learning interactions between mothers and their young children. As an illustration, watch a mother with a 1-year-old sitting on her knees in front of a collection of toys. A large part of her time is devoted to such quietly facilitative and scene-setting activities as holding a toy that seems to require three hands to manipulate, retrieving things that have been pushed out of range, clearing away those things that are not at present being used in order to provide the child with a sharper focus for the main activity, turning toys so that they become more easily grasped, demonstrating their less obvious properties, and all along molding her body in such a way as to provide maximal physical support and access to the play materials (Schaffer, 1977:73).

In addition to the research showing how adults arrange the environment to promote children's learning, a great deal of research has also been conducted on how adults guide children's understanding of how to act in new situations through their emotional cues regarding the nature of the situation, nonverbal models of how to behave, verbal and nonverbal interpretations of events, and verbal labels to classify objects and events (Rogoff, 1990; Walden and Ogan, 1988). Parents frame their language and behavior in ways that facilitate learning by young children (Bruner, 1981a, b, 1983; Edwards, 1987; Hoff-Ginsberg and Shatz, 1982). For example, in the earliest months, the restrictions of parental baby talk to a small number of melodic contours may enable infants to abstract vocal prototypes (Papousek et al., 1985). Parental labeling of objects and categories may assist children in understanding category hierarchies and learning appropriate labels (Callanan, 1985; Mervis, 1984). Communication with caregivers to accomplish everyday goals is the groundwork for children's early learning of the language and other cognitive tools of their community; see Box 4.5.

An extremely important role of caregivers involves efforts to help children connect new situations to more familiar ones. In our discussion of competent performance and transfer (see Chapter 3), we noted that knowledge appropriate to a particular situation is not necessarily accessed despite being relevant. Effective teachers help people of all ages make connections among different aspects of their knowledge.

Caregivers attempt to build on what children know and extend their competencies by providing supporting structures or scaffolds for the child's performance (Wood et al., 1976). Scaffolding involves several activities and tasks, such as:

- interesting the child in the task;
- reducing the number of steps required to solve a problem by simplifying the task, so that a child can manage components of the process and recognize when a fit with task requirements is achieved;
- maintaining the pursuit of the goal, through motivation of the child and direction of the activity;
- marking critical features of discrepancies between what a child has produced and the ideal solution;
- controlling frustration and risk in problem solving; and
- demonstrating an idealized version of the act to be performed.

Scaffolding can be characterized as acting on a motto of "Where before there was a spectator, let there now be a participant" (Bruner, 1983:60).

BOX 4.5 Which Toy?

Consider the efforts to reach an understanding between an adult and a 14-month-old about which toy the infant wants to play with. The adult is looking for a toy in the toy box. When he touches the tower of rings, the baby exclaims, "Aa!" The adult responds, "Aa?" picking up the tower. The infant continues looking at the toy box and ignores the tower, so the adult shows the baby the tower and again asks "Aa?" The baby points at something in the toy box grunting, "Aa . . . aa . . . " The adult reaches toward the toy box again, and the infant exclaims, "Tue!" The adult exclaimed "Aa!" as he picks up the peekaboo cloth and shows it to the infant. But the infant ignores the cloth and points again at something in the toy box, then, impatiently, waves his arm. The adult responds, "Aa?" But the baby points down to the side of the toy box. They repeat the cycle with another toy, and the baby waves his arm impatiently. The adult says "You show me!" and lifts the baby to his lap from the high chair. The adult then picks up the jack-in-the-box, asking, "This?"—the baby opens his hand toward the toy, and they began to play (Rogoff et al., 1984:42-43).

Learning to Read and Tell Stories

The importance of adult support of children's learning can be demonstrated by considering the question: How is it that children, born with no language, can develop most of the rudiments of story telling in the first three years of life? (Engle, 1995). A variety of literacy experiences prepare children for this prowess. Providing children with practice at telling or "reading" stories is an impetus to the growth of language skills and is related to early independent reading; see Box 4.6. For many years some parents and scholars have known about the importance of early reading, through picture book "reading" that is connected to personal experiences. Recently, the efficacy of this process has been scientifically validated—it has been shown to work (see National Research Council, 1998).

In the late nineteenth century, C. L. Dodgson—Lewis Carroll—prepared a nursery version of his famous *Alice in Wonderland/Through the Looking Glass* books. The majority of the book consisted of reprints of the famous Tenniel woodcut illustrations. The book was to stimulate "reading" in the sense that contemporary children's wordless picture books do. This was a first of its kind, and we quote Lewis Carroll (cited in Cohen, 1995:440).

> I have reason to believe that "Alice's Adventures in Wonderland" has been read by some hundreds of English Children, aged from Five to Fifteen: also by Children aged from Fifteen to Twenty-five: yet again by Children aged

BOX 4.6   Baby Reading

Sixteenth-month-old Julie is left alone temporarily with a visiting grandfather. Wishing to distract the child from her mother's absence, he starts "reading" a picture book to her. On each page is an animal and its "baby." Julie shows interest as a spectator until they came to a picture of a kangaroo and its "joey." She quickly says "Kanga, baby." Pointing to a shirt with Kanga and Roo (from *Winnie the Pooh*), she says again, "Kanga" "baby." Grandfather repeats each utterance. Then he says: "Where's Julie's Kanga?" knowing that she has recently received a large stuffed animal from Australia. With great excitement, Julie pulls the stuffed animal over to her grandfather and, pointing to the book, says "Kanga, baby," then points to the stuffed toy, "Kanga" and to the joey in the pouch, "baby." Communication had been reached with much laughter and repetition of the Kanga/baby routine. Even at the one-word utterance stage, children can "read," "refer," and "represent" across settings (Brown, personal communication).

> from Twenty-five to Thirty-five . . . And my ambition now (is it a vain one?)
> is that it will be read by Children aged from Nought to Five. To be read?
> Nay, not so! Say rather to be thumbed, to be cooed over, to be dogs'-eared,
> to be rumpled, to be kissed, by the illiterate, ungrammatical.

A preeminent educator, Dodgson had a pedagogical creed about how "Nursery Alice" should be approached. The subtext of the book is aimed at adults, almost in the fashion of a contemporary teacher's guide; they were asked to bring the book to life. The pictures were the primary focus; much of the original tale is left unspecified. For example, when looking at the famous Tenniel picture of Alice swimming with mouse in a pool of her own tears, Carroll tells the adult to read to the child as follows (cited in Cohen, 1995:441):

> Now look at the picture, and you'll soon guess what happened next. It looks just like the sea, doesn't it? But it really is the Pool of Tears—all made of Alice's tears, you know!
>
> And Alice has tumbled into the Pool: and the Mouse has tumbled in: and there they are swimming about together.
>
> Doesn't Alice look pretty, as she swims across the picture? You can just see her blue stockings, far away under the water.
>
> But Why is the Mouse swimming away from Alice is such a hurry? Well, the reason is, that Alice began talking about cats and dogs: and a Mouse always hates talking about cats and dogs!
>
> Suppose you were swimming about, in a Pool of your own Tears: and suppose somebody began talking to you about lesson-books and bottles of medicine, wouldn't you swim as hard as you could go?

Carroll, a natural teacher, guides caretakers through the task of concentrating the child's attention on the picture, prodding the child's curiosity by asking questions, and engaging the child in a dialogue—even if the child's contribution is initially limited. Carroll asks the adult to lead the child through literacy events by developing "habits of close observation." He cleverly suggests certain truths about human and animal nature, and he opens up a realm of fun and nonsense that the child can share with the adult reading the story (Cohen, 1995:442).

When caregivers engage in picture book "reading," they can structure children's developing narrative skills by asking questions to organize children's stories or accounts (Eisenberg, 1985; McNamee, 1980). If the child stops short or leaves out crucial information, adults may prompt, "What happened next?" or "Who else was there?" Such questions implicitly provide children with cues to the desired structure of narratives in their environment.

For example, one mother began reading with her child, Richard, when he was only 8 months old (Ninio and Bruner, 1978). The mother initially did all the "reading," but at the same time she was engaged in "teaching" Richard the ritual dialogue for picture book reading. At first she appeared to be content with any vocalization from the baby, but as soon as he produced actual words, she increased her demands and asked for a label with the query, "What's that?" The mother seemed to increase her level of expectation, first coaxing the child to substitute a vocalization for a nonvocal sign and later a well-formed word for a babbled vocalization. Initially, the mother did all the labeling because she assumed that the child could not; later, the mother labeled only when she believed that the child would not or could not label for himself. Responsibility for labeling was thereby transferred from the mother to the child in response to his increasing store of knowledge, finely monitored by the mother. During the course of the study the mother constantly updated her inventory of the words the child had previously understood and repeatedly attempted to make contact with his growing knowledge base.

Middle-class children between 1-1/2 and 3 years often provide labels spontaneously. One group of children did such labeling as "There's a horsie" or asked the mothers for information "What's this?" (DeLoache, 1984). With the 3-year-olds, the mothers went far beyond labeling; they talked about the relation among the objects in the picture, related them to the children's experiences, and questioned the children about their outside experience. For example, "That's right, that's a beehive. Do you know what bees make? They make honey. They get nectar from flowers and use it to make honey, and then they put the honey in the beehive." The mothers use the situation and the material to provide the children with a great deal of background information. They continually elaborate and question information, which are comprehension-fostering activities that must later be applied to "real" reading tasks.

In these reading activities, mothers are attempting to function in what psychologists call a child's zone of proximal development—to stretch what the child can do with a little assistance (see Box 4.1 above). As the child advances, so does the level of collaboration demanded by the mother. The mother systematically shapes their joint experiences in such a way that the child will be drawn into taking more and more responsibility for their joint work. In so doing, she not only provides an excellent learning environment, she also models appropriate comprehension-fostering activities; crucial regulatory activities are thereby made overt and explicit.

Story telling is a powerful way to organize lived and listened-to experiences, and it provides an entry into the ability to construe narrative from text. By the time children are 3 or 4, they are beginning narrators; they can tell many kinds of stories, including relating autobiographical events, retelling fiction, and recalling stories they have heard. The everyday experiences of children foster this story telling. Children like to talk and learn about familiar activities, scripts or schemes, the "going to bed" script or the "going to McDonald's" script (Nelson, 1986; Mandler, 1996). Children like to listen to and retell personal experiences. These reminiscences are stepping stones to more mature narratives. As they get older, children increase their levels of participation by adding elements to the story and taking on greater pieces of the authorial responsibility. By 3 years of age, children in families in which joint story telling is common can take over the leadership role in constructing personal narratives.

Reminiscing also enables children to relate upsetting experiences; such narratives act as "cooling vessels" (Bruner, 1972), distancing the experience and confirming the safe haven of homes and other supportive environments. This early interest in sharing experience, joint picture book reading, and narrative, in general, have obvious implications for literary appreciation in preschool and early grades. Indeed, the KEEP (Au, 1981; Au and Jordan, 1981) program in Hawaii and the Reciprocal Teaching Program (Palinscar and Brown, 1984) in urban U.S. cities were both explicitly modeled after the natural interactions; they attempted to build on them and model the style. Connection-making and scaffolding by parents to support children's mathematical learning has also proved a successful intervention (Saxe et al., 1984; Byrnes, 1996) that has been mimicked in school settings.

Cultural Variations in Communication

There are great cultural variations in the ways in which adults and children communicate, and there are wide individual differences in communication styles within any cultural community. All cultural variations provide strong supports for children's development. However, some variations are more likely than others to encourage development of the specific kinds of knowledge and interaction styles that are expected in typical U.S. school environments. It is extremely important for educators—and parents—to take these differences into account.

Conversing, Observing, or Eavesdropping

In some communities, children are seldom direct conversational partners with adults, but rather engage with adults by participating in adult activities. In such situations, children's learning occurs through observing adults and from the pointers and support provided by adults in the contexts of ongoing activities. Such engagements contrast sharply with patterns common in other communities, in which adults take the role of directly instructing young children in language and other skills through explicit lessons that are not embedded in the contexts of ongoing activities (Ochs and Schieffelin, 1984; Rogoff, 1990; Rogoff et al., 1993).

For example, Pueblo Indian children are provided access to many aspects of adult life and are free to choose how and with whom to participate (John-Steiner, 1984). Their reports of their own learning stress their role as "apprentices" to more experienced members of the community (Suina and Smolkin, 1994). Observation and verbal explanation occur in the contexts of involvement in the processes as they are being learned.

In an African-American community of Louisiana, in which children are expected to be "seen and not heard," language learning occurs by eavesdropping. "The silent absorption in community life, the participation in the daily commercial rituals, and the hours spent overhearing adults' conversations should not be underestimated in their impact on a child's language growth" (Ward, 1971:37). "Nothing is censored for children's ears; they go everywhere in the community except Saturday-night parties." Older children teach social and intellectual skills: "Alphabets, colors, numbers, rhymes, word games, pen and pencil games are learned . . . from older children. No child, even the firstborn, is without such tutelage, since cousins, aunts, and uncles of their own age and older are always on hand" (Ward, 1971:25).

In this community, small children are not conversational partners with adults, as in the sense of other people with whom one converses. If children have something important to say, parents will listen, and children had better listen when their parents speak to them. But for conversation, adults talk to adults. Questions between older children and adults involve straightforward requests for information, not questions asked for the sake of conversation or for parents to drill children on topics to which the parents already know the answers. Mothers' speech to children, while not taking the form of a dialogue, is carefully regularized, providing precise, workable models of the language used in the community (Ward, 1971).

Schooling and the Role of Questioning

Detailed ethnographic research studies have shown striking differences in how adults and children interact verbally. Because of the prevalence of the use of questions in classrooms, one particularly important difference is how people treat questions and answers. One classic study, a comparison between the questioning behavior of white middle-class teachers in their own homes and the home question interaction of their working-class African-American pupils, showed dramatic differences (Heath, 1981, 1983). The middle-class mothers began the questioning game almost from birth and well before a child could be expected to answer. For example, a mother questions her 8-week-old infant, "You want your teddy bear?" and responds for the child, "Yes, you want your bear" (see Box 4.6 above). These rituals set the stage for a general reliance on questioning and pseudo-questioning interactions that serve a variety of social functions. Children exposed to these interaction patterns seem compelled to provide an answer and are quite happy to provide information that they know perfectly well an adult already possesses.

Such "known-answer" questions, where the interrogator has the information being requested, occur frequently in classroom dialogues (Mehan, 1979). Teachers routinely call on children to answer questions that serve to display and practice their knowledge, rather than to provide information that the teacher does not know. Similarly, in middle-class homes, known-answer questions predominate. For example, in one 48-hour period, almost half the utterances (48% of 215) addressed to 27-month-old Missy were questions; of these questions, almost half (46%) were known-answer questions (Heath, 1981, 1983).

In general, questions played a less central role in the home social interaction patterns of the African-American children; in particular, there was a notable lack of known-answer rituals (Heath, 1981, 1983). The verbal interactions served a different function, and they were embedded within different communicative and interpersonal contexts. Common questioning forms were analogy, story-starting, and accusatory; these forms rarely occurred in the white homes. For example, the African-American children were commonly asked to engage in the sophisticated use of metaphors by responding to questions that asked for analogical comparisons. The children were more likely to be asked "What's that like?" or "Who's he acting like?" rather than "What's that?" Such questions reflected the African-American adults' assumptions that preschool children are adept at noting likenesses between things, assumptions that are also revealed in speech forms other than questioning, such as frequent use of similes and metaphors. The adults were asked about and value metaphorical thinking and narrative exposition initiated by a story-telling question: one participant indicated a willingness to tell a story using the question form, "Did you see Maggie's dog yesterday?" The appropriate answer to such a query is not "yes" or "no," but another question, "No, what happened to Maggie's dog yesterday?" that sets the stage for the initiator's narrative. Both adults and older preschool children were totally familiar with these questioning rituals and played them enthusiastically.

These examples emphasize the systematic differences between the form and function of questioning behaviors in the working-class black and middle-class white communities that were studied. Neither approach is "deficient," but the match between the activities that predominate in classrooms at the early grades is much greater with middle-class homes than with working-class ones in that community. As the middle-class teachers practiced their familiar questioning routines with their pupils, it is not surprising that the middle-class pupils, who shared the teacher's background, successfully ful-filled the answerer role, while the working-class African-American children were often perplexed (Heath, 1981, 1983). Moreover, teachers were some-times bewildered by what they regarded as the lack of responsible answer-ing behavior on the part of their black pupils. They commented (Heath, 1981:108):

> They don't seem to be able to answer even the simplest questions.
>
> I would almost think some of them have a hearing problem; it is as though they don't hear me ask a question. I get blank stares to my ques-tion. When I am making statements or telling stories which interest them, they always seem to hear me.
>
> The simplest questions are the ones they can't answer in the class-room; yet on the playground, they can explain a rule for a ballgame, etc. They can't be as dumb as they seem in my class.
>
> I sometimes feel that when I look at them and ask a question I'm staring at a wall I can't break through.

However, as the teachers learned about the types of metaphoric and narrative question sequences with which the children are familiar, they were able to gradually introduce the unfamiliar known-answer routines. This is an excellent example of the "two-way path, from school to the community and from the community to school" (Heath, 1981:125) that is needed if the transition to formal schooling is to be made less traumatic for ethnically diverse groups. Not only can interventions be devised to help minority-culture parents prepare children for school, but the schools themselves can be sensitive to the problems of cultural mismatches. The answer is not to concentrate exclusively on changing children or changing schools, but to encourage adaptive flexibility in both directions.

CONCLUSION

The concept of "development" is critical to understanding the changes in children's thinking, such as the development of language, causal reasoning, and rudimentary mathematical concepts.

Young children are actively engaged in making sense of their worlds. In some particular domains, such as biological and physical causality, number, and language, they have strong predispositions to learn rapidly and readily. These predispositions support and may even make possible early learning and pave the way for competence in early schooling. Yet even in these domains, children still have a great deal of learning to do.

Children's early understanding of the perceptual and physical world may jump-start the learning process, even making learning possible, but one should look with caution for ways in which early knowledge may impede later learning. For example, children who treat rational numbers as they had treated whole numbers will experience trouble ahead. Awareness of these roadblocks to learning could help teachers anticipate the difficulty.

Although children learn readily in some domains, they can learn practically anything by sheer will and effort. When required to learn about nonprivileged domains they need to develop strategies of intentional learning. In order to develop strategic competence in learning, children need to understand what it means to learn, who they are as learners, and how to go about planning, monitoring, revising, and reflecting upon their learning and that of others. Children lack knowledge and experience but not reasoning ability. Although young children are inexperienced, they reason facilely with the knowledge they have.

Children are both problem solvers and problem generators: children attempt to solve problems presented to them, and they also seek novel challenges. They refine and improve their problem-solving strategies not only in the face of failure, but also by building on prior success. They persist because success and understanding are motivating in their own right.

Adults help make connections between new situations and familiar ones for children. Children's curiosity and persistence are supported by adults who direct their attention, structure their experiences, support their learning attempts, and regulate the complexity and difficulty levels of information for them.

Children, thus, exhibit capacities that are shaped by environmental experiences and the individuals who care for them. Caregivers provide supports, such as directing children's attention to critical aspects of events, commenting on features that should be noticed, and in many other ways providing structure to the information. Structure is critical for learning and for moving toward understanding information. Development and learning are not two parallel processes. Early biological underpinnings enable certain types of interactions, and through various environmental supports from caregivers and other cultural and social supports, a child's experiences for learning are expanded. Learning is promoted and regulated both by children's biology and ecology, and learning produces development.

5

Mind and Brain

As the popular press has discovered, people have a keen appetite for research information about how the brain works and how thought processes develop (*Newsweek*, 1996, 1997; *Time*, 1997a, b). Interest runs particularly high in stories about the neuro-development of babies and children and the effect of early experiences on learning. The fields of neuroscience and cognitive science are helping to satisfy this fundamental curiosity about how people think and learn.

In considering which findings from brain research are relevant to human learning or, by extension, to education, one must be careful to avoid adopting faddish concepts that have not been demonstrated to be of value in classroom practice. Among these is the concept that the left and right hemispheres of the brain should be taught separately to maximize the effectiveness of learning. Another is the notion that the brain grows in holistic "spurts," within or around which specific educational objectives should be arranged: as discussed in this chapter, there is significant evidence that brain regions develop asynchronously, although any specific educational implications of this remain to be determined. Another widely held misconception is that people use only 20 percent of their brains—with different percentage figures in different incarnations—and should be able to use more of it. This belief appears to have arisen from the early neuroscience finding that much of the cerebral cortex consists of "silent areas" that are not activated by sensory or motor activity. However, it is now known that these silent areas mediate higher cognitive functions that are not directly coupled to sensory or motor activity.

Advances in neuroscience are confirming theoretical positions advanced by developmental psychology for a number of years, such as the importance of early experience in development (Hunt, 1961). What is new, and therefore important for this volume, is the *convergence* of evidence from a number of scientific fields. As the sciences of developmental psychology, cognitive psychology, and neuroscience, to name but three, have contributed vast numbers of research studies, details about learning and development have converged to form a more complete picture of how intellectual development occurs. Clarification of some of the mechanisms of learning by neuroscience has been advanced, in part, by the advent of non-invasive imaging technologies, such as positron emission tomography (PET) and functional magnetic resonance imaging (FMRI). These technologies have allowed researchers to observe human learning processes directly.

This chapter reviews key findings from neuroscience and cognitive science that are expanding knowledge of the mechanisms of human learning. Three main points guide the discussion in this chapter:

1. Learning changes the physical structure of the brain.
2. These structural changes alter the functional organization of the brain; in other words, learning organizes and reorganizes the brain.
3. Different parts of the brain may be ready to learn at different times.

We first explain some basic concepts of neuroscience and new knowledge about brain development, including the effects of instruction and learning on the brain. We then look at language in learning as an example of the mind-brain connection. Lastly, we examine research on how memory is represented in the brain and its implications for learning.

From a neuroscience perspective, instruction and learning are very important parts of a child's brain development and psychological development processes. Brain development and psychological development involve continuous interactions between a child and the external environment—or, more accurately, a hierarchy of environments, extending from the level of the individual body cells to the most obvious boundary of the skin. Greater understanding of the nature of this interactive process renders moot such questions as how much depends on genes and how much on environment. As various developmental researchers have suggested, this question is much like asking which contributes most to the area of a rectangle, its height or its width (Eisenberg, 1995)?

THE BRAIN: FOUNDATION FOR LEARNING

Neuroscientists study the anatomy, physiology, chemistry, and molecular biology of the nervous system, with particular interest in how brain activity relates to behavior and learning. Several crucial questions about early learning particularly intrigue neuroscientists. How does the brain develop? Are there stages of brain development? Are there critical periods when certain things must happen for the brain to develop normally? How is information encoded in the developing and the adult nervous systems? And perhaps most important: How does experience affect the brain?

Some Basics

A nerve cell, or neuron, is a cell that receives information from other nerve cells or from the sensory organs and then projects that information to other nerve cells, while still other neurons project it back to the parts of the body that interact with the environment, such as the muscles. Nerve cells are equipped with a cell body—a sort of metabolic heart—and an enormous treelike structure called the dendritic field, which is the input side of the neuron. Information comes into the cell from projections called axons. Most of the excitatory information comes into the cell from the dendritic field, often through tiny dendritic projections called spines. The junctions through which information passes from one neuron to another are called synapses, which can be excitatory or inhibitory in nature. The neuron integrates the information it receives from all of its synapses and this determines its output.

During the development process, the "wiring diagram" of the brain is created through the formation of synapses. At birth, the human brain has in place only a relatively small proportion of the trillions of synapses it will eventually have; it gains about two-thirds of its adult size after birth. The rest of the synapses are formed after birth, and a portion of this process is guided by experience.

Synaptic connections are added to the brain in two basic ways. The first way is that synapses are overproduced, then selectively lost. Synapse overproduction and loss is a fundamental mechanism that the brain uses to incorporate information from experience. It tends to occur during the early periods of development. In the visual cortex—the area of the cerebral cortex of the brain that controls sight—a person has many more synapses at 6 months of age than at adulthood. This is because more and more synapses are formed in the early months of life, then they disappear, sometimes in prodigious numbers. The time required for this phenomenon to run its course varies in different parts of the brain, from 2 to 3 years in the human visual cortex to 8 to 10 years in some parts of the frontal cortex.

Some neuroscientists explain synapse formation by analogy to the art of sculpture. Classical artists working in marble created a sculpture by chiseling away unnecessary bits of stone until they achieved their final form. Animal studies suggest that the "pruning" that occurs during synapse overproduction and loss is similar to this act of carving a sculpture. The nervous system sets up a large number of connections; experience then plays on this network, selecting the appropriate connections and removing the inappropriate ones. What remains is a refined final form that constitutes the sensory and perhaps the cognitive bases for the later phases of development.

The second method of synapse formation is through the addition of new synapses—like the artist who creates a sculpture by adding things together until the form is complete. Unlike synapse overproduction and loss, the process of synapse addition operates throughout the entire human life span and is especially important in later life. This process is not only sensitive to experience, it is actually driven by experience. Synapse addition probably lies at the base of some, or even most, forms of memory. As discussed later in this chapter, the work of cognitive scientists and education researchers is contributing to our understanding of synapse addition.

Wiring the Brain

The role of experience in wiring the brain has been illuminated by research on the visual cortex in animals and humans. In adults, the inputs entering the brain from the two eyes terminate separately in adjacent regions of the visual cortex. Subsequently, the two inputs converge on the next set of neurons. People are not born with this neural pattern. But through the normal processes of seeing, the brain sorts things out.

Neuroscientists discovered this phenomenon by studying humans with visual abnormalities, such as a cataract or a muscle irregularity that deviates the eye. If the eye is deprived of the appropriate visual experience at an early stage of development (because of such abnormalities), it loses its ability to transmit visual information into the central nervous system. When the eye that was incapable of seeing at a very early age was corrected later, the correction alone did not help—the afflicted eye still could not see. When researchers looked at the brains of monkeys in which similar kinds of experimental manipulations had been made, they found that the normal eye had captured a larger than average amount of neurons, and the impeded eye had correspondingly lost those connections.

This phenomenon only occurs if an eye is prevented from experiencing normal vision very early in development. The period at which the eye is sensitive corresponds to the time of synapse overproduction and loss in the visual cortex. Out of the initial mix of overlapping inputs, the neural connections that belong to the eye that sees normally tend to survive, while the connections that belong to the abnormal eye wither away. When both eyes see normally, each eye loses some of the overlapping connections, but both keep a normal number.

In the case of deprivation from birth, one eye completely takes over. The later the deprivation occurs after birth, the less effect it has. By about 6 months of age, closing one eye for weeks on end will produce no effect whatsoever. The critical period has passed; the connections have already sorted themselves out, and the overlapping connections have been eliminated.

This anomaly has helped scientists gain insights into normal visual development. In normal development, the pathway for each eye is sculpted (or "pruned") down to the right number of connections, and those connections are sculpted in other ways, for example, to allow one to see patterns. By overproducing synapses then selecting the right connections, the brain develops an organized wiring diagram that functions optimally. The brain development process actually uses visual information entering from outside to become more precisely organized than it could with intrinsic molecular mechanisms alone. This external information is even more important for later cognitive development. The more a person interacts with the world, the more a person needs information from the world incorporated into the brain structures.

Synapse overproduction and selection may progress at different rates in different parts of the brain (Huttenlocher and Dabholkar, 1997). In the primary visual cortex, a peak in synapse density occurs relatively quickly. In the medial frontal cortex, a region clearly associated with higher cognitive functions, the process is more protracted: synapse production starts before birth and synapse density continues to increase until 5 or 6 years of age. The selection process, which corresponds conceptually to the main organization of patterns, continues during the next 4-5 years and ends around early adolescence. This lack of synchrony among cortical regions may also occur upon individual cortical neurons where different inputs may mature at different rates (see Juraska, 1982, on animal studies).

After the cycle of synapse overproduction and selection has run its course, additional changes occur in the brain. They appear to include both the modification of existing synapses and the addition of entirely new synapses to the brain. Research evidence (described in the next section) suggests that activity in the nervous system associated with learning experiences somehow causes nerve cells to create new synapses. Unlike the process of synapse overproduction and loss, synapse addition and modification are lifelong processes, driven by experience. In essence, the quality of information to which one is exposed and the amount of information one acquires is reflected throughout one's life in the structure of the brain. This process is probably not the only way that information is stored in the brain, but it is a very important way that provides insight into how people learn.

EXPERIENCES AND ENVIRONMENTS FOR BRAIN DEVELOPMENT

Alterations in the brain that occur during learning seem to make the nerve cells more efficient or powerful. Animals raised in complex environments have a greater volume of capillaries per nerve cell—and therefore a greater supply of blood to the brain—than the caged animals, regardless of whether the caged animal lived alone or with companions (Black et al., 1987). (Capillaries are the tiny blood vessels that supply oxygen and other nutrients to the brain.) In this way experience increases the overall quality of functioning of the brain. Using astrocytes (cells that support neuron functioning by providing nutrients and removing waste) as the index, there are higher amounts of astrocyte per neuron in the complex-environment animals than in the caged groups. Overall, these studies depict an orchestrated pattern of increased capacity in the brain that depends on experience.

Other studies of animals show other changes in the brain through learning; see Box 5.1. The weight and thickness of the cerebral cortex can be measurably altered in rats that are reared from weaning, or placed as adults, in a large cage enriched by the presence both of a changing set of objects for play and exploration and of other rats to induce play and exploration (Rosenzweig and Bennett, 1978). These animals also perform better on a variety of problem-solving tasks than rats reared in standard laboratory cages. Interestingly, both the interactive presence of a social group and direct physical contact with the environment are important factors: animals placed in the enriched environment alone showed relatively little benefit; neither did animals placed in small cages within the larger environment (Ferchmin et al., 1978; Rosenzweig and Bennett, 1972). Thus, the gross structure of the cerebral cortex was altered both by exposure to opportunities for learning and by learning in a social context.

Does Mere Neural Activity Change the Brain or Is Learning Required?

Are the changes in the brain due to actual learning or to variations in aggregate levels of neural activity? Animals in a complex environment not only learn from experiences, but they also run, play, and exercise, which activates the brain. The question is whether activation alone can produce brain changes without the subjects actually learning anything, just as activation of muscles by exercise can cause them to grow. To answer this question, a group of animals that learned challenging motor skills but had relatively little brain activity was compared with groups that had high levels of brain activity but did relatively little learning (Black et al., 1990). There were four groups in all. One group of rats was taught to traverse an elevated obstacle course; these "acrobats" became very good at the task over a month or so of practice. A second group of "mandatory exercisers" was put on a treadmill once a day, where they ran for 30 minutes, rested for 10 minutes, then ran another 30 minutes. A third group of "voluntary exercisers" had free access to an activity wheel attached directly to their cage, which they used often. A control group of "cage potato" rats had no exercise.

What happened to the volume of blood vessels and number of synapses per neuron in the rats? Both the mandatory exercisers and the voluntary exercisers showed higher densities of blood vessels than either the cage potato rats or the acrobats, who learned skills that did not involve significant

BOX 5.1   Making Rats Smarter

How do rats learn? Can rats be "educated?" In classic studies, rats are placed in a complex communal environment filled with objects that provide ample opportunities for exploration and play (Greenough, 1976). The objects are changed and rearranged each day, and during the changing time, the animals are put in yet another environment with another set of objects. So, like their real-world counterparts in the sewers of New York or the fields of Kansas, these rats have a relatively rich set of experiences from which to draw information. A contrasting group of rats is placed in a more typical laboratory environment, living alone or with one or two others in a barren cage—which is obviously a poor model of a rat's real world. These two settings can help determine how experience affects the development of the normal brain and normal cognitive structures, and one can also see what happens when animals are deprived of critical experiences.

After living in the complex or impoverished environments for a period from weaning to rat adolescence, the two groups of animals were subjected to a learning experience. The rats that had grown up in the complex environment made fewer errors at the outset than the other rats; they also learned more quickly not to make any errors at all. In this sense, they were smarter than their more deprived counterparts. And with positive rewards, they performed better on complex tasks than the animals raised in individual cages. Most significant, learning altered the rats' brains: the animals from the complex environment had 20-25 percent more synapses per nerve cell in the visual cortex than the animals from the standard cages (see Turner and Greenough, 1985; Beaulieu and Colonnier, 1987). It is clear that when animals learn, they add new connections to the wiring of their brains—a phenomenon not limited to early development (see, e.g., Greenough et al., 1979).

amounts of activity. But when the number of synapses per nerve cell was measured, the acrobats were the standout group. Learning adds synapses; exercise does not. Thus, different kinds of experience condition the brain in different ways. Synapse formation and blood vessel formation (vascularization) are two important forms of brain adaptation, but they are driven by different physiological mechanisms and by different behavioral events.

Localized Changes

Learning specific tasks brings about localized changes in the areas of the brain appropriate to the task. For example, when young adult animals were taught a maze, structural changes occurred in the visual area of the cerebral cortex (Greenough et al., 1979). When they learned the maze with one eye blocked with an opaque contact lens, only the brain regions connected to the open eye were altered (Chang and Greenough, 1982). When they learned a set of complex motor skills, structural changes occurred in the motor region of the cerebral cortex and in the cerebellum, a hindbrain structure that coordinates motor activity (Black et al., 1990; Kleim et al., 1996).

These changes in brain structure underlie changes in the functional organization of the brain. That is, learning imposes new patterns of organization on the brain, and this phenomenon has been confirmed by electrophysiological recordings of the activity of nerve cells (Beaulieu and Cynader, 1990). Studies of brain development provide a model of the learning process at a cellular level: the changes first observed in rats have also proved to be true in mice, cats, monkeys, and birds, and they almost certainly occur in humans.

ROLE OF INSTRUCTION IN BRAIN DEVELOPMENT

Clearly, the brain can store information, but what kinds of information? The neuroscientist does not address these questions. Answering them is the job of cognitive scientists, education researchers, and others who study the effects of experiences on human behavior and human potential. Several examples illustrate how instruction in specific kinds of information can influence natural development processes. This section discusses a case involving language development.

Language and Brain Development

Brain development is often timed to take advantage of particular experiences, such that information from the environment helps to organize the brain. The development of language in humans is an example of a natural process that is guided by a timetable with certain limiting conditions. Like the development of the visual system, parallel processes occur in human language development for the capacity to perceive phonemes, the "atoms" of speech. A phoneme is defined as the smallest meaningful unit of speech sound. Human beings discriminate the "b" sound from the "p" sound largely by perceiving the time of the onset of the voice relative to the time the lips part; there is a boundary that separates "b" from "p" that helps to distinguish "bet" from "pet." Boundaries of this sort exist among closely related phonemes, and in adults these boundaries reflect language experience. Very young children discriminate many more phonemic boundaries than adults, but they lose their discriminatory powers when certain boundaries are not supported by experience with spoken language (Kuhl, 1993). Native Japanese speakers, for example, typically do not discriminate the "r" from the "l" sounds that are evident to English speakers, and this ability is lost in early childhood because it is not in the speech that they hear. It is not known whether synapse overproduction and elimination underlies this process, but it certainly seems plausible.

The process of synapse elimination occurs relatively slowly in the cerebral cortical regions that are involved in aspects of language and other higher cognitive functions (Huttenlocher and Dabholkar, 1997). Different brain systems appear to develop according to different time frames, driven in part by experience and in part by intrinsic forces. This process suggests that children's brains may be more ready to learn different things at different times. But, as noted above, learning continues to affect the structure of the brain long after synapse overproduction and loss are completed. New synapses are added that would never have existed without learning, and the wiring diagram of the brain continues to be reorganized throughout one's life. There may be other changes in the brain involved in the encoding of learning, but most scientists agree that synapse addition and modification are the ones that are most certain.

Examples of Effects of Instruction on Brain Development

Detailed knowledge of the brain processes that underlie language has emerged in recent years. For example, there appear to be separate brain areas that specialize in subtasks such as hearing words (spoken language of others), seeing words (reading), speaking words (speech), and generating words (thinking with language). Whether these patterns of brain organization for oral, written, and listening skills require separate exercises to promote the component skills of language and literacy remains to be determined. If these closely related skills have somewhat independent brain representation, then coordinated practice of skills may be a better way to encourage learners to move seamlessly among speaking, writing, and listening.

Language provides a particularly striking example of how instructional processes may contribute to organizing brain functions. The example is interesting because language processes are usually more closely associated with the left side of the brain. As the following discussion points out, specific kinds of experiences can contribute to other areas of the brain taking over some of the language functions. For example, deaf people who learn a sign language are learning to communicate using the visual system in place of the auditory system. Manual sign languages have grammatical structures, with affixes and morphology, but they are not translations of spoken languages. Each particular sign language (such as American Sign Language) has a unique organization, influenced by the fact that it is perceived visually. The perception of sign language depends on parallel visual perception of shape, relative spatial location, and movement of the hands—a very different type of perception than the auditory perception of spoken language (Bellugi, 1980).

In the nervous system of a hearing person, auditory system pathways appear to be closely connected to the brain regions that process the features of spoken language, while visual pathways appear to go through several stages of processing before features of written language are extracted (Blakemore, 1977; Friedman and Cocking, 1986). When a deaf individual learns to communicate with manual signs, different nervous system processes have replaced the ones normally used for language—a significant achievement.

Neuroscientists have investigated how the visual-spatial and language processing areas each come together in a different hemisphere of the brain, while developing certain new functions as a result of the visual language experiences. In the brains of all deaf people, some cortical areas that normally process auditory information become organized to process visual information. Yet there are also demonstrable differences among the brains of deaf people who use sign language and deaf people who do not use sign language, presumably because they have had different language experiences (Neville, 1984, 1995). Among other things, major differences exist in the electrical activities of the brains of deaf individuals who use sign language and those who do not know sign language (Friedman and Cocking, 1986; Neville, 1984). Also, there are similarities between sign language users with normal hearing and sign language users who are deaf that result from their common experiences of engaging in language activities. In other words, specific types of instruction can modify the brain, enabling it to use alternative sensory input to accomplish adaptive functions, in this case, communication.

Another demonstration that the human brain can be functionally reorganized by instruction comes from research on individuals who have suffered strokes or had portions of the brain removed (Bach-y-Rita, 1980, 1981; Crill and Raichle, 1982). Since spontaneous recovery is generally unlikely, the best way to help these individuals regain their lost functions is to provide them with instruction and long periods of practice. Although this kind of learning typically takes a long time, it can lead to partial or total recovery of functions when based on sound principles of instruction. Studies of animals with similar impairments have clearly shown the formation of new brain connections and other adjustments, not unlike those that occur when adults learn (e.g., Jones and Schallert, 1994; Kolb, 1995). Thus, guided learning and learning from individual experiences both play important roles in the functional reorganization of the brain.

MEMORY AND BRAIN PROCESSES

Research into memory processes has progressed in recent years through the combined efforts of neuroscientists and cognitive scientists, aided by positron emission tomography and functional magnetic resonance imaging (Schacter, 1997). Most of the research advances in memory that help scientists understand learning come from two major groups of studies: studies that show that memory is not a unitary construct and studies that relate features of learning to later effectiveness in recall.

Memory is neither a single entity nor a phenomenon that occurs in a single area of the brain. There are two basic memory processes: declarative memory, or memory for facts and events which occurs primarily in brain systems involving the hippocampus; and procedural or nondeclarative memory, which is memory for skills and other cognitive operations, or memory that cannot be represented in declarative sentences, which occurs principally in the brain systems involving the neostriatum (Squire, 1997).

Different features of learning contribute to the durability or fragility of memory. For example, comparisons of people's memories for words with their memories for pictures of the same objects show a superiority effect for pictures. The superiority effect of pictures is also true if words and pictures are combined during learning (Roediger, 1997). Obviously, this finding has direct relevance for improving the long-term learning of certain kinds of information.

Research has also indicated that the mind is not just a passive recorder of events, rather, it is actively at work both in storing and in recalling information. There is research demonstrating that when a series of events are presented in a random sequence, people reorder them into sequences that make sense when they try to recall them (Lichtenstein and Brewer, 1980). The phenomenon of the active brain is dramatically illustrated further by the fact that the mind can "remember" things that actually did not happen. In one example (Roediger, 1997), people are first given lists of words: sour-candy-sugar-bitter-good-taste-tooth-knife-honey-photo-chocolate-heart-cake-tart-pie. During the later recognition phase, subjects are asked to respond "yes" or "no" to questions of whether a particular word was on the list. With high frequency and high reliability, subjects report that the word "sweet" was on the list. That is, they "remember" something that is not correct. The finding illustrates the active mind at work using inferencing processes to relate events. People "remember" words that are implied but not stated with the same probability as learned words. In an act of efficiency and "cognitive economy" (Gibson, 1969), the mind creates categories for processing information. Thus, it is a feature of learning that memory processes make relational links to other information.

In view of the fact that experience alters brain structures and that specific experiences have specific effects on the brain, the nature of "experience" becomes an interesting question in relation to memory processes. For example, when children are asked if a false event has ever occurred (as verified by their parents), they will correctly say that it never happened to them (Ceci, 1997). However, after repeated discussions around the same false events spread over time, the children begin to identify these false events as true occurrences. After about 12 weeks of such discussions, children give fully elaborated accounts of these fictitious events, involving parents, siblings, and a whole host of supporting "evidence." Repeating lists of words with adults similarly reveals that recalling non-experienced events activates the same regions of the brain as events or words that were directly experienced (Schacter, 1997). Magnetic resonance imaging also shows that the same brain areas are activated during questions and answers about both true and false events. This may explain why false memories can seem so compelling to the individual reporting the events.

In sum, classes of words, pictures, and other categories of information that involve complex cognitive processing on a repeated basis activate the brain. Activation sets into motion the events that are encoded as part of long-term memory. Memory processes treat both true and false memory events similarly and, as shown by imaging technologies, activate the same brain regions, regardless of the validity of what is being remembered. Experience is important for the development of brain structures, and what is registered in the brain as memories of experiences can include one's own mental activities.

These points about memory are important for understanding learning and can explain a good deal about why experiences are remembered well or poorly. Particularly important is the finding that the mind imposes structure on the information available from experience. This parallels descriptions of the organization of information in skilled performance discussed in Chapter 3: one of the primary differences between the novice and the expert is the manner in which information is organized and utilized. From the perspective of teaching, it again suggests the importance of an appropriate overall framework within which learning occurs most efficiently and effectively (see evidence discussed in Chapters 3 and 4).

Overall, neuroscience research confirms the important role that experience plays in building the structure of the mind by modifying the structures of the brain: development is not solely the unfolding of preprogrammed patterns. Moreover, there is a convergence of many kinds of research on some of the rules that govern learning. One of the simplest rules is that practice increases learning; in the brain, there is a similar relationship between the amount of experience in a complex environment and the amount of structural change.

In summary, neuroscience is beginning to provide some insights, if not final answers, to questions of great interest to educators. There is growing evidence that both the developing and the mature brain are structurally altered when learning occurs. Thus, these structural changes are believed to encode the learning in the brain. Studies have found alterations in the weight and thickness of the cerebral cortex of rats that had direct contact with a stimulating physical environment and an interactive social group. Subsequent work has revealed underlying changes in the structure of nerve cells and of the tissues that support their function. The nerve cells have a greater number of the synapses through which they communicate with each other. The structure of the nerve cells themselves is correspondingly altered. Under at least some conditions, both astrocytes that provide support to the neurons and the capillaries that supply blood may also be altered. The learning of specific tasks appears to alter the specific regions of the brain involved in the task. These findings suggest that the brain is a dynamic organ, shaped to a great extent by experience—by what a living being does, and has done.

CONCLUSION

It is often popularly argued that advances in the understanding of brain development and mechanisms of learning have substantial implications for education and the learning sciences. In addition, certain brain scientists have offered advice, often with a tenuous scientific basis, that has been incorporated into publications designed for educators (see, e.g., Sylwester, 1995:Ch. 7). Neuroscience has advanced to the point where it is time to think critically about the form in which research information is made available to educators so that it is interpreted appropriately for practice—identifying which research findings are ready for implementation and which are not.

This chapter reviews the evidence for the effects of experience on brain development, the adaptability of the brain for alternative pathways to learning, and the impact of experience on memory. Several findings about the brain and the mind are clear and lead to the next research topics:

1. The functional organization of the brain and the mind depends on and benefits positively from experience.

2. Development is not merely a biologically driven unfolding process, but also an active process that derives essential information from experience.

3. Research has shown that some experiences have the most powerful effects during specific sensitive periods, while others can affect the brain over a much longer time span.

4. An important issue that needs to be determined in relation to educa-

tion is which things are tied to critical periods (e.g., some aspects of phonemic perception and language learning) and for which things is the time of exposure less critical.

From these findings, it is clear that there are qualitative differences among kinds of learning opportunities. In addition, the brain "creates" informational experiences through mental activities such as inferencing, category formation, and so forth. These are types of learning opportunities that can be facilitated. By contrast, it is a bridge too far, to paraphrase John Bruer (1997), to suggest that specific activities lead to neural branching (Cardellichio and Field, 1997), as some interpreters of neuroscience have implied.

III

TEACHERS

AND TEACHING

6

The Design of Learning Environments

In this chapter we discuss implications of new knowledge about learning for the design of learning environments, especially schools. Learning theory does not provide a simple recipe for designing effective learning environments; similarly, physics constrains but does not dictate how to build a bridge (e.g., Simon, 1969). Nevertheless, new developments in the science of learning raise important questions about the design of learning environments—questions that suggest the value of rethinking what is taught, how it is taught, and how it is assessed. The focus in this chapter is on general characteristics of learning environments that need to be examined in light of new developments in the science of learning; Chapter 7 provides specific examples of instruction in the areas of mathematics, science, and history—examples that make the arguments in the present chapter more concrete.

We begin our discussion of learning environments by revisiting a point made in Chapter 1—that the learning goals for schools have undergone major changes during the past century. Everyone expects much more from today's schools than was expected 100 years ago. A fundamental tenet of modern learning theory is that different kinds of learning goals require different approaches to instruction (Chapter 3); new goals for education require changes in opportunities to learn. After discussing changes in goals, we explore the design of learning environments from four perspectives that appear to be particularly important given current data about human learning, namely, the degree to which learning environments are learner centered, knowledge centered, assessment centered, and community centered. Later, we define these perspectives and explain how they relate to the preceding discussions in Chapters 1-4.

CHANGES IN EDUCATIONAL GOALS

As discussed in Chapter 1, educational goals for the twenty-first century are very different from the goals of earlier times. This shift is important to keep in mind when considering claims that schools are "getting worse." In many cases, schools seem to be functioning as well as ever, but the challenges and expectations have changed quite dramatically (e.g., Bruer, 1993; Resnick, 1987).

Consider the goals of schooling in the early 1800s. Instruction in writing focused on the mechanics of making notation as dictated by the teacher, transforming oral messages into written ones. It was not until the mid to late 1800s that writing began to be taught on a mass level in most European countries, and school children began to be asked to compose their own written texts. Even then, writing instruction was largely aimed at giving children the capacity to closely imitate very simple text forms. It was not until the 1930s that the idea emerged of primary school students expressing themselves in writing (Alcorta, 1994; Schneuwly, 1994). As in writing, it was not until relatively recently that analysis and interpretation of what is read became an expectation of skilled reading by all school children. Overall, the definition of functional literacy changed from being able to sign one's name to word decoding to reading for new information (Resnick and Resnick, 1977); see Box 6.1.

In the early 1900s, the challenge of providing mass education was seen by many as analogous to mass production in factories. School administrators were eager to make use of the "scientific" organization of factories to structure efficient classrooms. Children were regarded as raw materials to be efficiently processed by technical workers (the teachers) to reach the end product (Bennett and LeCompte, 1990; Callahan, 1962; Kliebard, 1975). This approach attempted to sort the raw materials (the children) so that they could be treated somewhat as an assembly line. Teachers were viewed as workers whose job was to carry out directives from their superiors—the efficiency experts of schooling (administrators and researchers).

The emulation of factory efficiency fostered the development of standardized tests for measurement of the "product," of clerical work by teachers to keep records of costs and progress (often at the expense of teaching), and of "management" of teaching by central district authorities who had little knowledge of educational practice or philosophy (Callahan, 1962). In short, the factory model affected the design of curriculum, instruction, and assessment in schools.

Today, students need to understand the current state of their knowledge and to build on it, improve it, and make decisions in the face of uncertainty (Talbert and McLaughlin, 1993). These two notions of knowledge were identified by John Dewey (1916) as "records" of previous cultural accomplishments and engagement in active processes as represented by the phrase "to do." For example, doing mathematics involves solving problems, abstracting, inventing, proving (see, e.g., Romberg, 1983). Doing history involves the construction and evaluation of historical documents (see, e.g., Wineberg, 1996). Doing science includes such activities as testing theories

BOX 6.1   Literacy: Then and Now

Colonists were literate enough if they could sign their name, or even an X, on deeds. When immigrants arrived in large numbers in the 1800s, educators urged schools to deliver "recitation literacy" to the foreign children who filled the school-rooms. That literacy was the ability to hold a book and reel off memorized portions of basic American texts such as the opening paragraph of the Declaration of Inde-pendence, a part of the Gettysburg address, or some Bryant or Longfellow. With the coming of World War I, and the prospect of large numbers of men handling new equipment in foreign countries, Army testers redefined reading. Suddenly, to the dismay of men used to reading familiar passages, passing the army reading test meant being able to make sense, on the spot, of never-before-seen text. Cur-rently, that kind of "extraction literacy," revolutionary in 1914, looks meager. Find-ing out who, what, when, where or how simply does not yield the inferences, questions, or ideas we now think of as defining full or "higher literacy." The idea of a classroom where young women, poor and minority students, and learning disabled students *all* read (not recite) and write about (not copy) Shakespeare or Steinbeck is a radical and hopeful departure from the long-running conception of literacy as serviceable skills for the many and generative, reflective reading and writing for the few (Wolf, 1988:1).

through experimentation and observation (e.g., Lehrer and Schauble, 1996a, b; Linn, 1992, 1994; Schwab, 1978). Society envisions graduates of school systems who can identify and solve problems and make contributions to society throughout their lifetime—who display the qualities of "adaptive expertise" discussed in Chapter 3. To achieve this vision requires rethinking what is taught, how teachers teach, and how what students learn is assessed.

The remainder of this chapter is organized around Figure 6.1, which illustrates four perspectives on learning environments that seem particularly important given the principles of learning discussed in earlier chapters. Al-though we discuss these perspectives separately, they need to be conceptu-alized as a system of interconnected components that mutually support one another (e.g., Brown and Campione, 1996); we first discuss each perspective separately and then describe how they interrelate.

LEARNER-CENTERED ENVIRONMENTS

We use the term "learner centered" to refer to environments that pay careful attention to the knowledge, skills, attitudes, and beliefs that learners bring to the educational setting. This term includes teaching practices that

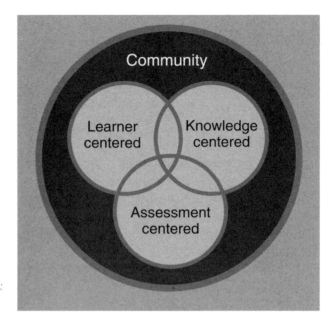

FIGURE 6.1 *Perspectives on learning environments. SOURCE: Bransford et al. (1998).*

have been called "culturally responsive," "culturally appropriate," "culturally compatible," and "culturally relevant" (Ladson-Billings, 1995). The term also fits the concept of "diagnostic teaching" (Bell et al., 1980): attempting to discover what students think in relation to the problems on hand, discussing their misconceptions sensitively, and giving them situations to go on thinking about which will enable them to readjust their ideas (Bell, 1982a:7). Teachers who are learner centered recognize the importance of building on the conceptual and cultural knowledge that students bring with them to the classroom (see Chapters 3 and 4).

Diagnostic teaching provides an example of starting from the structure of a child's knowledge. The information on which to base a diagnosis may be acquired through observation, questioning and conversation, and reflection on the products of student activity. A key strategy is to prompt children to explain and develop their knowledge structures by asking them to make predictions about various situations and explain the reasons for their predictions. By selecting critical tasks that embody known misconceptions, teachers can help students test their thinking and see how and why various ideas might need to change (Bell, 1982a, b, 1985; Bell et al., 1986; Bell and Purdy, 1985). The model is one of engaging students in cognitive conflict and then having discussions about conflicting viewpoints (see Piaget, 1973; Festinger, 1957). "To promote learning, it is important to focus on controlled changes of structure in a fixed context . . . or on deliberate transfer of a structure from one context to another" (Bell, 1985:72; see Chapter 7).

Learner-centered instruction also includes a sensitivity to the cultural practices of students and the effect of those practices on classroom learning. In a study of the Kamehameha School in Hawaii, teachers were deliberate in learning about students' home and community cultural practices and language use and incorporated them in classroom literacy instruction (Au and Jordan, 1981). After using the native Hawaiian "talk-story" (jointly produced student narratives), shifting the focus of instruction from decoding to comprehending, and including students' home experiences as a part of the discussion of reading materials, students demonstrated significant improvement in standardized test performance in reading.

Learner-centered teachers also respect the language practices of their students because they provide a basis for further learning. In science, one standard way of talking in both school and professional science is impersonal and expository, without any reference to personal or social intentions or experiences (Lemke, 1990; Wertsch, 1991). This way, which predominates in schools, privileges middle-class, mainstream ways of knowing and constitutes a barrier for students from other backgrounds who do not come to school already practiced in "school talk" (Heath, 1983). Everyday and scientific discourses need to be coordinated to assist students' scientific understanding.

In science discourse as it develops in most classrooms, students' talk frequently expresses multiple intentions or voices (see Ballenger, 1997; Bakhtin, 1984; Warren and Rosebery, 1996; Wertsch, 1991). In their narratives and arguments, students express both scientific and social intentions: scientific in that the students present evidence in support of a scientific argument; social in that they also talk about themselves as certain types of people (e.g., virtuous, honest, trustworthy). If the responses of other students and the teacher to these multivoiced narratives are always keyed to the scientific point, it helps to shape the meaning that is taken from them and relates them back to the context of the unfolding scientific argument (Ballenger, 1997). In standard science lessons, the scientific point in the talk of many students, particularly those whose discourse is not mainstream, is often missed, and the social intention is often devalued (Lemke, 1990; Michaels and Bruce, 1989; Wertsch, 1991; see Chapter 7).

In another example of connecting everyday talk and school talk, African American high school students were shown that many of their forms of everyday speech were examples of a very high form of literacy that was taught in school, but never before connected with their everyday experience (Lee, 1991, 1992). Like Proust who discovered he had been speaking prose all of his life, the students discovered that they were fluent in a set of competencies that were considered academically advanced.

Overall, learner-centered environments include teachers who are aware that learners construct their own meanings, beginning with the beliefs, understandings, and cultural practices they bring to the classroom. If teaching is conceived as constructing a bridge between the subject matter and the student, learner-centered teachers keep a constant eye on both ends of the bridge. The teachers attempt to get a sense of what students know and can do as well as their interests and passions—what each student knows, cares about, is able to do, and wants to do. Accomplished teachers "give learners reason," by respecting and understanding learners' prior experiences and understandings, assuming that these can serve as a foundation on which to build bridges to new understandings (Duckworth, 1987). Chapter 7 illustrates how these bridges can be built.

KNOWLEDGE-CENTERED ENVIRONMENTS

Environments that are solely learner centered would not necessarily help students acquire the knowledge and skills necessary to function effectively in society. As noted in Chapter 2, the ability of experts to think and solve problems is not simply due to a generic set of "thinking skills" or strategies but, instead, requires well-organized bodies of knowledge that support planning and strategic thinking. Knowledge-centered environments take seriously the need to help students become knowledgeable (Bruner, 1981) by learning in ways that lead to understanding and subsequent transfer. Current knowledge on learning and transfer (Chapter 3) and development (Chapter 4) provide important guidelines for achieving these goals. Standards in areas such as mathematics and science help define the knowledge and competencies that students need to acquire (e.g., American Association for the Advancement of Science, 1989; National Council of Teachers of Mathematics, 1989; National Research Council, 1996).

Knowledge-centered environments intersect with learner-centered environments when instruction begins with a concern for students' initial preconceptions about the subject matter. The story *Fish Is Fish* (Chapter 1) illustrates how people construct new knowledge based on their current knowledge. Without carefully considering the knowledge that students' bring to the learning situation, it is difficult to predict what they will understand about new information that is presented to them (see Chapters 3 and 4).

Knowledge-centered environments also focus on the kinds of information and activities that help students develop an understanding of disciplines (e.g., Prawat et al., 1992). This focus requires a critical examination of existing curricula. In history, a widely used history text on the American Revolution left out crucial information necessary to understand rather than merely memorize (Beck et al., 1989, 1991). In science, existing curricula tend to overemphasize facts and underemphasize "doing science" to explore and test big ideas (American Association for the Advancement of Science, 1989; National Research Council, 1996). As noted in Chapter 2, the Third International Mathematics and Science Study (Schmidt et al., 1997) characterized American curricula in mathematics and science as being "a mile wide and an inch deep." (Examples of teaching for depth rather than breadth are illustrated in Chapter 7.)

As discussed in the first part of this book, knowledge-centered environments also include an emphasis on sense-making—on helping students become metacognitive by expecting new information to make sense and asking for clarification when it doesn't (e.g., Palincsar and Brown, 1984; Schoenfeld, 1983, 1985, 1991). A concern with sense-making raises questions about many existing curricula. For example, it has been argued that many mathematics curricula emphasize

> . . . not so much a form of thinking as a substitute for thinking. The process of calculation or computation only involves the deployment of a set routine with no room for ingenuity or flair, no place for guess work or surprise, no chance for discovery, no need for the human being, in fact (Scheffler, 1975:184).

The argument here is not that students should never learn to compute, but that they should also learn other things about mathematics, especially the fact that it is possible for them to make sense of mathematics and to think mathematically (e.g., Cobb et al., 1992).

There are interesting new approaches to the development of curricula that support learning with understanding and encourage sense making. One is "progressive formalization," which begins with the informal ideas that students bring to school and gradually helps them see how these ideas can be transformed and formalized. Instructional units encourage students to build on their informal ideas in a gradual but structured manner so that they acquire the concepts and procedures of a discipline.

The idea of progressive formalization is exemplified by the algebra strand for middle school students using *Mathematics in Context* (National Center for Research in Mathematical Sciences Education and Freudenthal Institute, 1997). It begins by having students use their own words, pictures, or diagrams to describe mathematical situations to organize their own knowledge and work and to explain their strategies. In later units, students gradually begin to use symbols to describe situations, organize their mathematical work, or express their strategies. At this level, students devise their own symbols or learn some nonconventional notation. Their representations of problem situations and explanations of their work are a mixture of words and symbols. Later, students learn and use standard conventional algebraic notation for writing expressions and equations, for manipulating algebraic expressions and solving equations, and for graphing equations. Movement along this continuum is not necessarily smooth, nor all in one direction.

Although students are actually doing algebra less formally in the earlier grades, they are not forced to generalize their knowledge to a more formal level, nor to operate at a more formal level, before they have had sufficient experience with the underlying concepts. Thus, students may move back and forth among levels of formality depending on the problem situation or on the mathematics involved.

Central to curriculum frameworks such as "progressive formalization" are questions about what is developmentally appropriate to teach at various ages. Such questions represent another example of overlap between learner-centered and knowledge-centered perspectives. Older views that young children are incapable of complex reasoning have been replaced by evidence that children are capable of sophisticated levels of thinking and reasoning when they have the knowledge necessary to support these activities (see Chapter 4). An impressive body of research shows the potential benefit of early access by students to important conceptual ideas. In classrooms using a form of "cognitively guided" instruction in geometry, second-grade children's skills for representing and visualizing three-dimensional forms exceeded those of comparison groups of undergraduate students at a leading university (Lehrer and Chazan, 1998). Young children have also demonstrated powerful forms of early algebraic generalization (Lehrer and Chazan, 1998). Forms of generalization in science, such as experimentation, can be introduced before the secondary school years through a developmental approach to important mathematical and scientific ideas (Schauble et al., 1995; Warren and Rosebery, 1996). Such an approach entails becoming cognizant of the early origins of students' thinking and then identifying how those ideas can be fostered and elaborated (Brown and Campione, 1994).

Attempts to create environments that are knowledge centered also raise important questions about how to foster an integrated understanding of a discipline. Many models of curriculum design seem to produce knowledge and skills that are disconnected rather than organized into coherent wholes. The National Research Council (1990:4) notes that "To the Romans, a curriculum was a rutted course that guided the path of two-wheeled chariots." This rutted path metaphor is an appropriate description of the curriculum for many school subjects:

> Vast numbers of learning objectives, each associated with pedagogical strategies, serve as mile posts along the trail mapped by texts from kindergarten to twelfth grade. . . . Problems are solved not by observing and responding to the natural landscape through which the mathematics curriculum passes, but by mastering time tested routines, conveniently placed along the path (National Research Council, 1990:4).

An alternative to a "rutted path" curriculum is one of "learning the landscape" (Greeno, 1991). In this metaphor, learning is analogous to learning to live in an environment: learning your way around, learning what resources are available, and learning how to use those resources in conducting your activities productively and enjoyably (Greeno, 1991:175). The progressive formalization framework discussed above is consistent with this metaphor. Knowing where one is in a landscape requires a network of connections that link one's present location to the larger space.

Traditional curricula often fail to help students "learn their way around" a discipline. The curricula include the familiar scope and sequence charts that specify procedural objectives to be mastered by students at each grade: though an individual objective might be reasonable, it is not seen as part of a larger network. Yet it is the network, the connections among objectives, that is important. This is the kind of knowledge that characterizes expertise (see Chapter 2). Stress on isolated parts can train students in a series of routines without educating them to understand an overall picture that will ensure the development of integrated knowledge structures and information about conditions of applicability.

An alternative to simply progressing through a series of exercises that derive from a scope and sequence chart is to expose students to the major features of a subject domain as they arise naturally in problem situations. Activities can be structured so that students are able to explore, explain, extend, and evaluate their progress. Ideas are best introduced when students see a need or a reason for their use—this helps them see relevant uses of knowledge to make sense of what they are learning. Problem situations used to engage students may include the historic reasons for the development of the domain, the relationship of that domain to other domains, or the uses of ideas in that domain (see Webb and Romberg, 1992). In Chapter 7 we present examples from history, science, and mathematics instruction that emphasize the importance of introducing ideas and concepts in ways that promote deep understanding.

A challenge for the design of knowledge-centered environments is to strike the appropriate balance between activities designed to promote understanding and those designed to promote the automaticity of skills necessary to function effectively without being overwhelmed by attentional requirements. Students for whom it is effortful to read, write, and calculate can encounter serious difficulties learning. The importance of automaticity has been demonstrated in a number of areas (e.g., Beck et al., 1989, 1991; Hasselbring et al., 1987; LaBerge and Samuels, 1974; see Chapter 2).

ASSESSMENT-CENTERED ENVIRONMENTS

In addition to being learner centered and knowledge centered, effectively designed learning environments must also be assessment centered. The key principles of assessment are that they should provide opportunities for feedback and revision and that what is assessed must be congruent with one's learning goals.

It is important to distinguish between two major uses of assessment. The first, formative assessment, involves the use of assessments (usually administered in the context of the classroom) as sources of feedback to improve teaching and learning. The second, summative assessment, measures what students have learned at the end of some set of learning activities. Examples of formative assessments include teachers' comments on work in progress, such as drafts of papers or preparations for presentations. Examples of summative assessments include teacher-made tests given at the end of a unit of study and state and national achievement tests that students take at the end of a year. Ideally, teachers' formative and summative assessments are aligned with the state and national assessments that students take at the end of the year; often, however, this is not the case. Issues of summative assessment for purposes of national, state, and district accountability are beyond the scope of this volume; our discussion focuses on classroom-based formative and summative assessments.

Formative Assessments and Feedback

Studies of adaptive expertise, learning, transfer, and early development show that feedback is extremely important (see Chapters 2, 3, and 4). Students' thinking must be made visible (through discussions, papers, or tests), and feedback must be provided. Given the goal of learning with understanding, assessments and feedback must focus on understanding, and not only on memory for procedures or facts (although these can be valuable, too). Assessments that emphasize understanding do not necessarily require elaborate or complicated assessment procedures. Even multiple-choice tests can be organized in ways that assess understanding (see below).

Opportunities for feedback should occur continuously, but not intrusively, as a part of instruction. Effective teachers continually attempt to learn about their students' thinking and understanding. They do a great deal of on-line monitoring of both group work and individual performances, and they attempt to assess students' abilities to link their current activities to other parts of the curriculum and their lives. The feedback they give to students can be formal or informal. Effective teachers also help students build skills of self-assessment. Students learn to assess their own work, as well as the work of their peers, in order to help everyone learn more effectively (see, e.g., Vye et al., 1998a, b). Such self-assessment is an important part of the metacognitive approach to instruction (discussed in Chapters 3, 4, and 7).

In many classrooms, opportunities for feedback appear to occur relatively infrequently. Most teacher feedback—grades on tests, papers, worksheets, homework, and on report cards—represent summative assessments that are intended to measure the results of learning. After receiving grades, students typically move on to a new topic and work for another set of grades. Feedback is most valuable when students have the opportunity to use it to revise their thinking as they are working on a unit or project. The addition of opportunities for formative assessment increases students' learning and transfer, and they learn to value opportunities to revise (Barron et al., 1998; Black and William, 1998; Vye et al., 1998b). Opportunities to work collaboratively in groups can also increase the quality of the feedback available to students (Barron, 1991; Bereiter and Scardamalia, 1989; Fuchs et al., 1992; Johnson and Johnson, 1975; Slavin, 1987; Vye et al., 1998a), although many students must be helped to learn how to work collaboratively. New technologies provide opportunities to increase feedback by allowing students, teachers, and content experts to interact both synchronously and asynchronously (see Chapter 9).

A challenge of implementing good assessment practices involves the need to change many teachers', parents', and students' models of what effective learning looks like. Many assessments developed by teachers overly emphasize memory for procedures and facts (Porter et al., 1993). In addition, many standardized tests that are used for accountability still overemphasize memory for isolated facts and procedures, yet teachers are often judged by how well their students do on such tests. One mathematics teacher consistently produced students who scored high on statewide examinations by helping students memorize a number of mathematical procedures (e.g., proofs) that typically appeared on the examinations, but the students did not really understand what they were doing, and often could not answer questions that required an understanding of mathematics (Schoenfeld, 1988).

Appropriately designed assessments can help teachers realize the need to rethink their teaching practices. Many physics teachers have been surprised at their students' inabilities to answer seemingly obvious (to the expert) questions that assessed their students' understanding, and this outcome has motivated them to revise their instructional practices (Redish, 1996). Similarly, visually based assessments of "number sense" (see Case and Moss, 1996) have helped teachers discover the need to help their students develop important aspects of mathematical understanding (Bransford et al., 1998). Innovative assessments that reveal students' understanding of important concepts in science and mathematics have also been developed (Lehrer and Schauble, 1996a, b).

Formats for Assessing Understanding

Teachers have limited time to assess students' performances and provide feedback, but new advances in technology can help solve this problem (see Chapter 9). Even without technology, however, advances have been made in devising simple assessments that measure understanding rather than memorization. In the area of physics, assessments like those used in Chapter 2 to compare experts and novices have been revised for use in classrooms. One task presents students with two problems and asks them to state whether both would be solved using a similar approach and state the reason for the decision:

1. A 2.5-kilogram ball with a radius of 4 centimeters is traveling at 7 meters/second on a rough horizontal surface, but not spinning. At some later time, the ball is rolling without slipping 5 meters/second. How much work was done by friction?

2. A 0.5-kilogram ball with a radius of 15 centimeters is initially sliding at 10 meters/second without spinning. The ball travels on a horizontal surface and eventually rolls without slipping. Find the ball's final velocity.

Novices typically state that these two problems are solved similarly because they match on surface features—both involve a ball sliding and rolling on a horizontal surface. Students who are learning with understanding state that the problems are solved differently: the first can be solved by applying the work-energy theorem; the second can be solved by applying conservation of angular momentum (Hardiman et al., 1989); see Box 6.2. These kinds of assessment items can be used during the course of instruction to monitor the depth of conceptual understanding.

Portfolio assessments are another method of formative assessment. They provide a format for keeping records of students' work as they progress throughout the year and, most importantly, for allowing students to discuss their achievements and difficulties with their teachers, parents, and fellow students (e.g., Wiske, 1997; Wolf, 1988). They take time to implement and they are often implemented poorly—portfolios often become simply another place to store student work but no discussion of the work takes place—but used properly, they provide students and others with valuable information about their learning progress over time.

Theoretical Frameworks for Assessment

A challenge for the learning sciences is to provide a theoretical framework that links assessment practices to learning theory. An important step in this direction is represented by the work of Baxter and Glaser (1997), who

BOX 6.2   How Do You Know?

A 1-kilogram stick that is 2 meters long is placed on a frictionless surface and is free to rotate about a vertical pivot through one end. A 50-gram lump of putty is attached 80 centimeters from the pivot. Which of the following principles would allow you to determine the magnitude of the net force between the stick and the putty when the angular velocity of the system is 3 radians/second?

A. Newton's second law, $\vec{F}_{net} = M\vec{a}$
B. Angular momentum or conservation of angular momentum
C. Linear momentum or conservation of linear momentum
D. Work-energy theorem or conservation of mechanical energy
E. Conservation of linear momentum followed by conservation of mechanical energy

Performance on this item was near random for students finishing an introductory calculus-based physics course. The temptation is to match the "rotation" surface feature of the problem with "angular momentum," when in fact the problem is solved by a simple application of Newton's second law. Data such as these are important for helping teachers guide students toward the development of fluid, transferable knowledge (Leonard et al., 1996).

provide a framework for integrating cognition and context in assessing achievement in science. In their report, performance is described in terms of the content and process task demands of the subject matter and the nature and extent of cognitive activity likely to be observed in a particular assessment situation. The framework provides a basis for examining how developers' intentions are realized in performance assessments that purport to measure reasoning, understanding, and complex problem solving.

Characterizing assessments in terms of components of competence and the content-process demands of the subject matter brings specificity to generic assessment objectives such as "higher level thinking and deep understanding." Characterizing student performance in terms of cognitive activities focuses attention on the differences in competence and subject-matter achievement that can be observed in learning and assessment situations. The kind and quality of cognitive activities in an assessment is a function of the content and process demands of the task involved. For example, consider the content-process framework for science assessment shown in Figure 6.2 (Baxter and Glaser, 1997). In this figure, task demands for content

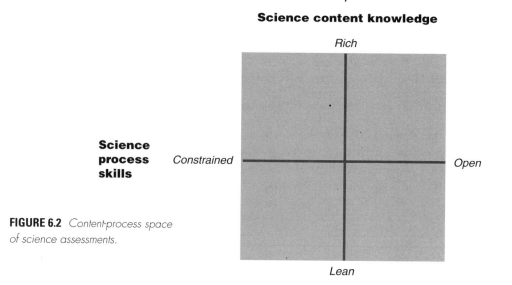

FIGURE 6.2 *Content-process space of science assessments.*

knowledge are conceptualized on a continuum from rich to lean (y axis). At one extreme are knowledge-rich tasks, tasks that require in-depth understanding of subject matter for their completion. At the other extreme are tasks that are not dependent on prior knowledge or related experiences; rather, performance is primarily dependent on the information given in the assessment situation. The task demands for process skills are conceptualized as a continuum from constrained to open (x axis). In open situations, explicit directions are minimized; students are expected to generate and carry out appropriate process skills for problem solution. In process-constrained situations, directions can be of two types: step-by-step, subject-specific procedures given as part of the task, or directions to explain the process skills that are necessary for task completion. In this situation, students are asked to generate explanations, an activity that does not require using the process skills. Assessment tasks can involve many possible combinations of content knowledge and process skills; Table 6.1 illustrates the relationship between the structure of knowledge and the organized cognitive activities.

COMMUNITY-CENTERED ENVIRONMENTS

New developments in the science of learning suggest that the degree to which environments are community centered is also important for learning. Especially important are norms for people learning from one another and continually attempting to improve. We use the term community centered to refer to several aspects of community, including the classroom as a commu-

TABLE 6.1 Cognitive Activity and Structure of Knowledge

Organized Cognitive Activity	Structure of Knowledge	
	Fragmented	Meaningful
Problem Representation	Surface features and shallow understanding	Underlying principles and relevant concepts
Strategy Use	Undirected trial-and-error problem solving	Efficient, informative, and goal oriented
Self-Monitoring	Minimal and sporadic	Ongoing and flexible
Explanation	Single statement of fact of description of superficial factors	Principled and coherent

nity, the school as a community, and the degree to which students, teachers, and administers feel connected to the larger community of homes, businesses, states, the nation, and even the world.

Classroom and School Communities

At the level of classrooms and schools, learning seems to be enhanced by social norms that value the search for understanding and allow students (and teachers) the freedom to make mistakes in order to learn (e.g., Brown and Campione, 1994; Cobb et al., 1992). Different classrooms and schools reflect different sets of norms and expectations. For example, an unwritten norm that operates in some classrooms is never to get caught making a mistake or not knowing an answer (see, e.g., Holt, 1964). This norm can hinder students' willingness to ask questions when they do not understand the material or to explore new questions and hypotheses. Some norms and expectations are more subject specific. For example, the norms in a mathematics class may be that mathematics is knowing how to compute answers; a much better norm would be that the goal of inquiry is mathematical understanding. Different norms and practices have major effects on what is taught and how it is assessed (e.g., Cobb et al., 1992). Sometimes there are different sets of expectations for different students. Teachers may convey expectations for school success to some students and expectations for school failure to others (MacCorquodale, 1988). For example, girls are sometimes discouraged from participating in higher level mathematics and science. Students, too, may share and convey cultural expectations that proscribe the participation of girls in some classes (Schofield et al., 1990).

BOX 6.3 **Talking in Class**

A speech-language pathologist working in an Inuit school (in northern Canada) asked a principal—who was not an Inuit—to compile a list of children who had speech and language problems in the school. The list contained a third of the students in the school, and next to several names the principal wrote, "Does not talk in class." The speech-language pathologist consulted a local Inuit teacher for help determining how each child functioned in his or her native language. She looked at the names and said, "Well-raised Inuit children should not talk in class. They should be learning by looking and listening."

When the speech-language pathologist asked that teacher about one toddler she was studying who was very talkative and seemed to the non-Inuit researcher to be very bright, the teacher said: "Do you think he might have a learning problem? Some of these children who don't have such high intelligence have trouble stopping themselves. They don't know when to stop talking" (Crago, 1988:219).

Classroom norms can also encourage modes of participation that may be unfamiliar to some students. For example, some groups rely on learning by observation and listening and then becoming involved in ongoing activities; school-like forms of talking may be unfamiliar for the children whose community has only recently included schools (Rogoff et al., 1993); see Box 6.3.

The sense of community in classrooms is also affected by grading practices, and these can have positive or negative effects depending on the students. For example, Navajo high school students do not treat tests and grades as competitive events the way that Anglo students do (Deyhle and Margonis, 1995). An Anglo high school counselor reported that Navajo parents complained about their children being singled out when the counselor started a "high achiever" bulletin board and wanted to put up the pictures of students with B averages or better. The counselor "compromised" by putting up happy stickers with the students' names on them. A Navajo student, staring at the board, said "The board embarrasses us, to be stuck out like that" (Deyhle and Margonis, 1995:28).

More broadly, competition among students for teacher attention, approval, and grades is a commonly used motivator in U.S. schools. And in some situations, competition may create situations that impede learning. This is especially so if individual competition is at odds with a community ethic of individuals' contributing their strengths to the community (Suina and Smolkin, 1994).

An emphasis on community is also imortant when attempting to borrow successful educational practices from other countries. For example, Japanese teachers spend considerable time working with the whole class, and they frequently ask students who have made errors to share their thinking with the rest of the class. This can be very valuable because it leads to discussions that deepen the understanding of everyone in the class. However, this practice works only because Japanese teachers have developed a classroom culture in which students are skilled at learning from one another and respect the fact that an analysis of errors is fruitful for learning (Hatano and Inagaki, 1996). Japanese students value listening, so they learn from large class discussions even if they do not have many chances to participate. The culture of American classrooms is often very different—many emphasize the importance of being right and contributing by talking. Teaching and learning must be viewed from the perspective of the overall culture of the society and its relationship to the norms of the classrooms. To simply attempt to import one or two Japanese teaching techniques into American classrooms may not produce the desired results.

The sense of community in a school also appears to be strongly affected by the adults who work in that environment. As Barth (1988) states:

> The relationship among adults who live in a school has more to do with the character and quality of the school and with the accomplishments of the students than any other factor.

Studies by Bray (1998) and Talbert and McLaughlin (1993) emphasize the importance of teacher learning communities. We say more about this in Chapter 8.

Connections to the Broader Community

An analysis of learning environments from the perspective of community also includes a concern for connections between the school environment and the broader community, including homes, community centers, after-school programs, and businesses. Chapters 3, 4, and 5 showed that learning takes time; ideally, what is learned in school can be connected to out-of-school learning and vice versa. Often, however, this ideal is not reached. As John Dewey (1916) noted long ago:

> From the standpoint of the child, the great waste in school comes from his inability to utilize the experience he gets outside . . . while on the other hand, he is unable to apply in daily life what he is learning in school. That is the isolation of the school—its isolation from life.

The importance of connecting the school with outside learning activities can be appreciated by considering Figure 6.3, which shows the percentage of time during a typical school year that students spend in school, sleeping, and engaged in other activities (see Bransford et al., 2000). The percentage of time spent in school is comparatively small. If students spend one-third of their nonsleeping time outside of school watching television, this means that they spend more time watching television in a year than they spend in school. (We say more about television and learning in the next section.)

A key environment for learning is the family. Even when family members do not focus consciously on instructional roles, they provide resources for children's learning, activities in which learning occurs, and connections to community (Moll, 1986a, b, 1990). Children also learn from the attitudes of family members toward skills and values of schooling.

The success of the family as a learning environment, especially in children's early years (see Chapter 4), has provided inspiration and guidance for some of the changes recommended in schools. The phenomenal development of children from birth to age 4 or 5 is generally supported by family interactions in which children learn by engaging with and observing others in shared endeavors. Conversations and other interactions that occur around events of interest with trusted and skilled adult and child companions are especially powerful environments for children's learning. Many of the recommendations for changes in schools can be seen as extensions of the learning activities that occur within families. In addition, recommendations

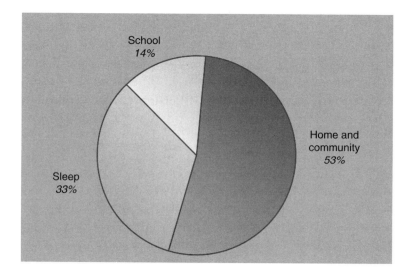

FIGURES 6.3 *Comparison of time spent in school, home and community, and sleep. Percentages were calculated using 180 school days each year, and each school day was estimated to be 6.5 hours in length.*

to include families in classroom activities and planning hold promise of bringing together two powerful systems for supporting children's learning.

Children participate in many other institutions outside their homes that can foster learning. Some of these institutions have learning as part of their goals, including many after-school programs, organizations such as Boy and Girl Scouts and 4-H Clubs, museums, and religious groups. Others make learning more incidental, but learning takes place nevertheless (see McLaughlin, 1990, on youth clubs; Griffin and Cole, 1984, on the Fifth Dimension Program).

Connections to experts outside of school can also have a positive influence on in-school learning because they provide opportunities for students to interact with parents and other people who take an interest in what students are doing. It can be very motivating both to students and teachers to have opportunities to share their work with others. Opportunities to prepare for these events helps teachers raise standards because the consequences go beyond mere scores on a test (e.g., Brown and Campione, 1994, 1996; Cognition and Technology Group at Vanderbilt, in press b).

The idea of outside audiences who present challenges (complete with deadlines) has been incorporated into a number of instructional programs (e.g., Cognition and Technology Group at Vanderbilt, 1997; Wiske, 1997). Working to prepare for outsiders provides motivation that helps teachers maintain student interest. In addition, teachers and students develop a better sense of community as they prepare to face a common challenge. Students are also motivated to prepare for outside audiences who do not come to the classroom but will see their projects. Preparing exhibits for museums represents an excellent example (see Collins et al., 1991). New technologies that enhance the ability to connect classrooms to others in the school, to parents, business leaders, college students, content area experts, and others around the world are discussed in Chapter 9.

TELEVISION

For better or for worse, most children spent a considerable amount of time watching television; it has played an increasingly prominent role in children's development over the past 50 years. Children watch a great deal of television before entering school, and television viewing continues throughout life. In fact, many students spend more hours watching television than attending school. Parents want their children to learn from television; at the same time they are concerned about what they are learning from the programs they watch (Greenfield, 1984).

Watching Different Kinds of Programs

Television programming for children ranges from educational to purely entertaining (see Wright and Huston, 1995). And there are different ways of watching programs—a child may watch in isolation or with an adult. Furthermore, just as in domains like chess, physics, or teaching (see Chapter 2), people's existing knowledge and beliefs affect what they notice, understand, and remember from viewing television (Newcomb and Collins, 1979). The same program can have different effects depending on who is watching and whether the viewing is a solo activity or part of an interactive group. An important distinction is whether the program is intended to be educational or not.

One group of preschoolers aged 2-4 and first-grade students aged 6-7 watched about 7-8 hours of noneducational programming per week; the preschool children also watched an average of 2 hours of educational programming per week, and the older students watched 1 hour. Despite the low ratio of educational to noneducational viewing, the educational programs seemed to have positive benefits. The 2- to 4-year-old preschoolers performed better than non-viewers of educational programs on tests of school readiness, reading, mathematics, and vocabulary as much as 3 years later (Wright and Huston, 1995). Specifically, viewing educational programs was a positive predictor of letter-word knowledge, vocabulary size, and school readiness on standardized achievement tests. For the older students, the viewing of educational programs was related to better performance on tests of reading comprehension and teachers' judgments of school adjustment in first and second grades, compared with children who were infrequent viewers. Overall, the effects of television viewing were not as widespread for the older students, and there were fewer significant effects for the older children than for the preschoolers. It is important to note that the effects of watching educational programs were evident "even when initial language skills, family education, income, and the quality of the home environment are taken into account" (Wright and Huston, 1995:22).

Effects on Beliefs and Attitudes

Television also provides images and role models that can affect how children view themselves, how they see others, attitudes about what academic subjects they should be interested in, and other topics related to person perception. These images can have both positive and negative effects. For example, when 8- to 14-year-olds watched programs designed to show positive attributes of children around the world, they were less likely to say that children from their own country were more interesting or more intelligent (O'Brien, 1981), and they began to see more similarities among people around the world (Greenfield, 1984). And children who watched episodes of Sesame Street featuring handicapped children had more positive feelings toward children with disabilities.

However, children can also misinterpret programs about people from different cultures, depending on what they already know (Newcomb and Collins, 1979). Stereotyping represents a powerful effect of watching television that is potentially negative. Children bring sex role stereotypes with them to school that derive from television programs and commercials (Dorr, 1982).

As a powerful visual medium, television creates stereotypes even when there is no intent to sell an image. But experimental studies indicate that such stereotyping effects decrease with children as young as 5 if adults offer critiques of the stereotypic portrayals as the children watch programs (Dorr, 1982). Thus, entertainment programs can educate in positive ways and learned information can be extended through adult guidance and commentary.

In sum, television has an impact on children's learning that must be taken seriously. But the medium is neither inherently beneficial nor harmful. The content that students watch, and how they watch it, has important effects on what they learn. Especially significant is the fact that informative or educational programming has been shown to have beneficial effects on school achievement and that a preponderance of non-educational, entertainment viewing can have negative effects. Furthermore, the benefits of informative viewing occur despite the fact that the ratio of young children's viewing tends to be 7:1 in favor of entertainment television. These findings support the wisdom of continued attempts to develop and study television programs that can help students acquire the kinds of knowledge, skills, and attitudes that support their learning in school.

THE IMPORTANCE OF ALIGNMENT

In the beginning of this chapter we noted that the four perspectives on learning environments (the degree to which they are learner, knowledge, assessment, and community centered) would be discussed separately but ultimately needed to be aligned in ways that mutually support one another. Alignment is as important for schools as for organizations in general (e.g., Covey, 1990). A key aspect of task analysis (see Chapter 2) is the idea of aligning goals for learning with what is taught, how it is taught, and how it is assessed (both formatively and summatively). Without this alignment, it is difficult to know what is being learned. Students may be learning valuable information, but one cannot tell unless there is alignment between what they are learning and the assessment of that learning. Similarly, students may be learning things that others don't value unless curricula and assessments are aligned with the broad learning goals of communities (Lehrer and Shumow, 1997).

A systems approach to promote coordination among activities is needed to design effective learning environments (Brown and Campione, 1996). Many schools have checklists of innovative practices, such as the use of collaborative learning, teaching for understanding and problem solving, and using formative assessment. Often, however, these activities are not coordinated with one another. Teaching for understanding and problem solving may be "what we do on Fridays"; collaborative learning may be used to promote memorization of fact-based tests; and formative assessments may focus on skills that are totally disconnected from the rest of the students' curriculum. In addition, students may be given opportunities to study collaboratively for tests yet be graded on a curve so that they compete with one another rather than trying to meet particular performance standards. In these situations, activities in the classroom are not aligned.

Activities *within* a particular classroom may be aligned yet fail to fit with the rest of the school. And a school as a whole needs to have a consistent alignment. Some schools communicate a consistent policy about norms and expectations for conduct and achievement. Others send mixed messages. For example, teachers may send behavior problems to the principal, who may inadvertently undermine the teacher by making light of the students' behavior. Similarly, schedules may or may not be made flexible in order to accommodate in-depth inquiry, and schools may or may not be adjusted to minimize disruptions, including nonacademic "pullout" programs and even the number of classroom interruptions made by a principal's overzealous use of the classroom intercom. Overall, different activities within a school may or may not compete with one another and impede overall progress. When principals and teachers work together to define a common vision for their entire school, learning can improve (e.g., Barth, 1988, 1991; Peterson et al., 1995).

Activities within schools must also be aligned with the goals and assessment practices of the community. Ideally, teachers' goals for learning fit with the curriculum they teach and the school's goals, which in turn fit the goals implicit in the tests of accountability used by the school system. Often these factors are out of alignment. Effective change requires a simultaneous consideration of all these factors (e.g., Bransford et al., 1998). The new scientific findings about learning provide a framework for guiding systemic change.

CONCLUSION

The goals and expectations for schooling have changed quite dramatically during the past century, and new goals suggest the need to rethink such questions as what is taught, how it is taught, and how students are assessed. We emphasized that research on learning does not provide a recipe for designing effective learning environments, but it does support the value of asking certain kinds of questions about the design of learning environments.

Four perspectives on the design of learning environments—the degree to which they are student centered, knowledge centered, assessment centered, and community centered—are important in designing these environments.

A focus on the degree to which environments are learner centered is consistent with the strong body of evidence suggesting that learners' use their current knowledge to construct new knowledge and that what they know and believe at the moment affects how they interpret new information. Sometimes learners' current knowledge supports new learning, sometimes it hampers learning: effective instruction begins with what learners bring to the setting; this includes cultural practices and beliefs as well as knowledge of academic content.

Learner-centered environments attempt to help students make connections between their previous knowledge and their current academic tasks. Parents are especially good at helping their children make connections. Teachers have a harder time because they do not share the life experiences of each of their students. Nevertheless, there are ways to systematically become familiar with each student's special interests and strengths.

Effective environments must also be knowledge centered. It is not sufficient only to attempt to teach general problem solving and thinking skills; the ability to think and solve problems requires well-organized knowledge that is accessible in appropriate contexts. An emphasis on being knowledge centered raises a number of questions, such as the degree to which instruction begins with students' current knowledge and skills, rather than simply presents new facts about the subject matter. While young students are capable of grasping more complex concepts than was believed previously, those concepts must be presented in ways that are developmentally appropriate. A knowledge-centered perspective on learning environments also highlights the importance of thinking about designs for curricula. To what extent do they help students learn with understanding versus promote the acquisition of disconnected sets of facts and skills? Curricula that emphasize an excessively broad range of subjects run the risk of developing disconnected rather than connected knowledge; they fit well with the idea of a curriculum as being a well-worn path in a road. An alternative metaphor for curriculum is to help students develop interconnected pathways within a discipline so that they "learn their away around in it" and not lose sight of where they are.

Issues of assessment also represent an important perspective for viewing the design of learning environments. Feedback is fundamental to learning, but opportunities to receive it are often scarce in classrooms. Students may receive grades on tests and essays, but these are summative assessments that occur at the end of projects; also needed are formative assessments that provide students opportunities to revise and hence improve the quality of their thinking and learning. Assessments must reflect the learning goals that define various environments. If the goal is to enhance understanding, it is not sufficient to provide assessments that focus primarily on memory for facts and formulas. Many instructors have changed their approach to teaching after seeing how their students failed to understand seemingly obvious (to the expert) ideas.

The fourth perspective on learning environments involves the degree to which they promote a sense of community. Ideally, students, teachers, and other interested participants share norms that value learning and high standards. Norms such as these increase people's opportunities to interact, receive feedback, and learn. There are several aspects of community, including the community of the classroom, the school, and the connections between the school and the larger community, including the home. The importance of connected communities becomes clear when one examines the relatively small amount of time spent in school compared to other settings. Activities in homes, community centers, and after-school clubs can have important effects on students' academic achievement.

Finally, there needs to be alignment among the four perspectives of learning environments. They all have the potential to overlap and mutually influence one another. Issues of alignment appear to be very important for accelerating learning both within and outside of schools.

7

Effective Teaching: Examples in History, Mathematics, and Science

The preceding chapter explored implications of research on learning for general issues relevant to the design of effective learning environments. We now move to a more detailed exploration of teaching and learning in three disciplines: history, mathematics, and science. We chose these three areas in order to focus on the similarities and differences of disciplines that use different methods of inquiry and analysis. A major goal of our discussion is to explore the knowledge required to teach effectively in a diversity of disciplines.

We noted in Chapter 2 that expertise in particular areas involves more than a set of general problem-solving skills; it also requires well-organized knowledge of concepts and inquiry procedures. Different disciplines are organized differently and have different approaches to inquiry. For example, the evidence needed to support a set of historical claims is different from the evidence needed to prove a mathematical conjecture, and both of these differ from the evidence needed to test a scientific theory. Discussion in Chapter 2 also differentiated between expertise in a discipline and the ability to help others learn about that discipline. To use Shulman's (1987) language, effective teachers need pedagogical content knowledge (knowledge about how to teach in particular disciplines) rather than only knowledge of a particular subject matter.

Pedagogical content knowledge is different from knowledge of general teaching methods. Expert teachers know the structure of their disciplines, and this knowledge provides them with cognitive roadmaps that guide the assignments they give students, the assessments they use to gauge students' progress, and the questions they ask in the give and take of classroom life. In short, their knowledge of the discipline and their knowledge of pedagogy interact. But knowledge of the discipline structure does not in itself guide the teacher. For example, expert teachers are sensitive to those aspects of the discipline that are especially hard or easy for new students to master.

This means that new teachers must develop the ability to "understand in a pedagogically reflective way; they must not only know their own way around a discipline, but must know the 'conceptual barriers' likely to hinder others" (McDonald and Naso, 1986:8). These conceptual barriers differ from discipline to discipline.

An emphasis on interactions between disciplinary knowledge and pedagogical knowledge directly contradicts common misconceptions about what teachers need to know in order to design effective learning environments for their students. The misconceptions are that teaching consists only of a set of general methods, that a good teacher can teach any subject, or that content knowledge alone is sufficient.

Some teachers *are* able to teach in ways that involve a variety of disciplines. However, their ability to do so requires more than a set of general teaching skills. Consider the case of Barb Johnson, who has been a sixth-grade teacher for 12 years at Monroe Middle School. By conventional standards Monroe is a good school. Standardized test scores are about average, class size is small, the building facilities are well maintained, the administrator is a strong instructional leader, and there is little faculty and staff turnover. However, every year parents sending their fifth-grade students from the local elementary schools to Monroe jockey to get their children assigned to Barb Johnson's classes. What happens in her classroom that gives it the reputation of being the best of the best?

During the first week of school Barb Johnson asks her sixth graders two questions: "What questions do you have about yourself?" and "What questions do you have about the world?" The students begin enumerating their questions, "Can they be about silly, little things?" asks one student. "If they're your questions that you really want answered, they're neither silly nor little," replies the teacher. After the students list their individual questions, Barb organizes the students into small groups where they share lists and search for questions they have in common. After much discussion each group comes up with a priority list of questions, rank-ordering the questions about themselves and those about the world.

Back together in a whole group session, Barb Johnson solicits the groups' priorities and works toward consensus for the class's combined lists of questions. These questions become the basis for guiding the curriculum in Barb's class. One question, "Will I live to be 100 years old?" spawned educational investigations into genetics, family and oral history, actuarial science, statistics and probability, heart disease, cancer, and hypertension. The students had the opportunity to seek out information from family members, friends, experts in various fields, on-line computer services, and books, as well as from the teacher. She describes what they had to do as becoming part of a "learning community." According to Barb Johnson, "We decide what are the most compelling intellectual issues, devise ways to investigate those issues and start off on a learning journey. Sometimes we fall short of our goal. Sometimes we reach our goal, but most times we exceed these goals—we learn more than we initially expected" (personal communication).

At the end of an investigation, Barb Johnson works with the students to help them see how their investigations relate to conventional subject-matter areas. They create a chart on which they tally experiences in language and literacy, mathematics, science, social studies and history, music, and art. Students often are surprised at how much and how varied their learning is. Says one student, "I just thought we were having fun. I didn't realize we were learning, too!"

Barb Johnson's teaching is extraordinary. It requires a wide range of disciplinary knowledge because she begins with students' questions rather than with a fixed curriculum. Because of her extensive knowledge, she can map students' questions onto important principles of relevant disciplines. It would not work to simply arm new teachers with general strategies that mirror how she teaches and encourage them to use this approach in their classrooms. Unless they have the relevant disciplinary knowledge, the teachers and the classes would quickly become lost. At the same time, disciplinary knowledge without knowledge about how students learn (i.e., principles consistent with developmental and learning psychology) and how to lead the processes of learning (i.e., pedagogical knowledge) would not yield the kind of learning seen in Barb Johnson's classes (Anderson and Smith, 1987).

In the remainder of this chapter, we present illustrations and discussions of exemplary teaching in history, mathematics, and science. The three examples of history, mathematics, and science are designed to convey a sense of the pedagogical knowledge and content knowledge (Shulman, 1987) that underlie expert teaching. They should help to clarify why effective teaching requires much more than a set of "general teaching skills."

HISTORY

Most people have had quite similar experiences with history courses: they learned the facts and dates that the teacher and the text deemed relevant. This view of history is radically different from the way that historians see their work. Students who think that history is about facts and dates miss exciting opportunities to understand how history is a discipline that is guided by particular rules of evidence and how particular analytical skills can be relevant for understanding events in their lives (see Ravitch and Finn, 1987). Unfortunately, many teachers do not present an exciting approach to history, perhaps because they, too, were taught in the dates-facts method.

Beyond Facts

In Chapter 2, we discussed a study of experts in the field of history and learned that they regard the available evidence as more than lists of facts (Wineburg, 1991). The study contrasted a group of gifted high school seniors with a group of working historians. Both groups were given a test of facts about the American Revolution taken from the chapter review section of a popular United States history textbook. The historians who had backgrounds in American history knew most of the items, while historians whose specialties lay elsewhere knew only a third of the test facts. Several students scored higher than some historians on the factual pretest. In addition to the test of facts, however, the historians and students were presented with a set of historical documents and asked to sort out competing claims and to formulate reasoned interpretations. The historians excelled at this task. Most students, on the other hand, were stymied. Despite the volume of historical information the students possessed, they had little sense of how to use it productively for forming interpretations of events or for reaching conclusions.

Different Views of History by Different Teachers

Different views of history affect how teachers teach history. For example, Wilson and Wineburg (1993) asked two teachers of American history to read a set of student essays on the causes of the American Revolution not as an unbiased or complete and definitive accounts of people and events, but to develop plans for the students' "remediation or enrichment." Teachers were provided with a set of essays on the question, "Evaluate the causes of the American Revolution," written by eleventh-graders for a timed, 45-minute test. Consider the different types of feedback that Mr. Barnes and Ms. Kelsey gave a student paper; see Box 7.1.

Mr. Barnes' comments on the actual content of the essays concentrated on the factual level. Ms. Kelsey's comments addressed broader images of the nature of the domain, without neglecting important errors of fact. Overall, Mr. Barnes saw the papers as an indication of the bell-shaped distribution of abilities; Ms. Kelsey saw them as representing the misconception that history is about memorizing a mass of information and recounting a series of facts. These two teachers had very different ideas about the nature of learning history. Those ideas affected how they taught and what they wanted their students to achieve.

Studies of Outstanding History Teachers

For expert history teachers, their knowledge of the discipline and beliefs about its structure interact with their teaching strategies. Rather than simply introduce students to sets of facts to be learned, these teachers help people to understand the problematic nature of historical interpretation and analysis and to appreciate the relevance of history for their everyday lives.

One example of outstanding history teaching comes form the classroom of Bob Bain, a public school teacher in Beechwood, Ohio. Historians, he notes, are cursed with an abundance of data—the traces of the past threaten to overwhelm them unless they find some way of separating what is important from what is peripheral. The assumptions that historians hold about significance shape how they write their histories, the data they select, and the narrative they compose, as well as the larger schemes they bring to organize and periodize the past. Often these assumptions about historical significance remain unarticulated in the classroom. This contributes to students' beliefs that their textbooks are *the* history rather than *a* history.

Bob Bain begins his ninth-grade high school class by having all the students create a time capsule of what they think are the most important artifacts from the past. The students' task, then, is to put down on paper why they chose the items they did. In this way, the students explicitly articulate their underlying assumptions of what constitutes historical significance. Students' responses are pooled, and he writes them on a large poster that he hangs on the classroom wall. This poster, which Bob Bain calls "Rules for Determining Historical Significance," becomes a lightening rod for class discussions throughout the year, undergoing revisions and elaborations as students become better able to articulate their ideas.

At first, students apply the rules rigidly and algorithmically, with little understanding that just as they made the rules, they can also change them. But as students become more practiced in plying their judgments of significance, they come to see the rules as tools for assaying the arguments of different historians, which allows them to begin to understand why historians disagree. In this instance, the students' growing ability to understand the interpretative nature of history is aided by their teacher's deep understanding of a fundamental principle of the discipline.

Leinhardt and Greeno (1991, 1994) spent 2 years studying a highly accomplished teacher of advanced placement history in an urban high school in Pittsburgh. The teacher, Ms. Sterling, a veteran of over 20 years, began her school year by having her students ponder the meaning of the statement, "Every true history is contemporary history." In the first week of the semester, Sterling thrust her students into the kinds of epistemological issues that one might find in a graduate seminar: "What is history?" "How do we know the past?" "What is the difference between someone who sits down to

BOX 7.1   Comments on Papers on the American Revolution

Student #7

When the French and Indian war ended, British expected Americans to help them pay back there war debts. That would be a reasonable request if the war was fought for the colonies, but it was fought for English imperialism so you can't blame them for not wanting to pay. The taxes were just the start of the slow turn toward rebellion another factor was when parliament decided to forbid the colonial government to make any more money, Specie became scarcer than ever, and a lot of merchants were pushed into a "two way squeeze" and faced bankruptcy. If I had the choice between being loyal, or rebelling and having something to eat, I know what my choice would be. The colonist who were really loyal never did rebel, and 1/3 support the revolution.

The main thing that turned most people was the amount of propaganda, speeches from people like Patrick Henry, and organizations like the "Association." After the Boston Massacre and the issuing of the Intolerable acts, people were convinced there was a conspiracy in the royal government to extinguish America's liberties. I think a lot of people also just were going with the flow, or were being pressured by the Sons of Liberty. Merchants who didn't go along with boycotts often became the victims of mob violence. Overall though, people were sick of getting overtaxed and walked on and decided let's do something about it.

'write history' and the artifacts that are produced as part of ordinary experience?" The goal of this extended exercise is to help students understand history as an *evidentiary* form of knowledge, not as clusters of fixed names and dates.

One might wonder about the advisability of spending 5 days "defining history" in a curriculum with so much to cover. But it is precisely Sterling's framework of subject-matter knowledge—her overarching understanding of the discipline as a whole—that permits students entry into the advanced world of historical sense-making. By the end of the course, students moved from being passive spectators of the past to enfranchised agents who could participate in the forms of thinking, reasoning, and engagement that are the hallmark of skilled historical cognition. For example, early in the school year, Ms. Sterling asked her students a question about the Constitutional Convention and "what were men able to do." Paul took the question literally: "Uh, I think one of the biggest things that they did, that we talked about yesterday, was the establishment of the first settlements in the Northwest

Mr. Barnes's Summary Comment

—your topic sentence is weak

—more factual detail would improve your essay

—note spelling and grammar corrections

C-

Ms. Kelsey's Summary Comment

—The greatest strength of this essay is its outstanding effort to grapple thoughtfully with the question, why did the colonists rebel? Keep thinking personally, "What if I were here?" It is a great place to start.

—To make the essay *work*, however, you need to refine your organization strategies significantly. Remember that your reader is basically ignorant, so you need to express your view as clearly as you can. Try to form your ideas from the beginning to a middle and then an end.

In the beginning, tell what side you're on: What made the colonists rebel—money, propaganda, conformity?

In the middle, justify your view. What factors support your idea and will convince your reader?

In the end, remind your reader again about your point of view.

Go back and revise and hand this in again!

SOURCE: Wilson and Wineburg (1993:Fig. 1). Reprinted by permission.

area states." But after 2 months of educating students into a way of thinking about history, Paul began to catch on. By January his responses to questions about the fall of the cotton-based economy in the South were linked to British trade policy and colonial ventures in Asia, as well as to the failure of Southern leaders to read public opinion accurately in Great Britain. Ms. Sterling's own understanding of history allowed her to create a classroom in which students not only mastered concepts and facts, but also used them in authentic ways to craft historical explanations.

Debating the Evidence

Elizabeth Jensen prepares her group of eleventh graders to debate the following resolution:

Resolved: The British government possesses the legitimate authority to tax the American colonies.

As her students enter the classroom they arrange their desks into three groups—on the left of the room a group of "rebels," on the right, a group of "loyalists," and in the front, a group of "judges." Off to the side with a spiral notebook on her lap sits Jensen, a short woman in her late 30s with a booming voice. But today that voice is silent as her students take up the question of the legitimacy of British taxation in the American colonies.

The rebels' first speaker, a 16-year-old girl with a Grateful Dead T-shirt and one dangling earring, takes a paper from her notebook and begins:

> England says she keeps troops here for our own protection. On face value, this seems reasonable enough, but there is really no substance to their claims. First of all, who do they think they are protecting us from? The French? Quoting from our friend Mr. Bailey on page 54, 'By the settlement in Paris in 1763, French power was thrown completely off the continent of North America.' Clearly not the French then. Maybe they need to protect us from the Spanish? Yet the same war also subdued the Spanish, so they are no real worry either. In fact, the only threat to our order is the Indians . . . but . . . we have a decent militia of our own. . . . So why are they putting troops here? The only possible reason is to keep us in line. With more and more troops coming over, soon every freedom we hold dear will be stripped away. The great irony is that Britain expects us to pay for these vicious troops, these British squelchers of colonial justice.

A loyalist responds:

> We moved here, we are paying less taxes than we did for two generations in England, and you complain? Let's look at why we are being taxed—the main reason is probably because England has a debt of £140,000,000. . . . This sounds a little greedy, I mean what right do they have to take our money simply because they have the power over us. But did you know that over one-half of their war debt was caused by defending us in the French and Indian War. . . . Taxation without representation isn't fair. Indeed, it's tyranny. Yet virtual representation makes this whining of yours an untruth. Every British citizen, whether he had a right to vote or not, is represented in Parliament. Why does this representation not extend to America?

A rebel questions the loyalist about this:

> Rebel: What benefits do we get out of paying taxes to the crown?
> Loyalist: We benefit from the protection.
> Rebel: (cutting in) Is that the only benefit you claim, protection?
> Loyalist: Yes—and all the rights of an Englishman.
> Rebel: Okay, then what about the Intolerable Acts . . . denying us rights of British subjects. What about the rights we are denied?
> Loyalist: The Sons of Liberty tarred and feather people, pillaged homes—they were definitely deserving of some sort of punishment.
> Rebel: So should all the colonies be punished for the acts of a few colonies?

For a moment, the room is a cacophony of charges and countercharges. "It's the same as in Birmingham," shouts a loyalist. A rebel snorts disparagingly, "Virtual representation is bull." Thirty-two students seem to be talking at once, while the presiding judge, a wiry student with horn-rimmed glasses, bangs his gavel to no avail. The teacher, still in the corner, still with spiral notebook in lap, issues her only command of the day. "Hold still!" she thunders. Order is restored and the loyalists continue their opening argument (from Wineburg and Wilson, 1991).

Another example of Elizabeth Jensen's teaching involves her efforts to help her high school students understand the debates between Federalists and anti-Federalists. She knows that her 15- and 16-year-olds cannot begin to grasp the complexities of the debates without first understanding that these disagreements were rooted in fundamentally different conceptions of human nature—a point glossed over in two paragraphs in her history textbook. Rather than beginning the year with a unit on European discovery and exploration, as her text dictates, she begins with a conference on the nature of man. Students in her eleventh-grade history class read excerpts from the writings of philosophers (Hume, Locke, Plato, and Aristotle), leaders of state and revolutionaries (Jefferson, Lenin, Gandhi), and tyrants (Hitler, Mussolini), presenting and advocating these views before their classmates. Six weeks later, when it is time to study the ratification of the Constitution, these now-familiar figures—Plato, Aristotle, and others—are reconvened to be courted by impassioned groups of Federalists and anti-Federalists. It is Elizabeth Jensen's understanding of what she wants to teach and what adolescents already know that allows her to craft an activity that helps students get a feel for the domain that awaits them: decisions about rebellion, the Constitution, federalism, slavery, and the nature of a government.

Conclusion

These examples provide glimpses of outstanding teaching in the discipline of history. The examples do not come from "gifted teachers" who know how to teach anything: they demonstrate, instead, that expert teachers have a deep understanding of the structure and epistemologies of their disciplines, combined with knowledge of the kinds of teaching activities that will help students come to understand the discipline for themselves. As we previously noted, this point sharply contradicts one of the popular—and dangerous—myths about teaching: teaching is a generic skill and a good teacher can teach any subject. Numerous studies demonstrate that any curriculum—including a textbook—is mediated by a teacher's understanding of the subject domain (for history, see Wineburg and Wilson, 1988; for math, see Ball, 1993; for English, see Grossman et al., 1989). The uniqueness of the content knowledge and pedagogical knowledge necessary to teach history becomes clearer as one explores outstanding teaching in other disciplines.

MATHEMATICS

As is the case in history, most people believe that they know what mathematics is about—computation. Most people are familiar with only the computational aspects of mathematics and so are likely to argue for its place in the school curriculum and for traditional methods of instructing children in computation. In contrast, mathematicians see computation as merely a tool in the real stuff of mathematics, which includes problem solving, and characterizing and understanding structure and patterns. The current debate concerning what students should learn in mathematics seems to set proponents of teaching computational skills against the advocates of fostering conceptual understanding and reflects the wide range of beliefs about what aspects of mathematics are important to know. A growing body of research provides convincing evidence that what teachers know and believe about mathematics is closely linked to their instructional decisions and actions (Brown, 1985; National Council of Teachers of Mathematics, 1989; Wilson, 1990a, b; Brophy, 1990; Thompson, 1992).

Teachers' ideas about mathematics, mathematics teaching, and mathematics learning directly influence their notions about what to teach and how to teach it—an interdependence of beliefs and knowledge about pedagogy and subject matter (e.g., Gamoran, 1994; Stein et al., 1990). It shows that teachers' goals for instruction are, to a large extent, a reflection of what they think is important in mathematics and how they think students best learn it. Thus, as we examine mathematics instruction, we need to pay attention to the subject-matter knowledge of teachers, their pedagogical knowledge (general and content specific), and their knowledge of children as learners of mathematics. Paying attention to these domains of knowledge also leads us to examine teachers' goals for instruction.

If students in mathematics classes are to learn mathematics with understanding—a goal that is accepted by almost everyone in the current debate over the role of computational skills in mathematics classrooms—then it is important to examine examples of teaching for understanding and to analyze the roles of the teacher and the knowledge that underlies the teacher's enactments of those roles. In this section, we examine three cases of mathematics instruction that are viewed as being close to the current vision of exemplary instruction and discuss the knowledge base on which the teacher is drawing, as well as the beliefs and goals which guide his or her instructional decisions.

Multiplication with Meaning

For teaching multidigit multiplication, teacher-researcher Magdelene Lampert created a series of lessons in which she taught a heterogeneous group of 28 fourth-grade students. The students ranged in computational skill from beginning to learn the single-digit multiplication facts to being able to accurately solve n-digit by n-digit multiplications. The lessons were intended to give children experiences in which the important mathematical principles of additive and multiplicative composition, associativity, commutativity, and the distributive property of multiplication over addition were all evident in the steps of the procedures used to arrive at an answer (Lampert, 1986:316). It is clear from her description of her instruction that both her deep understanding of multiplicative structures and her knowledge of a wide range of representations and problem situations related to multiplication were brought to bear as she planned and taught these lessons. It is also clear that her goals for the lessons included not only those related to students' understanding of mathematics, but also those related to students' development as independent, thoughtful problem solvers. Lampert (1986:339) described her role as follows:

> My role was to bring students' ideas about how to solve or analyze problems into the public forum of the classroom, to referee arguments about whether those ideas were reasonable, and to sanction students' intuitive use of mathematical principles as legitimate. I also taught new information in the form of symbolic structures and emphasized the connection between symbols and operations on quantities, but I made it a classroom requirement that students use their own ways of deciding whether something was mathematically reasonable in doing the work. If one conceives of the teacher's role in this way, it is difficult to separate instruction in mathematics content from building a culture of sense-making in the classroom, wherein teacher and students have a view of themselves as responsible for ascertaining the legitimacy of procedures by reference to known mathematical principles. On the part of the teacher, the principles might be known as a more formal abstract system, whereas on the part of the learners, they are known in relation to familiar experiential contexts. But what seems most important is that teachers and students together are disposed toward a particular way of viewing and doing mathematics in the classroom.

Magdelene Lampert set out to connect what students already knew about multidigit multiplication with principled conceptual knowledge. She did so in three sets of lessons. The first set used coin problems, such as "Using only two kinds of coins, make $1.00 using 19 coins," which encouraged children to draw on their familiarity with coins and mathematical principles that coin trading requires. Another set of lessons used simple stories and drawings to illustrate the ways in which large quantities could be grouped for easier counting. Finally, the third set of lessons used only numbers and arithmetic symbols to represent problems. Throughout the lessons, students were challenged to explain their answers and to rely on their arguments, rather than to rely on the teacher or book for verification of correctness. An example serves to highlight this approach; see Box 7.2.

Lampert (1986:337) concludes:

> . . . students used principled knowledge that was tied to the language of groups to explain what they were seeing. They were able to talk meaningfully about place value and order of operations to give legitimacy to procedures and to reason about their outcomes, even though they did not use technical terms to do so. I took their experimentations and arguments as evidence that they had come to see mathematics as more than a set of procedures for finding answers.

Clearly, her own deep understanding of mathematics comes into play as she teaches these lessons. It is worth noting that her goal of helping students see what is mathematically legitimate shapes the way in which she designs lessons to develop students' understanding of two-digit multiplication.

Understanding Negative Numbers

Helping third-grade students extend their understanding of numbers from the natural numbers to the integers is a challenge undertaken by another teacher-researcher. Deborah Ball's work provides another snapshot of teaching that draws on extensive subject content and pedagogical content knowledge. Her goals in instruction include "developing a practice that respects the integrity both of mathematics as a discipline *and* of children as mathematical thinkers" (Ball, 1993). That is, she not only takes into account what the important mathematical ideas are, but also how children think about the particular area of mathematics on which she is focusing. She draws on both her understanding of the integers as mathematical entities (subject-matter knowledge) and her extensive pedagogical content knowledge specifically about integers. Like Lampert, Ball's goals go beyond the boundaries of what is typically considered mathematics and include developing a culture in which students conjecture, experiment, build arguments, and frame and solve problems—the work of mathematicians.

Deborah Ball's description of work highlights the importance and difficulty of figuring out powerful and effective ways to represent key mathematical ideas to children (see Ball, 1993). A wealth of possible models for negative numbers exists and she reviewed a number of them—magic peanuts, money, game scoring, a frog on a number line, buildings with floors above and below ground. She decided to use the building model first and money later: she was acutely aware of the strengths and limitations of each

BOX 7.2 How Many Altogether?

The teacher begins with a request for an example of a basic computation.

Teacher: Can anyone give me a story that could go with this multiplication . . .12 × 4?

Jessica: There were 12 jars, and each had 4 butterflies in it.

Teacher: And if I did this multiplication and found the answer, what would I know about those jars and butterflies?

Jessica: You'd know you had that many butterflies altogether.

The teacher and students next illustrate Jessica's story and construct a procedure for counting the butterflies.

Teacher: Okay, here are the jars. The stars in them will stand for butterflies. Now, it will be easier for us to count how many butterflies there are altogether, if we think of the jars in groups. And as usual, the mathematician's favorite number for thinking about groups is? [Draw a loop around 10 jars.]

Sally: 10.

The lesson progresses as the teacher and students construct a pictorial representation of grouping 10 sets of four butterflies and having 2 jars not in the group; they recognize that 12 × 4 can be thought of as 10 × 4 plus 2 × 4. Lampert then has the children explore other ways of grouping the jars, for example, into two groups of 6 jars.

The students are obviously surprised that 6 × 4 plus 6 × 4 produces the same number as 10 × 4 plus 2 × 4. For Lampert, this is important information about the students' understanding (formative assessment—see Chapter 6). It is a sign that she needs to do many more activities involving different groupings. In subsequent lessons, students are challenged with problems in which the two-digit number in the multiplication is much bigger and, ultimately, in which both numbers are quite large—28 × 65. Students continue to develop their understanding of the principles that govern multiplication and to invent computational procedures based on those principles. Students defend the reasonableness of their procedures by using drawings and stories. Eventually, students explore more traditional as well as alternative algorithms for two-digit multiplication, using only written symbols.

model as a way for representing the key properties of numbers, particularly those of magnitude and direction. Reading Deborah Ball's description of her deliberations, one is struck by the complexity of selecting appropriate models for particular mathematical ideas and processes. She hoped that the positional aspects of the building model would help children recognize that negative numbers were not equivalent to zero, a common misconception. She was aware that the building model would be difficult to use for modeling subtraction of negative numbers.

Deborah Ball begins her work with the students, using the building model by labeling its floors. Students readily labeled the underground floors and accepted them as "below zero." They then explored what happened as little paper people entered an elevator at some floor and rode to another floor. This was used to introduce the conventions of writing addition and subtraction problems involving integers $4 - 6 = -2$ and $-2 + 5 = 3$. Students were presented with increasingly difficult problems. For example, "How many ways are there for a person to get to the second floor?" Working with the building model allowed students to generate a number of observations. For example, one student noticed that "any number below zero plus that same number above zero equals zero" (Ball, 1993:381). However, the model failed to allow for explorations for such problems $5 + (-6)$ and Ball was concerned that students were not developing a sense that -5 was less than -2—it was lower, but not necessarily less. Ball then used a model of money as a second representational context for exploring negative numbers, noting that it, too, has limitations.

Clearly, Deborah Ball's knowledge of the possible representations of integers (pedagogical content knowledge) and her understanding of the important mathematical properties of integers were foundational to her planning and her instruction. Again, her goals related to developing students' mathematical authority, and a sense of community also came into play. Like Lampert, Ball wanted her students to accept the responsibility of deciding when a solution is reasonable and likely to be correct, rather than depending on text or teacher for confirmation of correctness.

Guided Discussion

The work of Lampert and Ball highlights the role of a teacher's knowledge of content and pedagogical content knowledge in planning and teaching mathematics lessons. It also suggests the importance of the teacher's understanding of children as learners. The concept of cognitively guided instruction helps illustrate another important characteristic of effective mathematics instruction: that teachers not only need knowledge of a particular topic within mathematics and knowledge of how learners think about the particular topic, but also need to develop knowledge about how the individual children in their classrooms think about the topic (Carpenter and Fennema, 1992; Carpenter et al., 1996; Fennema et al., 1996). Teachers, it is claimed, will use their knowledge to make appropriate instructional decisions to assist students to construct their mathematical knowledge. In this approach, the idea of domains of knowledge for teaching (Shulman, 1986) is extended to include teachers' knowledge of individual learners in their classrooms.

Cognitively guided instruction is used by Annie Keith, who teaches a combination first- and second-grade class in an elementary school in Madison Wisconsin (Hiebert et al., 1997). Her instructional practices are an example of what is possible when a teacher understands children's thinking and uses that understanding to guide her teaching. A portrait of Ms. Keith's classroom reveals also how her knowledge of mathematics and pedagogy influence her instructional decisions.

Word problems form the basis for almost all instruction in Annie Keith's classroom. Students spend a great deal of time discussing alternative strategies with each other, in groups, and as a whole class. The teacher often participates in these discussions but almost never demonstrates the solution to problems. Important ideas in mathematics are developed as students explore solutions to problems, rather than being a focus of instruction per se. For example, place-value concepts are developed as students use base-10 materials, such as base-10 blocks and counting frames, to solve word problems involving multidigit numbers.

Mathematics instruction in Annie Keith's class takes place in a number of different settings. Everyday first-grade and second-grade activities, such as sharing snacks, lunch count, and attendance, regularly serve as contexts for problem-solving tasks. Mathematics lessons frequently make use of math centers in which the students do a variety of activities. On any given day, children at one center may solve word problems presented by the teacher while at another center children write word problems to present to the class later or play a math game.

She continually challenges her students to think and to try to make sense of what they are doing in math. She uses the activities as opportunities for her to learn what individual students know and understand about mathematics. As students work in groups to solve problems, she observes the various solutions and mentally makes notes about which students should present their work: she wants a variety of solutions presented so that students will have an opportunity to learn from each other. Her knowledge of the important ideas in mathematics serves as one framework for the selection process, but her understanding of how children think about the mathematical ideas they are using also affects her decisions about who should present. She might select a solution that is actually incorrect to be presented so that she can initiate a discussion of a common misconception. Or she may select a solution that is more sophisticated than most students have used in order to provide an opportunity for students to see the benefits of such a strategy. Both the presentations of solutions and the class discussions that follow provide her with information about what her students know and what problems she should use with them next.

Annie Keith's strong belief that children need to construct their understanding of mathematical ideas by building on what they already know guides her instructional decisions. She forms hypotheses about what her students understand and selects instructional activities based on these hypotheses. She modifies her instruction as she gathers additional information about her students and compares it with the mathematics she wants them to learn. Her instructional decisions give her clear diagnoses of individual students' current state of understanding. Her approach is not a free-for-all without teacher guidance: rather, it is instruction that builds on students' understandings and is carefully orchestrated by the teacher, who is aware of what is mathematically important and also what is important to the learner's progress.

Model-Based Reasoning

Some attempts to revitalize mathematics instruction have emphasized the importance of modeling phenomena. Work on modeling can be done from kindergarten through twelfth grade (K-12). Modeling involves cycles of model construction, model evaluation, and model revision. It is central to professional practice in many disciplines, such as mathematics and science, but it is largely missing from school instruction. Modeling practices are ubiquitous and diverse, ranging from the construction of physical models, such as a planetarium or a model of the human vascular system, to the development of abstract symbol systems, exemplified by the mathematics of algebra, geometry, and calculus. The ubiquity and diversity of models in these disciplines suggest that modeling can help students develop understanding about a wide range of important ideas. Modeling practices can and should be fostered at every age and grade level (Clement, 1989; Hestenes, 1992; Lehrer and Romberg, 1996a, b; Schauble et al., 1995; see Box 7.3).

Taking a model-based approach to a problem entails inventing (or selecting) a model, exploring the qualities of the model, and then applying the model to answer a question of interest. For example, the geometry of triangles has an internal logic and also has predictive power for phenomena ranging from optics to wayfinding (as in navigational systems) to laying floor tile. Modeling emphasizes a need for forms of mathematics that are typically underrepresented in the standard curriculum, such as spatial visualization and geometry, data structure, measurement, and uncertainty. For example, the scientific study of animal behavior, like bird foraging, is severely limited unless one also has access to such mathematical concepts as variability and uncertainty. Hence, the practice of modeling introduces the further explorations of important "big ideas" in disciplines.

Conclusion

Increasingly, approaches to early mathematics teaching incorporate the premises that all learning involves extending understanding to new situations, that young children come to school with many ideas about mathematics, that knowledge relevant to a new setting is not always accessed spontaneously, and that learning can be enhanced by respecting and encouraging children to try out the ideas and strategies that they bring to school-based learning in classrooms. Rather than beginning mathematics instruction by focusing solely on computational algorithms, such as addition and subtraction, students are encouraged to invent their own strategies for solving problems and to discuss why those strategies work. Teachers may also explicitly prompt students to think about aspects of their everyday life that are potentially relevant for further learning. For example, everyday experiences of walking and related ideas about position and direction can serve as a springboard for developing corresponding mathematics about the structure of large-scale space, position, and direction (Lehrer and Romberg, 1996b).

As research continues to provide good examples of instruction that help children learn important mathematics, there will be better understanding of the roles that teachers' knowledge, beliefs, and goals play in their instructional thinking and actions. The examples we have provided here make it clear that the selection of tasks and the guidance of students' thinking as they work through tasks is highly dependent on teachers' knowledge of mathematics, pedagogical content knowledge, and knowledge of students in general.

SCIENCE

Two recent examples in physics illustrate how research findings can be used to design instructional strategies that promote the sort of problem-solving behavior observed in experts. Undergraduates who had finished an introductory physics course were asked to spend a total of 10 hours, spread over several weeks, solving physics problems using a computer-based tool that constrained them to perform a conceptual analysis of the problems based on a hierarchy of principles and procedures that could be applied to solve them (Dufresne et al., 1996). This approach was motivated by research on expertise (discussed in Chapter 2). The reader will recall that, when asked to state an approach to solving a problem, physicists generally discuss principles and procedures. Novices, in contrast, tend to discuss

BOX 7.3   Qualitative Strategies Written by Students

Students enrolled in an introductory physics course were asked to write a strategy for an exam problem

Exam Problem:

A disk of mass, M = 2 kg, and radius, R = 0.4 m, has string wound around it and is free to rotate about an axle through its center. A block of mass, M = 1 kg, is attached to the end of the string, and the system is released from rest with no slack in the string. What is the speed of the block after it has fallen a distance, d = 0.5 m. Don't forget to provide both a strategy and a solution.

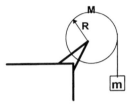

Strategy 1: Use the conservation of energy since the only nonconservative force in the system is the tension in the rope attached to the mass M and wound around the disk (assuming there is no friction between the axle and the disk, and the mass M and the air), and the work done by the tension to the disk and the mass cancel each other out. First, set up a coordinate system so the potential energy of the system at the start can be determined. There will be no kinetic energy at the start since it starts at rest. Therefore the potential energy is all the initial energy. Now set the initial energy equal to the final energy that is made up of the kinetic energy of the disk plus the mass M and any potential energy left in the system with respect to the chosen coordinate system.

Strategy 2: I would use conservation of mechanical energy to solve this problem. The mass M has some potential energy while it is hanging there. When the block starts to accelerate downward the potential energy is transformed into rotational kinetic energy

specific equations that could be used to manipulate variables given in the problem (Chi et al., 1981). When compared with a group of students who solved the same problems on their own, the students who used the computer to carry out the hierarchical analyses performed noticeably better in subsequent measures of expertise. For example, in problem solving, those who performed the hierarchical analyses outperformed those who did not, whether measured in terms of overall problem-solving performance, ability to arrive at the correct answer, or ability to apply appropriate principles to solve the problems; see Figure 7.1. Furthermore, similar differences emerged in problem categorization: students who performed the hierarchical analyses considered principles (as opposed to surface features) more often in of the disk and kinetic energy of the falling mass. Equating the initial and final states and using the relationship between v and ω the speed of M can be found. Mechanical energy is conserved even with the nonconservative tension force because the tension force is internal to the system (pulley, mass, rope).

Strategy 3: In trying to find the speed of the block I would try to find angular momentum kinetic energy, use gravity. I would also use rotational kinematics and moment of inertia around the center of mass for the disk.

Strategy 4: There will be a torque about the center of mass due to the weight of the block, M. The force pulling downward is mg. The moment of inertia about the axle is $1/2 MR^2$. The moment of inertia multiplied by the angular acceleration. By plugging these values into a kinematic expression, the angular speed can be calculated. Then, the angular speed times the radius gives you the velocity of the block.

The first two strategies display an excellent understanding of the principles, justification, and procedures that could be used to solve the problem (the what, why, and how for solving the problem). The last two strategies are largely a shopping list of physics terms or equations that were covered in the course, but the students are not able to articulate why or how they apply to the problem under consideration.

Having students write strategies (after modeling strategy writing for them and providing suitable scaffolding to ensure progress) provides an excellent formative assessment tool for monitoring whether or not students are making the appropriate links between problem contexts, and the principles and procedures that could be applied to solve them (see Leonard et al., 1996).

deciding whether or not two problems would be solved similarly; see Figure 7.2. (See Chapter 6 for an example of the type of item used in the categorization task of Figure 7.2.) It is also worth noting that both Figures 7.1 and 7.2 illustrate two other issues that we have discussed in this volume, namely that time on task is a major indicator for learning and that deliberate practice is an efficient way to promote expertise. In both cases, the control group made significant improvements simply as a result of practice (time on task), but the experimental group showed more improvements for the same amount of training time (deliberate practice).

Introductory physics courses have also been taught successfully with an approach for problem solving that begins with a qualitative hierarchical analy-

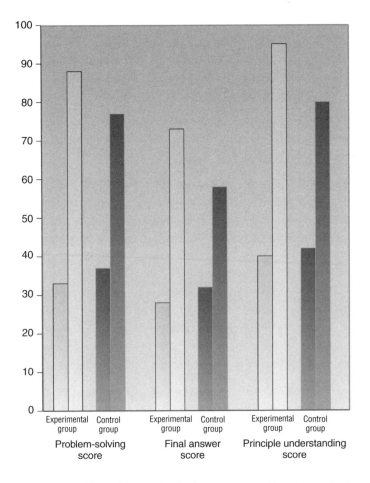

FIGURE 7.1 *Effects of two methods of training on problem-solving, final answer, and principle understanding. SOURCE: Dufresne et al. (1992).*

sis of the problems (Leonard et al., 1996). Undergraduate engineering students were instructed to write qualitative strategies for solving problems before attempting to solve them (based on Chi et al., 1981). The strategies consisted of a coherent verbal description of how a problem could be solved and contained three components: the major principle to be applied; the justification for why the principle was applicable; and the procedures for applying the principle. That is, the what, why, and how of solving the problem were explicitly delineated; see Box 7.4. Compared with students who took a traditional course, students in the strategy-based course per-

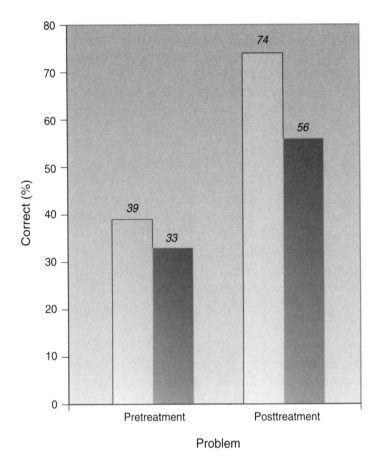

FIGURE 7.2 *Effects of two methods of training on considering principles for categorizing problems. SOURCE: Dufresne et al. (1992).*

formed significantly better in their ability to categorize problems according to the relevant principles that could be applied to solve them; see Figure 7.3.

Hierarchical structures are useful strategies for helping novices both recall knowledge and solve problems. For example, physics novices who had completed and received good grades in an introductory college physics course were trained to generate a problem analysis called a theoretical problem description (Heller and Reif, 1984). The analysis consists of describing force problems in terms of concepts, principles, and heuristics. With such an approach, novices substantially improved in their ability to solve problems, even though the type of theoretical problem description used in the study

BOX 7.4 Which Water Tastes Better?

The seventh- and eighth-grade students in a Haitian Creole bilingual program wanted to find the "truth" of a belief held by most of their classmates: that drinking water from the fountain on the third floor, where the junior high was located, was superior to the water from the other fountains in their school. Challenged by their teacher, the students set out to determine whether they actually preferred the water from the third floor or only thought they did.

As a first step, the students designed and took a blind taste test of the water from fountains on all three floors of the building. They found, to their surprise, that two-thirds of them chose the water from the first-floor fountain, even though they all said that they preferred drinking from the third-floor fountain. The students did not believe the data. They held firmly to their beliefs that the first-floor fountain was the worst because "all the little kids slobber in it." (The first-floor fountain is located near the kindergarten and first-grade classrooms.) Their teacher was also suspicious of the results because she had expected no differences among the three water fountains. These beliefs and suspicions motivated the students to conduct a second taste test with a larger sample drawn from the rest of the junior high.

The students decided where, when, and how to run their experiment. They discussed methodological issues: How to collect the water, how to hide the identity of the sources, and, crucially, how many fountains to include. They decided to include the same three fountains as before so that they could compare results.

was not a natural one for novices. Novices untrained in the theoretical descriptions were generally unable to generate appropriate descriptions on their own—even given fairly routine problems. Skills, such as the ability to describe a problem in detail before attempting a solution, the ability to determine what relevant information should enter the analysis of a problem, and the ability to decide which procedures can be used to generate problem descriptions and analyses, are tacitly used by experts but rarely taught explicitly in physics courses.

Another approach helps students organize knowledge by imposing a hierarchical organization on the performance of different tasks in physics (Eylon and Reif, 1984). Students who received a particular physics argument that was organized in hierarchical form performed various recall and problem-solving tasks better than subjects who received the same argument non-hierarchically. Similarly, students who received a hierarchical organization of problem-solving strategies performed much better than subjects who received the same strategies organized non-hierarchically. Thus, helping

They worried about bias in the voting process: What if some students voted more than once? Each student in the class volunteered to organize a piece of the experiment. About 40 students participated in the blind taste test. When they analyzed their data, they found support for their earlier results: 88 percent of the junior high students *thought* they preferred water from the third-floor fountain, but 55 percent actually chose the water from the first floor (a result of 33 percent would be chance).

Faced with this evidence, the students' suspicions turned to curiosity. Why was the water from the first-floor fountain preferred? How can they determine the source of the preference? They decided to analyze the school's water along several dimensions, among them acidity, salinity, temperature, and bacteria. They found that all the fountains had unacceptably high levels of bacteria. In fact, the first-floor fountain (the one most preferred) had the highest bacterial count. They also found that the water from the first-floor fountain was 20 degrees (Fahrenheit) colder than the water from fountains on the other floors. Based on their findings, they concluded that temperature was probably a deciding factor in taste preference. They hypothesized that the water was naturally cooled as it sat in the city's underground pipes during the winter months (the study was conducted in February) and warmed as it flowed from the basement to the third floor.

SOURCE: Rosebery et al. (1992).

students to organize their knowledge is as important as the knowledge itself, since knowledge organization is likely to affect students' intellectual performance.

These examples demonstrate the importance of deliberate practice and of having a "coach" who provides feedback for ways of optimizing performance (see Chapter 3). If students had simply been given problems to solve on their own (an instructional practice used in all the sciences), it is highly unlikely that they would have spent time efficiently. Students might get stuck for minutes, or even hours, in attempting a solution to a problem and either give up or waste lots of time. In Chapter 3, we discussed ways in which learners profit from errors and that making mistakes is not always time wasted. However, it is not efficient if a student spends most of the problem-solving time rehearsing procedures that are not optimal for promoting skilled performance, such as finding and manipulating equations to solve the problem, rather than identifying the underlying principle and procedures that apply to the problem and then constructing the specific equa-

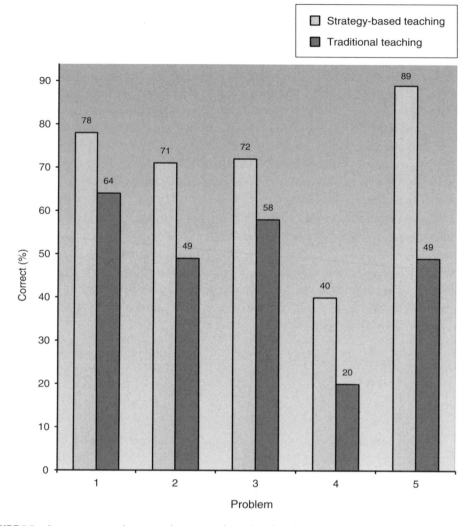

FIGURE 7.3 *Percent correct choices under strategy-based and traditional teaching conditions by problem number in a categorization, multiple-choice task. SOURCE: Dufresne et al. (1992).*

tions needed. In deliberate practice, a student works under a tutor (human or computer based) to rehearse appropriate practices that enhance performance. Through deliberate practice, computer-based tutoring environments have been designed that reduce the time it takes individuals to reach real-world performance criteria from 4 years to 25 hours (see Chapter 9)!

Conceptual Change

Before students can really learn new scientific concepts, they often need to re-conceptualize deeply rooted misconceptions that interfere with the learning. As reviewed above (see Chapters 3 and 4), people spend considerable time and effort constructing a view of the physical world through experiences and observations, and they may cling tenaciously to those views—however much they conflict with scientific concepts—because they help them explain phenomena and make predictions about the world (e.g., why a rock falls faster than a leaf).

One instructional strategy, termed "bridging," has been successful in helping students overcome persistent misconceptions (Brown, 1992; Brown and Clement, 1989; Clement, 1993). The bridging strategy attempts to bridge from students' correct beliefs (called anchoring conceptions) to their misconceptions through a series of intermediate analogous situations. Starting with the anchoring intuition that a spring exerts an upward force on the book resting on it, the student might be asked if a book resting on the middle of a long, "springy" board supported at its two ends experiences an upward force from the board. The fact that the bent board looks as if it is serving the same function as the spring helps many students agree that both the spring and the board exert upward forces on the book. For a student who may not agree that the bent board exerts an upward force on the book, the instructor may ask a student to place her hand on top of a vertical spring and push down and to place her hand on the middle of the springy board and push down. She would then be asked if she experienced an upward force that resisted her push in both cases. Through this type of dynamic probing of students' beliefs, and by helping them come up with ways to resolve conflicting views, students can be guided into constructing a coherent view that is applicable across a wide range of contexts.

Another effective strategy for helping students overcome persistent erroneous beliefs are interactive lecture demonstrations (Sokoloff and Thornton, 1997; Thornton and Sokoloff, 1997). This strategy, which has been used very effectively in large introductory college physics classes, begins with an introduction to a demonstration that the instructor is about to perform, such as a collision between two air carts on an air track, one a stationary light cart, the other a heavy cart moving toward the stationary cart. Each cart has an electronic "force probe" connected to it which displays on a large screen and in real-time the force acting on it during the collision. The teacher first asks the students to discuss the situation with their neighbors and then record a prediction as to whether one of the carts would exert a bigger force on the other during impact or whether the carts would exert equal forces.

The vast majority of students incorrectly predict that the heavier, moving cart exerts a larger force on the lighter, stationary cart. Again, this prediction seems quite reasonable based on experience—students know that a moving

Mack truck colliding with a stationary Volkswagen beetle will result in much more damage done to the Volkswagen, and this is interpreted to mean that the Mack truck must have exerted a larger force on the Volkswagen. Yet, notwithstanding the major damage to the Volkswagen, Newton's Third Law states that two interacting bodies exert equal and opposite forces on each other.

After the students make and record their predictions, the instructor performs the demonstration, and the students see on the screen that the force probes record forces of equal magnitude but oppositely directed during the collision. Several other situations are discussed in the same way: What if the two carts had been moving toward each other at the same speed? What if the situation is reversed so that the heavy cart is stationary and the light cart is moving toward it? Students make predictions and then see the actual forces between the carts displayed as they collide. In all cases, students see that the carts exert equal and opposite forces on each other, and with the help of a discussion moderated by the instructor, the students begin to build a consistent view of Newton's Third Law that incorporates their observations and experiences.

Consistent with the research on providing feedback (see Chapter 3), there is other research that suggests that students' witnessing the force displayed in real-time as the two carts collide helps them overcome their misconceptions; delays of as little as 20-30 minutes in displaying graphic data of an event occurring in real-time significantly inhibits the learning of the underlying concept (Brasell, 1987).

Both bridging and the interactive demonstration strategies have been shown to be effective at helping students permanently overcome misconceptions. This finding is a major breakthrough in teaching science, since so much research indicates that students often can parrot back correct answers on a test that might be erroneously interpreted as displaying the eradication of a misconception, but the same misconception often resurfaces when students are probed weeks or months later (see Mestre, 1994, for a review).

Teaching as Coaching

One of the best examples of translating research into practice is Minstrell's (1982, 1989, 1992) work with high school physics students. Minstrell uses many research-based instructional techniques (e.g., bridging, making students' thinking visible, facilitating students' ability to restructure their own knowledge) to teach physics for understanding. He does this through classroom discussions in which students construct understanding by making sense of physics concepts, with Minstrell playing a coaching role. The following quote exemplifies his innovative and effective instructional strategies (Minstrell, 1989:130-131):

Students' initial ideas about mechanics are like strands of yarn, some unconnected, some loosely interwoven. The act of instruction can be viewed as helping the students unravel individual strands of belief, label them, and then weave them into a fabric of more complete understanding. An important point is that later understanding can be constructed, to a considerable extent, from earlier beliefs. Sometimes new strands of belief are introduced, but rarely is an earlier belief pulled out and replaced. Rather than denying the relevancy of a belief, teachers might do better by helping students differentiate their present ideas from and integrate them into conceptual beliefs more like those of scientists.

Describing a lesson on force, Minstrell (1989:130-131) begins by introducing the topic in general terms:

Today we are going to try to explain some rather ordinary events that you might see any day. You will find that you already have many good ideas that will help explain those events. We will find that some of our ideas are similar to those of the scientist, but in other cases our ideas might be different. When we are finished with this unit, I expect that we will have a much clearer idea of how scientists explain those events, and I know that you will feel more comfortable about your explanations . . . A key idea we are going to use is the idea of force. What does the idea of force mean to you?

Many views emerge from the ensuing classroom discussion, from the typical "push or pull" to descriptions that include sophisticated terms, such as energy and momentum. At some point Minstrell guides the discussion to a specific example: he drops a rock and asks students how the event can be explained using their ideas about force. He asks students to individually formulate their ideas and to draw a diagram showing the major forces on the rock as arrows, with labels to denote the cause of each force. A lengthy discussion follows in which students present their views, views that contain many irrelevant (e.g., nuclear forces) or fictitious forces (e.g., the spin of the earth, air). In his coaching, Minstrell asks students to justify their choices by asking questions, such as "How do you know?" "How did you decide?" "Why do you believe that?"

With this approach, Minstrell has been able to identify many erroneous beliefs of students that stand in the way of conceptual understanding. One example is the belief that only active agents (e.g., people) can exert forces, that passive agents (e.g., a table) cannot. Minstrell (1992) has developed a framework that helps both to make sense of students' reasoning and to design instructional strategies. (For a related theoretical framework for classifying and explaining student reasoning, see the discussion of "phenomenological primitives" in DiSessa, 1988, 1993.) Minstrell describes identifiable pieces of students' knowledge as "facets," a facet being a convenient unit of thought, a piece of knowledge, or a strategy seemingly used by the student in addressing a particular situation. Facets may relate to conceptual knowledge (e.g., passive objects do not exert force), to strategic knowledge (e.g., average velocity can be determined by adding the initial and final velocities and dividing by two), or generic reasoning (e.g., the more the X, the more the Y). Identifying students' facets, what cues them in different contexts, and how students use them in reasoning are all helpful in devising instructional strategies.

Interactive Instruction in Large Classes

One of the obstacles to instructional innovation in large introductory science courses at the college level is the sheer number of students who are taught at one time. How does an instructor provide an active learning experience, provide feedback, accommodate different learning styles, make students' thinking visible, and provide scaffolding and tailored instruction to meet specific student needs when facing more than 100 students at a time? Classroom communication systems can help the instructor of a large class accomplish these objectives. One such system, called Classtalk, consists of both hardware and software that allows up to four students to share an input device (e.g., a fairly inexpensive graphing calculator) to "sign on" to a classroom communication network that permits the instructor to send questions for students to work on and permits students to enter answers through their input device. Answers can then be displayed anonymously in histogram form to the class, and a permanent record of each student's response is recorded to help evaluate progress as well as the effectiveness of instruction.

This technology has been used successfully at the University of Massachusetts-Amherst to teach physics to a range of students, from non-science majors to engineering and science majors (Dufresne et al., 1996; Wenk et al., 1997; Mestre et al., 1997). The technology creates an interactive learning environment in the lectures: students work collaboratively on conceptual questions, and the histogram of students' answers is used as a visual springboard for classwide discussions when students defend the reasoning they used to arrive at their answers. This technology makes students' thinking visible and promotes critical listening, evaluation, and argumentation in the class. The teacher is a coach, providing scaffolding where needed, tailoring "mini-lectures" to clear up points of confusion, or, if things are going well, simply moderating the discussion and allowing students to figure out things and reach consensus on their own. The technology is also a natural mechanism to support formative assessment during instruction, providing both the teacher and students with feedback on how well the class is grasping the concepts under study. The approach accommodates a wider variety of learning styles than is possible by lectures and helps to foster a community of learners focused on common objectives and goals.

Science for All Children

The examples above present some effective strategies for teaching and learning science for high school and college students. We drew some general principles of learning from these examples and stressed that the findings consistently point to the strong effect of knowledge structures on learning. These studies also emphasize the importance of class discussions for developing a language for talking about scientific ideas, for making students' thinking explicit to the teacher and to the rest of the class, and for learning to develop a line of argumentation that uses what one has learned to solve problems and explain phenomena and observations.

The question that immediately occurs is how to teach science to younger children or to students who are considered to be educationally "at risk." One approach that has been especially useful in science teaching was developed with language-minority grade-school children: Chèche Konnen, which in Haitian Creole means search for knowledge (Rosebery et al., 1992). The approach stresses how discourse is a primary means for the search for knowledge and scientific sense-making. It also illustrates how scientific ideas are constructed. In this way it mirrors science, in the words of Nobel Laureate Sir Peter Medawar (1982:111):

> Like other exploratory processes, [the scientific method] can be resolved into a dialogue between fact and fancy, the actual and the possible; between what could be true and what is in fact the case. The purpose of scientific enquiry is not to compile an inventory of factual information, nor to build up a totalitarian world picture of Natural Laws in which every event that is not compulsory is forbidden. We should think of it rather as a logically articulated structure of justifiable beliefs about a Possible World— a story which we invent and criticize and modify as we go along, so that it ends by being, as nearly as we can make it, a story about real life.

The Chèche Konnen approach to teaching began by creating "communities of scientific practice" in language-minority classrooms in a few Boston and Cambridge, MA public schools. "Curriculum" emerges in these classrooms from the students' questions and beliefs and is shaped in ongoing interactions that include both the teacher and students. Students explore their own questions, much as we described above in Barb Johnson's class. In addition, students design studies, collect information, analyze data and construct evidence, and they then debate the conclusions that *they* derive from their evidence. In effect, the students build and argue about theories; see Box 7.5.

Students constructed scientific understandings through an iterative process of theory building, criticism, and refinement based on their own questions, hypotheses, and data analysis activities. Question posing, theorizing, and argumentation formed the structure of the students' scientific activity.

Within this structure, students explored the implications of the theories they held, examined underlying assumptions, formulated and tested hypotheses, developed evidence, negotiated conflicts in belief and evidence, argued alternative interpretations, provided warrants for conclusions, and so forth. The process as a whole provided a richer, more scientifically grounded experience than the conventional focus on textbooks or laboratory demonstrations.

The emphasis on establishing communities of scientific practice builds on the fact that robust knowledge and understandings are socially constructed through talk, activity, and interaction around meaningful problems and tools (Vygotsky, 1978). The teacher guides and supports students as they explore problems and define questions that are of interest to them. A community of practice also provides direct cognitive and social support for the efforts of the group's individual members. Students share the responsibility for thinking and doing: they distribute their intellectual activity so that the burden of managing the whole process does not fall to any one individual. In addition, a community of practice can be a powerful context for constructing scientific meanings. In challenging one another's thoughts and beliefs, students must be explicit about their meanings; they must negotiate conflicts in belief or evidence; and they must share and synthesize their knowledge to achieve understanding (Brown and Palincsar, 1989; Inagaki and Hatano, 1987).

What do students learn from participating in a scientific sense-making community? Individual interviews with students before and after the water taste test investigation (see Box 7.4), first in September and again the following June, showed how the students' knowledge and reasoning changed. In the interviews (conducted in Haitian Creole), the students were asked to think aloud about two open-ended real-world problems—pollution in the Boston Harbor and a sudden illness in an elementary school. The researchers were interested in changes in students' conceptual knowledge about aquatic ecosystems and in students' uses of hypotheses, experiments, and explanations to organize their reasoning (for a complete discussion, see Rosebery et al., 1992).

Conceptual Knowledge

Not surprisingly, the students knew more about water pollution and aquatic ecosystems in June than they did in September. They were also able to use this knowledge generatively. One student explained how she would clean the water in Boston Harbor (Rosebery et al., 1992:86).

> Like you look for the things, take the garbage out of the water, you put a screen to block all the paper and stuff, then you clean the water; you put chemical products in it to clean the water, and you'd take all the micro-

BOX 7.5 Physical Models

Physical models, like models of solar systems or elbows, are microcosms of systems that draw heavily on children's intuitions about resemblance to sustain the relationship between the world being modeled and the model itself. The photograph below displays a child's model of the elbow. Note, for instance, the rubber bands that mimic the connective function of ligaments and the wooden dowels that are arranged so that their translation in the vertical plane cannot exceed 180 degrees. Though the search for function is supported by initial resemblance, what counts as resemblance typically changes as children revise their models. For example, attempts to make models exemplify elbow motion often lead to an interest in the way muscles might be arranged (from Lehrer and Schauble, 1996a, b).

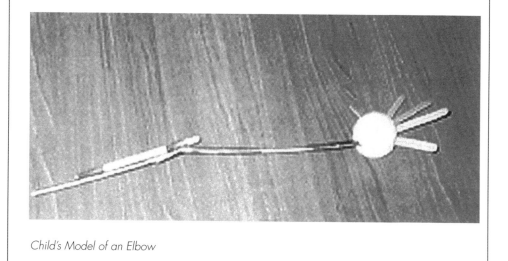

Child's Model of an Elbow

scopic life out. Chlorine and alum, you put in the water. They'd gather the little stuff, the little stuff would stick to the chemical products, and they would clean the water.

Note that this explanation contains misconceptions. By confusing the cleaning of drinking water with the cleaning of sea water, the student suggests adding chemicals to take all microscopic life from the water (good for drinking water, but bad for the ecosystem of Boston Harbor). This example illustrates the difficulties in transferring knowledge appropriately from one context to another (see Chapter 3). Despite these shortcomings, it is clear that this student is starting on the path to scientific thinking, leaving behind the more superficial "I'd take all the bad stuff out of the water" type of explanation. It is also clear that by making the student's thinking visible, the teacher is in an excellent position to refine her (and perhaps the class's) understanding.

Scientific Thinking

Striking changes appeared in students' scientific reasoning. In September, there were three ways in which the students showed little familiarity with scientific forms of reasoning. First, the students did not understand the function of hypotheses or experiments in scientific inquiry. When asked for their ideas about what could be making the children sick, the students tended, with few exceptions, to respond with short, unelaborated, often untestable "hypotheses" that simply restated the phenomena described in the problem: "That's a thing . . . . Ah, I could say a person, some person that gave them something . . . . Anything, like give poison to make his stomach hurt" (Rosebery et al., 1992:81).

Second, the students conceptualized evidence as information they already knew, either through personal experience or second-hand sources, rather than data produced through experimentation or observation. When asked to generate an experiment to justify an hypothesis—"How would you find out?"—they typically offered declarations: "Because the garbage is a poison for them . . . . The garbage made the fish die" (Rosebery et al., 1992:78).

Third, the students interpreted an elicitation for an experiment—"How would you be sure?"—as a text comprehension question for which there was a "right" answer. They frequently responded with an explanation or assertion of knowledge and consistently marked their responses as explanatory ("because"): "Because fish don't eat garbage. They eat plants under the water" (page 78).

In the June interviews, the students showed that they had become familiar with the function of hypotheses and experiments and with reasoning within larger explanatory frameworks. Elinor had developed a model of an integrated water system in which an action or event in one part of the system had consequences for other parts (Rosebery et al., 1992:87):

> You can't leave [the bad stuff] on the ground. If you leave it on the ground, the water that, the earth has water underground, it will still spoil the water underground. Or when it rains it will just take it and, when it rains, the water runs, it will take it and leave it in the river, in where the water goes in. Those things, poison things, you aren't supposed to leave it on the ground.

In June, the students no longer invoked anonymous agents, but put forward chains of hypotheses to explain phenomena, such as why children were getting sick (page 88):

> Like, you could test what the kids ate and, like, test the water, too; it could be the water that isn't good, that has microbes, that might have microscopic animals in it to make them sick.

The June interviews also showed that students had begun to develop a sense of the function and form of experimentation. They no longer depended on personal experience as evidence, but proposed experiments to test specific hypotheses. In response to a question about sick fish, Laure clearly understands how to find a scientific answer (page 91):

> I'd put a fish in fresh water and one fish in a water full of garbage. I'd give the fresh water fish food to eat and the other one in the nasty water, I'd give it food to eat to see if the fresh water, if the one in the fresh water would die with the food I gave it, if the one in the dirty water would die with the food I gave it. . . . I would give them the same food to see if the things they eat in the water and the things I give them now, which will make them healthy and which wouldn't make them healthy.

Conclusion

Teaching and learning in science have been influenced very directly by research studies on expertise (see Chapter 2). The examples discussed in this chapter focus on two areas of science teaching: physics and junior high school biology. Several of the teaching strategies illustrated ways to help students think about the general principles or "big" ideas in physics before jumping to formulas and equations. Others illustrate ways to help students engage in deliberate practice (see Chapter 3) and to monitor their progress.

Learning the strategies for scientific thinking have another objective: to develop thinking acumen needed to promote conceptual change. Often, the barrier to achieving insights to new solutions is rooted in a fundamental misconception about the subject matter. One strategy for helping students in physics begins with an "anchoring intuition" about a phenomenon and then gradually bridging it to related phenomena that are less intuitive to the student but involve the same physics principles. Another strategy involves the use of interactive lecture demonstrations to encourage students to make predictions, consider feedback, and then reconceptualize phenomena.

The example of Chèche Konnen demonstrates the power of a sense-making approach to science learning that builds on the knowledge that students bring with them to school from their home cultures, including their familiar discourse practices. Students learned to think, talk, and act scientifically, and their first and second languages mediated their learning in powerful ways. Using Haitian Creole, they designed their studies, interpreted data, and argued theories; using English, they collected data from their mainstream peers, read standards to interpret their scientific test results, reported their findings, and consulted with experts at the local water treatment facility.

CONCLUSION

Outstanding teaching requires teachers to have a deep understanding of the subject matter and its structure, as well as an equally thorough understanding of the kinds of teaching activities that help students understand the subject matter in order to be capable of asking probing questions.

Numerous studies demonstrate that the curriculum and its tools, including textbooks, need to be dissected and discussed in the larger contexts and framework of a discipline. In order to be able to provide such guidance, teachers themselves need a thorough understanding of the subject domain and the epistemology that guides the discipline (for history, see Wineburg and Wilson, 1988; for math and English, see Ball, 1993; Grossman et al., 1989; for science, see Rosebery et al., 1992).

The examples in this chapter illustrate the principles for the design of learning environments that were discussed in Chapter 6: they are learner, knowledge, assessment, and community centered. They are learner centered in the sense that teachers build on the knowledge students bring to the learning situation. They are knowledge centered in the sense that the teachers attempt to help students develop an organized understanding of important concepts in each discipline. They are assessment centered in the sense that the teachers attempt to make students' thinking visible so that ideas can be discussed and clarified, such as having students (1) present their arguments in debates, (2) discuss their solutions to problems at a qualitative level, and (3) make predictions about various phenomena. They are community centered in the sense that the teachers establish classroom norms that learning with understanding is valued and students feel free to explore what they do not understand.

These examples illustrate the importance of pedagogical content knowledge to guide teachers. Expert teachers have a firm understanding of their respective disciplines, knowledge of the conceptual barriers that students face in learning about the discipline, and knowledge of effective strategies for working with students. Teachers' knowledge of their disciplines provides a cognitive roadmap to guide their assignments to students, to gauge student progress, and to support the questions students ask. The teachers focus on understanding rather than memorization and routine procedures to follow, and they engage students in activities that help students reflect on their own learning and understanding.

The interplay between content knowledge and pedagogical knowledge illustrated in this chapter contradicts a commonly held misconception about teaching—that effective teaching consists of a set of general teaching strategies that apply to all content areas. This notion is erroneous, just as is the idea that expertise in a discipline is a general set of problem-solving skills that lack a content knowledge base to support them (see Chapter 2).

The outcomes of new approaches to teaching as reflected in the results of summative assessments are encouraging. Studies of students' discussions in classrooms indicate that they learn to use the tools of systematic inquiry to think historically, mathematically, and scientifically. How these kinds of teaching strategies reveal themselves on typical standardized tests is another matter. In some cases there is evidence that teaching for understanding can increase scores on standardized measures (e.g., Resnick et al., 1991); in other cases, scores on standardized tests are unaffected, but the students show sizable advantages on assessments that are sensitive to their comprehension and understanding rather than reflecting sheer memorization (e.g., Carpenter et al., 1996; Secules et al., 1997).

It is noteworthy that none of the teachers discussed in this chapter felt that he or she was finished learning. Many discussed their work as involving a lifelong and continuing struggle to understand and improve. What opportunities do teachers have to improve their practice? The next chapter explores teachers' chances to improve and advance their knowledge in order to function as effective professionals.

8

Teacher Learning

The findings from research on learning suggest roles for teachers that differ from their roles in the past. Education reform efforts in the United States cannot succeed without an effort to help teachers and administrators assume these new roles (Darling-Hammond, 1997:154):

> If teachers are to prepare an ever more diverse group of students for much more challenging work—for framing problems; finding, integrating and synthesizing information; creating new solutions; learning on their own; and working cooperatively—they will need substantially more knowledge and radically different skills than most now have and most schools of education now develop.

This chapter considers the kinds of learning opportunities available to teachers and analyzes them from the perspective of what is known about ways to help people learn.

Teacher learning is relatively new as a research topic, so there is not a great deal of data on it. But the research that does exist, generally in the form of rich case studies, provides important information about teachers as they attempt to change their practices. Our discussion of these cases is based on the assumption that what is known about learning applies to teachers as well as to their students.

We begin our discussion by examining opportunities for teacher learning that are available to practicing teachers. Some are formal; many others are informal. Understanding teachers' opportunities for learning—including the constraints on teachers' time—is important for developing a realistic picture of possibilities for lifelong learning. In some cases, teachers' opportunities for learning have been consistent with what is currently known about ways to facilitate learning; in other cases they have not (Koppich and Knapp, 1998).

After discussing opportunities for learning, we examine the topic of teacher as learner from the perspectives used in Chapter 6 to characterize effective learning environments. We end with a discussion of learning opportunities for preservice education—for college students who are in programs designed to help them learn how to teach.

OPPORTUNITIES FOR PRACTICING TEACHERS

Practicing teachers continue to learn about teaching in many ways. First, they learn from their own practice. Whether this learning is described as the monitoring and adjustment of good practice or analyzed more completely according to a model of pedagogical reasoning (Wilson et al., 1987), teachers gain new knowledge and understanding of their students, schools, curriculum, and instructional methods by living the practical experiments that occur as a part of professional practice (Dewey, 1963; Schön, 1983). Teachers also learn from their own practice through different types of teacher research or "action research," such as creating journals, essays, classroom studies, and oral inquiry processes (Cochran-Smith and Lytle, 1993).

Second, teachers learn through their interactions with other teachers. Some of this occurs during formal and informal mentoring that is similar to apprenticeship learning (Lave and Wenger, 1991; see also Little, 1990; Feiman-Nemser and Parker, 1993). Formal mentoring occurs when an experienced teacher takes a new teacher under his or her wing to provide insight and advice, sometimes for state programs (Feiman-Nemser and Parker, 1993); informal mentoring occurs through conversations in hallways, teachers' rooms, and other school settings. Novices also learn through supervision by department chairs, principals, and other supervisors.

To a small but increasing degree, teachers are teaching other teachers through formal inservice education. Administrators are beginning to recognize expertise in their schools and districts and are encouraging teachers to share that expertise as inservice presenters to their colleagues. Some states, such as Massachusetts, even recognize the preparation for these inservice programs as a form of professional learning for the presenters and award them with "professional development points" for time spent in preparing to teach, as well as time spent teaching their colleagues.

Teachers also teach teachers outside of schools. Meetings of professional associations and teachers' unions include numerous workshops and presentations in which teachers share their knowledge with other teachers. Other examples include the Physics Teacher Resource Agent Project of the American Association of Physics Teachers and the Woodrow Wilson Fellows, in which teachers are trained to provide workshops in instructional methods and materials, as well as content, for other teachers (Van Hise, 1986).

Third, teachers learn from teacher educators in their schools, in degree programs, and in specific teacher enhancement projects that are often provided by consultants. In the 1960s, teachers were trained in this way to use behavioral objectives; in the 1970s, they were taught Madeline Hunter's lesson structure; and currently, they are offered such topics as constructivism, alternative assessments, and cooperative learning. Teacher enhancement programs funded by federal agencies, such as the National Science Foundation and the U.S. Department of Education, tend to organize training by subject area and are often tied to innovations in curriculum or pedagogy.

Fourth, many teachers enroll in graduate programs. Some states require a master's degree or continuing education to maintain certification, and most school districts tie teachers' salaries to their level of education (Renyi, 1996). For the most part, teachers take graduate courses in education rather than in the subject matter of their teaching because of the lack of disciplinary graduate courses that are offered after school hours or during the summer.

Finally, teachers also learn about teaching in ways that are separate from their formal professional work. They learn about intellectual and moral development in their roles as parents. They learn about nondidactic forms of instruction through such activities as coaching (Lucido, 1988) and other youth-related work in their communities.

Because of the wide variety of ways in which teachers continue to learn about teaching and learning, it is difficult to generalize about or judge the quality of the teachers' learning experiences. One fact is clear, however: there are relatively few opportunities available if measured in financial terms. Overall, there is minimal public investment in formal opportunities for professional development for practicing teachers. Most school districts spend only between 1 and 3 percent of their operating budgets for professional development, even with salaries factored in. This lack of investment in personnel is unheard of either in leading corporations or in schools in other countries (Kearns, 1988).

QUALITY OF LEARNING OPPORTUNITIES

Even when resources are formally provided for teachers' continued development, opportunities for effective learning vary in terms of quality. In this section we analyze the quality of teachers' learning experiences from the perspectives on learning environments discussed in Chapter 6—namely, the degree to which they are learner centered, knowledge centered, assessment centered, and community centered (see Figure 6.1 in Chapter 6).

Learner-Centered Environments

As noted in Chapter 6, environments that are learner-centered attempt to build on the strengths, interests, and needs of the learners. Many efforts to facilitate teacher learning fall short in this regard; they often consist of required lectures and workshops that are not tailored to teachers' needs.

Two-thirds of U.S. teachers state that they have no say in what or how they learn in the professional development opportunities provided to them in schools (U.S. Department of Education, 1994).

The importance of learner-centered instruction can be illustrated by considering the case of Ellen and Molly, two teachers at a progressive urban high school. Ellen is a 25-year seasoned English teacher, a master at teaching writing, opening doors to literature for all students, and creating high standards for her students and ensuring that they achieve them. She is a strong mentor to beginning teachers. For her continuing professional growth, she craves meetings with other faculty members to develop curriculum. This is how she experiences strong intellectual camaraderie and maintains the interest and challenge she needs to keep vital in the classroom. Ellen wants the stimulus of talking about the big ideas with colleagues. She needs the adult interactions to balance and enhance her student interactions.

In contrast to Ellen, Molly is a second-year science teacher whose primary professional concerns involve classroom management and how to develop and maintain it. Molly must master these fundamentals before she can implement any new approach to curriculum, instruction, and assessment. She needs to see how to coordinate work on curriculum and assessment with the development of norms and responsibilities in the classroom that help all students learn. Obviously, Ellen and Molly have very different needs for professional growth, for becoming better teachers.

It can be difficult to meet the different needs of Ellen and Molly and all their colleagues. In a study of the development and implementation of *Minds on Physics* (Leonard et al., 1999a-f), it quickly became apparent to the development team and the evaluators that they did not have the resources available to tailor professional development to the needs of the individual teachers (Feldman and Kropf, 1997). The 37 teachers in the project taught at different levels (high school and community college), in different settings (urban, suburban, and rural), had different undergraduate majors and different amounts of graduate studies, and ranged from new teachers to 30-year veterans.

Some projects provide professional development opportunities that include different stages of participation. The Wisconsin Teacher Enhancement Program in Biology (WTEPB) provides teachers with multiple roles that change as they become more expert in teaching science. Betty Overland, an elementary teacher in Madison, went from avoiding the teaching of science to being "an enthusiastic missionary for reform in science in the elementary schools" (Renyi, 1996:51). She began by participating in a 2-week workshop. This led to her involvement with the members of the biology department at the University of Wisconsin, and she then borrowed their equipment and invited their faculty to visit her class. The next summer she was a facilitator for one of the classes offered to teachers by WTEPB, and she continued to participate in other workshops and served as a facilitator for others. Eventually, she found herself on a panel as an advocate for a new science education program (Renyi, 1996).

Other ways of dealing with diverse needs include encouraging teachers to form interest groups around particular topics and projects (see, e.g., Cognition and Technology Group at Vanderbilt, in press). New technologies provide opportunities for communication and on-line learning that can connect teachers with others who share their interests and needs (see Chapter 9).

Knowledge-Centered Environments

As discussed in Chapter 6, effective learning environments are knowledge centered as well as learner centered. Ideally, opportunities for teacher learning include a focus on pedagogical content knowledge (Shulman, 1966; see also Chapters 2 and 7), but many fall short of this ideal. For example, the "knowledge" taught by teachers to teachers and supplied by consultants is often not supported by research about learning (Barone et al., 1996). In addition, workshops for teachers often focus more on generic pedagogy (e.g., cooperative learning) than on the need to integrate pedagogy with the content of various disciplines.

A case study of Mrs. O illustrates the importance of helping teachers rethink their disciplinary knowledge as well as their teaching strategies. She attended several summer workshops that used the mathematics curriculum *Math Their Way* (Baratta-Lorton, 1976); the workshops introduced her to new teaching techniques. After the workshops she saw the transformation of her practice as complete as she made some changes in her teaching at the elementary school level that reflected the then-new California mathematics framework. However, she stopped short of rethinking her knowledge of mathematics and saw no need for additional education.

Mrs. O's lack of interest in continued learning seemed to be related to the nature of the workshops that she attended (Cohen, 1990). For Mrs. O to accept the new reform on a deeper level, she would have had to unlearn old mathematics, learn new concepts of teaching mathematics, and have a much more substantial understanding of mathematics itself. The workshops that Mrs. O attended provided her only with teaching techniques, not with the deep understanding of mathematics and mathematics teaching and learning that she would need to implement the reform as envisioned by policymakers.

Preliminary attempts to educate teachers to use *Minds on Physics* (Leonard et al., 1999a-f) also illustrate the difficulty of getting teachers to rethink the nature of their disciplines. Teachers were provided with an in-depth summer workshop, three academic year follow-ups, and contact with the curriculum developers through mail, electronic mail, and telephone. Even though the teachers changed their understanding of concepts, such as constructivism, and learned new teaching methods, such as collaborative group work, many of their fundamental beliefs about their students and about the purpose of high school physics did not change. For example, while the new curriculum focused on content organized around big ideas as a way to engender deep conceptual understanding of physics, the teachers believed that the purpose of their courses was to provide their students with an overview of all physics because their students would never take another physics course (Feldman and Kropf, 1997).

Several professional development projects for teachers use subject matter as the primary vehicle for learning; teachers learn how to teach a subject by focusing on their own experiences as learners. Examples include SummerMath (Schifter and Fosnot, 1993), the Bay Area and National Writing Project (Bay Area Writing Project, 1979; Freedman, 1985a, b), and the Chicago Teachers Academy for Mathematics and Science (Stake and Migotsky, 1995). In SummerMath, teachers solve mathematics problems together or actually participate in authoring texts. Teachers also write cases about their children's mathematics learning; this engages their own subject-matter knowledge—or lack thereof—which leads them to struggle with their own mathematics learning (Schifter and Fosnot, 1993).

In Project SEED (Science for Early Education Development), elementary school teachers in Pasadena were provided with opportunities to learn about science content and pedagogy by working with the curriculum kits that they would be using in the classroom. Teachers were introduced to content by experienced mentor teachers and scientists, who worked with them as they used the kits (Marsh and Sevilla, 1991).

It can be difficult for teachers to undertake the task of rethinking their subject matter. Learning involves making oneself vulnerable and taking risks, and this is not how teachers often see their role. Particularly in areas like mathematics and science, elementary teachers often lack confidence, and they worry about admitting that they don't know or understand for fear of colleagues' and administrators' reactions (see, e.g., Heaton, 1992; Ball and Rundquist, 1993; Peterson and Barnes, 1996; Lampert, 1998). In addition, teachers generally are accustomed to feeling efficacious—to knowing that they can affect students' learning—and they are accustomed to being in control. When they encourage students to actively explore issues and generate questions, it is almost inevitable that they will encounter questions that they cannot answer—and this can be threatening. Helping teachers become comfortable with the role of learner is very important. Providing them with access to subject-matter expertise is also extremely important. New developments in technology (see Chapter 9) provide avenues for helping teachers and their students gain wider access to expertise.

Assessment-Centered Environments

Environments that are assessment centered provide opportunities for learners to test their understanding by trying out things and receiving feedback. Such opportunities are important to teacher learning for a number of reasons. One is that teachers often don't know if certain ideas will work unless they are prompted to try them with their students and see what happens; see Box 8.1. In addition to providing evidence of success, feedback provides opportunities to clarify ideas and correct misconceptions. Especially important are opportunities to receive feedback from colleagues who observe attempts to implement new ideas in classrooms. Without feedback, it is difficult to correct potentially erroneous ideas.

A report from a group of researchers highlights the importance of classroom-based feedback (Cognition and Technology Group at Vanderbilt, 1997). They attempted to implement ideas for teaching that had been developed by several of their colleagues at different universities. The researchers were very familiar with the material and could easily recite relevant theory and data. However, once they faced the challenge of helping teachers implement the ideas in local classrooms in their area, they realized the need for

BOX 8.1 **"Exceptional Kids"**

> Mazie Jenkins was skeptical when first told that research shows that first-grade children can solve addition and subtraction word problems without being taught the procedures. When she saw videotapes of 5-year-old children solving word problems by counting and modeling, Mazie said they were exceptional kids because they could solve "difficult" word problems, such as:
>
> > You have five candy bars in your Halloween bag; the lady in the next house puts some more candy bars in your bag. Now you have eight candy bars. How many candy bars did the lady in the next house give you?
>
> Then Mazie tried out this problem with her first-grade class at the beginning of the year, and she excitedly reported, "My kids are exceptional too!" Mazie learned that, while she herself saw this problem as a "subtraction" problem—because she had been taught the procedure for doing the problem that way—her first graders solved the problem spontaneously, typically by counting out five unifix cubes (to represent candy bars), adding more cubes until they had eight, and then counting the number they had added to get to eight. Mazie's kids then proudly reported the answer as "three" (Carpenter et al., 1989).

much more guidance. They knew many facts about the colleagues' programs, but did not know how to translate them into action (see Chapter 2 for discussions of conditionalized expert knowledge). Without extended opportunities for more information and feedback, the researchers did not know how to proceed.

After several months, the researchers and their teacher collaborators began to feel comfortable with their attempts at implementation. The colleagues who had developed the new programs visited the classrooms in the researchers' city and provided feedback. There were numerous errors of implementation, which could be traced to an inadequate understanding of the new programs. The experience taught all participants a valuable lesson. The colleagues who had developed the programs realized that they had not been as clear as they should have been about their ideas and procedures. The researchers experienced the difficulty of implementing new programs and realized that their errors would have remained invisible without feedback about what was wrong.

Certification programs are being developed that are designed to help teachers reflect on and improve their practice. Suggestions for reflection help teachers focus on aspects of their teaching that they might otherwise have failed to notice. In addition, teachers preparing for certification often ask peers to provide feedback on their teaching and their ideas. Billie Hicklin, a seventh-grade teacher in North Carolina, was one of the first teachers to participate in the National Board certification process (Bunday and Kelly, 1996). She found that the structured reflection that was required for certification resulted in her making significant changes in her teaching practices and in the ways that she interacts with colleagues (Renyi, 1996).

Community-Centered Environments

Community-centered environments involve norms that encourage collaboration and learning. An important approach to enhancing teacher learning is to develop communities of practice, an approach that involves collaborative peer relationships and teachers' participation in educational research and practice (Lave and Wenger, 1991). Examples include the Bay Area Writing Project (1979); the Cognitively Guided Instruction Project (Carpenter and Fennema, 1992; Carpenter et al., 1989, 1996); Minstrell and Hunt's (Minstrell, 1989) physics and mathematics teacher group; the Annenberg Critical Friends Project; and Fredericksen and White (1994) "video clubs," where teachers share tapes of lessons they have taught and discuss the strengths and weaknesses of what they see.

As part of these communities, teachers share successes and failures with pedagogy and curriculum development. For example, the Annenberg Institute's critical friends groups are led by a teacher/coach, trained in process skills and diverse ways of looking at student work. The groups can be anything to which the teachers agree, but usually involve issues of student achievement, such as, "What is good work?" "How do we know?" and "How do we develop shared standards for good work?"

Some communities of practice are supported by school districts. For example, at the Dade Academy for the Teaching Arts (DATA) in Florida, "extern" teachers spend a 9-week sabbatical working with resident teachers, who have reduced teaching assignments at neighboring Miami Beach High School. The externs design their own programs, do research projects, and participate in group seminars. In DATA, the community of practice is supported by providing the extern teachers with sabbaticals, supporting the resident teachers through reduced loads, and by giving the program a home—portable classrooms next to Miami Beach High School (Renyi, 1996).

The notion of bringing teachers together to review student work in a nonjudgmental fashion is also embodied in the "Descriptive Review" (Carini, 1979). Again, the central questions involve looking deeply at student work, not trying to provide reasons (psychological, social, economic) that the student might not be producing strong academic work. This approach often uses student artwork to help teachers identify student strengths. Project Zero's "collaborative review process" (Perkins, 1992) for teachers builds on the descriptive review approach and adds some new elements as well, such as a variety of computer networks for teachers. Examples of computer networks include BreadNet, out of the Breadloaf Writing Project, LabNet (Ruopp, 1993), and Mathline (Cole, 1996). Other ways to foster collaboration include opportunities to score and discuss student essays or to compare and discuss student portfolios (Wiske, 1998).

Collaborative discussions become most valuable when two teachers are jointly involved in sense-making and understanding of the phenomena of learning (e.g., Peterson et al., 1989). For example, in creating a new functions-based approach to algebra teaching for all students, teacher colleagues at Holt High School report how important for learning it was for two teachers to "team" together in the same classroom and share decisions (Yerushalmy et al., 1990). Every day these two algebra teachers had to discuss and agree on what to do next. This joint decisionmaking required reflection and discussion on the texts of specific algebra problems, as well as discussion of students' understanding of functions, as reflected in the classroom discussions and in students' writings. Coming to joint decisions required these teachers to wrestle with issues of mathematics and mathematics learning around their own specific problems of practice as teachers, such as what constitutes valid evidence for students' understanding in the specific day-to-day situation.

Overall, two major themes emerge from studies of teacher collaborations: the importance of shared experiences and discourse around texts and data about student learning and a necessity for shared decisions. These findings are consistent with analyses of situated learning and discourse (Greeno et al., 1996); empirical studies of high school teachers' use of information in their work (Natriello et al., 1994), and models of assessment as situated discourse around texts (Case and Moss, 1996).

ACTION RESEARCH

Action research represents another approach to enhancing teacher learning by proposing ideas to a community of learners. Action research is an approach to professional development in which, typically, teachers spend 1 or more years working on classroom-based research projects. While action research has multiple forms and purposes, it is an important way for teachers to improve their teaching and their curricula, and there is also an assumption that what teachers learn through this process can be shared with others (Noffke, 1997). Action research contributes to sustained teacher learning and becomes a way for teachers to teach other teachers (Feldman, 1993). It encourages teachers to support each other's intellectual and pedagogical growth, and it increases the professional standing of teachers by recognizing their ability to add to knowledge about teaching. Ideally, active engagement in research on teaching and learning also helps set the stage for understanding the implications of new theories of how people learn.

The teachers of the Physics Teacher Action Research Group (PTARG) in the San Francisco Bay area practice a form of collaborative action research called enhanced normal practice (Feldman, 1996). In regular group meetings, the teachers discuss their students' work. Between the meetings they try out pedagogical and curricular ideas from the group. They then report to the group on successes and failures and critically analyze the implementation of the ideas. In addition to generating and sharing of pedagogical content knowledge, the PTARG teachers came to deeper understandings of their subject area (Feldman, 1993; see also Hollingsworth, 1994, on work with urban literacy teachers).

Action research can also be tailored to the level of expertise and the needs of the teachers, especially if the teachers set the goals for the research and work collaboratively. Because action research is a constructivist process set in a social situation, teachers' beliefs about learning, their students, and their conceptions of themselves as learners are explicitly examined, challenged, and supported. When action research is conducted in a collaborative mode among teachers, it fosters the growth of learning communities. In fact, some of these communities have flourished for as many as 20 years, such as the Philadelphia Teachers Learning Cooperative and the Classroom Action Research Network (Feldman, 1996; Hollingsworth, 1994; Cochran-Smith and Lytle, 1993).

Unfortunately, the use of action research as a model of sustained teacher learning is hampered by lack of time and other resources. Teachers in the United States are generally not provided with paid time for such professional activities as action research. To provide that time would require financial resources that are not available to most school districts. As a result, teachers either engage in action research on their own time, as part of credit-bearing courses, or as part of separately funded projects. Typically, when the course is over or when the project ends, teachers' formal action research ends. While teachers have claimed that they have incorporated action research into their practice in an informal manner, there is little research that has examined what that means.

The sustainability of action research is also hampered by the difference between practitioner research and academic research. If academicians are to encourage teachers to do action research, they need to have models that fit the temporal flow of school teaching (Feldman and Atkin, 1995) and rely on forms of validity that are appropriate to research in the practical domain (Feldman, 1994; Cochran-Smith and Lytle, 1993).

PRESERVICE EDUCATION

Preservice programs that prepare new teachers will play an especially important role during the next few decades (Darling-Hammond, 1997:162):

> The United States will need to hire 2 million teachers over the next decade to meet the demands of rapidly rising enrollments, growing retirements, and attrition that can reach 30% for beginning teachers in their initial years . . . . [All] will need to be prepared to teach an increasingly diverse group of learners to ever-higher standards of academic achievement.

Most of the nation's new teachers will come from teacher education programs that have considerable structural variation. First, teacher education can be an undergraduate major or a program that is in addition to an academic major. Second, there can be an expectation that the program can be completed within the traditional 4 years of undergraduate study or that it is a 5-year or masters degree program as advocated by the Holmes Group (1986). Third, programs for initial teacher preparation can be university or college based or located primarily in the field. Finally, programs can differ as to whether they are primarily academic programs or whether their main purpose is certification or licensing.

While programs can vary in these ways, they tend to have several components in common: some subject-matter preparation, usually liberal arts or general education for prospective elementary teachers and subject-matter concentration for prospective secondary teachers; a series of foundational courses, such as philosophy, sociology, history, psychology of education;

one or more developmental, learning, and cognitive psychology courses; methods ("how to") courses; and a sequence of field experiences (see Goodlad, 1990). What differs among the programs is the primacy of the different components, the instructors' goals for their program and their courses, and the attitudes and beliefs that students bring to them.

Four philosophical traditions of practice have dominated teacher education in the twentieth century (Zeichner and Liston, 1990:4):

1. an academic tradition that emphasizes teachers' knowledge of subject matter and their ability to transform that subject matter to promote student understanding;

2. a social efficiency tradition that emphasizes teachers' abilities to apply thoughtfully a "knowledge base" about teaching that has been generated through research on teaching;

3. a developmentalist tradition that stresses teachers' abilities to base their instruction on their direct knowledge of their students—their mental readiness for particular activities; and

4. a social reconstructionist tradition that emphasizes teachers' abilities to analyze social contexts in terms of their contribution to greater equality, justice, and elevation of the human condition in schooling and society.

Although these traditions can act as useful heuristics for understanding the guiding principles of particular teacher education programs, it is important to realize that most programs do not fit neatly within the categories (Zeichner, 1981). And even though these traditions underlie teacher education programs, students are often not aware of them explicitly (Zeichner and Liston, 1990). The actual experiences of many prospective teachers often obscure the philosophical or ideological notions that guide their preparatory years, which color evaluations of the quality of preservice experiences (see below).

The components of teacher education programs—collections of courses, field experiences, and student teaching—tend to be disjointed (Goodlad, 1990); they are often taught or overseen by people who have little ongoing communication with each other. Even when the components are efficiently organized, there may be no shared philosophical base among the faculty. Moreover, grading policies in college classes can undercut collaboration, and students rarely have a chance to form teams who stay together for a significant portion of their education (unlike the team approach to problem-based learning in medical schools (see, e.g., Barrows, 1985). Political factors have strong effects on teacher education. Many "misguided regulatory intrusions" (Goodlad, 1990:189)—from schools, colleges, accreditation boards, and state and federal departments of education—have a negative effect on teacher education programs. The regulations often interfere with attempts to develop coherent and innovative programs that can prepare teachers to teach. The majority of teachers are educated in state colleges and universities, the budgets of which are controlled by state legislators and governors, and they teach in public schools that are affected by local politics through school boards, as well as by the same statewide influences (Elmore and Sykes, 1992). It is not surprising that these many forces do not lead to the most innovative teacher education programs.

The National Commission on Teaching and America's Future (1996) identified several problems with current preservice teacher preparation programs:

- Inadequate time: 4-year undergraduate degrees make it difficult for prospective elementary teachers to learn subject matter and for prospective secondary teachers to learn about the nature of learners and learning.
- Fragmentation: The traditional program arrangement (foundations courses, developmental psychology sequence, methods courses, and field experiences) offers disconnected courses that novices are expected to pull together into some meaningful, coherent whole.
- Uninspired teaching methods: Although teachers are supposed to excite students about learning, teacher preparation methods courses are often lectures and recitation. So, prospective teachers who do not have hands-on, "minds-on" experiences with learning are expected to provide these kinds of experiences for students.
- Superficial curriculum: The need to fulfill certification requirements and degree requirements leads to programs that provide little depth in subject matter or in educational studies, such as research on teaching and learning. Not enough subject-matter courses are included in teachers' preparation.

The effects of these problems can be seen in the complaints that preservice teacher education students have about foundations courses that seem disjointed and irrelevant to practice, or are "too theoretical" and have no bearing on what "real" teachers do in "real" classrooms with "real" students. They also complain that methods courses are time consuming and without intellectual substance. When methods courses explore the theory and research bases for instructional methods and curricula, the students complain that they are not oriented enough toward practice.

These problems in preservice education impede lifelong learning in at least two ways. First, a message is sent to prospective teachers that research in education, whether on teaching or learning, has little to do with schooling and, therefore, that they do not need to learn about the findings from research. Second, the importance of viewing themselves as subject-matter experts is not emphasized to teachers—especially teachers in the early and middle grades: they fall into believing the old saw that "those who can, do;

those who can't, teach." Teachers are not encouraged to seek the knowledge and understanding that would allow them to teach academically rigorous curricula.

Even teachers who attend institutions that provide a strong preparation for teaching face major challenges after they graduate. They need to make the transition from a world dominated primarily by college courses, with only *some* supervised teaching experiences, to a world in which they are the teachers; hence, they face the challenge of transferring what they have learned. Yet even with strong levels of initial learning, transfer does not happen immediately nor automatically (see Chapter 3). People often need help in order to use relevant knowledge that they have acquired, and they usually need feedback and reflection so that they can try out and adapt their previously acquired skills and knowledge in new environments. These environments—the schools—have an extremely important effect on the beliefs, knowledge, and skills that new teachers will draw on. It is the difficult transition, in Lee Shulman's (1986) terms, from expert learner to novice teacher.

Many of the schools that teachers enter are organized in ways that are not consistent with new developments in the science of learning. The schools often favor "covering the curriculum," testing for isolated sets of skills and knowledge, and solo teaching, with limited use and understanding of new technologies (National Commission on Teaching and America's Future, 1996). When student teachers enter their first classrooms, the instructional methods, curricula, and resources can be very different from the ones they learned about in teacher education programs. So although prospective teachers are often anxious to begin their student teaching and find it the most satisfying aspect of their teacher preparation (Hollins, 1995), the dissonance between this experience and their course work supports the belief that educational theory and research have little to do with classroom practice.

Most new teachers are required to "sink or swim" in their initial teaching placement (National Commission on Teaching and America's Future, 1996:39). New teachers are often given the most challenging assignments—more students with special educational needs, the greatest number of class preparations (some outside of their field of expertise), and many extracurricular duties—and they are usually asked to take on these responsibilities with little or no support from administrators or senior colleagues. It is not surprising that turnover among new teachers is extremely high, particularly in the first 3 years of teaching.

CONCLUSION

Teachers are key to enhancing learning in schools. In order to teach in a manner consistent with new theories of learning, extensive learning opportunities for teachers are required.

We assume that what is known about learning applies to teachers as well as their students. Yet teacher learning is a relatively new topic of research, so there is not a great deal of data about it. Nevertheless, there are a number of rich case studies that investigate teachers' learning over extended time periods and these cases, plus other information, provide data on learning opportunities available to teachers from the perspective of what is known about how people learn.

Much of what constitutes the typical approaches to formal teacher professional development are antithetical to what research findings indicate as promoting effective learning. The typical workshops tend to occur once, deal with decontextualized information, and often do not resonate with teachers' perceived needs. By contrast, research evidence indicates that the most successful teacher professional development activities are those that are extended over time and encourage the development of teachers' learning communities. These kinds of activities have been accomplished by creating opportunities for shared experiences and discourse around shared texts and data about student learning, and focus on shared decisionmaking. The learning communities of teachers also allow for differing kinds of background training and for variations in their readiness to learn. Successful programs involve teachers in learning activities that are similar to ones that they will use with their students.

Many learning opportunities for teachers fall short when viewed from the perspectives of being learner, knowledge, assessment, and community centered. But there are examples of successful programs that appear to fit these conditions quite well. Many programs for preservice teachers also fall short of providing the kinds of learning experiences suggested by new developments in the science of learning. They need well-defined goals for learning, beliefs about how people learn that are grounded in theory, and a rigorous academic curriculum that emphasizes depth of understanding.

While the flaws of preservice and inservice programs have serious consequences for how well teachers are prepared to begin teaching, they may also significantly affect teachers' lifelong learning and development as professionals. In particular, the dissonance between what is taught in college courses and what happens in classrooms can lead to later rejection of educational research and theory by teachers. This is due, in part, to the ways in which they have been taught in the disciplines and how their colleagues teach. Although teachers are urged to use student-centered, constructivist, depth-versus-breadth approaches in their education classes, new teachers often see traditional teaching approaches in use at the college level and in the classroom next door. Beginning teachers are especially influenced by the nature of the schools in which they begin their teaching.

Successful learning for teachers requires a continuum of coordinated efforts that range from preservice education to early teaching to opportunities for lifelong development as professionals. Creating such opportunities, built out of the knowledge base from the science of learning, represents a major challenge, but it is not an impossible task.

9

Technology to Support Learning

Attempts to use computer technologies to enhance learning began with the efforts of pioneers such as Atkinson and Suppes (e.g., Atkinson, 1968; Suppes and Morningstar, 1968). The presence of computer technology in schools has increased dramatically since that time, and predictions are that this trend will continue to accelerate (U.S. Department of Education, 1994). The romanticized view of technology is that its mere presence in schools will enhance student learning and achievement. In contrast is the view that money spent on technology, and time spent by students using technology, are money and time wasted (see Education Policy Network, 1997). Several groups have reviewed the literature on technology and learning and concluded that it has great potential to enhance student achievement and teacher learning, but only if it is used appropriately (e.g., Cognition and Technology Group at Vanderbilt, 1996; President's Committee of Advisors on Science and Technology, 1997; Dede, 1998).

What is now known about learning provides important guidelines for uses of technology that can help students and teachers develop the competencies needed for the twenty-first century. The new technologies provide opportunities for creating learning environments that extend the possibilities of "old"—but still useful—technologies—books; blackboards; and linear, one-way communication media, such as radio and television shows—as well as offering new possibilities. Technologies do not guarantee effective learning, however. Inappropriate uses of technology can hinder learning—for example, if students spend most of their time picking fonts and colors for multimedia reports instead of planning, writing, and revising their ideas. And everyone knows how much time students can waste surfing the Internet. Yet many aspects of technology make it easier to create environments that fit the principles of learning discussed throughout this volume.

Because many new technologies are interactive (Greenfield and Cocking, 1996), it is now easier to create environments in which students can learn by doing, receive feedback, and continually refine their understanding and build new knowledge (Barron et al., 1998; Bereiter and Scardamalia,

1993; Hmelo and Williams, 1998; Kafai, 1995; Schwartz et al., 1999). The new technologies can also help people visualize difficult-to-understand concepts, such as differentiating heat from temperature (Linn et al., 1996). Students can work with visualization and modeling software that is similar to the tools used in nonschool environments, increasing their understanding and the likelihood of transfer from school to nonschool settings (see Chapter 3). These technologies also provide access to a vast array of information, including digital libraries, data for analysis, and other people who provide information, feedback, and inspiration. They can enhance the learning of teachers and administrators, as well as that of students, and increase connections between schools and the communities, including homes.

In this chapter we explore how new technologies can be used in five ways:

- bringing exciting curricula based on real-world problems into the classroom;
- providing scaffolds and tools to enhance learning;
- giving students and teachers more opportunities for feedback, reflection, and revision;
- building local and global communities that include teachers, administrators, students, parents, practicing scientists, and other interested people; and
- expanding opportunities for teacher learning.

NEW CURRICULA

An important use of technology is its capacity to create new opportunities for curriculum and instruction by bringing real-world problems into the classroom for students to explore and solve; see Box 9.1. Technology can help to create an active environment in which students not only solve problems, but also find their own problems. This approach to learning is very different from the typical school classrooms, in which students spend most of their time learning facts from a lecture or text and doing the problems at the end of the chapter.

Learning through real-world contexts is not a new idea. For a long time, schools have made sporadic efforts to give students concrete experiences through field trips, laboratories, and work-study programs. But these activities have seldom been at the heart of academic instruction, and they have not been easily incorporated into schools because of logistical constraints and the amount of subject material to be covered. Technology offers powerful tools for addressing these constraints, from video-based problems and computer simulations to electronic communications systems that connect

BOX 9.1   **Bringing Real-World Problems to Classrooms**

Children in a Tennessee middle-school math class have just seen a video adventure from the Jasper Woodbury series about how architects work to solve community problems, such as designing safe places for children to play. The video ends with this challenge to the class to design a neighborhood playground:

Narrator: Trenton Sand and Lumber is donating 32 cubic feet of sand for the sandbox and is sending over the wood and fine gravel. Christina and Marcus just have to let them know exactly how much they'll need. Lee's Fence Company is donating 280 feet of fence. Rodriguez Hardware is contributing a sliding surface, which they'll cut to any length, and swings for physically challenged children. The employees of Rodriguez want to get involved, so they're going to put up the fence and help build the playground equipment. And Christina and Marcus are getting their first jobs as architects, starting the same place Gloria did 20 years ago, designing a playground.

Students in the classroom help Christina and Marcus by designing swingsets, slides, and sandboxes, and then building models of their playground. As they work through this problem, they confront various issues of arithmetic, geometry, measurement, and other subjects. How do you draw to scale? How do you measure angles? How much pea gravel do we need? What are the safety requirements?

Assessments of students' learning showed impressive gains in their understanding of these and other geometry concepts (e.g., Cognition and Technology Group at Vanderbilt, 1997). In addition, students improved their abilities to work with one another and to communicate their design ideas to real audiences (often composed of interested adults). One year after engaging in these activities, students remembered them vividly and talked about them with pride (e.g., Barron et al., 1998).

classrooms with communities of practitioners in science, mathematics, and other fields (Barron et al., 1995).

A number of video- and computer-based learning programs are now in use, with many different purposes. The Voyage of the Mimi, developed by Bank Street College, was one of the earliest attempts to use video and computer technology to introduce students to real-life problems (e.g., Char and Hawkins, 1987): students "go to sea" and solve problems in the context of learning about whales and the Mayan culture of the Yucatan. More recent series include the Jasper Woodbury Problem Solving Series (Cognition and Technology Group at Vanderbilt, 1997), 12 interactive video environments that present students with challenges that require them to understand and apply important concepts in mathematics; see the example in Box 9.2. Students who work with the series have shown gains in mathematical problem solving, communication abilities, and attitudes toward mathematics (e.g., Barron et al., 1998; Crews et al., 1997; Cognition and Technology Group at Vanderbilt, 1992, 1993, 1994, 1997; Vye et al., 1998).

New learning programs are not restricted to mathematics and science. Problem-solving environments have also been developed that help students better understand workplaces. For example, in a banking simulation, students assume roles, such as the vice president of a bank, and learn about the knowledge and skills needed to perform various duties (Classroom Inc., 1996).

The interactivity of these technology environments is a very important feature for learning. Interactivity makes it easy for students to revisit specific parts of the environments to explore them more fully, to test ideas, and to receive feedback. Noninteractive environments, like linear videotapes, are much less effective for creating contexts that students can explore and reexamine, both individually and collaboratively.

Another way to bring real-world problems into the classroom is by connecting students with working scientists (Cohen, 1997). In many of these student-scientist partnerships, students collect data that are used to understand global issues; a growing number of them involve students from geographically dispersed schools who interact through the Internet. For example, Global Lab supports an international community of student researchers from more than 200 schools in 30 countries who construct new knowledge about their local and global environments (Tinker and Berenfeld, 1993, 1994). Global Lab classrooms select aspects of their local environments to study. Using shared tools, curricula, and methodologies, students map, describe, and monitor their sites, collect and share data, and situate their local findings into a broader, global context. After participating in a set of 15 skill-building activities during their first semester, Global Lab students begin advanced research studies in such areas as air and water pollution, background radiation, biodiversity, and ozone depletion. The global perspective helps learners identify environmental phenomena that can be observed around the world, including a decrease in tropospheric ozone levels in places where vegetation is abundant, a dramatic rise of indoor carbon dioxide levels by the end of the school day, and the substantial accumulation of nitrates in certain vegetables. Once participants see significant patterns in their data, this "telecollaborative" community of students, teachers, and scientists tackles the most rigorous aspects of science—designing experiments, conducting peer reviews, and publishing their findings.

BOX 9.2   Problem Solving and Attitudes

Students in classrooms in nine states received opportunities to solve four Jasper adventures distributed throughout the year. The average total time spent solving Jasper adventures ranged from 3 to 4 weeks. The students were compared with non-Jasper comparison classes on standardized test scores of mathematics, problems requiring complex problem solving, and attitudes toward mathematics and complex challenges. With no losses in standardized test scores, both boys and girls in the Jasper classrooms showed better complex problem solving and had more positive attitudes toward mathematics and complex challenges (see Cognition and Technology Group at Vanderbilt, 1992; Pellegrino et al., 1991).

The graphs show scores for Jasper and comparison students on questions that asked them to (a) identify the key data and steps needed to solve complex problems, (b) evaluate possible solutions to these problems, and (c) indicate their self-confidence with respect to mathematics, their belief in the utility of mathematics, their current interest in mathematics, and their feelings about complex math challenges. Figure 9.1 shows positive attitude changes from the beginning to the end of the school year for students in the interactive video challenge series, with negative changes falling below the midline of the graph, as shown for most of the students in the comparison groups. Figures 9.2 and 9.3 indicate positive changes for Jasper-video students' planning skills growth and comprehension on the problem-solving challenges. Clearly, the interactive video materials had positive effects on children's problem solving and comprehension.

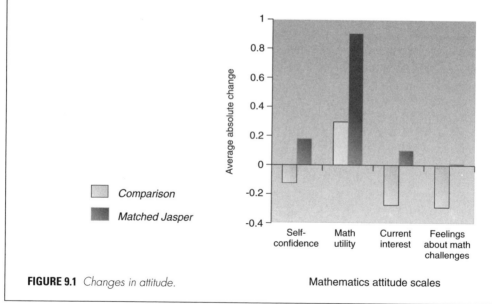

FIGURE 9.1 *Changes in attitude.*

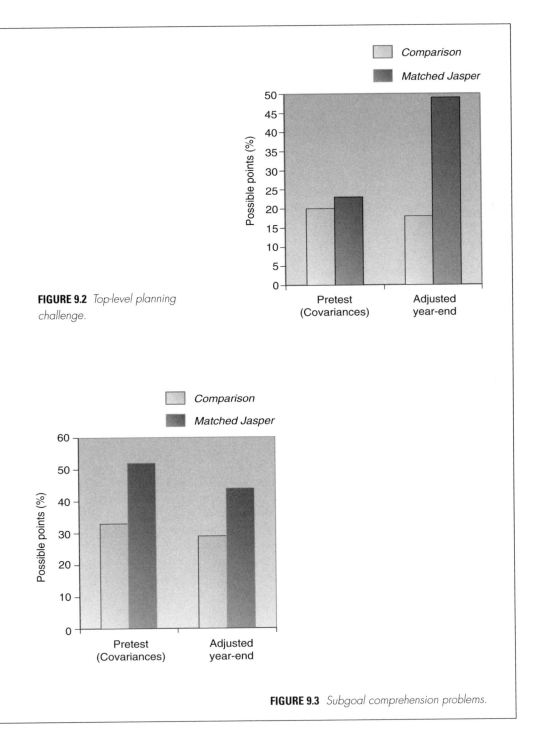

FIGURE 9.2 *Top-level planning challenge.*

FIGURE 9.3 *Subgoal comprehension problems.*

Similar approaches have been used in astronomy, ornithology, language arts, and other fields (Bonney and Dhondt, 1997; Riel, 1992; University of California Regents, 1997). These collaborative experiences help students understand complex systems and concepts, such as multiple causes and interactions among different variables. Since the ultimate goal of education is to prepare students to become competent adults and lifelong learners, there is a strong argument for electronically linking students not just with their peers, but also with practicing professionals. Increasingly scientists and other professionals are establishing electronic "collaboratories" (Lederberg and Uncapher, 1989), through which they define and conduct their work (e.g., Finholt and Sproull, 1990; Galegher et al., 1990). This trend provides both a justification and a medium for establishing virtual communities for learning purposes.

Through Project GLOBE (Global Learning and Observations to Benefit the Environment), thousands of students in grades kindergarten through 12 (K-12) from over 2,000 schools in more than 34 countries are gathering data about their local environments (Lawless and Coppola, 1996). Students collect data in five different earth science areas, including atmosphere, hydrology, and land cover, using protocols specified by principal investigators from major research institutions. Students submit their data through the Internet to a GLOBE data archive, which both the scientists and the students use to perform their analyses. A set of visualization tools provided on the GLOBE World Wide Web site enables students to see how their own data fit with those collected elsewhere. Students in GLOBE classrooms demonstrate higher knowledge and skill levels on assessments of environmental science methods and data interpretation than their peers who have not participated in the program (Means et al., 1997).

Emerging technologies and new ideas about teaching are being combined to reshape precollege science education in the Learning Through Collaborative Visualization (CoVis) Project (Pea, 1993a; Pea et al., 1997). Over wideband networks, middle and high school students from more than 40 schools collaborate with other students at remote locations. Thousands of participating students study atmospheric and environmental sciences—including topics in meteorology and climatology—through project-based activities. Through these networks, students also communicate with "telementors"—university researchers and other experts. Using scientific visualization software, specially modified for learning, students have access to the same research tools and datasets that scientists use.

In one 5-week activity, "Student Conference on Global Warming," supported by curriculum units, learner-centered scientific visualization tools and data, and assessment rubrics available through the CoVis GeoSciences web server, students across schools and states evaluate the evidence for global warming and consider possible trends and consequences (Gordin et al.,

1996). Learners are first acquainted with natural variation in climatic temperature, human-caused increases in atmospheric carbon dioxide, and uses of spreadsheets and scientific visualization tools for inquiry. These staging activities specify themes for open-ended collaborative learning projects to follow. In laying out typical questions and data useful to investigate the potential impact of global warming on a country or a country's potential impact on global warming, a general framework is used in which students specialize by selecting a country, its specific data, and the particular issue for their project focus (e.g., rise in carbon-dioxide emissions due to recent growth, deforestation, flooding due to rising sea levels). Students then investigate either a global issue or the point of view of a single country. The results of their investigations are shared in project reports within and across schools, and participants consider current results of international policy in light of their project findings.

Working with practitioners and distant peers on projects with meaning beyond the school classroom is a great motivator for K-12 students. Students are not only enthusiastic about what they are doing, they also produce some impressive intellectual achievements when they can interact with meteorologists, geologists, astronomers, teachers, or computer scientists (Means et al., 1996; O'Neill et al., 1996; O'Neill, 1996; Wagner, 1996).

SCAFFOLDS AND TOOLS

Many technologies function as scaffolds and tools to help students solve problems. This was foreseen long ago: in a prescient 1945 essay in the *Atlantic Monthly*, Vannevar Bush, science adviser to President Roosevelt, depicted the computer as a general-purpose symbolic system that could serve clerical and other supportive research functions in the sciences, in work, and for learning, thus freeing the human mind to pursue its creative capacities.

In the first generation of computer-based technologies for classroom use, this tool function took the rather elementary form of electronic "flashcards" that students used to practice discrete skills. As applications have spilled over from other sectors of society, computer-based learning tools have become more sophisticated (Atkinson, 1968; Suppes and Morningstar, 1968). They now include calculators, spreadsheets, graphing programs, function probes (e.g., Roschelle and Kaput, 1996), "mathematical supposers" for making and checking conjectures (e.g., Schwartz, 1994), and modeling programs for creating and testing models of complex phenomena (Jackson et al., 1996). In the Middle School Mathematics Through Applications Projects (MMAP), developed at the Institute for Research on Learning, innovative software tools are used for exploring concepts in algebra through such problems as designing insulation for arctic dwellings (Goldman and Moschkovich,

1995). In the Little Planet Literacy Series, computer software helps to move students through the phases of becoming better writers (Cognition and Technology Group at Vanderbilt, 1998a, b). For example, in the Little Planet Literacy Series, engaging video-based adventures encourage kindergarten, first-, and second-grade students to write books to solve challenges posed at the end of the adventures. In one of the challenges, students need to write a book in order to save the creatures on the Little Planet from falling prey to the wiles of an evil character named Wongo.

The challenge for education is to design technologies for learning that draw both from knowledge about human cognition and from practical applications of how technology can facilitate complex tasks in the workplace. These designs use technologies to scaffold thinking and activity, much as training wheels allow young bike riders to practice cycling when they would fall without support. Like training wheels, computer scaffolding enables learners to do more advanced activities and to engage in more advanced thinking and problem solving than they could without such help. Cognitive technologies were first used to help students learn mathematics (Pea, 1985) and writing (Pea and Kurland, 1987); a decade later, a multitude of projects use cognitive scaffolds to promote complex thinking, design, and learning in the sciences, mathematics, and writing.

The Belvedere system, for example, is designed to teach science-related public policy issues to high school students who lack deep knowledge of many science domains, have difficulty zeroing in on the key issues in a complex scientific debate, and have trouble recognizing abstract relationships that are implicit in scientific theories and arguments (Suthers et al., 1995). Belvedere uses graphics with specialized boxes to represent different types of relationships among ideas that provide scaffolding to support students' reasoning about science-related issues. As students use boxes and links within Belvedere to represent their understanding of an issue, an on-line adviser gives hints to help them improve the coverage, consistency, and evidence for their arguments (Paolucci et al., 1996).

Scaffolded experiences can be structured in different ways. Some research educators advocate an apprenticeship model, whereby an expert practitioner first models the activity while the learner observes, then scaffolds the learner (with advice and examples), then guides the learner in practice, and gradually tapers off support and guidance until the apprentice can do it alone (Collins et al., 1989). Others argue that the goal of enabling a solo approach is unrealistic and overrestrictive since adults often need to use tools or other people to accomplish their work (Pea, 1993b; Resnick, 1987). Some even contend that well-designed technological tools that support complex activities create a truly human-machine symbiosis and may reorganize components of human activity into different structures than they had in pretechnological designs (Pea, 1985). Although there are varying views on the exact goals and on how to assess the benefits of scaffolding technologies, there is agreement that the new tools make it possible for people to perform and learn in far more complex ways than ever before.

In many fields, experts are using new technologies to represent data in new ways—for example, as three-dimensional virtual models of the surface of Venus or of a molecular structure, either of which can be electronically created and viewed from any angle. Geographical information systems, to take another example, use color scales to visually represent such variables as temperature or rainfall on a map. With these tools, scientists can discern patterns more quickly and detect relationships not previously noticed (e.g., Brodie et al., 1992; Kaufmann and Smarr, 1993).

Some scholars assert that simulations and computer-based models are the most powerful resources for the advancement and application of mathematics and science since the origins of mathematical modeling during the Renaissance (Glass and Mackey, 1988; Haken, 1981). The move from a static model in an inert medium, like a drawing, to dynamic models in interactive media that provide visualization and analytic tools is profoundly changing the nature of inquiry in mathematics and science. Students can visualize alternative interpretations as they build models that can be rotated in ways that introduce different perspectives on the problems. These changes affect the kinds of phenomena that can be considered and the nature of argumentation and acceptable evidence (Bachelard, 1984; Holland, 1995).

The same kinds of computer-based visualization and analysis tools that scientists use to detect patterns and understand data are now being adapted for student use. With probes attached to microcomputers, for example, students can do real-time graphing of such variables as acceleration, light, and sound (Friedler et al., 1990; Linn, 1991; Nemirovsky et al., 1995; Thornton and Sokoloff, 1998). The ability of the human mind to quickly process and remember visual information suggests that concrete graphics and other visual representations of information can help people learn (Gordin and Pea, 1995), as well as help scientists in their work (Miller, 1986).

A variety of scientific visualization environments for precollege students and teachers have been developed by the CoVis Project (Pea, 1993a; Pea et al., 1997). Classrooms can collect and analyze real-time weather data (Fishman and D'Amico, 1994; University of Illinois, Urbana-Champaign, 1997) or 25 years of Northern Hemisphere climate data (Gordin et al., 1994). Or they can investigate the global greenhouse effect (Gordin et al., 1996). As described above, students with new technological tools can communicate across a network, work with datasets, develop scientific models, and conduct collaborative investigations into meaningful science issues.

Since the late 1980s, cognitive scientists, educators, and technologists have suggested that learners might develop a deeper understanding of phenomena in the physical and social worlds if they could build and manipulate models of these phenomena (e.g., Roberts and Barclay, 1988). These speculations are now being tested in classrooms with technology-based modeling tools. For example, the STELLA modeling environment, which grew out of research on systems dynamics at the Massachusetts Institute of Technology (Forrester, 1991), has been widely used for instruction at both the undergraduate and precollege level, in fields as diverse as population ecology and history (Clauset et al., 1987; Coon, 1988; Mintz, 1993; Steed, 1992; Mandinach, 1989; Mandinach et al., 1988).

The educational software and exploration and discovery activities developed for the GenScope Project use simulations to teach core topics in genetics as part of precollege biology. The simulations move students through a hierarchy of six key genetic concepts: DNA, cell, chromosome, organism, pedigree, and population (Neumann and Horwitz, 1997). GenScope also uses an innovative hypermodel that allows students to retrieve real-world data to build models of the underlying physical process. Evaluations of the program among high school students in urban Boston found that students not only were enthusiastic about learning this complex subject, but had also made significant conceptual developments.

Students are using interactive computer microworlds to study force and motion in the Newtonian world of mechanics (Hestenes, 1992; White, 1993). Through the medium of interactive computer microworlds, learners acquire hands-on and minds-on experience and, thus, a deeper understanding of science. Sixth graders who use computer-based learning tools develop a better conceptual understanding of acceleration and velocity than many 12th-grade physics students (White, 1993); see Box 9.3. In another project, middle school students employ easy-to-use computer-based tools (Model-It) to build qualitative models of systems, such as the water quality and algae levels in a local stream. Students can insert data they have collected into the model, observe outcomes, and generate what if scenarios to get a better understanding of the interrelationships among key variables (Jackson et al., 1996).

In general, technology-based tools can enhance student performance when they are integrated into the curriculum and used in accordance with knowledge about learning (e.g., see especially White and Frederiksen, 1998). But the mere existence of these tools in the classroom provides no guarantee that student learning will improve; they have to be part of a coherent education approach.

FEEDBACK, REFLECTION, AND REVISION

Technology can make it easier for teachers to give students feedback about their thinking and for students to revise their work. Initially, teachers working with the Jasper Woodbury playground adventure (described above) had trouble finding time to give students feedback about their playground

BOX 9.3   The Use of ThinkerTools in Physics Instruction

The ThinkerTools Inquiry Curriculum uses an innovative software tool that allows experimenters to perform physics experiments under a variety of conditions and compare the results with experiments performed with actual objects. The curriculum emphasizes a metacognitive approach to instruction (see Chapters 2, 3, and 4) by using an inquiry cycle that helps students see where they are in the inquiry process, plus processes called reflective assessment in which students reflect on their own and each others' inquiries.

Experiments conducted with typical seventh-, eighth-, and ninth-grade students in urban, public middle schools revealed that the software modeling tools made the difficult subject of physics understandable as well as interesting to a wide range of students. Students not only learned about physics, but also about processes of inquiry.

We found that, regardless of their lower grade levels (7-9) and their lower pretest scores, students who had participated in ThinkerTools outperformed high school physics students (grades 11-12) on qualitative problems in which they were asked to apply the basic principles of Newtonian mechanics to real-world situations. In general, this inquiry-oriented, model-based, constructivist approach to science education appears to make science interesting and accessible to a wider range of students than is possible with traditional approaches (White and Fredericksen, 1998:90-91).

designs, but a simple computer interface cut in half the time it took teachers to provide feedback (see, e.g., Cognition and Technology Group at Vanderbilt, 1997). An interactive Jasper Adventuremaker software program allows students to suggest solutions to a Jasper adventure, then see simulations of the effects of their solutions. The simulations had a clear impact on the quality of the solutions that students generated subsequently (Crews et al., 1997). Opportunities to interact with working scientists, as discussed above, also provide rich experiences for learning from feedback and revision (White and Fredericksen, 1994). The SMART (Special Multimedia Arenas for Refining Thinking) Challenge Series provides multiple technological resources for feedback and revision. SMART has been tested in various contexts, including the Jasper challenge. When its formative assessment resources are added to these curricula, students achieve at higher levels than without them (e.g. Barron et al., 1998; Cognition and Technology Group at Vanderbilt, 1994,

BOX 9.4   A Program for Diagnosing Preconceptions in Physics

A computer-based DIAGNOSER program has helped teachers increase student achievement in high school physics (Hunt and Minstrell, 1994). The program assesses students' beliefs (preconceptions) about various physical phenomena—beliefs that often fit their everyday experiences but are not consistent with physicists' views of the world (see Chapters 2, 3, 6, and 7). Given particular beliefs, sets of activities are recommended that help students reinterpret phenomena from a physicist's perspective. Teachers incorporate information from the diagnoser to guide how they teach. Data from experimental and comparison classrooms on students' understanding of important concepts in physics show strong superiority for those in the experimental groups; see the graph below.

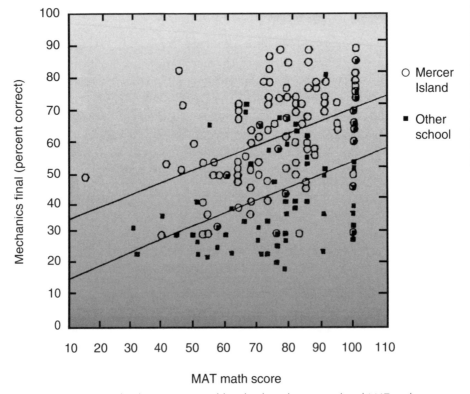

FIGURE 9.4   *Mercer Island versus comparable school mechanics vinal and MAT math scores. SOURCE: Hunt and Minstrell (1994).*

1997; Vye et al., 1998). Another way of using technology to support formative assessment is described in Box 9.4.

Classroom communication technologies, such as Classtalk, can promote more active learning in large lecture classes and, if used appropriately, highlight the reasoning processes that students use to solve problems (see Chapter 7). This technology allows an instructor to prepare and display problems that the class works on collaboratively. Students enter answers (individually or as a group) via palm-held input devices, and the technology collects, stores, and displays histograms (bar graphs of how many students preferred each problem solution) of the class responses. This kind of tool can provide useful feedback to students and the teacher on how well the students understand the concepts being covered and whether they can apply them in novel contexts (Mestre et al., 1997).

Like other technologies, however, Classtalk does not guarantee effective learning. The visual histograms are intended to promote two-way communication in large lecture classes: as a springboard for class discussions in which students justify the procedures they used to arrive at their answers, listen critically to the arguments of others, and refute them or offer other reasoning strategies. But the technology could be used in ways that have nothing to do with this goal. If, for example, a teacher used Classtalk merely as an efficient device to take attendance or administer conventional quizzes, it would not enhance two-way communication or make students' reasoning more visible. With such a use, the opportunity to expose students to varying perspectives on problem solving and the various arguments for different problem solutions would be lost. Thus, effective use of technology involves many teacher decisions and direct forms of teacher involvement.

Peers can serve as excellent sources of feedback. Over the last decade, there have been some very successful and influential demonstrations of how computer networks can support groups of students actively engaged in learning and reflection. Computer-Supported Intentional Learning Environments (CSILE) provide opportunities for students to collaborate on learning activities by working through a communal database that has text and graphics capabilities (Scardamalia et al., 1989; Scardamalia and Bereiter, 1991, 1993; Scardamalia et al., 1994). Within this networked multimedia environment (now distributed as Knowledge Forum), students create "notes" that contain an idea or piece of information about the topic they are studying. These notes are labeled by categories, such as question or new learning, that other students can search and comment on; see Box 9.5. With support from the instructor, these processes engage students in dialogues that integrate information and contributions from various sources to produce knowledge. CSILE also includes guidelines for formulating and testing conjectures and prototheories. CSILE has been used in elementary, secondary, and postgraduate classrooms for science, history, and social studies. Students in

BOX 9.5 **Slaminan Number System**

An example of how technology-supported conversations can help students refine each other's thinking comes from an urban elementary classroom. Students worked in small groups to design different aspects of a hypothetical culture of rain forest dwellers (Means et al., 1995).

The group that was charged with developing a number system for the hypothetical culture posted the following entry:

This is the slaminan's number system. It is a base 10 number system too. It has a pattern to it. The number of lines increase up to five then it goes upside down all the way to 10.

Another student group in the same classroom reviewed this CSILE posting and displayed impressive analytic skills (as well as good social skills) in a response pointing out the need to extend the system:

We all like the number system but we want to know how the number 0 looks like, and you can do more numbers not just 10 like we have right now.

Many students in this classroom speak a language other than English in their homes. CSILE provides opportunities to express their ideas in English and to receive feedback from their peers.

CSILE classes do better on standardized tests and portfolio entries and show greater depth in their explanations than students in classes without CSILE (see, e.g., Scardamalia and Bereiter, 1993). Furthermore, students at all ability levels participate effectively: in fact, in classrooms using the technology in the most collaborative fashion, CSILE's positive effects were particularly strong for lower- and middle-ability groups (Bryson and Scardamalia, 1991).

As one of its many uses to support learning, the Internet is increasingly being used as a forum for students to give feedback to each other. In the GLOBE Project (described above), students inspect each others' data on the project web site and sometimes find readings they believe may be in error. Students use the electronic messaging system to query the schools that report suspicious data about the circumstances under which they made their measurement; for another kind of use, see Box 9.6.

An added advantage of networked technologies for communication is that they help make thinking visible. This core feature of the cognitive apprenticeship model of instruction (Collins, 1990) is exemplified in a broad range of instructional programs and has a technological manifestation, as well (see, e.g., Collins, 1990; Collins and Brown, 1988; Collins et al., 1989). By prompting learners to articulate the steps taken during their thinking processes, the software creates a record of thought that learners can use to reflect on their work and teachers can use to assess student progress. Several projects expressly include software designed to make learners' thinking visible. In CSILE, for example, as students develop their communal hypermedia database with text and graphics, teachers can use the database as a record of students' thoughts and electronic conversations over time. Teachers can browse the database to review both their students' emerging understanding of key concepts and their interaction skills (Means and Olson, 1995b).

The CoVis Project developed a networked hypermedia database, the collaboratory notebook, for a similar purpose. The collaboratory notebook is divided into electronic workspaces, called notebooks, that can be used by students working together on a specific investigation (Edelson et al., 1995). The notebook provides options for making different kinds of pages—questions, conjectures, evidence for, evidence against, plans, steps in plans, information, and commentary. Using the hypermedia system, students can pose a question, then link it to competing conjectures about the questions posed by different students (perhaps from different sites) and to a plan for investigating the question. Images and documents can be electronically "attached" to pages. Using the notebook shortened the time between students' preparation of their laboratory notes and the receipt of feedback from their teachers (Edelson et al., 1995). Similar functions are provided by SpeakEasy, a software tool used to structure and support dialogues among engineering students and their instructors (Hoadley and Bell, 1996).

Sophisticated tutoring environments that pose problems are also now available and give students feedback on the basis of how experts reason and organize their knowledge in physics, chemistry, algebra, computer programming, history, and economics (see Chapter 2). With this increased understanding has come an interest in: testing theories of expert reasoning by translating them into computer programs, and using computer-based expert systems as part of a larger program to teach novices. Combining an expert model with a student model—the system's representation of the student's level of knowledge—and a pedagogical model that drives the system has produced intelligent tutoring systems, which seek to combine the advantages of customized one-on-one tutoring with insights from cognitive research about expert performance, learning processes, and naive reasoning (Lesgold et al., 1990; Merrill et al., 1992).

A variety of computer-based cognitive tutors have been developed for algebra, geometry, and LISP programming (Anderson et al., 1995). These cognitive tutors have resulted in a complex profile of achievement gains for the students, depending on the nature of the tutor and the way it is inte-

BOX 9.6 **Monsters, Mondrian, and Me**

As part of the Challenge 2000 Multimedia Project, elementary teachers Lucinda Surber, Cathy Chowenhill, and Page McDonald teamed up to design and execute an extended collaboration between fourth-grade classes at two elementary schools. In a unit they called "Monsters, Mondrian, and Me," students were directed to describe a picture so well in an e-mail message that their counterparts in the other classroom could reproduce it. The project illustrates how telecommunication can both make clear the need for clear, precise writing and provide a forum for feedback from peers.

During the Monster phase of the project, students in the two classes worked in pairs first to invent and draw monsters (such as "Voyager 999," "Fat Belly," and "Bug Eyes") and then to compose paragraphs describing the content of their drawings (e.g., "Under his body he has four purple legs with three toes on each one"). Their goal was to provide a complete and clear enough description that students in the other class could reproduce the monster without ever having seen it. The descriptive paragraphs were exchanged through electronic mail, and the matched student pairs made drawings based on their understanding of the descriptions.

The final step of this phase involved the exchange of the "second-generation drawings" so that the students who had composed the descriptive paragraphs could reflect on their writing, seeing where ambiguity or incomplete specification led to a different interpretation on the part of their readers.

The students executed the same steps of writing, exchange of paragraphs, drawing, and reflection, in the Mondrian stage, this time starting with the art of abstract expressionists such as Mondrian, Klee, and Rothko. In the Me stage, students studied self-portraits of famous painters and then produced portraits of themselves, which they attempted to describe with enough detail so that their distant partners could produce portraits matching their own.

grated into the classroom (Anderson et al., 1990, 1995); see Boxes 9.7 and 9.8.

Another example of the tutoring approach is the Sherlock Project, a computer-based environment for teaching electronics troubleshooting to Air Force technicians who work on a complex system involving thousands of parts (e.g., Derry and Lesgold, 1997; Gabrys et al., 1993). A simulation of this complex system was combined with an expert system or coach that offered advice when learners reached impasses in their troubleshooting attempts; and with reflection tools that allowed users to replay their performance and try out possible improvements. In several field tests of techni-

By giving students a distant audience for their writing (their partners at the other school), the project made it necessary for students to say everything in writing, without the gestures and oral communication that could supplement written messages within their own classroom. The pictures that their partners created on the basis of their written descriptions gave these young authors tangible feedback regarding the completeness and clarity of their writing.

The students' reflections revealed developing insights into the multiple potential sources for miscommunication:

> Maybe you skipped over another part, or maybe it was too hard to understand.

> The only thing that made it not exactly perfect was our mistake. . . . . We said, "Each square is down a bit, " What we should have said was, "Each square is all the way inside the one before it, " or something like that.

> I think I could have been more clear on the mouth. I should have said that it was closed. I described it [as if it were] open by telling you I had no braces or retainers.

The electronic technologies that students used in this project were quite simple (word processors, e-mail, scanners). The project's sophistication lies more in its structure, which required students to focus on issues of audience understanding and to make translations across different media (words and pictures), potentially increasing their understanding of the strengths and weaknesses of each.

The students' artwork, descriptive paragraphs, and reflections are available on a project website at http://www.barron.palo-alto.ca.us/hoover/mmm/mmm.html.

cians as they performed the hardest real-world troubleshooting tasks, 20 to 25 hours of Sherlock training was the equivalent of about 4 years of on-the-job experience. Not surprisingly, Sherlock has been deployed at several U.S. Air Force bases. Two of the crucial properties of Sherlock are modeled on successful informal learning: learners successfully complete every problem they start, with the amount of coaching decreasing as their skill increases; and learners replay and reflect on their performance, highlighting areas where they could improve, much as a football player might review a game film.

BOX 9.7   **Learning with the Geometry Tutor**

When the Geometry Tutor was placed in classes in a large urban high school, students moved through the geometry proofs more quickly than expected by either the teachers or the tutor developers. Average, below-average, and under-achieving high-ability students with little confidence in their math skills benefited most from the tutor (Wertheimer, 1990). Students in classes using the tutor showed higher motivation by starting work much more quickly—often coming early to class to get started—and taking more responsibility for their own progress. Teachers started spending more of their time assisting individual students who asked for help and giving greater weight to effort in assigning student grades (Schofield, 1995).

It is noteworthy that students can use these tutors in groups as well as alone. In many settings, students work together on tutors and discuss issues and possible answers with others in their class.

CONNECTING CLASSROOMS TO COMMUNITY

It is easy to forget that student achievement in school also depends on what happens outside of school. Bringing students and teachers in contact with the broader community can enhance their learning. In the previous chapter, we discussed learning through contacts with the broader community. Universities and businesses, for example, have helped communities upgrade the quality of teaching in schools. Engineers and scientists who work in industry often play a mentoring role with teachers (e.g., University of California-Irvine Science Education Program).

Modern technologies can help make connections between students' in-school and out-of-school activities. For example, the "transparent school" (Bauch, 1997) uses telephones and answering machines to help parents understand the daily assignments in classrooms. Teachers need only a few minutes per day to dictate assignments into an answering machine. Parents can call at their convenience and retrieve the daily assignments, thus becoming informed of what their children are doing in school. Contrary to some expectations, low-income parents are as likely to call the answering machines as are parents of higher socioeconomic status.

The Internet can also help link parents with their children's schools. School calendars, assignments, and other types of information can be posted on a school's Internet site. School sites can also be used to inform the community of what a school is doing and how they can help. For example, the American Schools Directory (www.asd.com), which has created Internet pages for each of the 106,000 public and private K-12 schools in the country,

BOX 9.8   Intelligent Tutoring in High School Algebra

A large-scale experiment evaluated the benefits of introducing an intelligent alge-bra tutoring system into an urban high school setting (Koedinger et al., 1997). An important feature of the project was a collaborative, client-centered design that coordinated the tutoring system with the teachers' goals and expertise. The col-laboration produced the PUMP (Pittsburgh urban mathematics program) curricu-lum, which focuses on mathematical analyses of real-world situations, the use of computational tools, and on making algebra accessible to all students. An intelli-gent tutor, PAT (for PUMP Algebra Tutor) supported this curriculum. Researchers compared achievement levels of ninth- grade students in the tutored classrooms (experimental group) with achievement in more traditional algebra classrooms. The results demonstrated strong benefits from the use of PUMP and PAT, which is currently used in 70 schools nationwide..

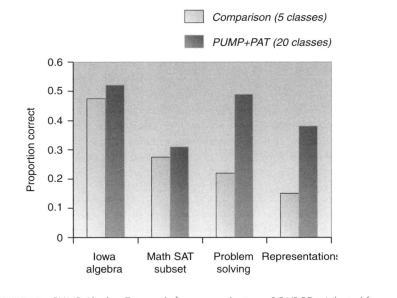

FIGURE 9.5   *PUMP Algebra Tutor end-of-course evaluation.   SOURCE: Adapted from Koedinger et al. (1997).*

includes a "Wish List" on which schools post requests for various kinds of help. In addition, the ASD provides free e-mail for every student and teacher in the country.

Several projects are exploring the factors required to create effective electronic communities. For example, we noted above that students can learn more when they are able to interact with working scientists, authors, and other practicing professionals. An early review of six different electronic communities, which included teacher and student networks and a group of university researchers, looked at how successful these communities were in relation to their size and location, how they organized themselves, what opportunities and obligations for response were built into the network, and how they evaluated their work (Riel and Levin, 1990). Across the six groups, three factors were associated with successful network-based communities: an emphasis on group rather than one-to-one communication; well-articulated goals or tasks; and explicit efforts to facilitate group interaction and establish new social norms.

To make the most of the opportunities for conversation and learning available through these kinds of networks, students, teachers, and mentors must be willing to assume new or untraditional roles. For example, a major purpose of the Kids as Global Scientists (KGS) research project—a worldwide clusters of students, scientist mentors, technology experts, and experts in pedagogy—is to identify key components that make these communities successful (Songer, 1993). In the most effective interactions, a social glue develops between partners over time. Initially, the project builds relationships by engaging people across locations in organized dialogues and multimedia introductions; later, the group establishes guidelines and scaffolds activities to help all participants understand their new responsibilities. Students pose questions about weather and other natural phenomena and refine and respond to questions posed by themselves and others. This dialogue-based approach to learning creates a rich intellectual context, with ample opportunities for participants to improve their understanding and become more personally involved in explaining scientific phenomena.

TEACHER LEARNING

The introduction of new technologies to classrooms has offered new insights about the roles of teachers in promoting learning (McDonald and Naso, 1986; Watts, 1985). Technology can give teachers license to experiment and tinker (Means and Olson, 1995a; U.S. Congress, Office of Technology Assessment, 1995). It can stimulate teachers to think about the processes of learning, whether through a fresh study of their own subject or a fresh perspective on students' learning. It softens the barrier between what students do and what teachers do.

When teachers learn to use a new technology in their classrooms, they model the learning process for students; at the same time, they gain new insights on teaching by watching their students learn. Moreover, the transfer of the teaching role from teacher to student often occurs spontaneously during efforts to use computers in classrooms. Some children develop a profound involvement with some aspect of the technology or the software, spend considerable time on it, and know more than anyone else in the group, including their teachers. Often both teachers and students are novices, and the creation of knowledge is a genuinely cooperative endeavor. Epistemological authority—teachers possessing knowledge and students receiving knowledge—is redefined, which in turn redefines social authority and personal responsibility (Kaput, 1987; Pollak, 1986; Skovsmose, 1985). Cooperation creates a setting in which novices can contribute what they are able and learn from the contributions of those more expert than they. Collaboratively, the group, with its variety of expertise, engagement, and goals, gets the job done (Brown and Campione, 1987:17). This devolution of authority and move toward cooperative participation results directly from, and contributes to, an intense cognitive motivation.

As teachers learn to use technology, their own learning has implications for the ways in which they assist students to learn more generally (McDonald and Naso, 1986):

- They must be partners in innovation; a critical partnership is needed among teachers, administrators, students, parents, community, university, and the computer industry.
- They need time to learn: time to reflect, absorb discoveries, and adapt practices.
- They need collegial advisers rather than supervisors; advising is a partnership.

Internet-based communities of teachers are becoming an increasingly important tool for overcoming teachers' sense of isolation. They also provide avenues for geographically dispersed teachers who are participating in the same kinds of innovations to exchange information and offer support to each other (see Chapter 8). Examples of these communities include the LabNet Project, which involves over 1,000 physics teachers (Ruopp et al., 1993); Bank Street College's Mathematics Learning project; the QUILL network for Alaskan teachers of writing (Rubin, 1992); and the HumBio Project, in which teachers are developing biology curricula over the network (Keating, 1997; Keating and Rosenquist, 1998). WEBCSILE, an Internet version of the CSILE program described above, is being used to help create teacher communities.

The worldwide web provides another venue for teachers to communicate with an audience outside their own institutions. At the University of Illinois, James Levin asks his education graduate students to develop web pages with their evaluations of education resources on the web, along with hot links to those web resources they consider most valuable. Many students not only put up these web pages, but also revise and maintain them after the course is over. Some receive tens of thousands of hits on their web sites each month (Levin et al., 1994; Levin and Waugh, 1998).

While e-mail, listservs, and websites have enabled members of teacher communities to exchange information and to stay in touch, they represent only part of technology's full potential to support real communities of practice (Schlager and Schank, 1997). Teacher communities of practice need chances for planned interactions, tools for joint review and annotation of education resources, and opportunities for on-line collaborative design activities. In general, teacher communities need environments that generate the social glue that Songer found so important in the Kids as Global Scientists community.

The Teacher Professional Development Institute (TAPPED IN), a multiuser virtual environment, integrates synchronous ("live") and asynchronous (such as e-mail) communication. Users can store and share documents and interact with virtual objects in an electronic environment patterned after a typical conference center. Teachers can log into TAPPED IN to discuss issues, create and share resources, hold workshops, engage in mentoring, and conduct collaborative inquiries with the help of virtual versions of such familiar tools as books, whiteboards, file cabinets, notepads, and bulletin boards. Teachers can wander among the public "rooms," exploring the resources in each and engaging in spontaneous live conversations with others exploring the same resources. More than a dozen major teacher professional development organizations have set up facilities within TAPPED IN.

In addition to supporting teachers' ongoing communication and professional development, technology is used in preservice seminars for teachers. A challenge in providing professional development for new teachers is allowing them adequate time to observe accomplished teachers and to try their own wings in classrooms, where innumerable decisions must be made in the course of the day and opportunities for reflection are few. Prospective teachers generally have limited exposure to classrooms before they begin student teaching, and teacher trainers tend to have limited time to spend in classes with them, observing and critiquing their work. Technology can help overcome these constraints by capturing the complexity of classroom interactions in multiple media. For example, student teachers can replay videos of classroom events to learn to read subtle classroom clues and see important features that escaped them on first viewing.

Databases have been established to assist teachers in a number of subject areas. One is a video archive of mathematics lessons from third- and fifth-grade classes, taught by experts Magdalene Lampert and Deborah Ball (1998). The lessons model inquiry-oriented teaching, with students working to solve problems and reason and engaging in lively discussions about the mathematics underlying their solutions. The videotapes allow student teachers to stop at any point in the action and discuss nuances of teacher performance with their fellow students and instructors. Teachers' annotations and an archive of student work associated with the lessons further enrich the resource.

A multimedia database of video clips of expert teachers using a range of instructional and classroom management strategies has been established by Indiana University and the North Central Regional Educational Laboratory (Duffy, 1997). Each lesson comes with such materials as the teacher's lesson plan, commentary by outside experts, and related research articles. Another technological resource is a set of video-based cases (on videodisc and CD-ROM) for teaching reading that shows prospective teachers a variety of different approaches to reading instruction. The program also includes information about the school and community setting, the philosophy of the school principals, a glimpse of what the teachers did before school started, and records of the students' work as they progress throughout the year (e.g., Kinzer et al., 1992; Risko and Kinzer, 1998).

A different approach is shown in interactive multimedia databases illustrating mathematics and science teaching, developed at Vanderbilt University. Two of the segments, for example, provide edited video tapes of the same teacher teaching two second-grade science lessons. In one lesson, the teacher and students discuss concepts of insulation presented in a textbook chapter; in the second lesson, the teacher leads the students in a hands-on investigation of the amount of insulation provided by cups made of different materials. On the surface, the teacher appears enthusiastic and articulate in both lessons and the students are well behaved. Repeated viewings of the tapes, however, reveal that the students' ability to repeat the correct words in the first lesson may mask some enduring misconceptions. The misconceptions are much more obvious in the context of the second lesson (Barron and Goldman, 1994).

In yet a different way in which technology can support preservice teacher preparation, education majors enrolled at the University of Illinois who were enrolled in lower division science courses like biology were electronically linked up to K-12 classrooms to answer student questions about the subject area. The undergraduates helped the K-12 students explore the science. More important, the education majors had a window into the kinds of questions that elementary or high school students ask in the subject domain, thus motivating them to get more out of their university science courses (Levin et al., 1994).

CONCLUSION

Technology has become an important instrument in education. Computer-based technologies hold great promise both for increasing access to knowledge and as a means of promoting learning. The public imagination has been captured by the capacity of information technologies to centralize and organize large bodies of knowledge; people are excited by the prospect of information networks, such as the Internet, linking students around the globe into communities of learners.

What has not yet been fully understood is that computer-based technologies can be powerful pedagogical tools—not just rich sources of information, but also extensions of human capabilities and contexts for social interactions supporting learning. The process of using technology to improve learning is never solely a technical matter, concerned only with properties of educational hardware and software. Like a textbook or any other cultural object, technology resources for education—whether a software science simulation or an interactive reading exercise—function in a social environment, mediated by learning conversations with peers and teachers.

Just as important as questions about learning and the developmental appropriateness of the products for children are issues that affect those who will use them as tools to promote learning; namely, teachers. In thinking about technology, the framework of creating learning environments that are learner, knowledge, assessment, and community centered is also useful. There are many ways that technology can be used to help create such environments, both for teachers and for the students whom they teach. Many issues arise in considering how to educate teachers to use new technologies effectively. What do they need to know about learning processes? About the technology? What kinds of training are most effective for helping teachers use high-quality instructional programs? What is the best way to use technology to facilitate teacher learning?

Good educational software and teacher-support tools, developed with a full understanding of principles of learning, have not yet become the norm. Software developers are generally driven more by the game and play market than by the learning potential of their products. The software publishing industry, learning experts, and education policy planners, in partnership, need to take on the challenge of exploiting the promise of computer-based technologies for improving learning. Much remains to be learned about using technology's potential: to make this happen, learning research will need to become the constant companion of software development.

IV

FUTURE DIRECTIONS

FOR THE

SCIENCE OF LEARNING

10

Conclusions

The pace at which science proceeds sometimes seems alarmingly slow, and impatience and hopes both run high when discussions turn to issues of learning and education. In the field of learning, the past quarter century has been a period of major research advances. Because of the many new developments, the studies that resulted in this volume were conducted to appraise the scientific knowledge base on human learning and its application to education. We evaluated the best and most current scientific data on learning, teaching, and learning environments. The objective of the analysis was to ascertain what is required for learners to reach deep understanding, to determine what leads to effective teaching, and to evaluate the conditions that lead to supportive environments for teaching and learning.

A scientific understanding of learning includes understanding about learning processes, learning environments, teaching, sociocultural processes, and the many other factors that contribute to learning. Research on all of these topics, both in the field and in laboratories, provides the fundamental knowledge base for understanding and implementing changes in education.

This volume discusses research in six areas that are relevant to a deeper understanding of students' learning processes: the role of prior knowledge in learning, plasticity and related issues of early experience upon brain development, learning as an active process, learning for understanding, adaptive expertise, and learning as a time-consuming endeavor. It reviews research in five additional areas that are relevant to teaching and environments that support effective learning: the importance of social and cultural contexts, transfer and the conditions for wide application of learning, subject matter uniqueness, assessment to support learning, and the new educational technologies.

LEARNERS AND LEARNING

Development and Learning Competencies

Children are born with certain biological capacities for learning. They can recognize human sounds; can distinguish animate from inanimate objects; and have an inherent sense of space, motion, number, and causality. These raw capacities of the human infant are actualized by the environment surrounding a newborn. The environment supplies information, and equally important, provides structure to the information, as when parents draw an infant's attention to the sounds of her or his native language.

Thus, developmental processes involve interactions between children's early competencies and their environmental and interpersonal supports. These supports serve to strengthen the capacities that are relevant to a child's surroundings and to prune those that are not. Learning is promoted and regulated by the children's biology and their environments. The brain of a developing child is a product, at the molecular level, of interactions between biological and ecological factors. Mind is created in this process.

The term "development" is critical to understanding the changes in children's conceptual growth. Cognitive changes do not result from mere accretion of information, but are due to processes involved in conceptual reorganization. Research from many fields has supplied the key findings about how early cognitive abilities relate to learning. These include the following:

• "Privileged domains:" Young children actively engage in making sense of their worlds. In some domains, most obviously language, but also for biological and physical causality and number, they seem predisposed to learn.

• Children are ignorant but not stupid: Young children lack knowledge, but they do have abilities to reason with the knowledge they understand.

• Children are problem solvers and, through curiosity, generate questions and problems: Children attempt to solve problems presented to them, and they also seek novel challenges. They persist because success and understanding are motivating in their own right.

• Children develop knowledge of their own learning capacities—metacognition—very early. This metacognitive capacity gives them the ability to plan and monitor their success and to correct errors when necessary.

• Children' natural capabilities require assistance for learning: Children's early capacities are dependent on catalysts and mediation. Adults play a critical role in promoting children's curiosity and persistence by directing children's attention, structuring their experiences, supporting their learning attempts, and regulating the complexity and difficulty of levels of information for them.

Neurocognitive research has contributed evidence that both the developing and the mature brain are structurally altered during learning. For example, the weight and thickness of the cerebral cortex of rats is altered when they have direct contact with a stimulating physical environment and an interactive social group. The structure of the nerve cells themselves is correspondingly altered: under some conditions, both the cells that provide support to the neurons and the capillaries that supply blood to the nerve cells may be altered as well. Learning specific tasks appears to alter the specific regions of the brain appropriate to the task. In humans, for example, brain reorganization has been demonstrated in the language functions of deaf individuals, in rehabilitated stroke patients, and in the visual cortex of people who are blind from birth. These findings suggest that the brain is a dynamic organ, shaped to a great extent by experience and by what a living being does.

Transfer of Learning

A major goal of schooling is to prepare students for flexible adaptation to new problems and settings. Students' abilities to transfer what they have learned to new situations provides an important index of adaptive, flexible learning; seeing how well they do this can help educators evaluate and improve their instruction. Many approaches to instruction look equivalent when the only measure of learning is memory for facts that were specifically presented. Instructional differences become more apparent when evaluated from the perspective of how well the learning transfers to new problems and settings. Transfer can be explored at a variety of levels, including transfer from one set of concepts to another, one school subject to another, one year of school to another, and across school and everyday, nonschool activities.

People's abilitiy to transfer what they have learned depends upon a number of factors:

- People must achieve a threshold of initial learning that is sufficient to support transfer. This obvious point is often overlooked and can lead to erroneous conclusions about the effectiveness of various instructional approaches. It takes time to learn complex subject matter, and assessments of transfer must take into account the degree to which original learning with understanding was accomplished.
- Spending a lot of time ("time on task") in and of itself is not sufficient to ensure effective learning. Practice and getting familiar with subject matter take time, but most important is how people use their time while

learning. Concepts such as "deliberate practice" emphasize the importance of helping students monitor their learning so that they seek feedback and actively evaluate their strategies and current levels of understanding. Such activities are very different from simply reading and rereading a text.

• Learning with understanding is more likely to promote transfer than simply memorizing information from a text or a lecture. Many classroom activities stress the importance of memorization over learning with understanding. Many, as well, focus on facts and details rather than larger themes of causes and consequences of events. The shortfalls of these approaches are not apparent if the only test of learning involves tests of memory, but when the transfer of learning is measured, the advantages of learning with understanding are likely to be revealed.

• Knowledge that is taught in a variety of contexts is more likely to support flexible transfer than knowledge that is taught in a single context. Information can become "context-bound" when taught with context-specific examples. When material is taught in multiple contexts, people are more likely to extract the relevant features of the concepts and develop a more flexible representation of knowledge that can be used more generally.

• Students develop flexible understanding of when, where, why, and how to use their knowledge to solve new problems if they learn how to extract underlying themes and principles from their learning exercises. Understanding how and when to put knowledge to use—known as conditions of applicability—is an important characteristic of expertise. Learning in multiple contexts most likely affects this aspect of transfer.

• Transfer of learning is an active process. Learning and transfer should not be evaluated by "one-shot" tests of transfer. An alternative assessment approach is to consider how learning affects subsequent learning, such as increased speed of learning in a new domain. Often, evidence for positive transfer does not appear until people have had a chance to learn about the new domain—and then transfer occurs and is evident in the learner's ability to grasp the new information more quickly.

• All learning involves transfer from previous experiences. Even initial learning involves transfer that is based on previous experiences and prior knowledge. Transfer is not simply something that may or may not appear after initial learning has occurred. For example, knowledge relevant to a particular task may not automatically be activated by learners and may not serve as a source of positive transfer for learning new information. Effective teachers attempt to support positive transfer by actively identifying the strengths that students bring to a learning situation and building on them, thereby building bridges between students' knowledge and the learning objectives set out by the teacher.

• Sometimes the knowledge that people bring to a new situation impedes subsequent learning because it guides thinking in wrong directions.

For example, young children's knowledge of everyday counting-based arithmetic can make it difficult for them to deal with rational numbers (a larger number in the numerator of a fraction does not mean the same thing as a larger number in the denominator); assumptions based on everyday physical experiences can make it difficult for students to understand physics concepts (they think a rock falls faster than a leaf because everyday experiences include other variables, such as resistance, that are not present in the vacuum conditions that physicists study), and so forth. In these kinds of situations, teachers must help students change their original conceptions rather than simply use the misconceptions as a basis for further understanding or leaving new material unconnected to current understanding.

Competent and Expert Performance

Cognitive science research has helped us understand how learners develop a knowledge base as they learn. An individual moves from being a novice in a subject area toward developing competency in that area through a series of learning processes. An understanding of the structure of knowledge provides guidelines for ways to assist learners acquire a knowledge base effectively and efficiently. Eight factors affect the development of expertise and competent performance:

- Relevant knowledge helps people organize information in ways that support their abilities to remember.
- Learners do not always relate the knowledge they possess to new tasks, despite its potential relevance. This "disconnect" has important implications for understanding differences between usable knowledge (which is the kind of knowledge that experts have developed) and less-organized knowledge, which tends to remain "inert."
- Relevant knowledge helps people to go beyond the information given and to think in problem representations, to engage in the mental work of making inferences, and to relate various kinds of information for the purpose of drawing conclusions.
- An important way that knowledge affects performances is through its influences on people's representations of problems and situations. Different representations of the same problem can make it easy, difficult, or impossible to solve.
- The sophisticated problem representations of experts are the result of well-organized knowledge structures. Experts know the conditions of applicability of their knowledge, and they are able to access the relevant knowledge with considerable ease.
- Different domains of knowledge, such as science, mathematics, and history, have different organizing properties. It follows, therefore, that to

have an in-depth grasp of an area requires knowledge about both the content of the subject and the broader structural organization of the subject.

• Competent learners and problem solvers monitor and regulate their own processing and change their strategies as necessary. They are able to make estimates and "educated guesses."

• The study of ordinary people under everyday cognition provides valuable information about competent cognitive performances in routine settings. Like the work of experts, everyday competencies are supported by sets of tools and social norms that allow people to perform tasks in specific contexts that they often cannot perform elsewhere.

Conclusions

Everyone has understanding, resources, and interests on which to build. Learning a topic does not begin from knowing nothing to learning that is based on entirely new information. Many kinds of learning require transforming existing understanding, especially when one's understanding needs to be applied in new situations. Teachers have a critical role in assisting learners to engage their understanding, building on learners' understandings, correcting misconceptions, and observing and engaging with learners during the processes of learning.

This view of the interactions of learners with one another and with teachers derives from generalizations about learning mechanisms and the conditions that promote understanding. It begins with the obvious: learning is embedded in many contexts. The most effective learning occurs when learners transport what they have learned to various and diverse new situations. This view of learning also includes the not so obvious: young learners arrive at school with prior knowledge that can facilitate or impede learning. The implications for schooling are many, not the least of which is that teachers must address the multiple levels of knowledge and perspectives of children's prior knowledge, with all of its inaccuracies and misconceptions.

• Effective comprehension and thinking require a coherent understanding of the organizing principles in any subject matter; understanding the essential features of the problems of various school subjects will lead to better reasoning and problem solving; early competencies are foundational to later complex learning; self-regulatory processes enable self-monitoring and control of learning processes by learners themselves.

• Transfer and wide application of learning are most likely to occur when learners achieve an organized and coherent understanding of the material; when the situations for transfer share the structure of the original learning; when the subject matter has been mastered and practiced; when subject domains overlap and share cognitive elements; when instruction includes specific attention to underlying principles; and when instruction explicitly and directly emphasizes transfer.

• Learning and understanding can be facilitated in learners by emphasizing organized, coherent bodies of knowledge (in which specific facts and details are embedded), by helping learners learn how to transfer their learning, and by helping them use what they learn.

• In-depth understanding requires detailed knowledge of the facts within a domain. The key attribute of expertise is a detailed and organized understanding of the important facts within a specific domain. Education needs to provide children with sufficient mastery of the details of particular subject matters so that they have a foundation for further exploration within those domains.

• Expertise can be promoted in learners. The predominant indicator of expert status is the amount of time spent learning and working in a subject area to gain mastery of the content. Secondarily, the more one knows about a subject, the easier it is to learn additional knowledge.

TEACHERS AND TEACHING

The portrait we have sketched of human learning and cognition emphasizes learning for in-depth comprehension. The major ideas that have transformed understanding of learning also have implications for teaching.

Teaching for In-Depth Learning

Traditional education has tended to emphasize memorization and mastery of text. Research on the development of expertise, however, indicates that more than a set of general problem-solving skills or memory for an array of facts is necessary to achieve deep understanding. Expertise requires well-organized knowledge of concepts, principles, and procedures of inquiry. Various subject disciplines are organized differently and require an array of approaches to inquiry. We presented a discussion of the three subject areas of history, mathematics, and science learning to illustrate how the structure of the knowledge domain guides both learning and teaching.

Proponents of the new approaches to teaching engage students in a variety of different activities for constructing a knowledge base in the subject domain. Such approaches involve both a set of facts and clearly defined principles. The teacher's goal is to develop students' understanding of a given topic, as well as to help them develop into independent and thoughtful problem solvers. One way to do this is by showing students that they already have relevant knowledge. As students work through different problems that a teacher presents, they develop their understanding into principles that govern the topic.

In mathematics for younger (first- and second-grade) students, for example, cognitively guided instruction uses a variety of classroom activities to bring number and counting principles into students' awareness, including snack-time sharing for fractions, lunch count for number, and attendance for part-whole relationships. Through these activities, a teacher has many opportunities to observe what students know and how they approach solutions to problems, to introduce common misconceptions to challenge students' thinking, and to present more advanced discussions when the students are ready.

For older students, model-based reasoning in mathematics is an effective approach. Beginning with the building of physical models, this approach develops abstract symbol system-based models, such as algebraic equations or geometry-based solutions. Model-based approaches entail selecting and exploring the properties of a model and then applying the model to answer a question that interests the student. This important approach emphasizes understanding over routine memorization and provides students with a learning tool that enables them to figure out new solutions as old ones become obsolete.

These new approaches to mathematics operate from knowledge that learning involves extending understanding to new situations, a guiding principle of transfer (Chapter 3); that young children come to school with early mathematics concepts (Chapter 4); that learners cannot always identify and call up relevant knowledge (Chapters 2, 3, and 4); and that learning is promoted by encouraging children to try out the ideas and strategies they bring with them to school-based learning (Chapter 6). Students in classes that use the new approaches do not begin learning mathematics by sitting at desks and only doing computational problems. Rather, they are encouraged to explore their own knowledge and to invent strategies for solving problems and to discuss with others why their strategies work or do not work.

A key aspect of the new ways of teaching science is to focus on helping students overcome deeply rooted misconceptions that interfere with learning. Especially in people's knowledge of the physical, it is clear that prior knowledge, constructed out of personal experiences and observations—such as the conception that heavy objects fall faster than light objects—can conflict with new learning. Casual observations are useful for explaining why a rock falls faster than a leaf, but they can lead to misconceptions that are difficult to overcome. Misconceptions, however, are also the starting point for new approaches to teaching scientific thinking. By probing students' beliefs and helping them develop ways to resolve conflicting views, teachers can guide students to construct coherent and broad understandings of scientific concepts. This and other new approaches are major breakthroughs in teaching science. Students can often answer fact-based questions on tests that *imply* understanding, but misconceptions will surface as the students are questioned about scientific concepts.

Chèche Konnen ("search for knowledge" in Haitian Creole) was presented as an example of new approaches to science learning for grade school children. The approach focuses upon students' personal knowledge as the foundations of sense-making. Further, the approach emphasizes the role of the specialized functions of language, including the students' own language for communication when it is other than English; the role of language in developing skills of how to "argue" the scientific "evidence" they arrive at; the role of dialogue in sharing information and learning from others; and finally, how the specialized, scientific language of the subject matter, including technical terms and definitions, promote deep understanding of the concepts.

Teaching history for depth of understanding has generated new approaches that recognize that students need to learn about the assumptions any historian makes for connecting events and schemes into a narrative. The process involves learning that any historical account is *a* history and not *the* history. A core concept guiding history learning is how to determine, from all of the events possible to enumerate, the ones to single out as significant. The "rules for determining historical significance" become a lightening rod for class discussions in one innovative approach to teaching history. Through this process, students learn to understand the interpretative nature of history and to understand history as an *evidentiary* form of knowledge. Such an approach runs counter to the image of history as clusters of fixed names and dates that students need to memorize. As with the Chèche Konnen example of science learning, mastering the concepts of historical analysis, developing an evidentiary base, and debating the evidence all become tools in the history toolbox that students carry with them to analyze and solve new problems.

Expert Teachers

Expert teachers know the structure of the knowledge in their disciplines. This knowledge provides them with cognitive roadmaps to guide the assignments they give students, the assessments they use to gauge student progress, and the questions they ask in the give-and-take of classroom life. Expert teachers are sensitive to the aspects of the subject matter that are especially difficult and easy for students to grasp: they know the conceptual barriers that are likely to hinder learning, so they watch for these tell-tale signs of students' misconceptions. In this way, both students' prior knowledge and teachers' knowledge of subject content become critical components of learners' growth.

Subject-matter expertise requires well-organized knowledge of concepts and inquiry procedures. Similarly, studies of teaching conclude that expertise consists of more than a set of general methods that can be applied across all subject matter. These two sets of research-based findings contradict the common misconception about what teachers need to know in order to design effective learning environments for students. Both subject-matter knowledge and pedagogical knowledge are important for expert teaching because knowledge domains have unique structures and methods of inquiry associated with them.

Accomplished teachers also assess their own effectiveness with their students. They reflect on what goes on in the classroom and modify their teaching plans accordingly. Thinking about teaching is not an abstract or esoteric activity. It is a disciplined, systematic approach to professional development. By reflecting on and evaluating one's own practices, either alone or in the company of a critical colleague, teachers develop ways to change and improve their practices, like any other opportunity for learning with feedback.

Conclusions

- Teachers need expertise in both subject matter content and in teaching.
- Teachers need to develop understanding of the theories of knowledge (epistemologies) that guide the subject-matter disciplines in which they work.
- Teachers need to develop an understanding of pedagogy as an intellectual discipline that reflects theories of learning, including knowledge of how cultural beliefs and the personal characteristics of learners influence learning.
- Teachers are learners and the principles of learning and transfer for student learners apply to teachers.
- Teachers need opportunities to learn about children's cognitive development and children's development of thought (children's epistemologies) in order to know how teaching practices build on learners' prior knowledge.
- Teachers need to develop models of their own professional development that are based on lifelong learning, rather than on an "updating" model of learning, in order to have frameworks to guide their career planning.

LEARNING ENVIRONMENTS

Tools of Technology

Technology has become an important instrument in education. Computer-based technologies hold great promise both for increasing access to knowledge and as a means of promoting learning. The public imagination has been captured by the capacity of information technologies to centralize and organize large bodies of knowledge; people are excited by the prospect of information networks, such as the Internet, for linking students around the globe into communities of learners.

There are five ways that technology can be used to help meet the challenges of establishing effective learning environments:

• Bringing real-world problems into classrooms through the use of videos, demonstrations, simulations, and Internet connections to concrete data and working scientists.

• Providing "scaffolding" support to augment what learners can do and reason about on their path to understanding. Scaffolding allows learners to participate in complex cognitive performances, such as scientific visualization and model-based learning, that is more difficult or impossible without technical support.

• Increasing opportunities for learners to receive feedback from software tutors, teachers, and peers; to engage in reflection on their own learning processes; and to receive guidance toward progressive revisions that improve their learning and reasoning.

• Building local and global communities of teachers, administrators, students, parents, and other interested learners.

• Expanding opportunities for teachers' learning.

An important function of some of the new technologies is their use as tools of representation. Representational thinking is central to in-depth understanding and problem representation is one of the skills that distinguish subject experts from novices. Many of the tools also have the potential to provide multiple contexts and opportunities for learning and transfer, for both student-learners and teacher-learners. Technologies can be used as learning and problem-solving tools to promote both independent learning and collaborative networks of learners and practitioners.

The use of new technologies in classrooms, or the use of any learning aid for that matter, is never solely a technical matter. The new electronic technologies, like any other educational resource, are used in a social environment and are, therefore, mediated by the dialogues that students have with each other and the teacher.

Educational software needs to be developed and implemented with a full understanding of the principles of learning and developmental psychology. Many new issues arise when one considers how to educate teachers to use new technologies effectively: What do they need to know about learning processes? What do they need to know about the technologies? What kinds of training are most effective for helping teachers use high-quality instructional programs? Understanding the issues that affect teachers who will be using new technologies is just as pressing as questions of the learning potential and developmental appropriateness of the technologies for children.

Assessment to Support Learning

Assessment and feedback are crucial for helping people learn. Assessment that is consistent with principles of learning and understanding should:

- Mirror good instruction.
- Happen continuously, but not intrusively, as a part of instruction.
- Provide information (to teachers, students, and parents) about the levels of understanding that students are reaching.

Assessment should reflect the *quality* of students' thinking, as well as what specific content they have learned. For this purpose, achievement measurement must consider cognitive theories of performance. Frameworks that integrate cognition and context in assessing achievement in science, for example, describe performance in terms of the content and process task demands of the subject matter and the nature and extent of cognitive activities likely to be observed in a particular assessment situation. The frameworks provide a basis for examining performance assessments that are designed to measure reasoning, understanding, and complex problem solving.

The nature and purposes of an assessment also influence the specific cognitive activities that are expressed by the student. Some assessment tasks emphasize a particular performance, such as explanation, but deemphasize others, such as self-monitoring. The kind and quality of cognitive activities observed in an assessment situation are functions of the content and process demands of the tasks involved. Similarly, the task demands for process skills can be conceived along a continuum from constrained to open. In open situations, explicit directions are minimized in order to see how students generate and carry out appropriate process skills as they solve problems. Characterizing assessments in terms of components of competence and the content and process demands of the subject matter brings specificity to assessment objectives, such as "higher level thinking" and "deep understanding." This approach links specific content with the underlying cognitive processes and the performance objectives that the teacher has in mind. With articulated objectives and an understanding of the correspondence between task features and cognitive activities, the content and process demands of tasks are brought into alignment with the performance objectives.

Effective teachers see assessment opportunities in ongoing classroom learning situations. They continually attempt to learn about students' thinking and understanding and make it relevant to current learning tasks. They do a great deal of on-line monitoring of both group work and individual performances, and they attempt to link current activities to other parts of the curriculum and to students' daily life experiences.

Students at all levels, but increasingly so as they progress through the grades, focus their learning attention and energies on the parts of the curriculum that are assessed. In fact, the art of being a good student, at least in the sense of getting good grades, is tied to being able to anticipate what will be tested. This means that the information to be tested has the greatest influence on guiding students' learning. If teachers stress the importance of understanding but then test for memory of facts and procedures, it is the latter that students will focus on. Many assessments developed by teachers overemphasize memory for procedures and facts; expert teachers, by contrast, align their assessment practices with their instructional goals of depth-of-understanding.

Learning and Connections to Community

Outside of formal school settings, children participate in many institutions that foster their learning. For some of these institutions, promoting learning is part of their goals, including after-school programs, as in such organizations as Boy and Girl Scout Associations and 4-H Clubs, museums, and religious education. In other institutions or activities, learning is more incidental, but learning takes place nevertheless. These learning experiences are fundamental to children's—and adults'—lives since they are embedded in the culture and the social structures that organize their daily activities. None of the following points about the importance of out-of-school learning institutions, however, should be taken to deemphasize the central role of schools and the kinds of information that can be most efficiently and effectively taught there.

A key environment for learning is the family. In the United States, many families hold a learning agenda for their children and seek opportunities for their children to engage with the skills, ideas, and information in their communities. Even when family members do not focus consciously on instructional roles, they provide resources for children's learning that are relevant to school and out-of-school ideas through family activities, the funds of knowledge available within extended families and their communities, and the attitudes that family members display toward the skills and values of schooling.

The success of the family as a learning environment, especially in the early years, has provided inspiration and guidance for some of the changes recommended in schools. The rapid development of children from birth to ages 4 or 5 is generally supported by family interactions in which children learn by observing and interacting with others in shared endeavors. Conversations and other interactions that occur around events of interest with trusted and skilled adults and child companions are especially powerful environments for learning. Many of the recommendations for changes in schools can be seen as extensions of the learning activities that occur within families. In addition, recommendations to include families in classroom activities and educational planning hold promise of bringing together two powerful systems for supporting children's learning.

Classroom environments are positively influenced by opportunities to interact with parents and community members who take interest in what they are doing. Teachers and students more easily develop a sense of community as they prepare to discuss their projects with people who come from outside the school and its routines. Outsiders can help students appreciate similarities and differences between classroom environments and everyday environments; such experiences promote transfer of learning by illustrating the many contexts for applying what they know.

Parents and business leaders represent examples of outside people who can have a major impact on student learning. Broad-scale participation in school-based learning rarely happens by accident. It requires clear goals and schedules and relevant curricula that permit and guide adults in ways to help children learn.

Conclusions

Designing effective learning environments includes considering the goals for learning and goals for students. This comparison highlights the fact that there are various means for approaching goals of learning, and furthermore, that goals for students change over time. As goals and objectives have changed, so has the research base on effective learning and the tools that students use. Student populations have also shifted over the years. Given these many changes in student populations, tools of technology, and society's requirements, different curricula have emerged along with needs for new pedagogical approaches that are more child-centered and more culturally sensitive, all with the objectives of promoting effective learning and adaptation (transfer). The requirement for teachers to meet such a diversity of challenges also illustrates why assessment needs to be a tool to help teachers determine if they have achieved their objectives. Assessment can guide teachers in tailoring their instruction to individual students' learning needs and, collaterally, inform parents of their children's progress.

- Supportive learning environments, which are the social and organizational structures in which students and teachers operate, need to focus on the characteristics of classroom environments that affect learning; the environments as created by teachers for learning and feedback; and the range of learning environments in which students participate, both in and out of school.
- Classroom environments can be positively influenced by opportunities to interact with others who affect learners, particularly families and community members, around school-based learning goals.
- New tools of technology have the potential of enhancing learning in many ways. The tools of technology are creating new learning environments, which need to be assessed carefully, including how their use can facilitate learning, the types of assistance that teachers need in order to incorporate the tools into their classroom practices, the changes in classroom organization that are necessary for using technologies, and the cognitive, social, and learning consequences of using these new tools.

11

Next Steps for Research

As noted above, an essential purpose of this volume is to expand on the original version of *How People Learn* by exploring how the findings of research on learning can be incorporated into classroom practice. The research agenda that follows includes both the recommendations in the original volume and a broad range of proposed project areas focused on bridging research and practice.

The paths through which research influences practice are depicted in Figure 11.1. To a limited extent, research directly influences classroom practce when teachers and researchers collaborate in design experiments, or when interested teachers incorporate ideas from research into their classroom practice. This appears as the only line directly linking research and practice in Figure 11.1. More typically, ideas from research are filtered through the development of education materials; through pre-service and in-service teacher and administrator education programs; through public policies at the national, state, and school district levels; and through the public's beliefs about learning and teaching, often gleaned from the popular media and from their own experiences in school. These are the four arenas that mediate the link between research and practice in Figure 11.1 The public includes teachers, whose beliefs may be influenced by popular presentations of research, and parents, whose beliefs about learning and teaching affect classroom practice as well.

Several aspects of Figure 11.1 are worth noting. First, the influence of research on the four mediating arenas—education materials, pre-service and in-service teacher and administrator education programs, public policy, and public opinion and the media—has typically been weak for a variety of reasons. Educators generally do not look to research for guidance. The concern of researchers for the validity and robustness of their work, as well as their focus on underlying constructs that explain learning, often differ from the focus of educators on the applicability of htose constructs in real classroom settings with many students, restricted time, and a variety of de-

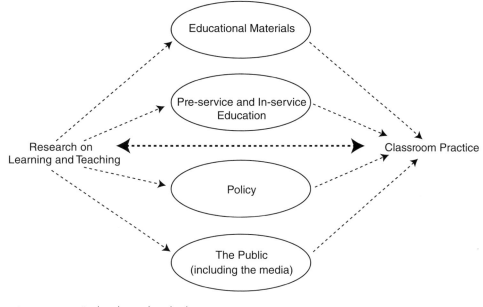

FIGURE 11.1 *Paths through which research influences practice.*

mands. Even the language used by researchers is very different from that familiar to teachers. And the full schedules of many teachers leaves them with little time to identify and read relevant research. These factors contribute to the feeling voiced by many teachers that research has largely been irrelevant to their work (Fleming, 1988). Without clear communication of a research-based theory of learning and teaching, the operational theories held by the various stakeholders are not aligned. Teachers, administrators, and parents frequently encounter conflicting ideas about the nature of learning and its implications for effective teaching.

Second, with the exception of the relatively small set of cases in which teachers and researchers work together on design experiments, the arrows between research and practice in Figure 11.1 are one-way. This reflects the fact that practitioners typically have few opportunities to shape the research agenda and contribute to an emerging knowledge base of learning and teaching. The task of bridging research and practice requires an agenda that allows for a flow of information, ideas, and research questions in both directions. It requires an agenda that consolidates the knowledge base and strengthens the links between that knowledge base and each of the components that together influence practice.

The potential benefits of bridging theory and practice are noted by Donald Stokes in his recent work, *Pasteur's Quadrant* (1997). Stokes observes that many of the advances in science are intimately connected to the search for solutions to practical problems. Pasteur appears in the book's title because his work contributed so clearly to scientific understanding while simultaneously focusing on practical problems. Such research is "use-inspired." As in Pasteur's case, when executed as part of a systematic and strategic program of inquiry, it can support new understandings at the most fundamental and basic scientific level.

A central theme of Stokes's argument is that the typical linear conceptualization of research as a sequence from basic to applied is an inaccurate characterization of much research, and it is highly limiting for the envisioning of a research agenda. He proposes instead a quadrant in two-dimensional space in which considerations of use and the quest for fundamental understanding define the horizontal and vertical axes respectively. The quadrant allows for the possibility that research can be high in both basic and applied values.

From this perspective, one can envision the need for a comprehensive program of use-driven strategic research and development focused on issues of improving classroom learning and teaching. The facts that schools and classrooms are the focus and that enhanced practice and learning are the desired goals render the program of research no less important with respect to advancing the theoretical base for how people learn. Indeed, many of the advances described in this volume are the product of use-inspired research and development focused on solving problems of classroom practice.

It is worth noting that a wide array of quantitative and qualitative methods drawn from the behavioral and social sciences are employed in education research. The methods often vary with the nature of the learning and teaching problem studied and the level of detail at which issues are pursued. Given the complexity of educational issues in real-world contexts in which variables are often difficult to control, the types of "use-inspired" research envisioned here will necessarily demand a variety of methods. These will range from controlled designs to case studies, with analytic methods for deriving conclusions and inferences including both quantitative and qualitative procedures of substantial rigor. To build an effective bridge between research and practice, such a multiplicity of methods is not only reasonable, it is essential. No single research method can suffice.

OVERARCHING THEMES

Adopting the perspective of use-inspired, strategic research and development focused on issues of learning and teaching is a powerful way to organize and justify the specific project areas described below. Five overarching themes can serve to guide our understanding of the change that is required to bridge research and practice more effectively. Three of these themes point to the consolidation of knowledge that would help link research and practice:

1. Elaborate the messages in this volume at a level of detail that makes them usable to educators and policy makers. The findings presented in the preceding chapters and their implications need to be substantially elaborated and incorporated into curricula, instructional tools, and assessment tools before their impact will be felt in the classroom. It is not enough to know, for example, that subject-matter information must be tied to related concepts if deep understanding and transfer of learning are the goals. Teachers must recognize which particular concepts are most relevant *for the subject matter that they teach.* And they need curriculum materials that support the effort to link information with concepts. Similarly, policy makers need to know quite specifically how the principles presented herein relate to state standards. In this sense, the *development* aspect of the agenda is critical.

2. Communicate the messages in this volume in the manner that is most effective for each of the audiences that influences educational practice. For teachers to teach differently and administrators and policy makers to support a different model of teaching, they need opportunities to learn about the recommended changes and to understand what they are designed to achieve. Research must be done on effective methods of communicating these ideas to teachers, administrators, and policy makers, each of whom have different information needs and different ways of learning. Similarly, teachers, administrators, and policy makers who participated in this study all emphasized that the public's beliefs regarding education influence how they do their jobs. They recommended research aimed at effectively communicating key ideas from this volume to the public.

3. Use the principles in this volume as a lens through which to evaluate existing education practices and policies. As discussed earlier, many existing school practices and policies are inconsistent with what is known about learning. But havens of exemplary educational practice have also been described. The education landscape is dotted with reform efforts and with institutes and centers that produce new ideas and new teaching materials. Educators, administrators, and policy makers are eager for help in sorting through what already exists. They want to know which of these current practices, training programs, and policies are in alignment with the principles in this volume and which are in clear violation.

Moreover, educators involved in this study emphasized that new ideas are introduced to schools one after another, and teachers become weary and skeptical that any new reform effort will be better than the last. Zealous efforts to promote the newest idea often overlook existing practices that are successful. An effort to identify such practices will build support from those who have long been engaged in teaching for understanding.

Together, these three themes suggest that an effective bridge between research and practice will require a consolidated knowledge base on learning and teaching that builds, or is cumulative, over time. Elaborating on the conceptualization in Figure 11.1, this knowledge base appears at the center of Figure 11.2. Fed by research, it organizes, synthesizes, interprets, and communicates research findings in a manner that allows easy access and effective learning for those in each of the mediating arenas. Attending to the communication and information links between the knowledge base and each of the components of the model simultaneously enhances the prospect for the alignment of research ideas and practice.

Two additional themes focus on *how* research should be conducted to strengthen its link to practice:

4. Conduct research in teams that combine the expertise of researchers and the wisdom of practitioners. Much of the work that is needed to bridge research and practice focuses on the education and professional development of teachers, the curriculum, instruction and assessment tools that support their teaching, and the policies that define the environment in which teaching takes place. These are areas about which practitioners have a great deal of knowledge and experience. Thus it is important to have educators partnered with researchers in undertaking these research projects. Such partnerships allow the perspectives and knowledge of teachers to be tapped, bringing an awareness to the research of the needs and dynamics of a classroom environment. Since such partnerships are novel to many researchers, exemplary cases and guiding principles will need to be developed to make more likely the successful planning and conduct of research team partnerships.

5. Extend the frontier of learning research by expanding the study of classroom practice. As the earlier discussion of the Stokes work suggests, research efforts that begin by observing the learning that takes place

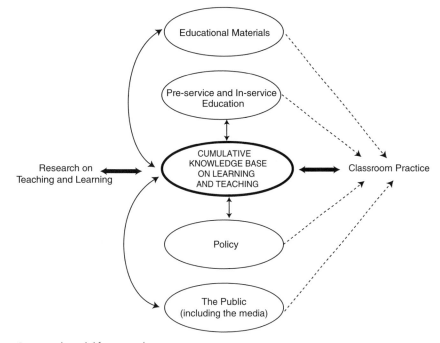

FIGURE 11.2 *Proposed model for strengthening the link between research and practice.*

in the classroom may advance understanding of the science of learning in important and useful ways.

Taken together, these latter two suggestions imply that the links between research and practice should routinely flow in both directions. The insights of researchers help shape the practitioner's understanding, and the insights of practitioners help shape the research agenda and the insights of researchers. Moreover, the link between each of the arenas and the knowledge base flows in both directions. Efforts to align teaching materials, teacher education, administration, public policy, and public opinion with the knowledge base are part of an ongoing, iterative research effort in which the implementation of new ideas, teaching techniques, or forms of communication are themselves the subject of study.

The agenda that follows proposes research and development that can help consolidate the knowledge base and can build the two-way links between the knowledge base and each of the arenas that influences practice. But that knowledge base is also fed by research on learning more generally and on classroom practice. The proposed agenda includes additional research that would strengthen the understanding of learning in areas that go beyond this volume.

Finally, since communication and access to knowledge are key to alignment, a new effort is proposed that would use interactive technologies to facilitate communication of the variety of findings that would emerge from these research and development projects.

In many of the proposed areas for research and development, work is already under way. Inclusion in the agenda is not meant to overlook the contributions of research already done or in progress. Rather, the agenda is inclusive in order to suggest that research findings need to be synthesized and integrated into the knowledge base and their implications tested through ongoing, iterative research.

RESEARCH AND DEVELOPMENT OF EDUCATIONAL MATERIALS

The goal of the recommended research and development in this area is to build on and elaborate findings in this volume so that they are "applications ready" and more usable to those responsible for developing curriculum, instructional, and assessment materials. The intent is to achieve three interrelated goals: (a) to identify existing educational materials that are aligned with the principles of learning suggested in earlier chapters and to develop and test new materials in areas of need; (b) to advance the knowledge base by significantly extending the work described herein to additional areas of curriculum, instructional techniques, and assessments that are in need of detailed analysis; and (c) to communicate the messages of this volume in a manner appropriate to developers of educational materials and teachers by using a variety of technologies (e.g., texts, electronic databases, interactive web sites). The recommended research is described in this section in seven project areas.

Examine Existing Practice

1. Review a sample of current curricula, instructional techniques, and assessments for alignment with principles discussed in this volume. It is recommended that teams of discipline-specific experts, researchers in pedagogy and cognitive science, and teachers review a sample of widely used curricula, as well as curricula that have a reputation for teaching for understanding. The envisioned research would involve two stages; these might be conducted together in a project, or as sequential projects.

Stage 1: These curricula and their companion instructional techniques and assessments should be evaluated with careful attention paid to alignment with the principles of learning outlined herein. The review might include consideration of the extent to which the curriculum emphasizes depth over breadth of coverage; the effectiveness of the opportunities provided to grasp key concepts related to the subject matter; the extent to which the curriculum provides opportunities to explore preconceptions about the subject matter; the adequacy of the factual knowledge base provided by the curriculum; the extent to which formative assessment procedures are built into the curriculum; and the extent to which accompanying summative assessment procedures measure understanding and ability to transfer rather than memory of fact.

The features that support learning should be highlighted and explained, as should the features that are in conflict. The report from this research should accomplish two goals. First, it should identify examples of curriculum components, instructional techniques, and assessment tools that incorporate the principles of learning. Second, the explication of features that support or conflict with the principles of learning should be provided in sufficient detail and in a format that allows the report to serve as a learning device for those in the education field who choose and use teaching and assessment tools. As such, it could serve as a reference document when new curricula and assessments are being considered.

Stage 2: The curricula that are considered promising should be evaluated to determine their effectiveness when used in practice. Curricula that are highly rated on paper may be very difficult for teachers to work with, or in the light of classroom practice may fail to achieve the level of understanding for which they are designed. Measures of student achievement take center stage in this effort. Achievement is indicated not only by a command of factual knowledge, but also by a student's conceptual understanding of subject matter and the ability to apply those concepts to future learning of new, related material. If existing assessments do not measure conceptual understanding and knowledge transfer, then this stage will require development and testing of such measures. In addition to achievement scores, feedback from teachers and curriculum directors who use the materials would provide additional input for stage 2.

Ideally, the review of curricula would take place at several levels: at the level of curriculum units, which may span several weeks of instructional time; at the level of semester-long and year-long sequences of units; and at the level of multiple grades, so that students have chances to progressively deepen their understanding over a number of years.

The curricula reviewed should not be limited to those that are print based. As a subset of this effort, a review of curricula that are multimedia should be undertaken. The number of computers in schools is expanding rapidly. For schools to use that equipment to support learning, they must be able to identify the computer-based programs that can enhance classroom teaching or class assignments. Research should be done to:

- Identify technology programs or computer-based curricula that are aligned with the principles of learning for understanding. The programs identified should go beyond those that are add-ons of factual information or that simply provide information in an entertaining fashion. The investigation should explore how the programs can be used as a tool to support knowledge building in the unit being studied, and how they can further enhance the development of understanding of key concepts in the unit. The study should also explore the adequacy of opportunities for learning about the programs and for ongoing support in using the programs in a classroom setting.
- Evaluate the aligned programs as teaching/learning tools by conducting empirical research on their distinctive contribution to achievement and other desired outcomes.
- Investigate computer programs that appear to be effective teaching devices but do not clearly align with the principles of learning. These might suggest productive areas for further study.

Extend the Knowledge Base by Developing and Testing New Educational Materials

2. In areas in which curriculum development has been weak, design and evaluate new curricula, with companion assessment tools, that teach and measure deep understanding. As an extension of project area 1 above, or in some cases as a substitute, the development and evaluation of new curriculum and assessment materials that reflect the principles of learning outlined herein should be undertaken. Again, the development should be done by teams of disciplinary experts, cognitive scientists, curriculum developers, and expert teachers. Ideally, research in this category will begin with existing curricula and modify them to better reflect key principles of learning. In some cases, however, exemplary curricula for particular kinds of subject matter may not exist, so the teams will need to create them. This research and development might be coordinated with the ongoing efforts of the National Science Foundation to ensure complementary rather than duplicative efforts.

The curricula should be designed to support learning for understanding. They will presumably emphasize depth over breadth. The designs should engage students' initial understanding, promote construction of a foundation of factual knowledge in the context of a general conceptual framework, and encourage the development of metacognitive skills.

Companion teacher materials for a curriculum should include a "meta-guide" that explains its links to principles of learning, reflects pedagogical content knowledge concerning the curriculum, and promotes flexible use of the curriculum by teachers. The guide should include discussion of expected prior knowledge (including typical preconceptions), expected competencies required of students, and ways to carry out formative assessments as learning proceeds. Potentially excellent curricula can fail because teachers are not given adequate support to use them. Although instructional guides cannot replace teacher training efforts, the meta-guide should be both comprehensive and user-friendly to supplement those efforts. Finally, both formative and summative tests of learning and transfer should be proposed as well.

Once developed, field-testing of the curricula should be conducted to amass data on student learning and teacher satisfaction, identifying areas for improvement. Clearly, it is easier to field-test short units rather than longer ones. Ideally, different research groups that are focusing on similar topics across different age groups (e.g., algebra in elementary, middle, and high school) would work to explore the degree to which each of the parts seems to merge into a coherent whole.

Once again, careful attention should be paid to the criteria used to evaluate the learning that is supported by the materials and accompanying pedagogy. Achievement should measure understanding of concepts and ability to transfer learning to new, related areas.

3. Conduct research on formative assessment. A separate research effort on formative assessment is recommended. The importance of making students' thinking visible by providing frequent opportunities for assessment, feedback, and revision, as well as teaching students to engage in self-assessment, is emphasized throughout this volume and in the proposals above. But the knowledge base on how to do this effectively is still weak. To bolster the understanding of formative assessment so that it can more effectively be built into curricula, this research effort should:

- Formulate design principles for formative assessments that promote the development of coherent, well-organized knowledge. The goal of these assessments is to tap understanding rather than memory for procedures and facts.
- Experiment with approaches to developing in students and teachers a view of formative assessment and self-assessment as an opportunity for providing useful information that allows for growth, rather than as an outcome measure of success or failure.

• Explore the potential of new technologies that provide the opportunity to incorporate formative assessment into teaching in an efficient and user-friendly fashion.

This research effort should consider as well the relationship between formative and summative assessments. If the goal of learning is to achieve deep understanding, then formative assessment should identify problems and progress toward that goal, and summative assessment should measure the level of success at reaching that goal. Clearly they are different stages of the same process and should be closely tied in design and purpose.

4. Develop and evaluate videotaped model lessons for broadly taught, common curriculum units that appear throughout the K-12 education system. Many lessons and units of study are taught almost universally to students in the United States. Examples include the rain cycle in science, the concept of gravity in physics, the Civil War in history, and *Macbeth* in English. A sample of familiar teaching topics should be chosen to illustrate teaching methods that are compatible with the findings in this volume. The research and development should be undertaken by teams composed of disciplinary experts, pedagogical experts, master teachers, and video specialists. The model lessons or units envisioned by the committee would in all cases:

• Illustrate a methodology for drawing out and working with student preconceptions and assessing progress toward understanding (results from project area 5 below could contribute to this endeavor).
• Present the conceptual framework for understanding or organizing the new material.
• Provide clear opportunities for transfer of knowledge to related areas.

When appropriate, they would also.

• Provide instruction on the use of meta-cognitive skills.
• Include examples of group processes in the development of understanding, illustrating the nature (and potential advantages) of capitalizing on shared expertise in the classroom.

The model units would be prefaced and heavily annotated to guide the viewer's understanding. Annotations would include both subject content and pedagogical technique. Companion assessment tools should be developed that measure understanding of the core concepts taught in the lessons. Multiple models of teaching the same unit in different school contexts are recommended. These could serve several purposes. First, the goal of the videotaped models is to illustrate effective approaches to teaching more generally, not just of teaching a particular unit. This learning is more likely to occur with multiple examples that allow for variation in the delivery of the lesson, holding constant the underlying principles of effective teaching.

Second, the classroom dynamics and level of preparation of the students can vary significantly from one school to the next. It may be difficult for a teacher to find relevant instruction in a videotape of a class that does not resemble the one in which she or he teaches. Finally, the art of teaching requires flexibility in responding to students' inquiries and reflections. Multiple cases can demonstrate flexibility in response to the particular students being taught while attending to a common body of knowledge.

Whether providing multiple models does indeed achieve these purposes is itself a research question worth pursuing. Such research should test the effect of each additional model provided on the level of understanding of key learning and teaching concepts, as well as the amount of variation between models that optimizes the flexibility of understanding that viewers achieve.

Once pilot versions of these lessons are designed, rigorous field-testing, with time built into the research plan for revision and retesting, should be undertaken. Video-based materials already developed and in use as part of the National Board for Professional Teaching Standards training and assessment development process should be considered as possible candidate materials for further study as part of this process.

The model lessons should be organized in widely accessible video and multimedia libraries that could serve multiple purposes:

- The lessons could be used as anchors for discussions of pre-service and in-service teachers and administrators, as they try to understand and master the pedagogy to accompany the new forms of learning described in this volume.
- The lessons could be instructive in administrative training programs. School administrators responsible for hiring and evaluating teachers need models of good practice that can inform their evaluations.
- With some modified annotations, the lessons could inform parents about teaching techniques that promote learning for understanding. Changing classroom teaching can be problematic if new methods run counter to parents' perceptions of the learning process. The model lessons could help parents understand the goals of the espoused approach to teaching.

5. Conduct extensive evaluation research through both small-scale studies and large-scale evaluations to determine the goals, assumptions, and uses of technologies in classrooms and the match or mismatch of these uses with the principles of learning and the transfer of learning. Because many computer-based technologies are relatively new to classrooms, basic premises about learning with these tools need to be examined with respect to the principles of learning described in this volume.

Extend the Knowledge Base Through Elaboration and Development of Key Research Findings

6. Conduct research on key conceptual frameworks, by discipline, for the units that are commonly taught in K-12 education. A key finding of the research reviewed in this volume is that deep understanding—and the transfer of learning that is one of its hallmarks—requires that the subject matter being taught be tied to the key concepts or organizing principles that the discipline uses to understand that subject. The goal of teaching about a given topic is not simply to convey factual information, although that information is a necessary component. The meaning of that information as it relates to basic concepts in the discipline, the related analytical methods that answer the question "How do we know," and the terms of discourse in a disciplinary field are all components in developing competence.

To illustrate, consider the topic of marine mammals as it might be taught in early elementary school. That unit would be likely to include identification of the various marine mammals, information on the features that distinguish marine mammals from fish, and perhaps more detailed information on the various types and sizes of whales, the relative size of male and female whales, etc. To the marine biologist, this information is the interesting detail in a larger story, which begins with the question: "Why are there mammals in the sea?" A unit organized around that question would engross students in an evolutionary tale in which the adaptation of sea creatures for life on the land takes a twist: land mammals now adapt to life in the sea. The core biological concepts of adaptation and natural selection would be at the center of the tale. Students would come to understand the puzzle that marine mammals posed for scientists: Could sea creatures evolve to mammals that live on land and then evolve again to mammals that return to the sea? They would come to understand the debate in the scientific community and the discovery of supporting evidence. And they would have cause to challenge the widespread misconception that evolution is a unidirectional process.

The approach of tying information on marine mammals to the concepts, language, and ways of knowing in that branch of science can be used in other areas of science, as well as in other disciplines. But the concepts and organizing principles that provide a framework for particular subject matter are often obvious only to those who are expert in the discipline. Discipline-specific research should be conducted in history, mathematics, natural sciences, and social sciences to systematically review units of study that commonly appear in K-12 curricula, specifying the conceptual framework to which the unit should be tied. The results of this effort will allow teachers and curriculum developers to see if a common conceptual basis exists for separate units of study. Making those underlying concepts explicit helps students construct a model for understanding that facilitates transfer.

It is also recommended that the work in each discipline be reviewed by a panel of disciplinary experts to identify consensus and contested areas. To the extent that there is a high level of agreement within a discipline about the organizing constructs as they apply to units of classroom study, the outcome of this research will be highly useful to those who design and evaluate curricula and to those who teach.

7. Identify and address preconceptions by field. The research reviewed in this volume makes the case that new learning is built on the foundation of existing knowledge and preconceived notions regarding the subject of study. Learning is enhanced when preconceived understandings are drawn out. When these are accurate, new knowledge can be directly tied to what is already known. And when they are inaccurate, students can be made aware of how their existing conceptions fall short and be provided with more robust alternatives. Teachers and curriculum developers can build learning experiences into curricula that challenge typical misconceptions, and that draw out and work with unpredictable preconceptions. Research by discipline and subject area is recommended:

- To identify common preconceptions that students bring to the classroom at different levels of education.
- To identify links that can be made between existing learner understandings and the disciplinary knowledge, when they are compatible.
- To identify progressive learning sequences that would allow students to bridge naïve and mature understandings of the subject matter.

The research would be conducted independently for mathematics, natural sciences, social sciences, and humanities. The research teams should combine disciplinary experts with cognitive scientists, expert teachers, and curriculum developers. The range of topics covered in each disciplinary area should allow for exploration of the key concepts in the field as they arise in commonly covered course topics in the K-12 curriculum.

In some disciplines (e.g., physics), substantial research has already been done to identify misconceptions. This project should build on those efforts but extend them by developing and testing strategies for working with preconceptions, providing tools and techniques for teachers to work with in the classroom.

The research, as envisioned, would involve several stages:

- Stage 1 would involve the identification of the subject areas for study and the key concepts that students must comprehend in order to understand each subject area. Assessment tools that allow for a test of comprehension of these concepts, including tests of the degree to which students' understanding supports new learning (transfer), would also be developed at this stage.
- Stage 2 would consist of a review of existing research that explores the preconceptions that students bring to that subject area and an extension of the research into areas that have not been adequately explored.
- Stage 3 would involve the development of learning opportunities and instructional strategies that build on, or challenge, those preconceptions. These might include experiments in physics that produce results contradicting initial understandings, or research tasks in history that show the same event from multiple perspectives, challenging good-guy/bad-guy stereotyping.
- Stage 4 would involve experimental testing of the newly developed learning tools and instructional strategies, with the assessment tools developed in stage 1 used as a measure of comprehension.

The final products of this research in each disciplinary area would include written reports of research results, as well as descriptions of tested instructional techniques for working with student preconceptions. The findings could be incorporated into videotaped model lessons (project area 4 above) or those used in the pedagogical laboratories proposed in project area 15.

Develop Tools for Effective Communication of the Principles of Learning as They Apply to Educational Materials

8. Develop an interactive communications site that provides information on curricula by field. Participants in this study suggested a high level of frustration with the task of sorting through and evaluating curricula. A central source of information on curricula and their major features would be highly valued. A means of meeting this need would be the development and maintenance of an interactive communications site that provides information about design principles for effective curricula, and relates these principles to particular curricula by subject area. The curriculum review and development recommended above would provide a solid foundation of information for creation of the site.

Comparing and rating curricula can be a difficult business. A good curriculum will need to balance coverage of information with in-depth exploration of concepts. But there is no magic balancing point. One curriculum may provide more opportunities to explore interesting scientific narratives, whereas another may offer more opportunities for valuable experimentation. But if the difficulty in evaluating curricula means backing away entirely from the effort to compare and evaluate, then the information available to those who must choose among curricula is diminished. Thousands of schools and teachers must then bear a much heavier burden of information collection.

A comprehensive evaluation process that does not rank-order curricula, but rather evaluates them on an array of relevant features is recommended. A sample of such features taken from this volume includes the extent to which the curriculum draws out preconceptions; whether it includes embedded assessment (both formative and summative), the extent to which it places information in the relevant conceptual framework, the extent to which curriculum modules can be reconfigured in ways that allow teachers to meet particular goals and needs, and the extent to which it encourages the development of metacognitive skills. Other useful information on the curriculum would include the extent and results of field-testing, the length of time it has been in use, the number of schools or school districts that have adopted it, the opportunities for teacher learning, and the amount and kind of support available to teachers using the curriculum. Information on student response to and interest in the curriculum would be useful as well.

Evaluating curricula in terms of their relevant features that align with the principles in this volume is a massive undertaking. For its ultimate success, such evaluations will need to represent expert judgments coming from different perspectives, including the subject-matter discipline, master teachers, learning and pedagogy experts, and curriculum developers. Users of an interactive communications site that publishes these judgments can then weigh the expertise they consider most useful for guiding their choice of curricula. The site should invite their feedback on experiences with using the curricula that this information led them to select. Ideally, the communications site will make it easy for teachers to access information that is directly relevant to their particular goals and needs.

Success will also require a growing group of constituencies and experts who can carry forward the principles in this volume to evaluating curricula.

RESEARCH ON PRE-SERVICE AND IN-SERVICE EDUCATION

The research and development proposed in this section is designed, once again, to achieve three goals: (a) to look first at existing practice through the lens of this volume, (b) to advance understanding in ways that would facilitate alignment of teacher preparation with principles of learning, and (c) to make the findings of this research more widely accessible and easily understood. The recommended research is described in seven project areas.

Examine Existing Practice Through the Lens of This Volume

9. Review the structure and practices of teacher education for alignment with the principles of learning. For teacher education and professional development programs to be aligned with the principles of learning, they need to prepare teachers to think about the enterprise of teaching as building on the existing knowledge base and preconceptions of their students, to teach skills for drawing out and working with existing understandings, and to continually assess the progress of students toward the goal of deep understanding. The programs need to provide for their students the opportunity to develop a deep understanding themselves of the subject matter they will teach and the ability to facilitate students' transfer of knowledge to related areas. They need to prepare teachers to be aware of and directly teach metacognitive skills. And they need to convey a model of the teacher as learner, who continually develops expertise that is flexible and adaptive.

These are implications for *what* schools of education and professional development programs should teach. But the students in those programs will themselves learn more effectively if they are taught according to these principles. The principles and findings in this volume therefore have implications for *how* schools of education do their job. Do those schools have program structures and practices that reflect the principles of learning discussed here?

It is recommended that evaluation research be conducted to examine current program structures and practices at schools of education through the lens of this volume. This effort should not only synthesize what is already known about teacher training programs, but also undertake a new evaluation. The sample of schools should be chosen to reflect the wide range of program formats (which currently include undergraduate and postbaccalaureate program designs), as well as the widely varying enrollment demographics that exist across the more than 1,000 universities and colleges that offer teacher certification programs. The goal of this research is largely descriptive: to understand better how teachers are being trained relative to current understandings of learning, teaching, and the development of expertise; how much variation currently exists in teacher education programs; and the factors that contribute to such variability. Of special concern are program structures, course content, and instructional practices that seriously conflict with the principles of this volume. The proposed research should also bring into focus features of teacher education programs that correspond to the principles of learning, and that enhance the capability of future teachers to incorporate the principles into their practice.

10. Review professional development programs for alignment with the principles of learning and for relative effectiveness in changing teaching practice. The issue of teacher preparedness is rapidly becoming one of intense focus in policy arenas. Professional development programs are an important policy tool available to concerned lawmakers. But there are vastly different models of professional development, and relatively little is known about the amount and type that is required to significantly change teacher performance and student achievement. Existing research efforts along these lines need to be extended and built on.

It is recommended that alternative models of professional development be reviewed for their alignment with the principles of learning. Features that promote or conflict with the principles should be highlighted. The research should also examine the effects of alternative types, and amounts, of professional development training on teacher performance and student achievement. As envisioned, the research would:

• Define a small set of common models of professional development. These should include individual workshops, more lengthy in-service programs, and university courses. They should include training that is tied to a specific curriculum, as well as training in teaching techniques.

• Review the features of those programs that do and do not support learning, including the opportunities they provide for exploring teachers' preconceptions, for assessing what teachers are learning as they go along, and for teachers to provide feedback and receive ongoing support as they attempt to use what they have learned in the classroom environment.

• Define measures of teacher knowledge and performance that would be expected to change as a result of the learning opportunity.

• Define measures of student achievement that would be expected to change as a result of the change in teaching.

• Estimate the effect of quantity and type of training on teacher performance and student achievement.

The envisioned research would require a major data collection effort. Success is likely to require that researchers work closely with school districts over a multiyear period. In states or school districts that are about to undergo an expansion in professional development spending, conditions may be particularly ripe for such a partnership.

The results of this research should be written up separately for the three communities who are likely to find them useful: (a) for those who provide professional development programs, the results should provide feedback that allows for improvement in program design; (b) for administrators and policy makers, the results should provide guidance in evaluating professional development programs; and (c) for researchers, the results should be reported in detail sufficient to support further meta-analytic research.

11. Explore the efficacy of various types of professional development activities for school administrators. School administrators at the individual school and school district levels are responsible for facilitating teacher learning and evaluating teacher performance. If they are to support teachers' efforts to incorporate the principles of learning into classroom practice, they will need professional development opportunities that provide an understanding of the principles and their enactment in a classroom environment.

It is recommended that research be conducted to identify the amount and type of professional development needed to create in administrators an ability to differentiate between teaching practices that do, and do not, incorporate what is known about how people learn. This research should go beyond an effort to identify whether a particular professional development opportunity effectively changes administrators' evaluations of teacher performance. It should vary the amount of such training and the model through which training is provided (intensive workshops, monthly seminars conducted over the course of a year, etc.). Measures of administrators' interpretations of teaching should be taken prior to training, at the point of program completion, and again a year after completion in order to ascertain the sustainability of change over time and the effect of prior beliefs on post-training performance.

Extend the Knowledge Base Through Elaboration and Development of Key Research Findings

12. Conduct research on the preconceptions of teachers regarding the process of learning. Adults, as well as children, have preconceptions that contribute to the ways in which they make sense of ideas and evidence and the decisions they make in undertaking tasks. For teachers to think about and conduct their teaching differently, they need to learn, and the principles of learning should guide that effort. It is therefore recommended that:

- Research be conducted that explores the prior conceptions and beliefs of teachers and those learning to become teachers, identifying the common pedagogical models that current and prospective teachers use.
- Learning opportunities be developed that challenge misconceptions about how people learn and support the development of a new model that is based on learning research.

- Evaluations be conducted of the effectiveness of those learning opportunities in changing understanding and conceptions of practice.

The outcome of this research would include both a description of common preconceptions about learning and tested techniques for working with those preconceptions that could be incorporated into the curricula of schools of education and professional development programs.

13. Conduct discipline-specific research on the level and type of education required for teaching that discipline in elementary, middle, and high school. This volume makes clear that to teach effectively in any discipline, the teacher must link the information being taught to the key organizing principles of the discipline. To achieve this, the teacher must be provided with the discipline-specific training that allows for deep understanding of those principles. This type of teaching is not now a consistent feature of teacher training programs.

It is recommended that discipline-specific research be conducted on the amount and type of training in content knowledge that teachers need for various levels of schooling (elementary, middle, high) in order to teach for understanding. The challenge in providing such training is to equip the future teacher with *both* content knowledge *and* an understanding of the thinking of children in the subject area at different developmental stages. Each is a critical component for effective teaching in a subject area. In light of this dual requirement, is content knowledge best obtained in disciplinary courses that also service majors in the discipline, or in courses in schools of education, or in jointly sponsored courses that emphasize effective teaching of the content of the discipline? When content and teaching methods are taught separately, are teachers able to bridge the two? When they are done together, is adequate attention given to the disciplinary content?

It is further recommended that the discipline-specific research teams evaluate existing tools for assessing teachers' content knowledge and knowledge of discipline-specific developmental trajectories and make recommendations regarding their adequacy.

Develop Tools for Effective Communication of the Principles of Learning to Teacher Education

14. Examine the efficacy of professional development activities. Much of what constitutes the typical approach to formal teacher professional development is antithetical to what promotes teacher learning.

Research studies are needed to determine the efficacy of various types of professional development activities, including pre-service and in-service seminars, workshops, and summer institutes. Studies should include professional activities that are extended over time and across broad teacher learning communities in order to identify the processes and mechanisms that contribute to the development of teachers' learning communities.

15. Develop model pedagogical laboratories. In many fields in which scientific principles must be put to work, laboratory experiences provide the opportunity to experiment with applications of general and specific principles. The expense of the laboratories is justified by the qualitatively different experience made possible when the boundaries of an idea can be tested or worked with in a laboratory or field-based setting.

To prepare students in schools of education to put to work the scientific principles of how people learn, laboratory experience could provide the opportunity to test the principles, become familiar with their boundaries, and learn how to make them operational. The development of pilot pedagogical laboratories is therefore recommended.

The teachers who participated in this study emphasized that a first classroom experience can so overwhelm a teacher that what was learned in a preparatory program can quickly be cast aside. Norms of operating in a school can quickly be adopted as survival techniques, however divergent those norms and the principles of learning might be. Laboratory experience could provide the opportunities for practice, as well as for observation and diagnosis of events that are likely to arise in the classroom, that could ease the transition into the classroom and allow for greater transfer of school-based learning to the practice of teaching.

The laboratories, as envisioned, would have multiple purposes, the most important of which would be to provide teaching practice. The laboratories would need to develop ongoing relationships with a body of students to be taught (e.g., partnerships with local schools or Saturday classes). How this relationship would be established and maintained should be given careful attention in the design proposal for such a laboratory. Expert teachers who staff the laboratory would provide feedback and diagnosis of the teacher's lessons. The process could be aided by the use of a videotaped record of the instruction. The analysis could be further augmented by viewing tapes of other teachers who have attempted similar lessons. The teacher in training would work to improve the lesson through an iterative process of feedback and revision.

The laboratory setting would be ideal for helping teachers to develop the ability to conduct formative assessment techniques. Teachers must be able to draw out and work with students' preconceptions and assess their progress toward understanding. The laboratory could provide opportunities to develop those techniques under guided instruction.

The laboratory, as envisioned, would not provide a teaching internship or serve the function of a professional development school. Rather, it would provide an opportunity for beginning teachers to experiment with the principles of learning that are relevant to teaching practice. The goal is not to decontextualize teaching, but to create an environment in which the immediate demands of the classroom do not prevent reflection on, or exploration of, the process of learning. Exercises could be developed for laboratory use that involve cognitive science findings of relevance to teaching, including findings on memory, the organization of information, the use of metacognitive strategies, and retrieval of knowledge when transfer is prompted and when it is not. In addition to creating a deeper appreciation of the science of learning, these opportunities would invite teachers to think of themselves as scientists, to observe and reflect on learning as a scientist would. To the extent that those skills transfer to the classroom, the goal of continuous learning and reflection on practice will be well served.

The laboratories would also serve as a locus of information for teachers in training, for practicing teachers in the community, and for researchers in the learning sciences. "Protocol materials," or materials for diagnosis and interpretation, could be housed here. These might include model lessons or units (project area 4) that could be incorporated into the teaching of diagnostic and interpretive competencies. They might also include protocols of student creativity in scientific thinking, insight, reasoning like a novice versus an expert in a task, failure to transfer, negative transfer, distributed cognition, using parental stores of knowledge in a class, concrete and operational thinking, and inferring causation. These protocols, then, provide vivid cases and examples that instantiate concepts relevant to teaching and learning. Videotaped lessons of teaching in other countries produced by the Third International Mathematics and Science Study project might also be made available. Faculty-directed course projects could develop evaluations of curricula in terms of the principles of learning and submit them to the interactive communications site described above (project area 8) for broad use.

Technology centers could be housed in the laboratory as well. Computer programs to support classroom learning and technology-based curricula could be made available for exploration in this setting. Opportunities to connect with relevant communities of teachers and researchers via the Internet could also be explored. Students graduating from these programs will then carry to the schools in which they teach an ability to be connected to outside communities with relevant knowledge that is not now a feature in many school districts.

Well-equipped laboratories would be an asset in professional development activities as well as in pre-service training. As such, the laboratories could be used on a year-round basis.

16. Develop tools for in-service education that communicate the principles of learning in this volume. For the principles of learning to be incorporated into classroom practice, practicing teachers are a key audience. They are also a very busy audience. The challenge of developing ways to effectively communicate to those teachers is a central one. Research and development are recommended that distill the messages of this volume for teachers and develop examples that are relevant to the classroom context. These messages should be communicated in a variety of formats, including text, audiotapes, videotapes, CD-ROMS, and Internet-based resources.

Researchers should design and study the effectiveness of the different media in communicating key ideas, as well as the satisfaction of teachers with the various media and the change in practice that ensues. This research should focus on the format of the material as well. For example, case-like stories could be compared with more didactic methods often used in texts and lectures.

RESEARCH ON EDUCATION POLICY

This volume suggests far-reaching reform of education. It has direct implications for what is taught in the classroom, how it is taught, the relationship between students and teachers, the content and role of assessments, and the preparation of those who undertake the daunting task of classroom teaching. Yet it is not a blueprint for redesigning schools.

Policy makers involved in this study were interested in the critical components of change implied herein, as well as their associated costs. Given the task that is before them, this focus can be easily understood. But just as a doctor who recommends a healthy diet, stress reduction, exercise, adequate rest, and a personal support system cannot say which is most critical to health, researchers cannot identify the most critical change in the education system. The parts of the system cannot be isolated; the interactions among them have powerful influences on outcome.

And just as the exercise requirement has no single attached cost—it can be met by a run through the park or an indoor tennis game at a posh racket club—teaching for understanding has no obvious price tag attached. Eliciting and working with student ideas and preconceptions will be easier in a small class than in a larger one, just as exercise in a sports club will be easier in inclement weather. But with a diverse clientele, a doctor will do best to focus on the principle of raising the heart rate for a sustained period of time rather than dictate the method for achieving the goal. Similarly, the focus here is on the principles of teaching for understanding with the recognition that, in the diverse landscape of schooling, the manifestations of those principles will vary. This does not diminish what is known with certainty: teaching for understanding is a clear goal with several well-defined components (discussed in Chapter 1).

Our focus here is on policies that have a direct impact on attainment of those goals. Many of the research efforts already recommended will help inform policy; research on the efficacy of professional development programs, for example, will be of use to policy makers who set requirements for receiving funds for that purpose. At the urging of both policy makers and educators who participated in this study, further research is proposed to review standards and assessments at the state level, and to examine teacher certification requirements at both the state and national levels.

At the district level, reform can be notoriously difficult to implement or extend. In order to identify the policies that appear to facilitate or impede the adoption and expansion of new teaching practices, case study research on schools and school districts that have successfully implemented reform is proposed. Although we don't envision a blueprint, there may be organizational features, operational policies, or incentive structures in these schools that create an environment conducive to change.

The recommended research is described in five project areas.

State Standards and Assessments

17. Review state education standards and the assessment tools used to measure compliance through the lens of this volume. Forty-nine states now have a set of education standards that apply to their schools, and most have or are developing assessment tools to hold school districts accountable for implementation. Standards vary considerably in the amount of control they exercise over what is taught, in the content they impose, and (implicitly or explicitly) in the model of learning that they imply. It is recommended that a sample of state standards be reviewed through the lens of this volume for the following purposes:

- To identify features of standards that support and violate the principles of learning set forth herein.
- To evaluate the alignment of desirable features in a state's standards with the assessment tools used for measuring compliance.
- To evaluate the features of compliance assessments that support and conflict with the principles of learning.
- To identify incentives and penalties that support the goal of effective education and those that appear to undermine that goal.

18. Conduct research on measures of student achievement that reflect the principles in this volume and that can be used by states for accountability purposes. Tests of student achievement that can be widely and uniformly administered across schools are the key mechanism by which policy makers hold schools accountable. This volume has clear implications for the measurement of student achievement. It suggests, for example, that recall of factual information is inadequate as a measure of deep understanding or as an indicator of the ability to transfer learning to new situations or problems.

Conventional psychological and educational testing is an outgrowth of theories of ability and intelligence that were current at the beginning of the century. Psychometrics has become increasingly sophisticated in its measurements, yet it does not attempt to look inside the "black box" of the mind. Now that the newer sciences of cognition and development have transformed our understanding of learning and the development of expertise, measurement theory and practice need fundamental rethinking. There is much in the traditional methods that is valuable, including a focus on objectivity and reliability of measurement. There is a problem, however, with what is being measured.

As a first step in the process of rethinking educational testing, the committee recommends that assessment tools be designed and tested with the goal of measuring deep understanding, as well as the acquisition of factual knowledge. This is both a modest beginning and a challenging task. To be useful for policy purposes, these assessments should be in a form that can be administered widely and scored objectively and that meets reasonable standards of validity and reliability. These requirements can be at odds with the measurement of deep understanding, at least in the current state of the art. But it is important to begin finding solutions that, for example, minimize the trade-off between assessing for understanding and scoring objectively. A variety of experiments is needed, both with new forms of standardized tests (including computer-based instruments that permit "virtual" experiments), and with alternative assessments (such as portfolios) that have become more popular in recent years.

Research on assessment tools of different types is recommended to determine:

- Whether alternative assessments yield significantly different measures of student achievement or highly correlated results.
- How alternative assessment measures might be combined to offer a balanced view of achievement.

19. Review teacher certification and recertification requirements. Currently, 42 of the 50 states assess teachers as part of the certification and licensure process. But states vary enormously in the criteria used and the amount and type of assessment they require. The federal government also has provided support for an assessment process for advanced certification that is developed and administered by the National Board for Professional Teaching Standards. It is recommended that research be conducted to review the requirements for teacher certification in a sample of states (selected for their diversity). Specific focus should be given to the types of assessments currently in use across the continuum of teacher development, from initial licensure to advanced status. This would include standardized tests, performance-based assessments under development (Interstate New Teacher Assessment and Support Consortium), and the National Board assessments. Efforts should be made to determine:

- The features of certification that are aligned with the principles of this volume and those that are in conflict.
- To the extent that data are available, the relationship between certification and increases in student learning.

This project should also lead, when appropriate, to recommendations for strategies to reform certification processes so that they provide better signals of a teacher's preparedness for the task of teaching for understanding.

Study District-Level Policy

20. Conduct case study research of successful "scaling-up" of new curricula. School districts set a variety of policies that influence the environment in which teachers operate. Even when a new curriculum is pilot-tested with positive results, it can be very difficult to extend that curriculum into other schools in the district, sometimes even to other classrooms in the same school. Case study research of successful scaling-up efforts is recommended determine which district-level and school-level policies facilitated reform. The case studies should include information on features that teachers often identify as obstacles to reform:

- How much scheduled time do teachers have in their work day that is not in the classroom and that can be used for reflection, study, or discussion with other teachers?
- How much training was offered to teachers who adopted the new curriculum? Is there ongoing support for the teacher who has questions during implementation? Is there evaluation of the teacher's success at implementation?
- Is there a community within the school, or extending beyond the school, that provides support, feedback, and an opportunity for discussion among teachers? Existing research suggests that the development of a professional community as part of the school culture is one of the most important determinants of successful school restructuring to implement a more demanding curriculum (Elmore, 1995; Elmore and Burney, 1996). These

studies should focus on the features that hold that community together. Are there key players? Are there structured or informal opportunities for the exchange of ideas? What can be learned from these successes about the opportunities for enhancing teacher access to communities of learning using Internet tools?

• Did the school attempt to involve parents and other community stake-holders in the change?

Some case study research of this type has already been done or is now under way. The effort to extend the knowledge base in this area should be coupled with an effort to synthesize the research results, making them easily accessible to school communities interested in reform.

Develop Tools for Effective Communication of the Principles in This Volume to Policy Makers

21. Conduct research on the effective communication of research results to policy makers. Policy makers do not routinely look to research as a source of information and ideas. But there are windows of opportunity for research in policy making. Researchers who study this issue suggest that the windows are more likely to open during crises, when issues are new and policy makers have not yet taken a position, or when issues have been fought to a stalemate. When those opportunities arise, information must be communicated to policy makers in a manner that optimizes the chance that they will learn from research findings.

It is recommended that research be conducted to:

• Assess preconceptions of education policy makers regarding the goals of K-12 education and the strategies for achieving those goals. Are they consistent with the principles of learning in this volume?

• Identify examples that engage the preconceptions of policy makers (if those preconceptions diverge from research findings on how people learn) and test their effectiveness at changing the initial understanding.

• Identify methods of communication that are most likely to reach, and teach, policy makers.

• Compare the effectiveness of alternative approaches, including concisely written materials, personal contact, and briefings or seminars.

The product of this research should be both a report of the findings regarding how policy makers learn most effectively and concisely written material that can be used for communicating effectively to policy makers.

PUBLIC OPINION AND THE MEDIA

Information communicated to the public through the media can influence practice in two ways. First, to the extent that the public is aware of the implications of learning research for classroom practice, teachers, administrators, and policy makers will receive more support for the types of changes that are suggested in this volume. Second, many teachers, administrators, and policy makers themselves are influenced by ideas that reach them through popular media. This volume is not a document that is likely to be widely read by educators and policy makers. Information presented in a more popular format will have far better prospects of reaching this audience.

22. Write a popular version of this volume for parents and the public. Everyone has preconceptions regarding the process of learning and effective methods of education. Those theories are put to work on a daily basis when we model behaviors for children, provide instructions to co-workers, or explain a problem to a friend. These models are likely to be influenced by personal experience.

The translations of these experience-based models to the evaluation of classroom teaching can lead to expectations that conflict with the principles of learning drawn from research. A parent who is accustomed to teaching a child through direct instruction, for example, may be baffled by mathematics homework that requires the child to find a method of adding five two-digit numbers, rather than instructing the child to line those numbers in columns and add the columns in turn. The importance of grappling with the problem and searching for a solution method, and the appreciation that such grappling brings to the conventional method of solution, can be lost on the parent.

This volume develops many concepts and ideas that could inform parents about models of learning that are research based, thus influencing the criteria that parents use to judge classroom practice. But those ideas are embedded in a report that is not designed specifically to communicate to parents. The writing of a popular version of this volume is therefore recommended. The popular presentation should address common preconceptions held by the public regarding learning. It should couch research findings in multiple examples that are relevant to parents' observations of children at a variety of ages. And it should help parents who are interested in understanding or evaluating a school formulate questions and make observations.

Some particularly effective examples and their implications for teaching should be highlighted in a manner that makes them easy to extract from the text. The children's book *Fish Is Fish* by Leo Lionni (1970), mentioned in Chapter 1, can serve as an effective example. In the story, a frog adventures onto the land and comes back to describe what it saw. The fish who listen to the frog imagine each description to be an adaptation of a fish: humans are imagined to have fish bodies but walk upright, etc. The visual image powerfully describes the problem of presenting new information without regard to the learner's existing conceptions. Examples such as these would allow the popular media to communicate key ideas to the broader public who might not read the report.

The popular version of this volume should itself be a subject of study. A second stage of this project should involve research to assess whether the popular version effectively communicates its messages to a sample of parents.

BEYOND *HOW PEOPLE LEARN*

The research and development agenda proposed thus far is focused largely on how the insights from this volume be incorporated into educational practice. *How People Learn* reviews a burgeoning literature that, taken collectively, provides the foundation for a science of learning. But more work needs to be done to extend that foundation.

23. Make a commitment to basic research programs in cognition, learning, and teaching. This volume has shown the payoff from investing in research on such topics as the foundational role of learners' prior knowledge in acquiring new information; plasticity and adaptability of learning; the importance of social and cultural contexts in learning; understanding the conditions of transfer of learning; how the organizational structure of a discipline affects learning; how time, familiarity, and exploration affect fluency in learning; and many other topics. While these areas have produced a substantial body of research findings, the research remains incomplete. The framework has been constructed from the earlier research; details now need to be provided in order to advance the science of learning by refining the principles.

24. Establish new research programs in emerging areas, including technology, neurocognition, and sociocultural factors that mediate learning. Research is needed on the interrelations between learning and learning environments and between teaching and learning. This research should build on current findings in areas such as: how children learn to apply their competencies as they encounter new information; how early competencies relate to later school learning; the conditions and experiences that support knowledge scaffolding; and how representational systems are challenged by new tools of technology, such as visual cognition and other types of symbolic thinking:

25. Conduct new assessment research to focus on improving and implementing formative assessments. Research conclusions indicate that teachers need a variety of supports and learning opportunities for making their classrooms assessment centered in ways that support learning. Research questions that remain to be addressed include: How does a teacher use assessment? What skills do teachers need in order to be able to use formative assessments in ways that will improve their teaching? What kinds of supports do teachers need for learning and adopting innovative assessment processes?

26. Explore the foundations for science learning. Research is recommended that would explore such questions as the following:

• How can the field "scale up" successful demonstrations of research-based curricula so that they can be implemented in many diverse settings under the guidance of many different kinds of teachers?

• Which factors influence the conversion of research knowledge into effective instructional methods in real settings?

• Do strategies that work for science education also work to improve instruction in other subject areas?

• How can preschool children be assisted in developing representational structures so that there are bridges, rather than gaps, between early and later school learning?

• How can collaborative learning environments be organized in ways that counteract societal stereotypes and tap diversity as a positive resource for learning?

• Which kinds of assessments can effectively measure new kinds of science learning?

• How do the features of a constructivist curriculum interact with other social factors in classrooms?

• What is the impact of new technologies on school performance?

27. Enhance the methodologies of the learning sciences. The research areas relevant to the science of learning are demonstratively broad, including cognitive development, cognitive science, developmental psychology, neuroscience, anthropology, social psychology, sociology, cross-cultural research, research on learning in subject areas such as science, mathematics, history, and research on effective teaching, pedagogy, and the design of learning environments. New technologies for assessing learning in ways that track the growth of learning, not just cumulative of facts, are needed. Developing effective research methodologies is particularly important for research from this diverse array of disciplines. Advancement of learning research methodologies is critical for such diverse and complex data.

Government agencies and research foundations should develop initiatives and mechanisms of support specifically aimed at strengthening the methodological underpinnings of the learning sciences. Such mechanisms should include cross-field collaborations, internships, visiting scholar programs, training junior scholars in interdisciplinary approaches, and other procedures to foster collaborations for learning and developing new methodologies that can lead to more rigorous investigations in the science of learning.

Research aimed at developing and standardizing new measures and methods is also needed. Studies should be conducted and validated with diverse populations. New statistical techniques should be developed for analyzing the complex systems of learning. New qualitative measurement techniques are also needed, as is new research that is focused on ways to integrate qualitative and quantitative methods across the learning sciences.

28. Foster collaborations in the science of learning. This volume emphasizes the breadth of knowledge areas that affect learners and the significant advances that have been the direct result of collaborative research efforts across disciplines. That kind of collaboration is critical to further development of the learning sciences. It is recommended that government agencies and research foundations explicitly support a wide variety of interdisciplinary collaborations in the learning sciences. Such work should include teachers.

The field of learning research needs to become more integrated in focus and draw together relevant fields for interdisciplinary collaborations. To this end, mechanisms are needed to prepare a new generation of learning scientists by supporting interdisciplinary training for students and scientists to work together. It is important to expand the research scope so that basic researchers and educational researchers can work together on basic and applied issues and to facilitate ways for teachers and researchers to work together. While fields such as neuroscience and cognitive science have made important advances through their joint efforts, researchers had to learn the methodologies and techniques of each discipline before new research studies could be conducted. Efforts are needed to direct training programs in order to foster such interdisciplinary learning.

National databases to encourage collaboration are also recommended to capitalize on the new developments in information systems, research scientists of varying disciplines should be linked together, and teachers should be included in these virtual dialogues. In addition to electronic linkages, scientists should begin to share databases with one another and to work with national databases that they can access electronically.

Databases that link physics researchers with classroom physics educators, for example, have the potential to bring the two sectors closer to the core issues of the field. Basic researchers often have poor understanding of why learners fail to grasp basic concepts of the field; teachers often fail to see relationships of core concepts that, if better understood from the standpoint of theory, could facilitate their teaching. National databases can foster interdisciplinary collaboration and uses of cross-disciplinary data; promote broader exploration of testable questions across datasets; increase the quality of data by maintaining accurate and uniform records; and promote cost-effectiveness through the sharing of research data. Furthermore, national databases that are built from representative samples of the changing school population have the potential of broadening the scope and power of research findings.

29. Investigate successful and creative educational practice. There are well-known cases of exceptional teaching by educators who, often without the help of educational researchers, have created innovative and successful classrooms, programs, curricula, and teaching techniques. It is recommended that case study research be conducted to investigate the principles of learning that underlie successful educational experiments. The conceptual framework provided by this volume can be employed as a lens through which that practice can be viewed, and such case studies could challenge and inform the science of learning.

The research would have several potential benefits. It would ground in sound theory innovations that often exist in isolation, that often cannot be evaluated well by traditional methods, and that cannot be explained well to others. This research could contribute an understanding of why the innovations work, perhaps leading to improvements in them. Moreover, it may stimulate researchers to pursue new theoretical questions regarding cognition. In innovative classrooms, students may engage in forms and levels of learning that are not anticipated by current cognitive theory. From studying such classrooms and the learning that takes place in them, researchers may modify their conceptions about learning.

30. Investigate the potential benefits of collaborative learning in the classroom and the design challenges that it imposes. Outside the classroom, much learning and problem solving takes place as individuals engage with each other, inquire of those with skills and expertise, and use resources and tools that are available in the surrounding environment. The benefits of this "distributed cognition" are tapped inside the classroom when students work collaboratively on problems or projects, learning from each others' insights, and clarifying their own thinking through articulation and argument (Vye et al., 1998). Some research indicates that group problem solving is superior to individual problem solving (e.g., Evans, 1989; Newstead and Evans, 1995), and that developmental changes in cognition can be generated from peer argumentation (Goldman, 1994; Habermas, 1990; Kuhn, 1991; Moshman, 1995a, 1995b; Salmon and Zeitz, 1995; Youniss and Damon, 1992) and peer interaction (Dimant and Bearison, 1991; Kobayashi, 1994). For these reasons, the community-centered classroom described in Chapter 1, in which students learn from each other, can have substantial benefits.

But working in groups can have drawbacks for learning as well, particularly in the early grades. Societal stereotypes or classroom reputations can determine who takes the lead, and whose ideas are respected or dismissed. Differences in temperament can produce consistent leaders and followers. Group products can advance each member's understanding of a problem, or they can mask a lack of understanding by some.

It is recommended that research be conducted by teams of cognitive scientists, developmental psychologists, curriculum developers, and teachers to investigate the potential benefits of collaborative learning in the classroom and the problems that must be addressed to make it beneficial for all students. The research should explore and field-test alternative design strategies. The results should be presented both as scholarly research, and as a discussion addressed to teachers who are interested in collaborative learning in the classroom.

31. Investigate the interaction between cognitive competence and motivational factors. Much of the research on learning has been conducted outside the classroom. Inside the classroom, issues of cognitive competence are intertwined with issues of motivation to perform. The challenges of learning for today's world require disciplined study and problem solving from the earliest grades. To meet the challenges, learners must be motivated to pay attention, complete assignments, and engage in thinking.

Although cognitive psychologists have long posited a relationship between learning and motivation, they have paid little attention to the latter, despite its vital interest to teachers. Research has been done on motivation, but there is no commonly accepted unifying theory, nor a systematic application of what is known to educational practice (National Research Council, 1999b).

It is recommended that research be conducted to elucidate how student interests, identities, self-knowledge, self-regulation, and emotion interact with cognitive competence. This research should combine the efforts of social and developmental psychologists with those of cognitive psychologists. A variety of approaches should be considered, including case studies of small numbers of individual children and the study of the classroom practice of teachers with reputations for promoting achievement among average students, as well as those at high risk for failure.

32. Investigate the relationship between the organization and representation of knowledge and the purpose of learning that knowledge. Research in cognitive science suggests that knowledge is organized differently depending on the uses that need to be made of it. In other words, the structure of knowledge and memory and the conditions under which it is retrieved for application evolves to fit the uses to which it is put. Similarly, what counts as understanding will also be defined in terms of means, rather than as an end in itself. Just as there is no perfect map, but only maps that are useful for particular kinds of tasks and answering particular kinds of questions, there is no perfect state of understanding, but only knowledge organizations that are more or less useful for particular kinds of tasks and questions.

For example, relatively superficial knowledge of the concept of gold may be sufficient to differentiate a gold-colored watch from a silver-colored watch. But it would not be sufficient to differentiate a genuine gold watch from one made of other gold-colored metals or alloys, or fool's gold from the real thing.

This empirical insight has profound implications for the organization of education, teacher education, and curriculum development. Research to deepen understanding of the kinds of knowledge organizations that will best support particular kinds of activities is recommended. For example, the kinds of biology needed to know how to take care of plants (e.g., knowing when, where, and how to plant them in different climates and soil conditions) differs from the knowledge necessary to genetically engineer them.

These kinds of issues become particularly important when considering the nature of the content knowledge that teachers need in order to teach various disciplines. For example, the most useful knowledge for a middle school mathematics teacher may not come from taking a higher-level course in a traditional mathematics sequence, particularly if that course was designed for the uses of that knowledge by mathematics and engineering students in problems suited to the work activities of those disciplines. Instead, it may come from a course that integrates mathematics with particular kinds of inquiry involving design and other tasks.

These considerations are also important for curriculum. Research investigations could yield better understanding for guiding curriculum design so that the knowledge that learners develop from their experiences in courses will be better retrieved in anticipated contexts of use for that knowledge. For example, too little is known about the kinds of activities in which an educated person—but not a future scientist—will be expected to use the scientific knowledge that they may acquire in science courses. Research on these considerations is important to pursue.

COMMUNICATON OF RESEARCH KNOWLEDGE

When one considers the complexity of the ways in which research influences practice (as depicted in Figure 11.1), the heterogeneous audiences for research and their very different needs become apparent. As noted earlier, the ways in which the principles of learning depicted in this volume will be incorporated into practice raise unique problems for pre-service and in-service education, for educational materials, for policy, and for the public (including the media). The pathways by which research knowledge travels, and the transformations it must undertake for each of these audiences, raise striking challenges for communications design. To be effective, such communications cannot serve merely as disseminations of research knowledge. Translating and elaborating that knowledge for each audience has been a theme throughout the agenda. In this final section, we propose an effort to make these translations widely accessible.

33. Design and evaluate ways to easily access the cumulative knowledge base. There is a strong need for adaptive communications about the science of learning that can evolve to fit the distinctive needs of the various education audiences for knowledge derived from research. For such conversations to occur between the research communities and these diverse constituencies, experimentation with Internet-based communications forums is needed.

The Internet is becoming a social place for the formation and ongoing activities of distributed communities, not only a digital library for browsing and downloading information. Current electronic communities with tens of thousands of members share information and convene around a broad range of topics. High-quality resources on the science of learning will be needed to spur on-line discussions among the communities they are designed to serve, and to invite suggestions about how communications concerning the science of learning can better fit the needs of those who will use their results (Pea, 1999). Today one may find a great range of web sites that are devoted to education. But far fewer are devoted to research advances, much less their alignment with educational materials, practices, or policies that are depicted in the web sites.

The development and continuous improvement of a national communications forum for research knowledge on learning and teaching are recommended. This new media communications forum would be accessible through the Internet and would provide illustrative cases and usable information about both the research depicted in this volume and new findings that will continue to emerge in ongoing research. It would provide opportunities for different contributors who are stakeholders in education to post messages and rate the usefulness of documents and materials. Experimentation is needed in establishing "virtual places" online where diverse groups could convene to reflect on how these research advances could be incorporated to improve the practices of education and learning. Such a "learning improvement portal" would provide a vital national resource, guiding research-informed improvements of education.

CONCLUSION

The research efforts proposed herein represent a serious effort to combine the strengths of the research community with the insights gained from the wisdom and challenges of classroom practice. Our suggestions for research do not assume that basic research should first be conducted in isolation and then handed down to practitioners. Instead, we propose that researchers and practitioners work together to identify important problems of inquiry and define the kinds of research and communication strategies that would be most helpful to both groups.

Because of our emphasis on bridging research and practice, many of the efforts proposed here are nontraditional. They combine research and development, rather than undertaking the two separately. It is our view that such combined efforts are most likely to focus the attention of researchers on problems that are central to education, and they are more likely to ensure rigor and consistency with the principles of learning in the programs and products that are developed.

Moreover, many of the efforts combine research and communication. Often, the two are considered separate domains. But the goal of communication is learning, and this volume provides guidance for effective communication. For each audience, preconceived understandings must be identified and addressed in the effort to communicate. And examples that situate ideas in experiences relevant for that audience are crucial.

Combining expertise for the proposed projects will be challenging. There are still relatively few arenas in which researchers work as partners with teachers, administrators, and communications developers (who might film model lessons, develop web sites, produce brochures, etc.). But to be effective, systematic efforts to reform education will require that more of these partnerships be forged. Research and development grants that reward existing partnerships and encourage new ones to be formed could provide a much-needed impetus.

And finally, the agenda proposed is expansive. Many of the recommended projects are time-intensive, multiyear efforts. The nation's decentralized education system is vast. To use the lens of *How People Learn* to evaluate the various facets of that system is in itself a daunting task. We propose in addition the development and testing of new classroom teaching tools, techniques of teacher and administrator training, further research on human learning, and applications of technology that could provide dynamic mechanisms for bringing advances in how people learn and how people teach into continual cycles of coordination and improvement. We believe the integration of these efforts holds the potential to bring research and practice together in the interest of improved education.

References

CHAPTER 1

Anderson, J.R.
  1982   Acquisition of cognitive skill. *Psychological Review* 89:369-406.
  1987   Skill acquisition: Compilation of weak-method problem solutions. *Psychological Review* 94:192-210.
Bloom, B.S.
  1964   *Stability and Change in Human Characteristics.* New York: Wiley.
Bransford, J.D., and B.S. Stein
  1993   *The IDEAL Problem Solver* (2nd ed.). New York: Freeman.
Brice-Heath, S.
  1981   Toward an ethnohistory of writing in American. Pp. 25-45 in *Writing: The Nature, Development, and Teaching of Written Communication* (Vol. 1), M.F. Whiteman, ed. Hillsdale, NJ: Erlbaum.
  1983   *Ways with Words: Language, Life and Work in Communities and Classrooms.* Cambridge, England: Cambridge University Press.
Brown, A.L.
  1975   The development of memory: Knowing, knowing about knowing, and knowing how to know. In *Advances in Child Development and Behavior* (Vol. 10), H.W. Reese, ed. New York: Academic Press.
Brown, A.L., and J.C. Campione
  1994   Guided discovery in a community of learners. Pp. 229-270 in *Classroom Lessons: Integrating Cognitive Theory and Classroom Practices*, K. McGilly, ed. Cambridge, MA: MIT Press.
Carey, S., and R. Gelman
  1991   *The Epigenesis of Mind: Essays on Biology and Cognition.* Hillsdale, NJ: Erlbaum.
Chase, W.G., and H.A. Simon
  1973   Perception in chess. *Cognitive Psychology* 1:33-81.
Chi, M.T.H., P.J. Feltovich, and R. Glaser
  1981   Categorization and representation of physics problems by experts and novices. *Cognitive Science* 5:121-152.

Clement, J.
  1982   Student preconceptions of introductory mechanics. *American Journal of Physics* 50:66-71.

Cobb, P.
  1994   Theories of Mathematical Learning and Constructivism: A Personal View. Paper presented at the Symposium on Trends and Perspectives in Mathematics Education, Institute for Mathematics, University of Klagenfurt, Austria.

Cole, B.
  1996   Characterizing On-line Communication: A First Step. Paper presented at the Annual Meeting of the American Educational Research Association, April 8-12, New York, NY.

Confrey, J.
  1990   A review of research on student conceptions in mathematics, science programming. In *Review of Research in Education* 16:3-55, C.B. Cazden, ed. Washington, DC: American Educational Research Association.

deGroot, A.D.
  1965   *Thought and Choice in Chess.* The Hague, the Netherlands: Mouton.
  1969   *Methodology: Foundations of Inference and Research in the Behavioral Sciences.* New York and the Hague, the Netherlands: Mouton.

Diamat, R.J., and D.J. Bearison
  1991   Development of formal reasoning during successive peer interactions. *Developmental Psychology* 27:277-284.

DiSessa, A.
  1982   Unlearning Aristotelian physics: A study of knowledge-base learning. *Cognitive Science* 6:37-75.

Duckworth, E.
  1987   *"The Having of Wonderful Ideas" and Other Essays on Teaching and Learning.* New York: Teachers College Press, Columbia University.

Dweck, C.S.
  1989   Motivation. Pp. 87-136 in *Foundation for a Psychology of Education,* A. Lesgold and R. Glaser, eds. Hillsdale, NJ: Erlbaum.

Dweck, C., and E. Legget
  1988   A social-cognitive approach to motivation and personality. *Psychological Review* 95:256-273.

Elmore, R.F., P.L. Peterson, and S.J. McCarthey
  1996   *Restructuring in the Classroom: Teaching, Learning, and School Organization.* San Francisco: Jossey-Bass.

Erickson, F.
  1986   Qualitative methods in research on teaching. Pp. 119-161 in *Handbook of Research on Teaching.* New York: Macmillan.

Ericsson, K.A., and N. Charness
  1994   Expert performance: Its structure and acquistion. *American Psychologist* 49:725-745.

Evans, J. St. B. T.
  1989   *Bias in Human Reasoning.* Hillsdale, NJ: Erlbaum.

Flavell, J.H.
 1973   Metacognitive aspects of problem-solving. In *The Nature of Intelligence,*
         L.B. Resnick, ed. Hillsdale, NJ: Erlbaum.
Gardner, H.
 1991   *The Unschooled Mind: How Children Think and How Schools Should Teach.*
         New York: Basic Books.
Gelman, R., and C.R. Gallistel
 1978   *The Children's Understanding of Number.* Cambridge, MA: Harvard University Press.
         versity Press.
Goldman, A.I.
 1994   Argument and social epistemology. *Journal of Philosophy* 91:27-49.
Greenfield, P.M., and R.R. Cocking
 1996   *Interacting with Video.* Norwood, NJ: Ablex.
Greeno, J.
 1991   Number sense as situated knowing in a conceptual domain. *Journal for Research in Mathematics Education* 22(3):170-218.
         Research in Mathematics Education 22(3):170-218.
Habermas, J.
 1990   *Moral Consciousness and Communicative Action.* Cambridge, MA: MIT Press.
         Press.
Hammersly, M., and P. Atkinson
 1983   *Ethnography: Principles and Practices.* London: Travistock.
Harvard-Smithsonian Center for Astrophysics, Science Education Department
 1987   *A Private Universe.* Video. Cambridge, MA: Science Media Group.
Hatano, G., and K. Inagaki
 1986   Two courses of expertise. In *Child Development and Education in Japan,*
         H. Stevenson, H. Azuma, and K. Hakuta, eds. New York: W.H. Freeman.
Heath, S.
 1982   Ethnography in education: Defining the essential. Pp. 33-58 in *Children In and Out of School,* P. Gilmore and A. Gilmore, eds. Washington, DC:
         In and Out of School, P. Gilmore and A. Gilmore, eds. Washington, DC:
         Center for Applied Linguistics.
Holyoak, K.J.
 1984   Analogical thinking and human intelligence. Pp. 199-230 in *Advances in the Psychology of Human Intelligence* (Vol. 2), R.J. Sternberg, ed. Hillsdale,
         the Psychology of Human Intelligence (Vol. 2), R.J. Sternberg, ed. Hillsdale,
         NJ: Erlbaum.
Hull, C.L.
 1943   *Principles of Behavior.* New York: Appleton-Century-Crofts.
Hutchins, E.
 1995   *Cognition in the Wild.* Cambridge, MA: MIT Press.
James, W.
 1890   *Principles of Psychology.* New York: Holt.
Kuhn, D.
 1991   *The Skills of Argument.* Cambridge, England: Cambridge University Press.
Lamon, M., D. Caswell, M. Scardamalia, and R. Chandra
 1997   Technologies of Use and Social Interaction in Classroom Knowledge Building
         Communities. Paper presented at the Symposium on Computer-Supported
         Collaborative Learning: Advancements and Challenges, K. Lonka, chair,

European Association for Research in Learning and Instruction, August, Athens, Greece.

Lave, J.
1988   *Cognition in Practice: Mind, Mathematics, and Culture in Everyday Life.* Cambridge, MA: Cambridge University Press.

Lave, J., and E. Wegner
1991   *Situated Learning: Legitimate Peripheral Participation.* New York: Cambridge University Press.

Lehrer, R., and D. Chazan
1998a   *Designing Learning Environments for Developing Understanding of Geometry and Space.* Mahwah, NJ: Erlbaum.
1998b   *New Directions for Teaching and Learning Geometry.* Hillsdale, NJ: Erlbaum.

Lincoln, Y.S., and E.G. Guba
1985   *Naturalistic Inquiry.* Beverly Hills, CA: Sage.

Lionni, L.
1970   *Fish Is Fish.* New York: Scholastic Press.

Marshall, C., and G.B. Rossman
1955   *Designing Qualitative Research.* Thousand Oaks, CA: Sage.

McClelland, J.L ,and M. Chappell
1998   Familiarity breeds differentiation: A subject-likelihood approach to the effects of experience in recognition memory. *Psychological Review.* 105: 724-760.

McClelland, J.L., B.L. McNaughton, and R.C. O'Reilly
1995   Why there are complementary learning systems in hippocampus and neocortex: Insights from the successes and failures of connectionist models of learning and memory. *Psychological Review* 102:419-447.

Mestre, J.P.
1994   Cognitive aspects of learning and teaching science. Pp. 3-1 - 3-53 in *Teacher Enhancement for Elementary and Secondary Science and Mathematics: Status, Issues, and Problems*, S.J. Fitzsimmons and L.C. Kerpelman, eds. NSF 94-80. Arlington, VA: National Science Foundation.

Miles, M.B., and A.M. Huberman
1984   *Qualitative Data Analysis: A Sourcebook of New Methods.* Newbury Park, CA: Sage.

Minstrell, J.A.
1989   Teaching science for understanding. Pp. 130-131 in *Toward the Thinking Curriculum: Current Cognitive Research,* L.B. Resnick and L.E. Klopfer, eds. Alexandria, VA: Association for Supervision and Curriculum Development.

Moll, L.C.
1986a   Creating Strategic Learning Environments for Students: A Community-Based Approach. Paper presented at the S.I.G. Language Developed Invited Symposium Literacy and Schooling, Annual Meeting of the American Educational Research Association, San Francisco, California.
1986b   Writing as a communication: Creating strategic learning environments for students. *Theory into Practice* 25:102-108.

1990   *Vygotsky and Education.* New York: Cambridge University Press.

Moll, L.C., J. Tapia, and K.F. Whitmore
    1993   Living knowledge: The social distribution of cultural sources for thinking. Pp. 139-163 in *Distributed Cognitions*, G. Salomon, ed. Cambridge, UK: Cambridge University Press

Moshman, D.
    1995a   Reasoning as self-constrained thinking. *Human Development* 38:53-64.
    1995b   The construction of moral rationality. *Human Development* 38:265-281.

Munkata, Y., J.L McClelland, M.H. Johnson, and R.S. Siegler
    1997   Rethinking infant knowledge: Toward an adaptive process account of successes and failures in object permanence tasks. *Psychological Review* 104:686-713.

Newell, A., and H.A. Simon
    1972   *Human Problem Solving.* Englewood Cliffs, NJ: Prentice-Hall.

Newstead, S.E., and J. St. B.T. Evans, eds.
    1995   *Perspectives on Thinking and Reasoning: Essays in Honour of Peter Wason.* Hillsdale, NJ: Erlbaum.

Norman, D.A.
    1980   Twelve issues for cognitive science. *Cognitive Science* 4:1-32.
    1993   *Things That Make Us Smart: Defending Human Attributes in the Age of the Machine.* New York: Addison-Wesley.

Novick, L.R., and K.J. Holyoak
    1991   Mathematical problem solving by analogy. *Journal of Experimental Psychology: Learning, Memory, and Cognition* 17(3)(May):398-415.

Palincsar, A.S., and A.L. Brown
    1984   Reciprocal teaching of comprehension monitoring activities. *Cognition and Instruction* 1:117-175.

Piaget, J.
    1952   *The Origins of Intelligence in Children.* M. Cook, trans. New York: International Universities Press.
    1973a   *The Child and Reality: Problems of Genetic Psychology.* New York: Grossman.
    1973b   *The Language and Thought of the Child.* London: Routledge and Kegan Paul.
    1977   *The Grasp of Consciousness.* London: Routledge and Kegan Paul.
    1978   *Success and Understanding.* Cambridge, MA: Harvard University Press.

Plaut, D.C., J.L. McClelland, M.S. Seidenberg, and K.E. Patterson
    1996   Understanding normal and impaired word reading: Computational principles in quasi-regular domains. *Psychological Review* 103:56-115.

Prawaf, R.S., J. Remillard, R.T. Putnam, and R.M. Heaton
    1992   Teaching mathematics for understanding: Case study of four fifth-grade teachers. *Elementary School Journal* 93:145-152.

Redish, E.F.
    1996   Discipline-Specific Science Education and Educational Research: The Case of Physics. Paper prepared for the Committee on Developments in the Science of Learning, for The Sciences of Science Learning: An Interdisciplinary Discussion.

Rogoff, B.
1990   *Apprenticeship in Thinking: Cognitive Development in Social Context.* New York: Oxford University Press.

Rogoff, B., J. Mistry, A. Goncu, and C. Mosier
1993   Guided Participation in Cultural Activity by Toddlers and Caregivers. *Monographs of the Society for Research in Child Development* 58(7): Serial No. 236.

Salmon, M.H., and C.M. Zeitz
1995   Analyzing conversational reasoning. *Informal Logic* 17:1-23.

Scardamalia, M., and C. Bereiter
1991   Higher levels of agency for children in knowledge-building: A challenge for the design of new knowledge media. *Journal of the Learning Sciences* 1:37-68.

Scardamalia, M., C. Bereiter, and R. Steinbach
1984   Teachability of reflective processes in written composition. *Cognitive Science* 8:173-190.

Schauble, L., R. Glaser, R. Duschl, S. Schulze, and J. John.
1995   Students' understanding of the objectives and procedures of experimentation in the science classroom. *Journal of the Learning Sciences* 4(2):131-166.

Schoenfeld, A.H.
1983   Problem solving in the mathematics curriculum: A report, recommendation and annotated bibliography. *Mathematical Association of America Notes* No. 1.
1984   *Mathematical Problem Solving.* Orlando, FL: Academic Press.
1991   On mathematics as sense making: An informal attack on the unfortunate divorce of formal and informal mathematics. Pp. 331-343 in *Informal Reasoning and Education,* J.F. Voss, D.N. Perkins, and J.W. Segal, eds. Hillsdale, NJ: Erlbaum.

Schwartz, D.L., and J.D. Bransford
1998   A time for telling. *Cognition and Instruction* 16(4):475-522.

Simon, H.A.
1996   Observations on the Sciences of Science Learning. Paper prepared for the Committee on Developments in the Science of Learning for the Sciences of Science Learning: An Interdisciplinary Discussion. Department of Psychology, Carnegie Mellon University.

Skinner, B.F.
1950   Are theories of learning necessary? *Psychological Review* 57:193-216.

Spence, K.W.
1942   Theoretical interpretations of learning. In *Comparative Psychology,* F.A. Moss, ed. New York: Prentice-Hall.

Spradley, J.
1979   *The Ethnographic Interview.* New York: Harcourt, Brace, Javanovich.

Suina, J.H., and L.B. Smolkin
   1994   From natal culture to school culture to dominant society culture: Support-
           ing transitions for Pueblo Indian students. Pp. 115-130 in *Cross-cultural
           Roots of Minority Child Development*, P.M. Greenfield and R.R. Cocking,
           eds. Hillsdale, NJ: Erlbaum.
Thorndike, E.L.
   1913   *Educational Psychology* (Vols. 1 and 2). New York: Columbia University
           Press.
Vosniadou, S., and W.F. Brewer
   1989   The Concept of the Earth's Shape: A Study of Conceptual Change in Child-
           hood. Unpublished paper. Center for the Study of Reading, University of
           Illinois, Champaign.
Vye, N.J.., S.R. Goldman, C. Hmelo, J.F. Voss, S. Williams, and Cognition and Tech-
nology Group at Vanderbilt
   1998a   Complex mathematical problem solving by individuals and dyads. *Cogni-
           tion and Instruction* 15(4).
Vye, N.J., D.L. Schwartz, J.D. Bransford, B.J. Barron, L. Zech, and Cognition and
Technology Group at Vanderbilt
   1998b   SMART environments that support monitoring, reflection, and revision. In
           Metacognition in Educational Theory and Practice, D. Hacker, J. Dunlosky,
           and A. Graessner, eds. Mahwah, NJ: Erlbaum.
Vygotsky, L.S.
   1962   *Thought and Language.* Cambridge, MA: MIT Press.
   1978   *Mind in Society: The Development of the Higher Psychological Processes.*
           Cambridge, MA: The Harvard University Press. (Originally published 1930,
           New York: Oxford University Press.)
Warren, B., and A. Rosebery
   1996   This question is just too, too easy: Perspectives from the classroom on
           accountability in science. Pp. 97-125 in the *Contributions of Instructional
           Innovation to Understanding Learning*, L. Schauble and R. Glaser, eds.
           Mahwah, NJ: Erlbaum.
Watson, J.B.
   1913   Psychology as a behaviorist views it. *Psychological Review* 20:158-177.
Wellman, H.M.
   1990   *The Child's Theory of Mind.* Cambridge, MA: MIT Press.
White, B.Y., and J.R. Fredrickson
   1997   *The ThinkerTools Inquiry Project: Making Scientific Inquiry Accessible to
           Students.* Princeton, New Jersey: Center for Performance Assessment,
           Educational Testing Service.
   1998   Inquiry, modeling, and metacognition: Making science accessible to all
           students. *Cognition and Science* 16:90-91.
Youniss, J., and W. Damon.
   1992   Social construction in Piaget's theory. Pp. 267-286 in *Piaget's Theory: Pros-
           pects and Possibilities*, H. Berlin and P.B. Pufal, eds. Hillsdale, NJ: Erlbaum.

CHAPTER 2

American Association for the Advancement of Science
  1989   *Science for All Americans: A Project 2061 Report on Literacy Goals in Science, Mathematics, and Technology.* Washington, DC: American Association for the Advancement of Science.

Anderson, J.R.
  1981   *Cognitive Skills and Their Acquisition.* Hillsdale, NJ: Erlbaum.
  1982   Acquisition of cognitive skill. *Psychological Review* 89:369-406.

Beck I.L., M.G. McKeown, and E.W. Gromoll, et al.
  1989   Learning from social studies texts. *Cognition and Instruction* 6:99-158.

Beck, I.L., M.G. McKeown, G.M. Sinatra, and J.A. Loxterman
  1991   Revising social studies text from a text-processing perspective: Evidence of improved comprehensibility. *Reading Research Quarterly* 26:251-276.

Bransford, J.D.
  1979   *Human Cognition: Learning, Understanding, and Remembering.* Belmont, CA: Wadsworth.

Bransford J., T. Hasselbring, B. Barron, S. Kulweicz, J. Littlefield, and L. Goin
  1988   Uses of macro-contexts to facilitate mathematical thinking. Pp. 125-147 in *The Teaching and Assessing of Mathematical Problem Solving*, R.I. Charles and E.A. Silver, eds. Hillsdale, NJ: Erlbaum.

Bransford, J.D., J.J. Franks, N.J. Vye, and R.D. Sherwood
  1989   New approaches to instruction: Because wisdom can't be told. In *Similarity and Analogical Reasoning*, S. Vosniadou and A. Ortony, eds. Cambridge, UK: Cambridge University Press.

Bransford, J.D., and B.S. Stein
  1993   *The IDEAL Problem Solver* (2nd ed.). New York: Freeman.

Brophy, J. E.
  1983   Research on the self-fulfilling prophecy and teacher expectations. *Journal of Educational Psychology* 61:365-374.

Brown, A.L.
  1980   Metacognitive development and reading. In *Theoretical Issues in Reading Comprehension: Perspectives from Cognitive Psychology, Linguistics, Artificial Intelligence, and Education*, R.J. Spiro, B.C. Bruce, and W.F. Brewer, eds. Hillsdale, NJ: Erlbaum.

Brown, J.S., A Collins, and P. Durgid
  1989   Situated cognition and the culture of learning. *Educational Researcher* 18:32-41.

Case, R.
  1978   Implications of developmental psychology for the design of effective instruction. Pp. 441-463 in *Cognitive Psychology and Instruction*, A.M. Lesgold, J.W. Pellegrino, S.D. Fokkema, and R. Glaser, eds. New York: Plenum.

Chase, W.G., and H.A. Simon
  1973   Perception in chess. *Cognitive Psychology* 1:33-81.

Chi, M.T.H.
  1978   Knowledge structures and memory development. Pp. 73-96 in *Children's Thinking: What Develops*, R. Siegler, ed. Hillsdale, NJ: Erlbaum.

Chi, M.T.H., P.J. Feltovich, and R. Glaser
   1981   Categorization and representation of physics problems by experts and nov-
           ices. *Cognitive Science* 5:121-152.
Chi M.T.H., R. Glaser, and E. Rees
   1982   Expertise in problem solving. In *Advances in the Psychology of Human
           Intelligence* (Vol. 1). R.J. Sternberg, ed. Hillsdale, NJ: Erlbaum.
Cognition and Technology Group at Vanderbilt
   1997   *The Jasper Project: Lessons in Curriculum, Instruction, Assessment, and
           Professional Development.* Mahwah, NJ: Erlbaum.
deGroot, A.D.
   1965   *Thought and Choice in Chess.* The Hague, the Netherlands: Mouton.
Dweck, C.S.
   1989   Motivation. Pp. 87-136 in *Foundations for a Psychology of Education*, A.
           Lesgold and R. Glaser, eds. Hillsdale, NJ: Erlbaum.
Egan, D.E., and B.J. Schwartz
   1979   Chunking in recall of symbolic drawings. *Memory and Cognition* 7:149-
           158.
Ehrlich, K., and E. Soloway
   1984   An empirical investigation of the tacit plan knowledge in programming.
           Pp. 113-134 in *Human Factors in Computer Systems*, J. Thomas and M.L.
           Schneider, eds. Norwood, NJ: Ablex.
Ericsson, K.A., and H.A. Simon
   1993   *Protocol Analysis: Verbal Reports as Data.* 1984/1993. Cambridge, MA:
           MIT Press.
Ericsson, K.A., and J.J. Staszewski
   1989   Skilled memory and expertise: Mechanisms of exceptional performance.
           Pp. 235-267 in *Complex Information Processing: The Impact of Herbert A.
           Simon*, D. Klahr and K. Kotovsky, eds. Hillsdale, NJ: Erlbaum.
Flavell, J.H.
   1985   *Cognitive Development.* Englewood Cliffs, NJ: Prentice Hall.
   1991   Understanding memory access. Pp. 281-299 in *Cognition and the Sym-
           bolic Processes: Applied and Ecological Perspectives*, R. Hoffman and D.
           Palermo, eds. Hillsdale, NJ: Erlbaum.
Getzels, J., and M. Csikszentmihalyi
   1976   *The Creative Vision.* New York: Wiley.
Glaser, R.
   1992   Expert knowledge and processes of thinking. Pp. 63-75 in *Enhancing
           Thinking Skills in the Sciences and Mathematics.* D.F. Halpern, ed. Hillsdale,
           NJ: Erlbaum.
Glaser, R., and M.T.H. Chi
   1988   Overview. Pp. xv-xxvii in *The Nature of Expertise*, M.T.H. Chi, R. Glaser,
           and M.J. Farr, eds. Hillsdale, NJ: Erlbaum.
Grossman, P.L.
   1987   A Tale of Two Teachers: The Role of Subject Matter Orientation in Teach-
           ing. Paper presented at the meeting of the American Educational Research
           Association, Washington, DC.

1990   *The Making of a Teacher*. New York: Teachers College Press, Columbia University.

Hasselbring, T.S., L. Goin, and J.D. Bransford
1987   Effective mathematics instruction: Developing automaticity. *Teaching Exceptional Children* 19(3):30-33.

Hatano, G.
1990   The nature of everyday science: A brief introduction. *British Journal of Developmental Psychology* 8:245-250.

Hinsley, D.A., J.R. Hayes, and H.A. Simon
1977   From words to equations: Meaning and representation in algebra word problems. Pp. 89-106 in *Cognitive Processes in Comprehension*, M.A. Just and P.A. Carpenter, eds. Hillsdale, NJ: Erlbaum.

LaBerge, D., and S.J. Samuels
1974   Toward a theory of automatic information processing in reading. *Cognitive Psychology* 6:293-323.

Larkin, J.H.
1979   Information processing models in science instruction. Pp. 109-118 in *Cognitive Process Instruction*, J. Lochhead and J. Clement, eds. Hillsdale, NJ: Erlbaum.
1981   Enriching formal knowledge: A model for learning to solve problems in physics. Pp. 311-334 in *Cognitive Skills and Their Acquisition*, J.R. Anderson, ed. Hillsdale, NJ: Erlbaum.
1983   The role of problem representation in physics. Pp. 75-98 in *Mental Models*, D. Gentner and A.L. Stevens, eds. Hillsdale, NJ: Erlbaum.

Larkin, J., J. McDermottt, D.P. Simon, and H.A. Simon
1980   Expert and novice performance in solving physics problems. *Science* 208:1335-1342.

Larkin, J.H., and H.A. Simon
1987   Why a diagram is (sometimes) worth ten thousand words. *Cognitive Science* 11:65-69.

Lesgold, A.M.
1984   Acquiring expertise. Pp. 31-60 in *Tutorials in Learning and Memory: Essays in Honor of Gordon Bower*, J.R. Anderson and S.M. Kosslyn, eds. Hillsdale, NJ: Erlbaum.
1988   Problem solving. In *The Psychology of Human Thoughts*, R.J. Sternberg and E.E. Smith, eds. New York: Cambridge University Press.

Lesgold, A.M., H. Rubison, P. Feltovich, R. Glaser, D. Klopfer, and Y. Wang
1988   Expertise in a complex skill: Diagnosing x-ray pictures. Pp. 311-342 in *The Nature of Expertise*, M.T.H. Chi, R. Glaser, and M. Farr, eds. Hillsdale, NJ: Erlbaum.

Miller, G.A.
1956   The magical number seven, plus or minus two. Some limits on our capacity to process information. *Psychological Review* 63:81-87.

Miller, R.B.
1978   The information system designer. Pp. 278-291 in *The Analysis of Practical Skills*, W.T. Singleton, ed. Baltimore, MD: University Park Press.

National Research Council
1996   *National Science Education Standards*. Washington, DC: National Academy Press. Available: http://www.nap.edu.

Paige, J.M., and H.A. Simon
1966   Cognition processes in solving algebra word problems. Pp. 119-151 in *Problem Solving*, B. Kleinmutz, ed. New York: Wiley.

Redish, E.F.
1996   Discipline-specific Science Education and Educational Research: The Case of Physics. Paper prepared for the Committee on Developments in the Science of Learning for the Sciences of Science Learning: An Interdisciplinary Discussion.

Reusser, K.
1993   Tutoring systems and pedagogical theory: Representational tools for understanding, planning, and reflection in problem solving. Pp. 143-177 in *Computers as Cognitive Tools*, S.P. Lajoie and S.J. Derry, eds. Hillsdale, NJ: Erlbaum.

Robinson, C.S., and J.R. Hayes
1978   Making inferences about relevance in understanding problems. In *Human Reasoning*, R. Revlin and R.E. Mayer, eds. Washington, DC: Winston.

Sabers, D.S., K.S. Cushing, and D.C. Berliner
1991   Differences among teachers in a task characterized by simultaneity, multidimensionality, and immediacy. *American Educational Research Journal* 28(1):63-88.

Schmidt, W.H., C.C. McKnight, and S. Raizen
1997   *A Splintered Vision: An Investigation of U.S. Science and Mathematics Education*. U.S. National Research Center for the Third International Mathematics and Science Study. Dordrecht/Boston/London: Kluwer Academic Publishers. Available: gopher://gopher.wkap.nl.70/00gopher_root1%3A%5B book.soci.f500%5Df5101601.txt.

Schneider, W., and R.M. Shiffrin
1977   Controlled and automatic human information processing: Detection, search and attention. *Psychological Review* 84:1-66.
1985   Categorization (restructuring) and automatization: Two separable factors. *Psychological Review* 92(3):424-428.

Schneider, W., H. Gruber, A. Gold, and K. Opivis
1993   Chess expertise and memory for chess positions in children and adults. *Journal of Experimental Child Psychology* 56:323-349.

Shulman, L.
1986   Those who understand: Knowledge growth in teaching. *Educational Researcher* 15(2):4-14.
1987   Knowledge and teaching: Foundations of the new reform. *Harvard Educational Review* 57:1-22.

Simon, D.P., and H.A. Simon
1978   Individual differences in solving physics problems. Pp. 325-348 in *Children's Thinking: What Develops?* R. Siegler, ed. Hillsdale, NJ: Erlbaum.

Simon, H.A.
   1980   Problem solving and education. Pp. 81-96 in *Problem Solving and Educa-
           tion: Issues in Teaching and Research*, D.T. Tuma and R. Reif, eds. Hillsdale,
           NJ: Erlbaum.
Spiro, R.J., P.L. Feltovich, M.J. Jackson, and R.L. Coulson
   1991   Cognitive flexibility, constructivism, and hypertext: Random access in-
           struction for advanced knowledge acquisition in ill-structured domains.
           Educational Technology 31(5):24-33.
Voss, J.F., T.R. Greene, T.A. Post, and B.C. Penner
   1984   Problem solving skills in the social science. In *The Psychology of Learning
           and Motivation: Advances in Research Theory* (Vol. 17), G.H. Bower, ed.
           New York: Academic Press.
Whitehead, A.N.
   1929   *The Aims of Education*. New York: MacMillan.
Wineburg, S.S.
   1991   Historical problem solving: A study of the cognitive processes used in the
           evaluation of documentary and pictorial evidence. *Journal of Educational
           Psychology* 83(1):73-87.
   1998   Reading Abraham Lincoln: An expert-expert study in the interpretation of
           historical texts. *Cognitive Science* 22:319-346.
Wineburg, S.S., and J.E. Fournier
   1994   Contextualized thinking in history. Pp. 285-308 in *Cognitive and Instruc-
           tional Processes in History and the Social Sciences*, M. Carretero and J.F.
           Voss, eds. Hillsdale, NJ: Erlbaum.

CHAPTER 3

Allen, B., and A.W. Boykin
   1992   African American children and the educational process: Alleviating cul-
           tural discontinuity through prescriptive pedagogy. *School Psychology Re-
           view* 21(4):586-596.
Anderson, J.R., L.M. Reder, and H.A. Simon
   1996   Situated learning and education. *Educational Researcher* 25:4(May)5-96.
Au, K., and C. Jordan
   1981   Teaching reading to Hawaiian children: Finding a culturally appropriate
           solution. Pp. 139-152 in *Culture and the Bilingual Classroom: Studies in
           Classroom Ethnography*, H. Tureba, G. Guthrie, and K. Au, eds. Rowley,
           MA: Newbury House.
Barron, B.J., D.L. Schwartz, N.J. Vye, A. Moore, A. Petrosino, L. Zech, J.D. Bransford,
and Cognition and Technology Group at Vanderbilt
   1998   Doing with understanding: Lessons from research on problem and project-
           based learning. *Journal of Learning Sciences* 7(3 and 4):271-312.
Barrows, H.S.
   1985   *How to Design a Problem-Based Curriculum for the Preclinical Years*. New
           York: Springer.

Bassok, M., and K.J. Holyoak

1989a   Interdomain transfer between isomorphic topics in algebra and physics. *Journal of Experimental Psychology: Learning, Memory, and Cognition* 15:153-166.

1989b   Transfer of domain-specific problem solving procedures. *Journal of Experimental Psychology: Learning, Memory, and Cognition* 16:522-533.

Bassok, M., and K.L. Olseth

1995   Object-based representations: Transfer between cases of continuous and discrete models of change. *Journal of Experimental Psychology: Learning, Memory, and Cognition* 21:1522-1588.

Behr, M.J., G. Harel, T.R. Post, and R. Lesh

1992   Rational number, ratio, and proportion. Pp. 308-310 in *Handbook of Research on Mathematics Teaching and Learning: A Project of the National Council of Teachers of Mathematics*, D.A. Grouws, ed. New York: Macmillan.

Bereiter, C.

1997   Situated cognition and how to overcome it. Pp. 281-300 in *Situated Cognition: Social, Semiotic, and Psychological Perspectives*, D. Kirshner and J.A. Whitson, eds. Hillsdale, NJ: Erlbaum.

Biederman, I., and M.M. Shiffrar

1987   Sexing day-old chicks: A case study and expert systems analysis of a difficult perceptual-learning task. *Journal of Experimental Psychology: Learning, Memory, and Cognition* 13(4)(October):640-645.

Bielaczyc, K., P. Pirolli, and A.L. Brown

1995   Training in self-explanation and self-regulation strategies: Investigating the effects of knowledge acquisition activities on problem solving. *Cognition and Instruction* 13:221-252.

Bjork, R.A., and A. Richardson-Klavhen

1989   On the puzzling relationship between environment context and human memory. In *Current Issues in Cognitive Processes: The Tulane Flowerree Symposium on Cognition*, C. Izawa, ed. Hillsdale, NJ: Erlbaum.

Blake, I.K.

1994   Language development and socialization in young African-American children. Pp. 167-195 in *Cross Cultural Roots of Minority Child Development*, P.M. Greenfield and R.R. Cocking, eds. Hillsdale, NJ: Erlbaum.

Boykin, A.W., and F. Tom

1985   Black child socialization: A conceptual framework. Pp. 33-51 in *Black Children: Social, Educational, and Parental Environments*, H. McAdoo and J. McAdoo, eds. Beverly Hills, CA: Sage.

Bransford, J.D.

1979   *Human Cognition: Learning, Understanding, and Remembering*. Belmont, CA: Wadsworth.

Bransford, J.D., J.J. Franks, N.J. Vye, and R.D. Sherwood

1989   New approaches to instruction: Because wisdom can't be told. In *Similarity and Analogical Reasoning*, S. Vosniadou and A. Ortony, eds. Cambridge, UK: Cambridge University Press.

Bransford, J.D., and R. Johnson

1972   Contextual prerequisites for understanding: Some investigations of comprehension and recall. *Journal of Verbal Learning and Verbal Behavior* 11:717-726.

Bransford, J.D., and D. Schwartz

1999   Rethinking transfer: A simple proposal with multiple implications. *Review of Research in Education* 24:61-100.

Bransford, J.D., and B.S. Stein

1993   *The IDEAL Problem Solver* (2nd ed.). New York: Freeman.

Bransford, J.D., B.S. Stein, N.J. Vye, J.J. Franks, P.M. Auble, K.J. Mezynski, and G.A. Perfetto

1983   Differences in approaches to learning: An overview. *Journal of Experimental Psychology: General* 3(4):390-398.

Bransford, J.D., L. Zech, D. Schwartz, B. Barron, N.J. Vye, and Cognition and Technology Group at Vanderbilt

1998   Designs for environments that invite and sustain mathematical thinking. In *Symbolizing, Communicating, and Mathematizing: Perspectives on Discourse, Tools, and Instructional Design*, P. Cobb, ed. Mahwah, NJ: Erlbaum.

Brice-Heath, S.

1981   Toward an ethnohistory of writing in American education. Pp. 25-45 in *Writing: The Nature, Development and Teaching of Written Communication* (Vol. 1), M.F. Whiteman, ed. Hillsdale, NJ: Erlbaum.

1983   *Ways with Words: Language, Life and Work in Communities and Classrooms*. Cambridge, UK: Cambridge University Press.

Broudy, H.S.

1977   Types of knowledge and purposes in education. Pp. 1-17 in *Schooling and the Acquisition of Knowledge*, R.C. Anderson, R.J. Spiro, and W.E. Montague, eds. Hillsdale, NJ: Erlbaum.

Brown, A.L.

1975   The development of memory: Knowing, knowing about knowing, and knowing how to know. In *Advances in Child Development and Behavior* (Vol. 10), H.W. Reese, ed. New York: Academic Press.

Brown, A.L., J.D. Bransford, R.A. Ferrara, and J.C. Campione

1983   Learning, remembering, and understanding. Pp. 78-166 in *Handbook of Child Psychology: Vol. 3 Cognitive Development* (4th ed.), J.H. Flavell and E.M. Markman, eds. New York: Wiley.

Brown, G.

1986   Investigating listening comprehension in context. *Applied Linguistics* 7(3)Autumn):284-302.

Bruer, J.T.

1993   *Schools for thought*. Cambridge, MA: MIT Press.

Byrnes, J.P.

1996   *Cognitive Development and Learning in Instructional Contexts*. Boston: Allyn and Bacon.

Campione, J., and A.L. Brown

1987   Linking dynamic assessment with school achievement. Pp. 82-114 in *Dynamic Assessment: An Interactional Approach to Evaluating Learning Potential*, C.S. Lidz, ed. New York: Guilford.

Carraher, T.N.
   1986   From drawings to buildings: Mathematical scales at work. *International Journal of Behavioural Development* 9:527-544.
Carraher, T.N., D.W. Carraher, and A.D. Schliemann
   1985   Mathematics in the street and in school. *British Journal of Developmental Psychology* 3:21-29.
Cazden, C.
   1988   *Classroom Discourse.* Portsmouth, NH: Heinemann.
Cazden, C., S. Michaels, and P. Tabors
   1985   Spontaneous repairs in sharing time narratives: The intersection of metalinguistic awareness, speech event and narrative style. In *The Acquisition of Written Language: Revision and Response*, S. Freedman, ed. Norwood, NJ: Ablex.
Chase, W.G., and H.A. Simon
   1973   Perception in chess. *Cognitive Psychology* 1:33-81.
Chi, M.T.H., M. Bassok, M.W. Lewis, P. Reimann, and R. Glaser
   1989   Self-explanations: How students study and use examples in learning to solve problems. *Cognitive Science* 13:145-182.
Chi, M.T.H., N. deLeeuw, M. Chiu, and C. LaVancher
   1994   Eliciting self-explanations improves understanding. *Cognitive Science* 18:439-477.
Clement, J.J.
   1982a   Algebra word problem solutions: Thought processes underlying a common misconception. *Journal of Research in Mathematics Education* 13:16-30.
   1982b   Students' preconceptions in introductory mechanics. *American Journal of Physics* 50:66-71.
Cognition and Technology Group at Vanderbilt
   1996   Looking at technology in context: A framework for understanding technology and education research. Pp. 807-840 in *The Handbook of Educational Psychology*, D.C. Berliner and R.C. Calfee, eds. New York: Simon and Schuster-MacMillan.
   1997   *The Jasper Project: Lessons in Curriculum, Instruction, Assessment, and Professional Development.* Mahwah, NJ: Erlbaum.
   1998   Designing environments to reveal, support, and expand our children's potentials. Pp. 313-350 in *Perspectives on Fundamental Processes in Intellectual Functioning* (Vol. 1), S.A. Soraci and W. McIlvane, eds. Greenwich, CN: Ablex.
Cohen, P.
   1983   *A Calculating People: The Spread of Numeracy in Early America.* Chicago: University of Chicago Press.
Dooling, D.J., and R. Lachman
   1971   Effects of comprehension on retention of prose. *Journal of Experimental Psychology* 88:216-222.
Dunbar, K.
   1996   Problem Solving Among Geneticists. Paper prepared for the Committee on Developments in the Science of Learning for the Sciences of Science Learning: An Interdisciplinary Discussion.

Dweck, C.S.
  1989   Motivation. Pp. 87-136 in *Foundations for a Psychology of Education*, A. Lesgold and R. Glaser, eds. Hillsdale, NJ: Erlbaum.
Eich, E.
  1985   Context, memory, and integrated item/context imagery. *Journal of Experimental Psychology: Learning, Memory, and Cognition* 11:764-770.
Erickson, F., and G. Mohatt
  1982   Cultural organization and participation structures in two classrooms of Indian students. Pp. 131-174 in *Doing the Ethnography of Schooling*, G. Spindler, ed. New York: Holt, Rinehart and Winston.
Ericsson, K., W. Chase, and S. Faloon
  1980   Acquisition of a memory skill. *Science* 208:1181-1182.
Ericsson, K.A., R.T. Krampe, and C. Tesch-Romer
  1993   The role of deliberate practice in the acquisition of expert performance. *Psychological Review* 100:363-406.
Fasheh, M.
  1990   Community education: To reclaim and transform what has been made invisible. *Harvard Educational Review* 60:19-35.
Fishbein, E., M. Deri, M.S. Nello, and M.S. Marino
  1985   The role of implicit models in solving verbal problems in multiplication and division. *Journal for Research in Mathematics Education* 16(1)(January):3-17.
Flavell, J.H.
  1973   Metacognitive aspects of problem-solving. In *The Nature of Intelligence*, L.B. Resnick, ed. Hillsdale, NJ: Erlbaum.
Gagné, R., and J.J. Gibson
  1947   Research on the recognition of aircraft. In *Motion Picture Training and Research*, J.J. Gibson, ed. Washington, DC: U.S. Government Printing Office.
Garner, W.R.
  1974   *The Processing of Information and Structure.* Potomac, MD: Erlbaum.
Gee, J.P.
  1989   What is literacy? *Journal of Education* 171:18-25.
Gelman, R.
  1967   Conservation acquisition: A problem of learning to attend to the relevant attributes. *Journal of Experimental Child Psychology* 7:167-187.
Gibson, J.J, and E.J. Gibson
  1955   Perceptual learning: Differentiation or enrichment. *Psychological Review* 62:32-51.
Gick, M.L., and K.J. Holyoak
  1980   Analogical problem solving. *Cognitive Psychology* 12:306-355.
  1983   Schema induction and analogical transfer. *Cognitive Psychology* 15:1-38.
Gragg, C.I.
  1940   Because wisdom can't be told. *Harvard Alumni Bulletin* (October 19):78-84.

Greenfield, P.M., and L.K. Suzuki
    1998   Culture and human development: Implications for parenting, education, pediatrics, and mental health. Pp. 1059-1109 in *Handbook of Child Psychology* (Vol. 4), I.E. Sigel and K.A. Renninger, eds. New York: Wiley and Sons.

Hallinger, P., K. Leithwood, and J. Murphy, eds.
    1993   *Cognitive Perspectives on Educational Leadership.* New York: Teachers College Press, Columbia University.

Heath, S.B.
    1983   *Ways with Words: Language, Life, and Work in Communities and Classrooms.* Cambridge, UK: Cambridge University Press.

Hendrickson, G., and W.H. Schroeder
    1941   Transfer of training in learning to hit a submerged target. *Journal of Educational Psychology* 32:205-213.

Hestenes, D., M. Wells, and G. Swackhamer
    1992   Force concept inventory. *The Physics Teacher* 30(March):159-166.

Hmelo, C.E.
    1995   Problem-based learning: Development of knowledge and reasoning strategies. Pp. 404-408 in *Proceedings of the Seventeenth Annual Conference of the Cognitive Science Society.* Pittsburgh, PA: Erlbaum.

Holyoak, K.J.
    1984   Analogical thinking and human intelligence. Pp. 199-230 in *Advances in the Psychology of Human Intelligence* (Vol. 2), R.J. Sternberg, ed. Hillsdale, NJ: Erlbaum.

Judd, C.H.
    1908   The relation of special training to general intelligence. *Educational Review* 36:28-42.

Klahr, D., and S.M. Carver
    1988   Cognitive objectives in a LOGO debugging curriculum: Instruction, learning, and transfer. *Cognitive Psychology* 20:362-404.

Klausmeier, H.J.
    1985   *Educational Psychology* (5th ed.). New York: Harper and Row.

Lave, J.
    1988   *Cognition in Practice: Mind, Mathematics, and Culture in Everyday Life.* Cambridge, MA: Cambridge University Press.

Lave, J., M. Murtaugh, and O. de la Rocha
    1984   The dialectic of arithmetic in grocery shopping. Pp. 67-94 in *Everyday Cognition*, B. Rogoff and J. Lave, eds. Cambridge, MA: Harvard University Press.

Lee, C.D., and D. Slaughter-Defoe
    1995   Historical and sociocultural influences of African American education. Pp. 348-371 in *Handbook of Research on Multicultural Education*, J.A. Banks and C.M. Banks, eds. New York: Macmillan.

Lionni, L.
    1970   *Fish Is Fish.* New York: Scholastic Press.

Littlefield, J., V. Delclos, S. Lever, K. Clayton, J. Bransford, and J. Franks
1988   Learning LOGO: Method of teaching, transfer of general skills, and attitudes toward school and computers. Pp. 111-135 in *Teaching and Learning Computer Programming*, R.E. Mayer, ed. Hillsdale, NJ: Erlbaum.

Luchins, A.S. and Luchins, E.H.
1970   *Wertheimer's Seminar Revisited: Problem Solving and Thinking* (Vol. 1). Albany, NY: State University of New York.

Mayer, R.E.
1988   Introduction to research on teaching and learning computer programming. Pp. 1-12 in *Teaching and Learning Computer Programming: Multiple Research Perspectives*, R.E. Mayer, ed. Hillsdale, NJ: Erlbaum.

McCombs, B.L.
1996   Alternative perspectives for motivation. Pp. 67-87 in *Developing Engaged Readers in School and Home Communities*, L. Baker, P. Afflerback, and D. Reinking, eds. Mahwah, NJ: Erlbaum.

Mestre, J.P.
1994   Cognitive aspects of learning and teaching science. Pp. 3-1 - 3-53 in *Teacher Enhancement for Elementary and Secondary Science and Mathematics: Status, Issues, and Problems*, S.J. Fitzsimmons and L.C. Kerpelman, eds. NSF 94-80. Arlington, VA: National Science Foundation.

Michaels, S.
1981a "Sharing time," children's narrative styles and differential access to literacy. *Language in Society* 10:423-442.
1981b Discourses of the Seasons. Technical report. Urbana, IL: Reading Research and Education Center.
1986   Narrative presentations: An oral preparation for literacy with first graders. Pp. 94-115 in *The Social Construction of Literacy*, J. Cook-Gumperz, ed. New York: Cambridge University Press.

Moll, L.C., J. Tapia, and K.F. Whitmore
1993   Living knowledge: The social distribution of cultural sources for thinking. Pp. 139-163 in *Distributed Cognitions*, G. Salomon, ed. Cambridge, UK: Cambridge University Press.

Moll, L.C., and K.F. Whitmore
1993   Vygotsky in classroom practice. Moving from individual transmission to social transaction. Pp. 19-42 in *Contexts for Learning*, E.A. Forman, N. Minick, and C.A. Stone, eds. New York: Oxford University Press.

National Research Council
1994   *Learning, Remembering, Believing: Enhancing Human Performance*, D. Druckman, and R.A. Bjork, eds. Committee on Techniques for the Enhancement of Human Performance, Commission on Behavioral and Social Sciences and Education. Washington, DC: National Academy Press.

Newman, D., P. Griffin, and M. Cole
1989   *The Construction Zone: Working for Cognitive Change in School.* New York: Cambridge University Press.

Norman, D.A.
1993   *Things That Make Us Smart: Defending Human Attributes in the Age of the Machine.* New York: Addison-Wesley.

Novick, L.R., and K.J. Holyoak
    1991   Mathematical problem solving by analogy. *Journal of Experimental Psychology: Learning, Memory, and Cognition* 17(3)(May):398-415.

Palinscar, A.S., and A.L. Brown
    1984   Reciprocal teaching of comprehension monitoring activities. *Cognition and Instruction* 1:117-175.

Papert, S.
    1980   *Mindstorms: Computers, Children, and Powerful Ideas.* New York: Basic Books.

Patel, V.L., D.R. Kaufman, and S.A. Magder
    1996   The acquisition of medical expertise in complex dynamic environments. Pp. 127-165 in *The Road to Excellence: The Acquisition of Expert Performance in the Arts and Sciences, Sports and Games*, K.A. Ericsson, ed. Mahwah, NJ: Erlbaum.

Perfetto, G.A., J.D. Bransford, and J.J. Franks
    1983   Constraints on access in a problem solving context. *Memory and Cognition* 11:24-31.

Pezdek, K. and L. Miceli
    1982   Life span differences in memory integration as a function of processing time. *Developmental Psychology* 18(3)(May):485-490.

Pintrich, P.R., and D. Schunk
    1996   *Motivation in Education: Theory, Research and Application.* Columbus, OH: Merrill Prentice-Hall.

Polya, G.
    1957   *How to Solve It: A New Aspect of Mathematical Method.* Princeton, NJ: Princeton University Press.

Resnick, L.B.
    1987   *Education and Learning to Think.* Committee on Mathematics, Science, and Technology Education, Commission on Behavioral and Social Sciences and Education, National Research Council. Washington, DC: National Academy Press. Available: http://www.nap.edu.

Resnick, L.B., V.L. Bill, S.B. Lesgold, and M.N. Leer
    1991   Thinking in arithmetic class. Pp. 27-53 in *Teaching Advanced Skills to At-Risk Students*, B. Means. C. Chelemer, and M.S. Knapp, eds. San Francisco: Jossey-Bass.

Rogoff, B.
    1990   *Apprenticeship in Thinking: Cognitive Development in Social Context.* New York: Oxford University Press.
    1998   Cognition as a collaborative process. Pp. 679-744 in *Handbook of Child Psychology: Cognition, Perception, and Language* (5th ed.), W. Damon, D.Kuhn, and R.S. Siegler, eds. New York: Wiley.

Saxe, G.B.
    1990   *Culture and Cognitive Development: Studies in Mathematical Understanding.* Hillsdale, NJ: Erlbaum.

Scardamalia, M., C. Bereiter, and R. Steinbach
    1984   Teachability of reflective processes in written composition. *Cognitive Science* 8:173-190.

Schliemann, A.D., and N.M. Acioly
  1989   Mathematical knowledge developed at work: The contribution of practice versus the contribution of schooling. *Cognition and Instruction* 6:185-222.
Schoenfeld, A.H.
  1983   Problem solving in the mathematics curriculum: A report, recommendation and an annotated bibliography. *Mathematical Association of America Notes*, No. 1.
  1985   *Mathematical Problem Solving.* Orlando, FL: Academic Press.
  1991   On mathematics as sense-making: An informal attack on the unfortunate divorce of formal and informal mathematics. Pp. 311-343 in *Informal Reasoning and Education*, J.F. Voss, D.N. Perkins, and J.W. Segal, eds. Hillsdale, NJ: Erlbaum.
Schwartz, D., and J.D. Bransford
  1998   A time for telling. *Cognition and Instruction* 16(4):475-522.
Schwartz, D.L., X. Lin, S. Brophy, and J.D. Bransford
  1999   Toward the development of flexibly adaptive instructional designs. Pp. 183-213 in *Instructional Design Theories and Models: Volume II,* C.M. Reigelut, ed. Hillsdale, NJ: Erlbaum.
Scribner, S.
  1984   Studying working intelligence. Pp. 9-40 in *Everyday Cognition*, B. Rogoff and J. Lave, eds. Cambridge, MA: Harvard University Press.
Silver, E.A., L.J. Shapiro, and A. Deutsch
  1993   Sense making and the solution of division problems involving remainders: An examination of middle school students' solution processes and their interpretations of solutions. *Journal for Research in Mathematics Education* 24(2):117-135.
Simon, H.A.
  1972   On the development of the processes. In *Information Processing in Children*, L.B. Resnick and L.E. Klopfer, eds. Alexandria, VA: ASCD Books.
Simon, H.A., and W.G. Chase
  1973   Skill in chess. *American Scientist* 61:394-403.
Singley, K., and J.R. Anderson
  1989   *The Transfer of Cognitive Skill.* Cambridge, MA: Harvard University Press.
Spiro, R.J., P.L. Feltovich, M.J. Jackson, and R.L. Coulson
  1991   Cognitive flexibility, constructivism, and hypertext: Random access instruction for advanced knowledge acquisition in ill-structured domains. *Educational Technology* 31(5):24-33.
Suina, J.H.
  1988   And then I went to school. Pp. 295-299 in *Cultural and Linguistic Influences on Learning Mathematics*, R.R. Cocking and J.P. Mestre, eds. Hillsdale, NJ: Erlbaum.
Suina, J.H., and L.B. Smolkin
  1994   From natal culture to school culture to dominant society culture: Supporting transitions for Pueblo Indian students. Pp. 115-130 in *Cross-cultural Roots of Minority Child Development*, P.M. Greenfield and R.R. Cocking, eds. Hillsdale, NJ: Erlbaum.

Tate, W.
  1994   Race, retrenchment, and the reform of school mathematics. *Phi Delta Kappan* 75:477-486.

Taylor, O., and D. Lee
  1987   Standardized tests and African American children: Communication and language issues. *Negro Educational Review* 38:67-80.

Thorndike, E.L.
  1913   *Educational Psychology* (Vols. 1 and 2). New York: Columbia University Press.

Thorndike, E.L., and R.S. Woodworth
  1901   The influence of improvement in one mental function upon the efficiency of other functions. *Psychological Review* 8:247-261.

Vosniadou, S., and W.F. Brewer
  1989   The Concept of the Earth's Shape: A study of Conceptual Change in Childhood. Unpublished paper. Center for the Study of Reading, University of Illinois, Champaign, Illinois.

Wandersee, J.H.
  1983   Students' misconceptions about photosynthesis: A cross-age study. Pp. 441-465 in *Proceedings of the International Seminar on Misconceptions in Science and Mathematics,* H. Helm and J. Novak eds. Ithaca, NY: Cornell University.

Wason, P.C., and P.N. Johnson-Laird
  1972   *Psychology of Reasoning: Structure and Content.* Cambridge, MA: Harvard University Press.

Wertheimer, M.
  1959   *Productive Thinking.* New York: Harper and Row.

White, B.Y., and J.R. Frederickson
  1998   Inquiry, modeling and metacognition: Making science accessible to all students. *Cognition and Instruction* 16(1):3-117.

White, R.W.
  1959   Motivation reconsidered: The concept of competence. *Psychological Review* 66:297-333.

Williams, S.M.
  1992   Putting case-based instruction into context: Examples from legal and medical education. *The Journal of the Learning Sciences* 2(4):367-427.

Wineburg, Samuel S.
  1989a   Are cognitive skills context-bound? *Educational Researcher* 18(1):16-25.
  1989b   Remembrance of theories past. *Educational Researcher* 18:7-10.
  1996   The psychology of learning and teaching history. Pp. 423-437 in *Handbook of Research in Educational Psychology,* D. Berliner and R. Calfee, eds. NY: Macmillan.

Woodworth, R.S.
  1938   *Experimental Psychology.* New York, NY: Holt.

CHAPTER 4

Ashcraft, M.H.
   1985   Is it farfetched that some of us remember arithmetic facts? *Journal for Research in Mathematical Education* 16:99-105.
Au, K.
   1981   Participant structures in a reading lesson with Hawaiian children. *Anthropology and Education Quarterly* 2:91-115.
Au, K., and C. Jordan
   1981   Teaching reading to Hawaiian children: Finding a culturally appropriate solution. Pp. 139-152 in *Culture and the Bilingual Classroom: Studies in Classroom Ethnography*, H. Tureba, G. Guthrie, and K. Au, eds. Rowley, MA: Newbury House.
Bahrick, L.E., and J.N. Pickens
   1988   Classification of bimodal English and Spanish language passages by infants. *Infant Behavior and Development* 11:277-296.
Baillargeon, R.
   1995   Physical reasoning in infancy. Pp. 181-204 in *The Cognitive Neurosciences*, M.S. Gazzaniga, ed. Cambridge, MA: MIT Press.
Baillargeon, R., A. Needham, and J. DeVos
   1992   The development of young infants' intuitions about support. *Early Development Parenting* 1:69-78.
Bates, E., V. Carlson-Luden, and I. Bretherton
   1980   Perceptual aspects of tool using in infancy. *Infant Behavior and Development* 3:127-140.
Belmont, J.M., and E.C. Butterfield
   1971   Learning strategies as determinants of memory deficiencies. *Cognitive Psychology* 2:411-420.
Bereiter, C., and M. Scardamalia
   1989   Intentional learning as a goal of instruction. Pp. 361-392 in *Knowing, Learning, and Instruction*, L.B. Resnick, ed. Hillsdale, NJ: Erlbaum.
Bertenthal, B.I.
   1993   Infants' perception of biomechanical motions: Instrinsic image and knowledge-based constraints. In *Carnegie-Mellon Symposia in Cognition, Vol. 23: Visual Perception and Cognition in Infancy*, C.E. Granrud, ed. Hillsdale, NJ: Erlbaum.
Bidell, T.R., and K.W. Fischer
   1997   Between nature and nurture: The role of human agency in the epigenesis of intelligence. Pp. 193-242 in *Intelligence, Heredity, and Environment*, R.J. Sternberg and E.L. Grigorenko, eds. New York: Cambridge University Press.
Bijou, S., and D.M. Baer
   1961   *Child Development: Vol. 1: A Systematic and Empirical Theory.* New York: Appleton-Century-Crofts.
Brown, A.L.
   1975   The development of memory: Knowing, knowing about knowing, and knowing how to know. In *Advances in Child Development and Behavior* (Vol. 10), H.W. Reese, ed. New York: Academic Press.

1978   Knowing when, and how to remember: A problem of metacognition. Pp. 77-165 in *Advances in Instructional Psychology* (Vol. 1), R. Glaser, ed. Hillsdale, NJ: Erlbaum.

1990   Domain-specific principles affect learning and transfer in children. *Cognitive Science* 14:107-133.

Brown, A.L., and J.C. Campione

1994   Guided discovery in a community of learners. Pp. 229-270 in *Classroom Lessons: Integrating Cognitive Theory and Classroom Practice*, K. McGilly, ed. Cambridge, MA: MIT Press.

1996   Psychological theory and the design of innovative learning environments: On procedures, principles, and systems. Pp. 289-325 in *Innovations in Learning: New Environments for Education*, L. Schauble and R. Glaser, eds. Mahwah, NJ: Erlbaum.

Brown, A.L., and J.D. Day

1984   Macrorules for summarizing texts: The development of expertise. *Journal of Verbal Learning and Verbal Behavior* 22:1-14.

Brown, A.L., J.D. Bransford, R.A. Ferrara, and J.C. Campione

1983   Learning, remembering, and understanding. Pp. 78-166 in *Handbook of Child Psychology: Vol. 3 Cognitive Development* (4th ed.), J.H. Flavell and E.M. Markman, eds. New York: Wiley.

Brown, A.L., and J.S. DeLoache

1978   Skills, plans, and self-regulation. Pp. 3-35 in *Children's Thinking: What Develops?* R. Siegler, ed. Hillsdale, NJ: Erlbaum.

Brown, A.L., and S.Q.C. Lawton

1977   The feeling of knowing experience in educable retarded children. *Developmental Psychology* 11:401-412.

Brown, A.L., and R.A. Reeve

1987   Bandwidths of competence: The role of supportive contexts in learning and development. Pp. 173-223 in *Development and Learning: Conflict or Congruence?* The Jean Piaget Symposium Series, L.S. Liben, ed. Hillsdale, NJ: Erlbaum.

Brown, R.

1958   *Words and Things*. Glencoe, IL: Free Press.

Bruner, J.S.

1972   Toward a sense of community. Review of Gartner et al. (1971), "Children Teach Children." *Saturday Review* 55:62-63.

1981a   Intention in the structure of action and interaction. In *Advances in Infancy Research, Vol. 1*, L.P. Lipsitt, ed. Norwood, NJ: Ablex.

1981b   The organization of action and the nature of adult-infant transaction: Festschrift for J. R. Nuttin. Pp. 1-13 in *Cognition in Human Motivation and Learning*, D. d'Ydewalle and W. Lens, eds. Hillsdale, NJ: Erlbaum.

1983   *Child's Talk: Learning to Use Language*. New York: Norton.

Byrnes, J.P.

1996   *Cognitive Development and Learning in Instructional Contexts*. Boston: Allyn and Bacon.

Callanan, M.A.
1985   How parents label objects for young children: The role of input in the acquisition of category hierarchies. *Child Development* 56:508-523.

Canfield, R.L., and E.G. Smith
1996   Number-based expectations and sequential enumeration by 5-month-old infants. *Developmental Psychology* 32:269-279.

Carey, S., and R. Gelman
1991   *The Epigenesis of Mind: Essays on Biology and Cognition.* Hillsdale, NJ: Erlbaum.

Case, R.
1992   *The Mind's Staircase: Exploring the Conceptual Underpinning of Children's Thought and Knowledge.* Hillsdale, NJ: Erlbaum.

Chapman, R.S.
1978   Comprehension strategies in children. Pp. 308-329 in *Speech and Language in the Laboratory, School, and Clinic,* J. Kavanaugh and W. Strange, eds. Cambridge, MA: MIT Press.

Chi, M.T.H.
1978   Knowledge structures and memory development. Pp. 73-96 in *Children's Thinking: What Developes,* R. Siegler, ed. Hillsdale, NJ: Erlbaum.

Cognition and Technology Group at Vanderbilt
1994   From visual word problems to learning communities: Changing conceptions of cognitive research. Pp. 157-200 in Classroom Lessons: *Integrating Cognitive Theory and Classroom Practice,* K. McGilly, ed. Cambridge, MA: MIT Press/Bradford Books.

Cohen, A.
1994   The Effect of a Teacher-Designed Assessment Tool on an Instructor's Cognitive Activity While Using CSILE. Unpublished paper.

Cohen, M.N.
1995   *Lewis Carroll: A Biography.* New York: Knopf.

Colombo, J., and R.S. Bundy
1983   Infant response to auditing familiarity and novelty. *Infant Behavior* 6:305-311.

Cooney, J.B., H.L. Swanson, and S.F. Ladd
1988   Acquisition of mental multiplication skill: Evidence for the transition between counting and retrieval strategies. *Cognition and Instruction* 5(4):323-345.

Coyle, T.R., and D.F. Bjorklund
1997   The development of strategic memory: A modified microgenetic assessment of utilization deficiencies. *Cognitive Development* 11(2):295-314.

DeLoache, J.S.
1984   What's this? Maternal questions in joint picturebook reading with toddlers. *Quarterly Newsletter of the Laboratory for Comparative Human Cognition* 6:87-95.

DeLoache, J.S., D.J. Cassidy, and A.L. Brown
1985a   Precursors of mnemonic strategies in very young children's memory. *Child Development* 56:125-137.

DeLoache, J.S., K.F. Miller, and S.L. Pierroutsakos
   1998   Reasoning and problem-solving. Pp. 801-850 in *Handbook of Child Psychology* (Vol. 2), D. Kuhn and R.S. Siegler, eds. New York: Wiley.

DeLoache, J.S., S. Sugarman, and A.L. Brown
   1985b   The development of error correction strategies in young children's manipulative play. *Child Development* 56:928-939.

Dichter-Blancher, T.B., N.A. Bush-Rossnagel, and Knauf-Jensen
   1997   Mastery-motivation: Appropriate tasks for toddlers. *Infant Behavior and Development* 20(4):545-548.

Dweck, C.S.
   1989   Motivation. Pp. 87-136 in *Foundations for a Psychology of Education*, A. Lesgold and R. Glaser, eds. Hillsdale, NJ: Erlbaum.

Dweck, C., and E. Elliott
   1983   Achievement motivation. Pp. 643-691 in *Handbook of Child Psychology, Vol. IV: Socialization, Personality, and Social Development*, P.H. Mussen, ed. New York: Wiley.

Dweck, C., and E. Legget
   1988   A social-cognitive approach to motivation and personality. *Psychological Review* 95:256-273.

Edwards, C.P.
   1987   Culture and the construction of moral values: A comparative ethnography of moral encounters in two cultural settings. Pp. 123-150 in *Emergence of Morality in Young Children*, J. Kagan and L. Lamb, eds. Chicago: University of Chicago Press.

Eimas, P.D., E.R. Siqueland, P.W. Jusczyk, and J. Vigorito
   1971   Speech perception in infants. *Science* 171:303-306.

Eisenberg, A.R.
   1985   Learning to describe past experiences in conversation. *Discourse Processes* 8:177-204.

Engle, S.
   1995   *The Stories Children Tell: Making Sense of the Narratives of Childhood*. New York: Freeman.

Fantz, R.L.
   1961   The origin of form perception. *Scientific American* 204:66-72.

Flavell, J.H., and H.M. Wellman
   1977   Metamemory. Pp. 3-33 in *Perspectives on the Development of Memory and Cognition*, R.V. Kail and J.W. Hagen, eds. Hillsdale, NJ: Erlbaum.

Gardner, H.
   1983   *Frames of Mind*. New York: Basic Books.
   1991   *The Unschooled Mind: How Children Think, and How Schools Should Teach*. New York: Basic Books.
   1997   *Extraordinary Minds: Portraits of Exceptional Individuals and an Examination of Our Extraordinariness*. New York: Basic Books.

Geary, D.
   1994   *Children's Mathematical Development: Research and Practice Applications*. Washington, DC: American Psychological Association.

Geary, D.C., and M. Burlingham-Dubree
1989   External validation of the strategy choice model for addition. *Journal of Experimental Child Psychology* 47:175-192.

Gelman, R.
1990   First principles organize attention to and learning about relevant data: Number and the animate-inanimate distinction as examples. *Cognitive Science* 14:79-106.

Gelman, R., and A.L. Brown
1986   Changing views of cognitive competence in the young. Pp. 175-207 in *Discoveries and Trends in Behavioral and Social Sciences*, N. Smelser and D. Gerstein, eds. Commission on Behavioral and Social Sciences and Education, National Research Council. Washington, DC: National Academy Press.

Gelman, R., and C.R. Gallistel
1978   *The Child's Understanding of Number.* Cambridge, MA: Harvard University Press.

Gelman, S.A.
1988   The development of induction within natural kind and artifact categories. *Cognitive Psychology* 20:65-95.

Gibson, E.J.
1969   *Principles of Perceptual Learning and Development.* New York: Appleton-Century-Crofts.

Goldman, S.R., J.W. Pelligrino, and D.L. Mertz
1988   Extended practices of basic addition facts: Strategy changes in learning disabled students. *Cognition and Instruction* 5:223-265.

Gopnik, M.
1990   Feature-blind grammar and sysphasia. *Nature* 344:615.

Griffin, S., and R. Case
1997   Wrap-Up: Using peer commentaries to enhance models of mathematics teaching and learning. *Issues in Education* 3(1):115-134.

Griffin, S., R. Case, and A. Capodilupo
1992   Rightstart: A program designed to improve children's conceptual structure on which this performance depends. In *Development and Learning Environments*, S. Strauss, ed. Norwood, NJ: Ablex.

Groen, G.J., and L.B. Resnick
1977   Can preschool children invent addition algorithms? *Journal of Educational Psychology* 69:645-652.

Hatano, G., and K. Inagaki
1996   Cultural Contexts of Schooling Revisited: A Review of the Learning Gap from a Cultural Psychology Perspective. Paper presented at the Conference on Global Prospects for Education: Development, Culture and Schooling. University of Michigan.

Heath, S.B.
1981   Questioning at home and school: A comprehensive study. In *Doing Ethnography: Educational Anthopology in Action*, G. Spindler, ed. New York: Holt, Rinehart, and Winston.

1983 *Ways with Words: Language, Life, and Work in Communities and Classrooms.* Cambridge, England: Cambridge University Press.

Hoff-Ginsberg, E., and M. Shatz
1982 Linguistic input and the child's acquisition of language. *Psychological Bulletin* 92(1)(July):3-26.

John-Steiner, V.
1984 Learning styles among Pueblo children. *Quarterly Newsletter of the Laboratory of Comparative Human Cognition* 6:57-62.

Jorm, A.F., and D.L. Share
1983 Phonological recoding and reading acquisition. *Applied Psycholinguistics* 4(2)(June):103-147.

Kahan, L.D., and D.D. Richards
1986 The effects of context on referential communication strategies. *Child Development* 57(5)(October):1130-1141.

Kalnins, I.V., and J.S. Bruner
1973 The coordination of visual observation and instrumental behavior in early infancy. *Perception* 2:307-314.

Karmiloff-Smith, A.
1992 *Beyond Modularity: A Developmental Perspective on Cognitive Science.* Cambridge, MA: MIT Press.

Karmiloff-Smith, A., and B. Inhelder
1974 If you want to get ahead, get a theory. *Cognition* 3:195-212.

Klahr, D., and J.G. Wallace
1973 The role of quantification operators in the development of conservation of quantity. *Cognitive Psychology* 4:301-327.

Kolstad, V., and R. Baillargeon
1994 Appearance- and Knowledge-Based Responses to Containers in 5 1/2- to 8 1/2-Month-Old Infants. Unpublished paper.

Kuhara-Koijma, K., and G. Hatano
1989 Strategies of recognizing sentences among high and low critical thinkers. *Japanese Psychological Research* 3(1):1-9.

Kuhl, P.K., K.A. Williams, F. Lacerda, N. Stevens, and B. Lindblom
1992 Linguistic experience alters phonetic perception in infants by 6 months of age. *Science* 255:606-608.

Kuhn, D., ed.
1995 Development and learning: Reconceptualizing the intersection: Introduction. *Human Development* 38(special issue):293-294.

Lave, J., and E. Wenger
1991 *Situated Learning: Legitimate Peripheral Participation.* New York: Cambridge University Press.

Lehrer, R., and L. Schauble
1996 Developing Model-Based Reasoning in Mathematics and Science. Paper prepared for the Workshop on the Sciences of Science of Learning. National Research Council, Washington, DC.

Lemaire, P., and R.S. Siegler
1995 Four aspects of strategic change: Contributions to children's learning of multiplication. *Journal of Experimental Psychology: General* 124(1)(March):83-97.

Leslie, A.M.
    1994a   Pretending and believing: Issues in the theory ToMM. *Cognition* 50:211-238.
    1994b   ToMM, ToBy, and agency: Core architecture and domain specificity. Pp. 119-148 in *Domain Specificity in Cognition and Culture*, L.A. Hirshfeld and S. Gelman, eds.

Lewis, M., and R. Freedle
    1973   Mother-infant dyad: The cradle of meaning. Pp. 127-155 in *Communication and Affect*, P. Pliner, ed. New York: Academic Press.

Linberg, M.
    1980   The role of knowledge structure in the ontogeny of learning. *Journal of Experimental Child Psychology*, 30:401-410.

MacNamara, J.
    1972   Cognitive bases of language learning in infants. *Psychological Review* 79(1):1-13.

Mandler, J.M.
    1996   Development of categorization: Perceptual and conceptual categories. In *Infant Development: Recent Advances*, G. Bremner, A. Slater, and G. Butterworth, eds. Hove, England: Erlbaum.

Massey, C.M., and R. Gelman
    1988   Preschoolers decide whether pictured unfamiliar objects can move themselves. *Developmental Psychology* 24:307-317.

Mayes, L.C., R. Feldman, R.N. Granger, M.H. Bornstein, and R. Schottenfeld
    1998   The effects of polydrug use with and without cocaine on the mother-infant interaction at 3 and 6 months. *Infant Behavior and Development* 20(4):489-502.

McNamee, G.D.
    1980   The Social Origins of Narrative Skills. Unpublished doctoral dissertation. Northwestern University.

Mehan, H.
    1979   *Learning Lessons: Social Organization in the Classroom.* Cambridge, MA: Harvard University Press.

Mehler, J., and A. Christophe
    1995   Maturation and learning of language in the first year of life. Pp. 943-954 in *The Cognitive Neurosciences*, M.S. Gazzaniga, ed. Cambridge, MA: MIT Press.

Mervis, C.B.
    1984   Early lexical development: The contributions of mother and child. Pp. 339-370 in *Origins of Cognitive Skills*, C. Sophian, ed. Hillsdale, NJ: Erlbaum.

Miller, G.A.
    1956   The magical number seven, plus or minus two. Some limits on our capacity to process information. *Psychological Review* 63:81-87.

Moll, L.C. and K. Whitmore
    1993   Vygotsky in classroom practice: Moving from indidividual transmission to social transaction. Pp. 19-42 in *Contexts for Learning,* E.A.Forman, N. Minick, and C.A. Stone, eds. New York: Oxford University Press.

National Research Council

1998   *Preventing Reading Difficulties in Young Children*, C.E. Snow, M.S. Burns, and P. Griffin, eds. Committee on Prevention of Reading Difficulties in Young Children. Washington, DC: National Academy Press.

Needham, A., and R. Baillargeon

1993   Intuitions about support in 4 1/2-month-old infants. *Cognition* 47:121-148.

Nelson, K.

1986   *Event Knowledge: Structure and Function in Development*. Hillsdale, NJ: Erlbaum.

Newell, A., J.C. Shaw, and H.A. Simon

1958   Elements of a theory of human problem solving. *Psychological Review* 65:151-166.

Newell, A., and H.A. Simon

1972   *Human Problem Solving*. Englewood Cliffs, NJ: Prentice-Hall.

Newman, D., P. Griffin, and M. Cole

1989   *The Construction Zone: Working for Cognitive Change in School*. New York: Cambridge University Press.

Newsweek

1996   How kids are wired for music, math, and emotions, by E. Begley. *Newsweek* (February 19):55-61.

Ninio, A., and J.S. Bruner

1978   The achievement and antecedents of labeling. *Child Development* 24(2):131-144.

Ochs, E., and B.B. Schieffelin

1984   Language acquisition and socialization: Three developmental stories and their implications. Pp. 276-320 in *Culture and Its Acquisition*, R. Shweder and R. Levine, eds. Chicago: University of Chicago Press.

Ohlsson, S.

1991   Young Adults' Understanding of Evolutional Explanations: Preliminary Observations. Unpublished paper. Learning Research and Development Center, University of Pittsburgh.

Palinscar, A.S., and A.L. Brown

1984   Reciprocal teaching of comprehension monitoring activities. *Cognition and Instruction* 1:117-175.

Papousek, M., H. Papousek, and M.H. Bornstein

1985   The naturalistic vocal environment of young infants. Pp. 269-298 in *Social Perception in Infants*, T.M. Field and N. Fox, eds. Norwood, NJ: Ablex.

Pascual-Leone, J.

1988   Affirmations and negations, disturbances and contradictions in understanding Piaget: Is his later theory causal? *Contemporary Psychology* 33:420-421.

Piaget, J.

1952   *The Origins of Intelligence in Children*, M. Cook, trans. New York: International Universities Press.

1970   Piaget's theory. In *Carmichael's Manual of Child Psychology*, P.H. Musen, ed. New York: Wiley.

1977   *The Grasp of Consciousness*. London: Routledge and Kegan Paul.

1978   *Success and Understanding*. Cambridge, MA: Harvard University Press.

Pressley, M.J., P.B. El-Dinary, M.B. Marks, R. Brown, and S. Stein
    1992   Good strategy instruction is motivating and interesting. Pp. 333-358 in *The Role of Interest in Learning and Development*, K.A. Renninger, S. Hidi, and A. Krapp, eds. Hillsdale, NJ: Erlbaum.

Reder, L. and J.R. Anderson
    1980   A comparison of texts and their summaries: Memorial consequences. *Journal of Verbal Learning and Verbal Behavior* 198:121-134.

Resnick, L.B., and W.W. Ford
    1981   *The Psychology of Mathematics Instruction.* Hillsdale, NJ: Erlbaum.

Resnick, L.B., and S. Nelson-LeGall
    1998   Socializing intelligences. In *Piaget, Vygotsky, and Beyond: Future Issues for Developmental Psychology and Education*, L. Smith, J. Dockrell, and P. Tomlinson, eds. London, UK: Routledge.

Rogoff, B.
    1990   *Apprenticeship in Thinking: Cognitive Development in Social Context.* New York: Oxford University Press.

Rogoff, B., C. Malkin, and K. Gilbride
    1984   Interaction with babies as guidance in development. Pp. 31-44 in *Children's Learning in the "Zone of Proximal Development,"* B. Rogoff and J.V. Wertsch, eds. San Francisco: Jossey-Bass.

Rogoff, B., J. Mistry, A. Goncu, and C. Mosier
    1993   Guided Participation in Cultural Activity by Toddlers and Caregivers. *Monographs of the Society for Research in Child Development* 58(7): Serial no. 236.

Rogoff, B., and J.V. Wertsch, eds.
    1984   *Childrens' Learning in the "Zone of Proximal Development."* San Francisco: Jossey-Bass.

Rovee-Collier, C.
    1989   The joy of kicking: Memories, motives, and mobiles. Pp. 151-180 in *Memory: Interdisciplinary Approaches*, P.R. Solomon, G.R. Goethals, C.M. Kelly, and B.R. Stephens, eds. New York: Springer-Verlag.

Salomon, G.
    1993   No distribution without individuals' cognition: A dynamic interactional view. Pp. 111-138 in *Distributed Cognitions.* New York: Cambridge University Press.

Saxe, G.B., M. Gearhart, and S.B. Guberman
    1984   The social organization of early number development. Pp. 19-30 in *Children's Learning in the "Zone of Proximal Development,"* B. Rogoff and J.V. Wertsch, eds. San Francisco: Jossey-Bass.

Schaffer, H., ed.
    1977   *Studies in Infant-Mother Interaction.* London: Academic Press.

Schauble, L.
    1990   Belief revision in children: The role of prior knowledge and strategies for generating evidence. *Journal of Experimental Child Psychology* 49:31-57.

Schilling, T.H., and R.K. Clifton
    1998   Nine-month-old infants learn about a physical event in a single session: Implications for infants' understanding of physical phenomena. *Cognitive Development* 133:165-184.

Shultz, T.R.
1982   Rules for causal attribution. *Monographs of the Society for Research in Child Development* 47:serial no. 194.

Siegler, R.S.
1988   Individual differences in strategy choices: Good students, not-so-good students, and perfectionists. *Child Development* 59:833-851.
1996   A grand theory of development. *Monographs of the Society for Research in Child Development* 61:266-275.

Siegler, R.S., ed.
1978   *Children's Thinking: What Develops?* Hillsdale, NJ: Erlbaum.

Siegler, R.S., and K. Crowley
1991   The microgenetic method: A direct means for studying cognitive development. *American Psychologist* 46:606-620.
1994   Constraints on learning in nonprivileged domains. *Cognitive Psychology* 27:194-226.

Siegler, R.S., and K. McGilly
1989   Strategy choices in children's time-telling. In *Time and Human Cognition: A Life-span Perspective*, I. Levin and D. Zakay, eds. Amsterdam, the Netherlands: Elsevier.

Siegler, R.S., and M. Robinson
1982   The development of numerical understanding. In *Advances in Child Development and Behavior*, H.W. Reese and L.P. Lipsitt, eds. New York: Academic Press.

Simon, H.A.
1972   On the development of the processes. In *Information Processing in Children*, S. Farnham-Diggory, ed. New York: Academic Press.

Skinner, B.F.
1950   Are theories of learning necessary? *Psychological Review* 57:193-216.

Sophian, C.
1994   *Children's Numbers*. Madison, WI: WCB Brown and Benchmark.

Spelke, E.S.
1990   Principles of object perception. *Cognitive Science* 14:29-56.

Starkey, P.
1992   The early development of numerical reasoning. *Cognition* 43:93-126.

Starkey, P., and R. Gelman
1982   The development of addition and subtraction abilities prior to formal schooling. In *Addition and Subtraction: A Developmental Perspective*, T.P. Carpenter, J.M. Moser, and T.A. Romberg, eds. Hillsdale, NJ: Erlbaum.

Starkey, P., E.S. Spelke, and R. Gelman
1990   Numerical abstraction by human infants. *Cognition* 36:97-127.

Suina, J.H.
1988   And then I went to school. Pp. 295-299 in *Cultural and Linguistic Influences on Learning Mathematics*, R.R. Cocking and J.P. Mestre, eds. Hillsdale, NJ: Erlbaum.

Suina, J.H., and L.B. Smolkin
1994   From natal culture to school culture to dominant society culture: Supporting transitions for Pueblo Indian students. Pp. 115-130 in *Cross-Cultural*

Roots of Minority Child Development, P.M. Greenfield and R.R. Cocking, eds. Hillsdale, NJ: Erlbaum.

Vygotsky, L.S.
1978   *Mind in Society.* Cambridge: Harvard University Press.

Walden, T.A., and T.A. Ogan
1988   The development of social referencing. *Child Development* 59:1230-1240.

Ward, M.
1971   *Them Children.* New York: Holt, Rinehart and Winston.

Wellman, H.M.
1990   *The Child's Theory of Mind.* Cambridge, MA: MIT Press.

Wellman, H.M., and S.A. Gelman
1992   Cognitive development: Foundational theories of core domains. *Annual Review of Psychology* 43:337-375.

Wellman, H.M., and A.K. Hickey
1994   The mind's "I": Children's conceptions of the mind as an active agent. *Child Development* 65:1564-1580.

Wellman, H.M., K. Ritter, and J.H. Flavell
1975   Deliberate memory behavior in the delayed reactions of very young children. *Developmental Psychology* 11:780-787.

White, R.W.
1959   Motivation reconsidered: The concept of competence. *Psychological Review* 66:297-333.

Wood, D., J.S. Bruner, and G. Ross
1976   The role of tutoring in problem-solving. *Journal of Child Psychology and Psychiatry* 17:89-100.

Wright, J.C., and A.C. Huston
1995   Effects of Educational TV Viewing of Lower Income Preschoolers on Academic Skills, School Readiness, and School Adjustment One to Three Years Later. A report to Children's Television Workshop. Lawrence, KS: University of Kansas.

Wynn, K.
1990   Children's understanding of counting. *Cognition* 36:155-193.
1992a   Addition and subtraction by human infants. *Nature* 358:749-750.
1992b   Evidence against empirical accounts of the origins of numerical knowledge. *Mind and Language* 7:209-227.
1996   Infants' individuation and enumeration of actions. *Psychological Science* 7:164-169.

Yarrow, L.J., and D.J. Messer
1983   Motivation and cognition in infancy. Pp. 451-477 in *Origins of Intelligence: Infancy and Early Childhood*, M. Lewis, ed. New York: Plenum.

CHAPTER 5

Bach-y-Rita, P.
1980   Brain plasticity as a basis for therapeutic procedures. In *Recovery of Function: Theoretical Considerations for Brain Injury Rehabilitation*, P. Bach-y-Rita, ed. Baltimore, MD: University Park Press.

1981   Brain plasticity as a basis of the development of rehabilitation procedures for hemiplegia. *Scandinavian Journal of Rehabilitation Medicine* 13:73-83.

Beaulieu, C., and M. Colonnier

1987   Effects of the richness of the environment on the cat visual cortex. *Journal of Comparative Neurology* 266:478-494.

Beaulieu, C., and M. Cynader

1990   Effect of the richness of the environment on neurons in cat visual cortex. I. Receptive field properties. *Developmental Brain Research* 53:71-81.

Bellugi, U.

1980   Clues from the similarities between signed and spoken language. In *Signed and Spoken Language: Biological Constraints on Linguistic Form*, U. Bellugi and M. Studdert-Kennedy, eds. Weinheim, Germany: Venlag Chemie.

Black, J.E., K.R. Isaacs, B.J. Anderson, A.A. Alcantara, and W.T. Greenough

1990   Learning causes synaptogenesis, whereas motor activity causes angiogenesis, in cerebellar cortex of adult rats. *Proceedings of the National Academy of Sciences U.S.A.* 87:5568-5572.

Black, J.E., A.M. Sirevaag, and W.T. Greenough

1987   Complex experience promotes capillary formation in young rat visual cortex. *Neuroscience Letters* 83:351-355.

Blakemore, C.

1977   *Mechanics of the Mind.* Cambridge, UK: Cambridge University Press.

Bruer, J.T.

1997   Education and the brain: A bridge too far. *Educational Researcher* 26(8)(November):4-16.

Cardellichio, T., and W. Field

1997   Seven strategies to enhance neural branching. *Educational Leadership* 54(6)(March).

Ceci, S.J.

1997   Memory: Reproductive, Reconstructive, and Constructive. Paper presented at a symposium, Recent Advances in Research on Human Memory, April 29, National Academy of Sciences, Washington, DC.

Chang, F.L., and W.T. Greenough

1982   Lateralized effects of monocular training on dendritic branching in adult split-brain rats. *Brain Research* 232:283-292.

Crill, W.E., and M.E. Raichle

1982   Clinical evaluation of injury and recovery. In *Repair and Regeneration of the Nervous System*, J.G. Nicholls, ed. New York: Springer-Verlag.

Eisenberg, L.

1995   The social construction of the human brain. *American Journal of Psychiatry* 152:1563-1575.

Ferchmin, P.A., E.L. Bennett, and M.R. Rosenzweig

1978   Direct contact with enriched environment is required to alter cerebral weights in rats. *Journal of Comparative and Psysiological Psychology* 88:360-367.

Friedman, S.L., and R.R. Cocking

1986   Instructional influences on cognition and on the brain. Pp. 319-343 in *The Brain, Cognition, and Education*, S.L. Friedman, K.A. Klivington, and R.W. Peterson, eds. Orlando, FL: Academic Press.

Gibson, E.J.
  1969   *Principles of Perceptual Learning and Development.* New York: Appleton-Century-Crofts.
Greenough, W.T.
  1976   Enduring brain effects of differential experience and training. Pp. 255-278 in *Neural Mechanisms of Learning and Memory*, M.R. Rosenzweig and E.L. Bennett, eds. Cambridge, MA: MIT Press.
Greenough, W.T., J.M. Juraska, and F.R. Volkmar
  1979   Maze training effects on dendritic branching in occipital cortex of adult rats. *Behavioral and Neural Biology* 26:287-297.
Hunt, J.M.
  1961   *Intelligence and experience.* New York: Ronald Press.
Huttenlocher, P.R., and A.S. Dabholkar
  1997   Regional differences in synaptogenesis in human cerebral cortex. *Journal of Comparative Neurology* 387:167-178.
Jones, T.A., and T. Schallert
  1994   Use-dependent growth of pyramidal neurons after neocortex damage. *Journal of Neuroscience* 14:2140-2152.
Juraska, J.M.
  1982   The development of pyramidal neurons after eye opening in the visitual cortex of hooded rats: A quantitative study. *Journal of Comparative Neurology* 212:208-213.
Kleim, J.A., E. Lussnig, E.R. Schwarz, T.A. Comery, and W.T. Greenough
  1996   Synaptogenesis and Fos expression in the motor cortex of the adult rat following motor skill learning. *Journal of Neuroscience* 16:4529-4535.
Kolb, B.
  1995   *Brain Plasticity and Behavior.* Hillsdale, NJ: Erlbaum.
Kuhl, P.K.
  1993   Innate predispositions and the effects of experience in speech perception: The native language magnet theory. Pp. 259-274 in *Developmental Neurocognition: Speech and Face Processing in the First Year of Life*, B. deBoysson-Bardies, S. deSchonen, P. Juscyzyk, P. McNeilage, and J. Morton, eds. Dordrecht, NL: Kluwer Academic Publishers.
Lichtenstein, E.H., and W.F. Brewer
  1980   Memory for goal-directed events. *Cognitive Psychology* 12:415-445.
Neville, H.J.
  1984   Effects of early sensory and language experience on the development of the human brain. In *Neonate Cognition: Beyond the Blooming Buzzing Confusion*, J. Mehler and R. Fox, eds. Hillsdale, NJ: Erlbaum.
  1995   Effects of Experience on the Development of the Visual Systems of the Brain on the Language Systems of the Brain. Paper presented in the series Brain Mechanisms Underlying School Subjects, Part 3. University of Oregon, Eugene.
Newsweek
  1996   How kids are wired for music, math, and emotions, by E. Begley. *Newsweek* (February 19):55-61.
  1997   How to build a baby's brain, by E. Begley. *Newsweek* (Summer special issue):28-32.

Roediger, H.
   1997   Memory: Explicit and Implicit. Paper presented at the Symposium, Recent Advances in Research on Human Memory, National Academy of Sciences. Washington, DC.

Rosenzweig, M.R., and E.L. Bennett
   1972   Cerebral changes in rats exposed individually to an enriched environment. *Journal of Comparative and Physiological Psychology* 80:304-313.
   1978   Experiential influences on brain anatomy and brain chemistry in rodents. Pp. 289-330 in *Studies on the Development of Behavior and the Nervous System: Vol. 4. Early Influences*, G. Gottlieb, ed. New York: Academic Press.

Schacter, D.L.
   1997   Neuroimaging of Memory and Consciousness. Paper presented at the Symposium: Recent Advances in Research on Human Memory, National Academy of Sciences. Washington, DC.

Squire, L.R.
   1997   Memory and Brain Systems. Paper presented at the Symposium: Recent Advances in Research on Human Memory, National Academy of Sciences. Washington, DC.

Sylwester, R.
   1995   A Celebration of Neurons: An Educator's Guide to the Human Brain. Association for Supervision and Curriculum Development, Alexandria, VA.

Time
   1997a   The day-care dilemma, by J. Collins. *Time* (February 3):57-97.
   1997b   Fertile minds, by J.M. Nash. *Time* (February 3):49-56.

Turner, A.M., and W. Greenough
   1985   Differential rearing effects on rat visual cortex synapses. I. Synaptic and neuronal density and synapses per neuron. *Brain Research* 328:195-203.

CHAPTER 6

Alcorta, M.
   1994   Text writing from a Vygotskyan perspective: A sign-mediated operation. *European Journal of Psychology of Education* 9:331-341.

American Association for the Advancement of Science
   1989   *Science for All Americans: A Project 2061 Report on Literacy Goals in Science, Mathematics, and Technology*. Washington, DC: American Association for the Advancement of Science.

Au, K., and C. Jordan
   1981   Teaching reading to Hawaiian children: Finding a culturally appropriate solution. Pp. 139-152 in *Culture and the Bilingual Classroom: Studies in Classroom Ethnography*, H. Tureba, G. Guthrie, and K. Au, eds. Rowley, MA: Newbury House.

Bakhtin, M.
   1984   *Problems of Dostoevsky's Poetics*. Minneapolis: University of Minnesota Press.

Ballenger, C.
  1997   Social identities, moral narratives, scientific argumentation: Science talk in a bilingual classroom. *Language and Education* 11(1):1-14.
Barron, B.
  1991   Collaborative Problem Solving: Is Team Performance Greater Than What Is Expected from the Most Competent Member? Unpublished doctoral dissertation. Vanderbilt University.
Barron, B.J., D.L. Schwartz, N.J. Vye, A. Moore, A. Petrosino, L. Zech., J.D. Bransford, and Cognition and Technology Group at Vanderbilt
  1998   Doing with understanding: Lessons from research on problem and project-based learning. *Journal of Learning Sciences* 7(3 and 4):271-312.
Barth, R.S.
  1988   School as a community of leaders. In *Building a Professional Culture in Schools*, A. Lieberman, ed. New York: Teachers College Press.
  1991   *Improving Schools from Within: Teachers, Parents, and Principals Can Make the Difference*. San Francisco: Jossey-Bass Publishers.
Baxter, G.P., and R. Glaser
  1997   A Cognitive Framework for Performance Assessment. CSE Technical Report. National Center for Research on Evaluation, Standards, and Student Testing, Graduate School of Education, University of California, Los Angeles.
Beck, I.L., M.G. McKeown, and W.E. Gromoll
  1989   Learning from social studies texts. *Cognition and Instruction*, 6:99-158.
Beck, I.L., M.G. McKeown, G.M. Sinatra, and J.A. Loxterman
  1991   Revising social studies text from a text-processing perspective: Evidence of improved comprehensibility. *Reading Research Quarterly* 26:251-276.
Bell, A.W.
  1982a Diagnosing students' misconceptions. *The Australian Mathematics Teacher* 1:6-10.
  1982b Treating students' misconceptions. *The Australian Mathematics Teacher* 2:11-13.
  1985   Some implications of research on the teaching of mathematics. Pp. 61-79 in *Theory, Research and Practice in Mathematical Education*, A. Bell, B. Low, and J. Kilpatrick, eds. Proceedings of Fifth International Congress on Mathematical Education, Adelaide, South Australia. Nottingham, England: Shell Centre for Mathematical Education, University of Nottingham.
Bell, A.W., D. O'Brien, and C. Shiu
  1980   Designing teaching in the light of research on understanding. In *Proceedings of the Fourth International Conference for the Psychology of Mathematics Education*, R. Karplus, ed. ERIC Document Reproduction Service No. ED 250 186. Berkeley, CA: The International Group for the Psychology of Mathematics.
Bell, A.W., K. Pratt, and D. Purdy
  1986   Teaching by Conflict Discussion—A Comparative Experiment. Shell Centre for Mathematical Education, University of Nottingham, England.

Bell, A.W., and D. Purdy
  1985   Diagnostic Teaching—Some Problems of Directionality. Shell Centre for Mathematical Education, University of Nottingham, England.

Bennett, K.P., and M.D. LeCompte
  1990   *The Way Schools Work: A Sociological Analysis of Education*. New York: Longman.

Bereiter, C., and M. Scardamalia
  1989   Intentional learning as a goal of instruction. Pp. 361-392 in *Knowing, Learning, and Instruction: Essays in Honor of Robert Glaser*, L.B. Resnick, ed. Hillsdale, NJ: Erlbaum.

Black, P., and William, D.
  1998   Assessment and classroom learning. *In Assessment and Education*. Special issue of Assessment in Education: Principles, policy and practice 5(1):7-75. Carfax Pub. Co.

Bransford, J.D., with Cognition and Technology Group at Vanderbilt
  1998   Designing environments to reveal, support, and expand our children's potentials. Pp. 313-350 in *Perspectives on Fundamental Processes in Intellectual Functioning* (Vol. 1), S.A. Soraci and W. McIlvane, eds. Greenwich, CT: Ablex.
  2000   Adventures in anchored instruction: Lessons from beyond the ivory tower. In *Advances in Instructional Psychology* (Vol. 5), R. Glaser, ed. Mahwah, NJ: Erlbaum.

Bray, M.H.
  1998   Leading in Learning: An Analysis of Teachers' Interactions with Their Colleagues as They Implement a Constructivist Approach to Learning. Unpublished doctoral dissertation. Vanderbilt University, Peabody College, Nashville, TN.

Brown, A.L., and J.C. Campione
  1994   Guided discovery in a community of learners. Pp. 229-270 in *Classroom Lessons: Integrating Cognitive Theory and Classroom Practice*, K. McGilly, ed. Cambridge, MA: MIT Press.
  1996   Psychological theory and the design of innovative learning environments: On procedures, principles, and systems. Pp. 289-325 in *Innovations in Learning: New Environments for Education*, L. Schauble and R. Glaser, eds. Mahwah, NJ: Erlbaum.

Bruer, J.T.
  1993   *Schools for Thought*. Cambridge, MA: MIT Press.

Bruner, J.
  1981   The organization of action and the nature of adult-infant transaction: Festschrift for J. R. Nuttin. Pp. 1-13 in *Cognition in Human Motivation and Learning*, D. d'Ydewalle and W. Lens, eds. Hillsdale, NJ: Erlbaum.

Callahan, R.E.
  1962   *Education and the Cult of Efficiency*. Chicago: University of Chicago Press.

Case R., and J. Moss
  1996   Developing Children's Rational Number Sense: An Approach Based on Cognitive Development Theory. Paper presented at the annual conference on the Psychology of Mathematics Education, Orlando, Florida.
Cobb, P., E. Yackel, and T. Wood
  1992   A constructivist alternative to the representational view of mind in mathematics education. *Journal for Research in Mathematics Education* 19:99-114.
Cognition and Technology Group at Vanderbilt
  1997   *The Jasper Project: Lessons in Curriculum, Instruction, Assessment, and Professional Development.* Mahwah, NJ: Erlbaum.
Collins, A., J. Hawkins, and S.M. Carver
  1991   A cognitive apprenticeship for disadvantaged students. Pp. 216-243 in *Teaching Advanced Skills to At-Risk Students*, B. Means, C. Chelemer, and M.S. Knapp, eds. San Francisco: Jossey-Bass.
Covey, S.R.
  1990   *Principle-Centered Leadership.* New York: Simon and Schuster.
Crago, M.B.
  1988   Cultural Context in the Communicative Interaction of Young Inuit Children. Unpublished doctoral dissertation. McGill University.
Dewey, J.
  1916   *Democracy and Education.* New York: Macmillan.
Deyhle, D., and F. Margonis
  1995   Navajo mothers and daughters. Schools, jobs, and the family. *Anthropology and Education Quarterly* 26:135-167.
Dorr, A.
  1982   Television and the socialization of the minority child. In *Television and the Socialization of the Minority Child*, G.L. Berry and C. Mitchell-Kernan, eds. New York: Academic Press.
Duckworth, E.
  1987   *"The Having of Wonderful Ideas" and Other Essays on Teaching and Learning.* New York: Teachers College Press, Columbia University.
Festinger, L.
  1957   *A Theory of Cognitive Dissonance.* Stanford, CA: Stanford University Press.
Fuchs, L.S., D. Fuchs, and C.L. Hamlett
  1992   Computer applications to facilitate curriculum-based measurement. *Teaching Exceptional Children* 24(4):58-60.
Greenfield, P.M.
  1984   *Mind and Media: The Effects of Television, Video, Games, and Computers.* Cambridge, MA: Harvard University Press.
Greeno, J.
  1991   Number sense as situated knowing in a conceptual domain. *Journal for Research in Mathematics Education* 22(3):170-218.
Griffin, P., and M. Cole
  1984   Current activity for the future: The zo-ped. Pp. 45-64 in *Children's Learning in the "Zone of Proximal Development,"* B. Roscoff and J. Wertsch, eds. San Francisco: Jossey-Bass.

Hardiman, P., R. Dufresne, and J.P. Mestre
  1989   The relation between problem categorization and problem solving among experts and novices. *Memory & Cognition* 17(5):627-638.

Hasselbring, T.S., L. Goin, and J.D. Bransford
  1987   Effective mathematics instruction: Developing automaticity. *Teaching Exceptional Children* 19(3):30-33.

Hatano, G., and K. Inagaki
  1996   Cultural Contexts of Schooling Revisited: A Review of the Learning Gap from a Cultural Psychology Perspective. Paper presented at the conference on Global Prospects for Education: Development, Culture and Schooling. University of Michigan.

Heath, S.B.
  1983   *Ways with Words: Language, Life, and Work in Communities and Classrooms.* Cambridge, UK: Cambridge University Press.

Holt, J.
  1964   *How Children Fail.* New York: Dell.

Johnson, D.W., and R. Johnson
  1975   *Learning Together and Alone: Cooperation, Competition, and Individualization.* Englewood Cliffs, NJ: Prentice-Hall.

Kliebard, H.M.
  1975   Metaphorical roots of curriculum design. In *Curriculum Theorizing: The Reconceptualists*, W. Pinar, ed. Berkeley: McCutchan.

LaBerge, D., and S.J. Samuels
  1974   Toward a theory of automatic information processing in reading. *Cognitive Psychology* 6:293-323.

Ladson-Billings, G.
  1995   Toward a theory of culturally relevant pedagogy. *American Educational Research Journal* 32:465-491.

Lee, C.D.
  1991   Big picture talkers/words walking without masters: The instructional implications of ethnic voices for an expanded literacy. *Journal of Negro Education* 60:291-304.
  1992   Literacy, cultural diversity, and instruction. *Education and Urban Society* 24:279-291.

Lehrer, R., and D. Chazan
  1998   *Designing learning environments for developing understanding of geometry and space.* Mahwah, NJ: Erlbaum.

Lehrer, R., and L. Schauble
  1996a   Developing Model-Based Reasoning in Mathematics and Science. Paper prepared for the Workshop on the Science of Learning, National Research Council, Washington, DC.
  1996b   Building Bridges Between Mathematics and Science: Progress Report to James S. McDonnell Foundation. Meeting of Cognitive Studies for Educational Practice Program Investigators, November, Vanderbilt University, Nashville, TN.

Lehrer, R., and L. Shumow
   1997   Aligning the construction zones of parents and teachers for mathematics reform. *Cognition and Instruction* 15:41-83.

Lemke, J.
   1990   *Talking Science: Language, Learning and Values.* Norwood, NJ: Ablex.

Leonard, W.J., R.J. Dufresne, and J.P. Mestre
   1996   Using qualitative problem-solving strategies to highlight the role of conceptual knowledge in solving problems. *American Journal of Physics* 64:1495-1503.

Linn, M.C.
   1992   The computer as learning partner: Can computer tools teach science? In *This Year in School Science, 1991.* Washington, DC: American Association for the Advancement of Science.
   1994   Teaching for Understanding in Science. Paper presented at the National Science Foundation Conference on Research Using a Cognitive Science Perspective to Facilitate School-Based Innovation in Teaching Science and Mathematics. May 5-8, Sugarloaf Conference Center, Chestnut Hill, PA.

MacCorquodale, P.
   1988   Mexican American women and mathematics: Participation, aspirations, and achievement. Pp. 137-160 in *Linguistic and Cultural Influences on Learning Mathematics*, R.R. Cocking and J.P. Mestre, eds. Hillsdale, NJ: Erlbaum.

McLaughlin, M.W.
   1990   The Rand change agent study revisited: Macro perspectives and micro realities. *Educational Researcher* 19(9):11-16.

Moll, L.C.
   1986a   Creating Strategic Learning Environments for Students: A Community-Based Approach. Paper presented at the S.I.G. Language Development Invited Symposium Literacy and Schooling, Annual Meeting of the American Educational Research Association, San Francisco, CA.
   1986b   Writing as a communication: Creating strategic learning environments for students. *Theory into Practice* 25:102-108.

Moll, L.C., ed.
   1990   *Vygotsky and Education.* New York: Cambridge University Press.

National Center for Research in Mathematical Sciences Education and Freudenthal Institute, eds.
   1997   *Mathematics in Context: A Connected Curriculum for Grades 5-8.* Chicago: Encyclopaedia Britannica Educational Corporation.

National Council of Teachers of Mathematics
   1989   *Curriculum and Evaluation Standards for School Mathematics.* Reston, VA: National Council of Teachers of Mathematics.

National Research Council
   1990   *Reshaping School Mathematics.* Mathematical Sciences Education Board. Washington, DC: National Academy Press. Available: http://www.nap.edu.
   1996   *National Science Education Standards.* Washington, DC: National Academy Press: Available: http://www.nap.edu.

Newcomb, A.F., and W.E. Collins
    1979   Children's comprehension of family role portrayals in televised dramas: Effect of socio-economic status, ethnicity, and age. *Developmental Psychology* 15:417-423.
O'Brien, C.L.
    1981   The Big Blue Marble story. *Television and Children* 4/5:18-22.
Palinscar, A.S., and A.L. Brown
    1984   Reciprocal teaching of comprehension monitoring activities. *Cognition and Instruction* 1:117-175.
Peterson, P., S.J. McCarthey, and R.F. Elmore
    1995   Learning from school restructuring. *American Educational Research Journal* 33(1):119-154.
Piaget, J.
    1973   *The Child and Reality: Problems of Genetic Psychology.* New York: Grossman.
Porter, A.C., M.W. Kirst, E.J. Osthoff, J.S. Smithson, and S.A. Schneider
    1993   Reform Up Close: A Classroom Analysis. Draft final report to the National Science Foundation on Grant No. SPA-8953446 to the Consortium for Policy Research in Education. Wisconsin Center for Education Research, University of Wisconsin-Madison.
Prawat, R.S., J. Remillard, R.T. Putnam, and R.M. Heaton
    1992   Teaching mathematics for understanding: Case study of four fifth-grade teachers. *Elementary School Journal* 93:145-152.
Redish, E.F.
    1996   Discipline-Specific Science Education and Educational Research: The Case of Physics. Paper prepared for the Committee on Developments in the Science of Learning for the Sciences of Science Learning: An Interdisciplinary Discussion.
Resnick, D.P., and L.B. Resnick
    1977   The nature of literacy: An historical exploration. *Harvard Educational Review* 47:370-385.
Resnick, L.B.
    1987   *Education and Learning to Think.* Committee on Mathematics, Science, and Technology Education, Commission on Behavioral and Social Sciences and Education, National Research Council. Washington, DC: National Academy Press. Available: http://www.nap.edu.
Rogoff, B., J. Mistry, A. Goncu, and C. Mosier
    1993   Guided Participation in Cultural Activity by Toddlers and Caregivers. *Monographs of the Society for Research in Child Development* 58(7), serial no. 236.
Romberg, T.A.
    1983   A common curriculum for mathematics. Pp. 121-159 in *Individual Differences and the Common Curriculum: Eighty-second Yearbook of the National Society for the Study of Education, Part I.* G.D. Fenstermacher and J.I. Goodlad, eds. Chicago: University of Chicago Press.

Schauble, L.R. Glaser, R. Duschl, S. Schulze, and J. John
1995   Students' understanding of the objectives and procedures of experimentation in the science classroom. *The Journal of the Learning Sciences* 4(2):131-166.

Scheffler, I.
1975   Basic mathematical skills: Some philosophical and practical remarks. In *National Institute of Education Conference on Basic Mathematical Skills and Learning, Vol. 1.* Euclid, OH: National Institute of Education.

Schmidt, W.H., C.C. McKnight, and S. Raizen
1997   *A Splintered Vision: An Investigation of U.S. Science and Mathematics Education.* U.S. National Research Center for the Third International Mathematics and Science Study. Dordrecht/Boston/London: Kluwer Academic Publishers. Available: gopher://gopher.wkap.nl.70/00gopher_root1%3A%5Bbook.soci.f500%5Df5101601.txt.

Schneuwly, B.
1994   Tools to master writing: Historical glimpses. Pp. 137-147 in *Literacy and Other Forms of Mediated Action, Vol. 2: Explorations in Socio-Cultural Studies,* J.V. Wertsch and J.D. Ramirez, eds. Madrid: Fundación Infancia y Aprendizaje.

Schoenfeld, A.H.
1983   Problem solving in the mathematics curriculum: A report, recommendation, and an annotated bibliography. *Mathematical Association of American Notes,* No. 1.
1985   *Mathematical Problem Solving.* Orlando, FL: Academic Press.
1988   When good teaching leads to bad results: The disasters of well taught mathematics classes. *Educational Psychologist* 23(2):145-166.
1991   On mathematics as sense-making: An informal attack on the unfortunate divorce of formal and informal mathematics. Pp. 311-343 in *Informal Reasoning and Education,* J.F. Voss, D.N. Perkins, and J.W. Segal, eds. Hillsdale, NJ: Erlbaum.

Schofield, J.W., D. Evans-Rhodes, and B.R. Huber
1990   Artificial intelligence in the classroom: The impact of a computer-based tutor on teachers and students. *Social Science Computer Review* 8(1)24-41 (Special issue on Computing: Social and Policy Issues).

Schwab, J.
1978   Education and the structure of the disciplines. In *Science, Curriculum, and Liberal Education: Selected Essays of Joseph J. Schwab,* I. Westbury and N. Wilkof, eds. Chicago: University of Chicago Press.

Simon, H.A.
1969   *The Sciences of the Artificial.* Cambridge, MA: MIT Press.
1996   Observations on The Sciences of Science Learning. Paper prepared for the Committee on Developments in the Science of Learning for the Sciences of Science Learning: An Interdisciplinary Discussion.

Slavin, R.
1987   Grouping for instruction in the elementary school: Equity and effectiveness. *Equity and Excellence* 23:31-36.

Suina, J.H., and L.B. Smolkin
  1994 From natal culture to school culture to dominant society culture: Support-
         ing transitions for Pueblo Indian students. Pp. 115-130 in *Cross-Cultural
         Roots of Minority Child Development*, P.M. Greenfield and R.R. Cocking,
         eds. Hillsdale, NJ: Erlbaum.
Talbert, J.E., and M.W. McLaughlin
  1993 Understanding teaching in context. Pp. 167-206 in *Teaching for Under-
         standing: Challenges for Policy and Practice*, D.K. Cohen, M.W. McLaughlin,
         and J.E. Talbert, eds. San Francisco: Jossey-Bass.
Vye, N.J., S.R. Goldman, J.F. Voss, C. Hmelo, S. Williams, and Cognition and Technol-
ogy Group at Vanderbilt
  1998a Complex mathematical problem solving by individuals and dyads. *Cogni-
         tion and Instruction* 15(4).
Vye, N.J., D.L. Schwartz, J.D. Bransford, B.J. Barron, L. Zech, and Cognition and
Technology Group at Vanderbilt
  1998b SMART environments that support monitoring, reflection, and revision. In
         Metacognition in Educational Theory and Practice, D. Hacker, J. Dunlosky,
         and A. Graesser, eds. Mahwah, NJ: Erlbaum.
Warren, B., and A. Rosebery
  1996 This question is just too, too easy: Perspectives from the classroom on
         accountability in science. Pp. 97-125 in the *Contributions of Instructional
         Innovation to Understanding Learning*, L. Schauble and R. Glaser, eds.
         Mahwah, NJ: Erlbaum.
Webb, N., and T. Romberg
  1992 Implications of the NCTM Standards for mathematics assessment. In *Math-
         ematics Assessment and Evaluation*, T. Romberg, ed. Albany, NY: State
         University of New York Press.
Wertsch, J.V.
  1991 *Voices of the Mind.* Cambridge, MA: Harvard University Press.
Wineburg, S.S.
  1996 The psychology of learning and teaching history. Pp. 423-437 in *Hand-
         book of Research in Educational Psychology*, D.C. Berliner and R.C. Calfee,
         eds. NY: Macmillan.
Wiske, M.S.
  1997 *Teaching for Understanding: Linking Research with Practice.* San Fran-
         cisco: Jossey-Bass.
Wolf, D.P.
  1988 Becoming literate. *Academic Connections: The College Board* 1(4).
Wright, J.C., and A.C. Huston
  1995 Effects of Educational TV Viewing of Lower Income Preschoolers on Aca-
         demic Skills, School Readiness, and School Adjustment One to Three Years
         Later. Report to Children's Televsion Workshop, Center for Research on
         the Influence of Television on Children. University of Kansas.

CHAPTER 7

Anderson, C.W., and E.L. Smith
1987   Teaching science. Pp. 84-111 in *Educators' Handbook: A Research Perspective*, V. Richardson-Koehler, ed. White Plains, NY: Longman.

Ball, D.L.
1993   With an eye on the mathematical horizon: Dilemmas of teaching elementary school mathematics. *Elementary School Journal* 93:373-397.

Barth, R.S.
1991   *Improving Schools from Within: Teachers, Parents, and Principals Can Make the Difference.* San Francisco: Jossey-Bass.

Brasell, H.
1987   The effect of real-time laboratory graphing on learning graphic representations of distance and velocity. *Journal of Research in Science Teaching* 24:385-395.

Brophy, J.E.
1990   Teaching social studies for understanding and higher-order applications. *Elementary School Journal* 90:351-417.

Brown, A.L., and A.S. Palinscar
1989   Guided, cooperative learning and individual knowledge acquisition. Pp. 393-451 in *Knowing, Learning, and Instruction: Essays in Honor of Robert Glaser*, L. Resnick, ed. Hillsdale, NJ: Erlbaum.

Brown, C.A.
1985   A Study of the Socialization to Teaching of a Beginning Secondary Mathematics Teacher. Unpublished doctoral dissertation. University of Georgia.

Brown, D.
1992   Using examples to remediate misconceptions in physics: Factors influencing conceptual change. *Journal of Research in Science Teaching* 29:17-34.

Brown, D., and J. Clement
1989   Overcoming misconceptions via analogical reasoning: Factors influencing understanding in a teaching experiment. *Instructional Science* 18:237-261.

Carpenter, T., and E. Fennema
1992   Cognitively guided instruction: Building on the knowledge of students and teachers. Pp. 457-470 in *International Journal of Educational Research. Special issue: The Case of Mathematics in the United States*, W. Secada, ed.

Carpenter, T., E. Fennema, and M. Franke
1996   Cognitively guided instruction: A knowledge base for reform in primary mathematics instruction. *Elementary School Journal* 97(1):3-20.

Chi, M.T.H., P.J. Feltovich, and R. Glaser
1981   Categorization and representation of physics problems by experts and novices. *Cognitive Science* 5:121-152.

Clement, J.
1989   Learning via model construction and criticism. Pp. 341-381 in *Handbook of Creativity: Assessment, Theory, and Research*, G. Glover, R. Ronning and C. Reynolds, eds. New York: Plenum.
1993   Using bridging analogies and anchoring intuitions to deal with students' preconceptions in physics. *Journal of Research in Science Teaching* 30(10):1241-1257.

diSessa, A.
  1988   Knowledge in pieces. Pp. 49-70 in *Constructivism in the Computer Age*, G. Forman and P. Pufall, eds. Hillsdale, NJ: Erlbaum.
  1993   Toward an epistemology of physics. *Cognition and Instruction* 10(2):105-125.

Dufresne, R.J., W.J. Gerace, P. Hardiman, and J.P. Mestre
  1992   Constraining novices to perform expertlike problem analyses: Effects of schema acquisition. *The Journal of Learning Sciences* 2(3):307-331.

Dufresne, R.J., W.J. Gerace, W.J. Leonard, J.P. Mestre, and L. Wenk
  1996   Classtalk: A classroom communication system for active learning. *Journal of Computing in Higher Education* 7:3-47.

Eylon, B.S., and F. Reif
  1984   Effects of knowledge organization on task performance. *Cognition and Instruction* 1:5-44.

Fennema, E., T. Carpenter, M. Franke, L. Levi, V. Jacobs, and S. Empson
  1996   A longitudinal study of learning to use children's thinking in mathematics instruction. *Journal for Research in Mathematics Education* 27(4):403-434.

Gamoran, M.
  1994   Content knowledge and teaching innovation curricula. Paper presented at the annual meeting of the American Educational Research Association, New Orleans, Louisiana.

Grossman, P.L., S.M. Wilson, and L.S. Shulman
  1989   Teachers of substance: Subject matter for teaching. Pp. 23-36 in *Knowledge Base for the Beginning Teacher*, M.C. Reynolds, ed. New York: Pergamon Press.

Heller, J.I., and F. Reif
  1984   Prescribing effective human problem solving processes: Problem description in physics. *Cognition and Instruction* 1:177-216.

Hestenes, D.
  1992   Modeling games in the Newtonian world. *American Journal of Physics* 60:440-454.

Hiebert, J., T. Carpenter, E. Fennema, K. Fuson, H. Murray, A. Oliver, P. Human, and D. Wearne
  1997   *Designing Classrooms for Learning Mathematics with Understanding.* Portsmouth, NH: Heinemann Educational Books.

Inagaki, K., and G. Hatano
  1987   Young children's spontaneous personification as analogy. *Child Development* 58:1013-1020.

Lampert, M.
  1986   Knowing, doing, and teaching multiplication. *Cognition and Instruction* 3:305-342.

Lehrer, R., and T. Romberg
  1996a   Exploring children's data modeling. *Cognition and Instruction* 14:69-108.
  1996b   Springboards to geometry. Pp. 53-61 in *Perspectives on the Teaching of Geometry for the 21st Century*, G. Mammana and V. Villani, eds. Norwell, MA: Kluwer Academic Publishers.

Lehrer, R., and L. Schauble

1996a   Building Bridges Between Mathematics and Science. Progress report to James S. McDonnell Foundation. Meeting of Cognitive Studies for Educational Practice Program Investigators. November. Vanderbilt University, Nashville, TN.

1996b   Developing Model-Based Reasoning in Mathematics and Science. Paper presented at the Workshop on the Science of Learning, September, National Research Council, Washington, DC.

Leinhardt, G., and J.G. Greeno

1991   The cognitive skill of teaching. Pp. 233-268 in *Teaching Knowledge and Intelligent Tutoring*, Peter Goodyear, ed. Norwood, NJ: Ablex.

1994   History: A time to be mindful. Pp. 209-225 in *Teaching and Learning in History*, G. Leinhardt, I.L. Beck, and C. Stainton, eds. Hillsdale, NJ: Erlbaum.

Leonard, W.J., R.J. Dufresne, and J.P. Mestre

1996   Using qualitative problem-solving strategies to highlight the role of conceptual knowledge in solving problems. *American Journal of Physics* 64:1495-1503.

McDonald, J.P., and P. Naso

1986   Teacher as Learner: The Impact of Technology. Educational Technology Center, Graduate School of Education, Harvard University.

Medawar, P.

1982   *Pluto's Republic.* Oxford, UK: Oxford University Press.

Mestre, J.P.

1994   Cognitive aspects of learning and teaching science. Pp. 3-1 - 3-53 in *Teacher Enhancement for Elementary and Secondary Science and Mathematics: Status, Issues, and Problems*, S.J. Fitzsimmons and L.C. Kerpelman, eds. NSF 94-80. Arlington, VA: National Science Foundation.

Mestre, J.P., W.J. Gerace, R.J. Dufresne, and W.J. Leonard

1997   Promoting active learning in large classes using a classroom communication system. Pp. 1019-1036 in *The Changing Role of Physics Departments in Modern Universities: Proceedings of the International Conference on Undergraduate Physics Education.* Woodbury, NY: American Institute of Physics.

Minstrell, J.

1982   Explaining the "at rest" condition of an object. *The Physics Teacher* 20:10.

1989   Teaching science for understanding. Pp. 129-149 in *Toward the Thinking Curriculum: Current Cognitive Research,* L.B. Resnick and L.E. Klopfer, eds. Alexandria, VA: Association for Supervision and Curriculum Development.

1992   Facets of students' knowledge and relevant instruciton. Pp. 110-128 in *Proceedings of the International Workshop on Research in Physics Education: Theoretical Issues and Empirical Studies,* R. Duit, F. Goldberg, and H. Niedderer, eds. Kiel, Germany: Institüt für die Pädagogik der Naturwissenshaften.

National Council of Teachers of Mathematics

1989   *Curriculum and Evaluation Standards for School Mathematics.* Reston, VA: National Council on Teachers of Mathematics.

Ravitch, D.R., and C.E. Finn
   1987   *What Do Our 17-Year-Olds Know? A Report on the First National Assessment in History and Literature.* New York: Harper and Row.

Resnick, L.B., V.L. Bill, S.B. Lesgold, and M.N. Leer
   1991   Thinking in arithmetic class. Pp. 27-53 in *Teaching Advanced Skills to At-Risk Students*, B. Means, C. Chelemer, and M.S. Knapp, eds. San Francisco: Jossey-Bass.

Rosebery, A.S., B. Warren, and F.R. Conant
   1992   Appropriating scientific discourse: Findings from language minority classrooms. *The Journal of the Learning Sciences* 2(1):61-94.

Schauble, L., R. Glaser, R. Duschl, S. Schulze, and J. John
   1995   Students' understanding of the objectives and procedures of experimentation in the science classroom. *The Journal of the Learning Sciences* 4(2):131-166.

Secules, T., C.D. Cottom, M.H. Bray, L.D. Miller, and the Cognition and Technology Group at Vanderbilt
   1997   Schools for thought: Creating learning communities. *Educational Leadership* 54(6):56-60.

Shulman, L.
   1986   Paradigms and research programs in the study of teaching: A contemporary perspective. In *Handbook of Research in Teaching, 3rd ed.*, M.C. Witrock, ed. New York: Macmillan.
   1987   Knowledge and teaching: Foundations of the new reform. *Harvard Educational Review* 57:1-22.
   1996   Teacher Development: Roles of Domain Expertise and Pedagogical Knowledge. Paper prepared for the Committee on Developments in the Science of Learning for The Sciences of Science Learning: An Interdisciplinary Discussion.

Sokoloff, D.R., and R.K. Thornton
   1997   Using interactive lecture demonstrations to create an active learning environment. *The Physics Teacher* 35(6)(September):340-347.

Stein, M.K., J.A. Baxter, and G. Leinhardt
   1990   Subject matter knowledge and elementary instruction: A case from functions and graphing. *American Educational Research Journal* 27(4):639-663.

Talbert, J.E., and M.W. McLaughlin
   1993   Understanding teaching in context. Pp. 167-206 in *Teaching for Understanding: Challenges for Policy and Practice*, D.K. Cohen, M.W. McLaughlin, and J.E. Talbert, eds. San Francisco: Jossey-Bass.

Thompson, A.G.
   1992   Teachers' beliefs and conceptions: A synthesis of the research. Pp. 127-146 in *Handbook of Research in Mathematics Teaching and Learning*, D.A. Grouws, ed. New York: Macmillan.

Thornton, R.K., and D.R. Sokoloff
   1998   Assessing student learning of Newton's laws: The force and motion conceptual evaluation and the evaluation of active learning laboratory and lecture curricula. *American Journal of Physics* 64:338-352.

Vygotsky, L.S.
1978   *Mind in Society: The Development of the Higher Psychological Processes.*
Cambridge, MA: The Harvard University Press.

Wenk, L., R. Dufresne, W. Gerace, W. Leonard, and J. Mestre
1997   Technology-assisted active learning in large lectures. Pp. 431-452 in *Student-Active Science: Models of Innovation in College Science Teaching*, C. D'Avanzo and A. McNichols, eds. Philadelphia, PA: Saunders College Publishing.

Wilson, M.
1990a   Investigation of structured problem solving items. Pp. 137-203 in *Assessing Higher Order Thinking in Mathematics*, G. Kulm, ed. Washington, DC: American Association for the Advancement of Science.
1990b   Measuring a van Hiele geometry sequence: A reanalysis. *Journal for Research in Mathematics Education* 21:230-237.

Wilson, S.M., and S.S. Wineburg
1993   Wrinkles in time and place: Using performance assessments to understand the knowledge of history teachers. *American Educational Research Journal* 30(4)(Winter):729-769.

Wineburg, S.S.
1991   Historical problem solving: A study of the cognitive processes used in evaluating documentary and pictorial evidence. *Journal of Educational Psychology* 83(1):73-87.

Wineburg, S.S, and S.M. Wilson
1988   Peering at history through different lenses: The role of disciplinary perspectives in teaching history. *Teachers College Record* 89(4):525-539.
1991   Subject matter knowledge in the teaching of history. Pp. 303-345 in *Advances in Research on Teaching*, J.E. Brophy, ed. Greenwich, CT: JAI Press.

CHAPTER 8

Ball, D., and S. Rundquist
1993   Collaboration as a context for joining teacher learning with learning about teaching. Pp. 13-42 in *Teaching for Understanding: Challenges for Policy and Practice*, D.K. Cohen, M.W. McLaughlin, and J.E. Talbert, eds. San Francisco: Jossey-Bass.

Baratta-Lorton, M.
1976   *Math Their Way.* Boston: Addison-Wesley.

Barone, T., D. Berliner, J. Blanchard, U. Casanova, and T. McGowan
1996   A future for teacher education: Developing a strong sense of professionalism. Pp. 1108-1149 in *Handbook of Research on Teacher Education* (2nd ed.), J. Silula, ed. New York: Macmillan.

Barrows, H.S.
1985   *How to Design a Problem-Based Curriculum for the Preclinical Years.* New York: Springer.

Bay Area Writing Project
  1979   Bay Area Writing Project/California Writing Project/National Writing Project:
          An Overview. Unpublished paper, ED184123. University of California,
          Berkeley.
Bunday, M., and J. Kelly
  1996   National board certification and the teaching profession's commitment to
          quality assurance. *Phi Delta Kappan* 78(3):215-219.
Carini, P.
  1979   The Art of Seeing and the Visibility of the Person. Unpublished paper,
          North Dakota Study Group on Evaluation, University of North Dakota,
          Grand Forks, ND.
Carpenter, T., and E. Fennema
  1992   Cognitively guided instruction: Building on the knowledge of students
          and teachers. Pp. 457-470 in *International Journal of Educational Re-
          search*, (Special issue: The Case of Mathematics in the United States, W.
          Secada, ed.)
Carpenter, T., E. Fennema, and M. Franke
  1996   Cognitively guided instruction: A knowledge base for reform in primary
          mathematics instruction. *Elementary School Journal* 97(1):3-20.
Carpenter, T.P., E. Fennema, P.L. Peterson, C.P. Chiang, and M. Loef
  1989   Using knowledge of children's mathematics thinking in classroom teach-
          ing: An experimental study. *American Educational Research Journal*
          26:499-532.
Case, R.
  1996   Introduction: Reconceptualizing the nature of children's conceptual struc-
          tures and their development in middle childhood. Pp. 1-26 in The role of
          central conceptual structures in the development of children's thought.
          Monographs of the Society for Research in Child Development, serial no.
          246. 61(nos. 1-2).
Cochran-Smith, M., and S. Lytle
  1993   *Inside/Outside: Teacher Research and Knowledge.* New York: Teachers
          College Press, Columbia University.
Cognition and Technology Group at Vanderbilt
  1997   *The Jasper Project: Lessons in Curriculum, Instruction, Assessment, and
          Professional Development.* Mahwah, NJ: Erlbaum.
Cohen, D.K.
  1990   A revolution in one classroom: The case of Mrs. Oublier. *Educational
          Evolution and Policy Analysis* 12:330-338.
Cole, B.
  1996   Characterizing On-line Communication: A First Step. Paper presented at
          the Annual Meeting of the American Educational Research Association,
          April 8-12, New York, NY.
Darling-Hammond, L.
  1997   School reform at the crossroads: Confronting the central issues of teach-
          ing. *Educational Policy* 11(2):151-166.

Dewey, J.
1963   *Experience and Education.* New York: Collier.

Elmore, R., and G. Sykes
1992   Curriculum policy. Pp. 185-215 in *Handbook of Research on Curriculum,* P.W. Jackson, ed. New York: Macmillan.

Feiman-Nemser, S., and M. Parker
1993   Mentoring in context: A comparison of two US programs for beginning teachers. *International Journal of Educational Research* 19(8):699-718.

Feldman, A.
1993   Teachers Learning from Teachers: Knowledge and Understanding in Collaborative Action Research. Unpublished dissertation. Stanford University.
1994   Erzberger's dilemma: Validity in action research and science teachers' need to know. *Science Education* 78(1):83-101.
1996   Enhancing the practice of physics teachers: Mechanisms for the generation and sharing of knowledge and understanding in collaborative action research. *Journal of Research in Science Teaching* 33(5):513-540.

Feldman, A., and J. Atkin
1995   Embedding action research in professional practice. In *Educational Action Research: Becoming Practically Critical,* S. Noffke and R. Stevenson, eds. New York: Teachers College Press.

Feldman, A., and A. Kropf
1997   The Evaluation of Minds-On Physics: An Integrated Curriculum for Developing Concept-Based Problem Solving in Physics. Unpublished paper. Physics Education Research Group, Amherst, MA.

Fredericksen, J., and B. White
1994   Mental models and understanding: A problem for science education. In *New Directions in Educational Technology,* E. Scanlon and T. O'Shea, eds. New York: Springer-Verlag.

Freedman, S.W., ed.
1985a   The role of Response in the Acquisition of Written Language. Final Report. Graduate School of Education, University of California, Berkeley.
1985b   *The Acquisition of Written Language: Response and Revision.* Harwood, NJ: Ablex.

Goodlad, J.
1990   *Teachers for Our Nation's Schools.* San Francisco: Jossey-Bass.

Greeno, J.G., A.M. Collins, and L.B. Resnick
1996   Cognition and learning. Pp. 15-46 in *Handbook of Educational Psychology,* D.C. Berliner and R.C. Calfee, eds. NY: Macmillan.

Heaton, R.M.
1992   Who is minding the mathematics content? A case study of a fifth-grade teacher. *Elementary School Journal* 93:151-192.

Hollingsworth, S.
1994   *Teacher Research and Urban Literacy: Lessons and Conversations in a Feminist Key.* New York: Teachers College Press.

Hollins, E.
1995   Research, Culture, Teacher Knowledge and Development. Paper presented at the annual meeting of the American Educational Research Association, April, San Francisco.

Holmes Group
1986   Tomorrow's Teachers: A Report of the Holmes Group. Unpublished paper, Holmes Group, East Lansing, Michigan.

Kearns, D.T.
1988   An education recovery plan for America. *Phi Delta Kappan* 69(8):565-570.

Knapp, N.F., and P.L. Peterson
1995   Meanings and practices: Teachers' interpretation of "CGI" after four years. *Journal for Research in Mathematics Education* 26(1):40-65.

Koppich, J.E., and M.S. Knapp
1998   *Federal Research Investment and the Improvement of Teaching: 1980-1997.* Seattle, WA: Center for the Study of Teaching and Policy.

Lampert, M.
1998   Studying teaching as a thinking practice. Pp. 53-78 in *Thinking Practices,* J. Greene and S.G. Goldman, eds. Hillsdale, NJ: Erlbaum.

Lave, J., and E. Wenger
1991   *Situated Learning: Legitimate Peripheral Participation.* New York: Cambridge University Press.

Leonard, W.J., R.J Dufresne, W.J. Gerace, and J.P Mestre
1999a   *Minds on Physics: Motion Activities and Reader.* Dubuque, IA: Kendall/Hunt Publishing.
1999b   *Minds on Physics: Motion-Teacher's Guide.* Dubuque, IA: Kendall/Hunt Publishing.
1999c   *Minds on Physics: Interactions-Activities and Reader.* Dubuque, IA: Kendall/Hunt Publishing.
1999d   *Minds on Physics: Interactions-Teacher's Guide.* Dubuque, IA: Kendall/Hunt Publishing.
1999e   *Minds on Physics: Conservation Laws and Concept-Based Problem Solving-Activities and Reader.* Dubuque, IA: Kendall/Hunt Publishing.
1999f   *Minds on Physics: Conservation Laws and Concept-Based Problem Solving-Teacher's Guide.* Dubuque, IA: Kendall/Hunt Publishing.

Little, J.W.
1990   The mentor phenomenon and the social organization of teaching. *Review of Research in Education,* 16:297-351.

Lucido, H.
1988   Coaching physics. *Physics Teacher* 26(6):333-340.

Marsh, D., and J. Sevilla
1991   An Analysis of the Implementation of Project SEED: An Interim Report. Technical report. University of Southern California.

Minstrell, J.A.
1989   Teaching science for understanding. In *Toward the Thinking Curriculum: Current Cognitive Research,* L.B. Resnick and L.E. Klopfer, eds. Alexandria, VA: ASCD Books.

National Commission on Teaching and America's Future
1996   What Matters Most: Teaching for America's Future. New York: Teachers College, Columbia University.

Natriello, G., C.J. Riehl, and A.M. Pallas
1994   Between the Rock of Standards and the Hard Place of Accommodation: Evaluation Practices of Teachers in High Schools Serving Disadvantaged Students. Center for Research on Effective Schooling for Disadvantaged Students, Johns Hopkins University.

Noffke, S.
1997   Professional, personal, and political dimensions of action research. *Review of Research in Education* 22:305-343.

Perkins, D.
1992   *Smart Schools: From Training Memories to Educating Minds.* New York: Free Press.

Peterson, P.L., and C. Barnes
1996   Learning together: Challenges of mathematics, equity, and leadership. *Phi Delta Kappan* 77(7):485-491.

Peterson, P., T. Carpenter, and E. Fennema
1989   Teachers' knowledge of students' knowledge in mathematics problem solving: Correlational and case analyses. *Journal of Educational Psychology* 81:558-569.

Renyi, J.
1996   Teachers Take Charge of Their Learning: Transforming Professional Development for Student Success. Unpublished paper. National Foundation for the Improvement of Education, Washington, DC.

Ruopp, R.
1993   *LabNet: Toward a Community of Practice.* Hillsdale, NJ: Erlbaum.

Schifter, D., and C.T. Fosnot
1993   *Reconstructing Mathematics Education: Stories of Teachers Meeting the Challenge of Reform.* New York: Teachers College Press.

Schön, D.
1983   *The Reflective Practitioner: How Professionals Think in Action.* New York: Basic Books.

Shulman, L.
1986   Those who understand: Knowledge growth in teaching. *Educational Researcher* 15(2):4-14.

Stake, R., and C. Migotsky
1995   Evaluation Study of the Chicago Teachers Academy: Methods and Findings of the CIRCE Internal Evaluation Study. Paper presented at the Annual Meeting of the American Educational Research Association, April 18-22, San Francisco, California.

U.S. Department of Education
1994   National Assessment of Educational Progress (NAEP), 1994 Long-Term Assessment. Office of Educational Research and Improvement, U.S. Department of Education, Washington, DC.

Van Hise, Y.
    1986   Physics teaching resource agent institute reports of regional convocations. *AAPT Announcer* 16(2):103-110.

Wilson, S., L. Shulman, and A. Richert
    1987   '150 different ways' of knowing: Representations of knowledge in teaching. Pp. 104-124 in *Exploring Teachers' Thinking*, J. Calderhead, ed. London: Cassell.

Wiske, M.S.
    1998   *Teaching for Understanding: Linking Research with Practice.* San Francisco: Jossey-Bass.

Yerushalmy, M., D. Chazan, and M. Gordon
    1990   Guided inquiry and technology: A yearlong study of children and teachers using the Geometry Supposer. Newton, MA: Education Development Center, Center for Learning Technology.

Zeichner, K.
    1981-   Reflective teaching and field-based experience in teacher education. *Interchange* 12:1-22.

Zeichner, K., and Liston, D.
    1990   *Reflective teaching: An Introduction.* Mahwah, NJ: Erlbaum.

CHAPTER 9

Anderson, J.R., C.F. Boyle, A. Corbett, and M.W. Lewis
    1990   Cognitive modeling and intelligent tutoring. *Artificial Intelligence* 42:7-49.

Anderson, J.R., A.T. Corbett, K. Koedinger, and R. Pelletier
    1995   Cognitive tutors: Lessons learned. *The Journal of Learning Sciences* 4:167-207.

Atkinson, R.
    1968   Computerized instruction and the learning process. *American Psychologist* 23:225-239.

Bachelard, G.
    1984   *The New Scientific Spirit.* Boston: Beacon Press.

Barron, B., N. Vye, L. Zech, D. Schwartz, J. Bransford, S. Goldman, J. Pellegrino, J. Morris, S. Garrison, and R. Kantor
    1995   Creating contexts for community based problem solving: The Jasper Challenge Series. Pp. 47-71 in *Thinking and Literacy: The Mind at Work*, C. Hedley, P. Antonacci, and M. Rabinowitz, eds. Hillsdale, NJ: Erlbaum.

Barron, B.J., D.L. Schwartz, N.J. Vye, A. Moore, A. Petrosino, L. Zech., J.D. Bransford, and Cognition and Technology Group at Vanderbilt
    1998   Doing with understanding: Lessons from research on problem and project-based learning. *Journal of Learning Sciences* 7(3 and 4):271-312.

Barron, L.C., and E.S. Goldman
    1994   Integrating technology with teacher preparation. Pp. 81-110 in *Technology and Education Reform*, B. Means, ed. San Francisco: Jossey-Bass.

Bauch, J.P., ed.
  1997   The Bridge Project: Connecting Parents and Schools Through Voice Messaging. Report on the Pilot Projects. Vanderbilt University and Work/Family Directions, Inc., Nashville, TN.

Bereiter, C., and M. Scardamalia
  1993   *Surpassing Ourselves: An Inquiry into the Nature and Implicaitons of Expertise*. Chicago and La Salle, IL: Open Court Publishing.

Bonney, R., and A.A. Dhondt
  1997   FeederWatch: An example of a student-scientist partnership. In *Internet Links for Science Education: Student-Scientist Partnerships*, K.C. Cohen, ed. New York: Plenum.

Brodie, K.W., L.A. Carpenter, R.A. Earnshaw, J.R. Gallop, R.J. Hubbold, A.M. Mumford, C.D. Osland, and P. Quarendon
  1992   *Scientific Visualization*. Berlin: Springer-Verlag.

Brown, A.L., and J.C. Campione
  1987   On the importance of knowing what you are doing: Metacognition and mathematics. In *Teaching and Evaluating Mathematical Problem Solving*, R. Charles and E. Silver, eds. Reston, VA: National Council of Teachers of Mathematics.

Bryson, M., and M. Scardamalia
  1991   Teaching writing to students at risk for academic failure. Pp. 141-167 in *Teaching Advanced Skills to At-Risk Students: Views from Research and Practice*, B. Means, C. Chelemer, and M.S. Knapp, eds. San Francisco: Jossey Bass.

Char, C., and J. Hawkins
  1987   Charting the course: Involving teachers in the formative research and design of the Voyage of the Mimi. Pp. 211-222 in *Mirrors of Minds: Patterns of Experience in Educational Computing*, R.D. Pea and K. Sheingold, eds. Norwood, NJ: Ablex.

Classroom, Inc.
  1996   *Learning for Life Newsletter* (Sept. 24):1-10, B. Lewis, ed. NY: Classroom, Inc.

Clauset, K., C. Rawley, and G. Bodeker
  1987   STELLA: Softward for structural thinking. *Collegiate Microcomputer* 5(4):311-319.

Cognition and Technology Group at Vanderbilt
  1992   The Jasper series as an example of anchored instruction: Theory, program description, and assessment data. *Educational Psychologist* 27:291-315.
  1993   The Jasper series: Theoretical foundations and data on problem solving and transfer. Pp. 113-152 in *The Challenge in Mathematics and Science Education: Psychology's Response*, L.A. Penner, G.M. Batsche, H.M. Knoff, and D.L. Nelson, eds. Washington, DC: American Psychological Association.
  1994   From visual word problems to learning communities: Changing conceptions of cognitive research. Pp. 157-200 in *Classroom Lessons: Integrating Cognitive Theory and Classroom Practice*, K. McGilly, ed. Cambridge, MA: MIT Press/Bradford Books.

1996   Looking at technology in context: A framework for understanding tech-
        nology and education research. Pp. 807-840 in *The Handbook of Educa-
        tional Psychology*, D.C. Berliner and R.C. Calfee, eds. New York: Macmillan.
1997   *The Jasper Project: Lessons in Curriculum, Instruction, Assessment, and
        Professional Development.* Mahwah, NJ: Erlbaum.
1998a   Adventures in anchored instruction: Lessons from beyond the ivory tower.
        Burgess 1996 study in *Advances in Instructional Psychology, Vol. 5*, R.
        Glaser, ed. Mahwah, NJ: Erlbaum.
1998b   Designing environments to reveal, support, and expand our children's po-
        tentials. Pp. 313-350 in *Perspectives on Fundamental Processes in Intellec-
        tual Functioning* (Vol. 1), S.A. Soraci and W. McIlvane, eds. Greenwich,
        CT: Ablex.
Cohen, K.C., ed.
1997   *Internet Links for Science Education: Student-Scientist Partnerships.* New
        York: Plenum.
Collins, A.
1990   Cognitive apprenticeship and instructional technology. Pp. 121-138 in *Di-
        mensions of Thinking and Cognitive Instruction*, B.F. Jones and L. Idol,
        eds. Hillsdale, NJ: Erlbaum.
Collins, A., and J.S. Brown
1988   The computer as a tool for learning through reflection. Pp. 1-18 in *Learn-
        ing Issues for Intelligent Tutoring Systems*, H. Mandl and A. Lesgold, eds.
        New York: Springer-Verlag.
Collins, A., J.S. Brown, and S.E. Newman
1989   Cognitive apprenticeship: Teaching the crafts of reading, writing, and math-
        ematics. Pp. 453-494 in *Knowing, Learning, and Instruction: Essays in
        Honor of Robert Glaser*, L.B. Resnick, ed. Hillsdale, NJ: Erlbaum.
Coon, T.
1988   Using STELLA simulation software in life science education. *Computers in
        Life Science Education* 5(9):57-71.
Crews, T.R., G. Biswas, S.R. Goldman, and J.D. Bransford
1997   Anchored interactive learning environments. *International Journal of Ar-
        tificial Intelligence in Education* 8:142-178.
Dede, C., ed.
1998   Introduction. Pp. v-x in *Association for Supervision and Curriculum De-
        velopment (ASCD) Yearbook: Learning with Technology.* Alexandria, VA:
        Association for Supervision and Curriculum Development.
Derry, S.P., and A.M. Lesgold
1996   Toward a situated social practice model for instructional design. Pp. 787-
        806 in *Handbook of Educational Psychology*, R.C. Calfee and D.C. Berliner,
        eds. New York: Macmillan.
Duffy, T.M.
1997   Strategic teaching framework: An instructional model for learning com-
        plex interactive skills. Pp. 571-592 in *Instructional Development State of
        the Art: Vol. 3, Paradigms and Educational Technology*, C. Dills and A.
        Romiszowski, eds. Englewood Cliffs, NJ: Educational Technology Publi-
        cations.

Edelson, D.C., R.D. Pea, and L. Gomez
1995   Constructivism in the collaboratory. Pp. 151-164 in *Constructivist Learning Environments: Case Studies in Instructional Design*, B. G. Wilson, ed. Englewood Cliffs, NJ: Educational Technology Publications.

Education Policy Network
1997   The Daily Report Card. December 5. Available: http://www.negp.gov.

Finholt, T., and L.S. Sproull
1990   Electronic groups at work. *Organizational Science* 1:41-64.

Fishman, B., and L. D'Amico
1994   Which way will the wind blow? Network computer tool for studying the weather. Pp. 209-216 in *Educational Multimedia and Hypermedia, 1994: Proceedings of the Ed-Media '94*, T. Ottman and I. Tomek, eds. Charlottesville, VA: AACE.

Forrester, J.
1991   Systems dynamics: Adding structure and relevance to pre-college education. In *Shaping the Future*, K.R. Manning, ed. Boston, MA: MIT Press.

Friedler, Y., R. Nachmias, and M.C. Linn
1990   Learning scientific reasoning skills in microcomputer-based laboratories. *Journal of Research on Science Teaching* 27:173-191.

Gabrys, C., A. Weiner, and A. Lesgold
1993   Learning by problem solving in a coached apprenticeship system. Pp. 119-147 in *Cognitive Science Foundations of Instruction*, M. Rabinowitz, ed. Hillsdale, NJ: Erlbaum.

Galegher, J., R.E. Kraut, and C. Egido, eds.
1990   *Intellectual Teamwork: The Social and Technological Foundations of Cooperative Work*. Hillsdale, NJ: Erlbaum.

Glass, L., and M. Mackey
1988   *From Clocks to Chaos*. Princeton: Princeton University Press.

Goldman, S., and J.N. Moschkovich
1995   Environments for collaborating mathematically. Pp. 143-146 in *Proceedings of the First International Conference on Computer Support for Collaborative Learning*. October. Bloomington, Indiana.

Gordin, D., D. Edelson, and R.D. Pea
1996   The Greenhouse effect visualizer: A tool for the science classroom. *Proceedings of the Fourth American Meteorological Society Education Symposium*.

Gordin, D.N., D.C. Edelson, L.M. Gomez, E.M. Lento, and R.D. Pea
1996   Student conference on global warming: A collaborative network-supported ecologically hierarchic geosciences curriculum. *Proceedings of the Fifth American Meteorological Society Education Symposium*.

Gordin, D.N., and R.D. Pea
1995   Prospects for scientific visualization as an educational technology. *The Journal of the Learning Sciences* 4:249-279.

Gordin, D., J. Polman, and R.D. Pea
1994   The Climate Visualizer: Sense-making through scientific visualization. *Journal of Science Education and Technology* 3:203-226.

Greenfield, P.M., and R.R. Cocking, eds.
1996   *Interacting with Video*. Greenwich, CT: Ablex.

Haken, H.
1981 *Chaos and Order in Nature. Proceeding of the International Symposium on Synergetics.* New York: Springer-Verlag.

Hestenes, D.
1992 Modeling games in the Newtonian world. *American Journal of Physics* 60:440-454.

Hmelo, C., and S.M. Williams, eds.
1998 Special issue: Learning through problem solving. *The Journal of the Learning Sciences* 7(3 and 4).

Hoadley, C.M., and P. Bell
1996 Web for your head: The design of digital resources to enhance lifelong learning. *D-Lib Magazine.* September. Available: http://www.dlib.org/dlib/september96/kie/09hoadley.html

Holland, J.H.
1995 *Hidden Order: How Adaptation Builds Complexity.* New York: Addison-Wesley.

Hunt, E., and Minstrell, J.
1994 A cognitive approach to the teaching of physics. Pp. 51-74 in *Classroom Lessons: Integrating Cognitive Theory and Classroom Practice,* K. McGilly, ed. Cambridge, MA: MIT Press.

Jackson, S., S. Stratford, J. Krajcik, and E. Soloway
1996 Making system dynamics modeling accessible to pre-college science students. *Interactive Learning Environments* 4:233-257.

Kafai, Y.B.
1995 *Minds in Play: Computer Game Design as a Context for Children's Learning.* Hillsdale, NJ: Erlbaum.

Kaput, J.J.
1987 Representation systems and mathematics. In *Problems of Representation in the Teaching and Learning of Mathematics,* C. Jonvier, ed. Hillsdale, NJ: Erlbaum.

Kaufmann II, W.J., and L.L. Smarr
1993 Supercomputing and Transformation of Science. New York: Scientific American Library.

Keating, T.
1997 Electronic Community: The Role of an Electronic Network in the Development of a Community of Teachers Engaged in Curriculum Development and Implementation. Unpublished doctoral dissertation, Stanford University.

Keating, T., and A. Rosenquist
1998 The Role of an Electronic Network in the Development of a Community of Teachers Implementing a Human Biology Curriculum. Paper presented at the annual meeting of the National Association for Research in Teaching, San Diego, CA.

Kinzer, C.K., V. Risko, J. Carson, L. Meltzer, and F. Bigenho
1992 Students' Perceptions of Instruction and Instructional Needs: First Steps Toward Implementing Case-based Instruction. Paper presented at the 42nd annual meeting of the National Reading Conference, San Antonio, Texas. December.

Koedinger, K.R., J.R. Anderson, W.H. Hadley, and M.A. Mark
1997   Intelligent tutoring goes to school in the big city. *International Journal of Artificial Intelligence in Education* 8:30-43.

Lampert, M., and D.L. Ball
1998   *Teaching, Multimedia, and Mathematics: Investigations of Real Practice.* New York: Teachers College Press.

Lawless, J.G., and R. Coppola
1966   GLOBE: Earth as our backyard. *Geotimes* 41(9):28-30.

Lederberg, J., and K. Uncapher, eds.
1989   Towards a National Collaboratory: Report of an Invitational Workshop at the Rockefeller University, March 17-18. National Science Foundation Directorate for Computer and Information Science, Washington, DC.

Lesgold, A., S. Chipman, J.S. Brown, and E. Soloway
1990   Prospects for information science and technology focused on intelligent training systems concerns. Pp. 383-394 in *Annual Review of Computer Science.* Palo Alto, CA: Annual Review Press.

Levin, J., M. Waugh, D. Brown, and R. Clift
1994   Teaching teleapprenticeships: A new organizational framework for improving teacher education using electronic networks. *Journal of Machine-Mediated Learning* 4(2 and 3):149-161.

Linn, M.C.
1991   The computer as lab partner: Can computer tools teach science? In *This Year in School Science 1991*, L. Roberts, K. Sheingold, and S. Malcolm, eds. Washington, DC: American Association for the Advancement of Science.

Linn, M.C., N.B. Songer, and B.S. Eylon
1996   Shifts and convergences in science learning and instruction. Pp. 438-490 in *Handbook of Educational Psychology*, R.C. Calfee and D.C. Berliner, eds. Riverside, NJ: Macmillan.

Mandinach, E.
1989   Model-building and the use of computer simulation of dynamic systems. *Journal of Educational Computing Research* 5(2):221-243.

Mandinach, E., M. Thorpe, and C. Lahart
1988   *The Impact of the Systems Thinking Approach on Teaching and Learning Activities.* Princeton, NJ: Educational Testing Service.

McDonald, J.P., and P. Naso
1986   Teacher as Learner: The Impact of Technology. Unpublished paper, Educational Technology Center, Harvard Graduate School of Education. May.

Means, B., E. Coleman, A. Klewis, E. Quellamlz, C. Marder, and K. Valdes.
1997   *GLOBE Year 2 Evaluation.* Menlo Park, CA: SRI International.

Means, B., T. Middleton, A. Lewis, E. Quellmaiz, and K. Valdes
1996   *GLOBE Year 1 Evaluation.* Menlo Park, CA: SRI International.

Means, B., and K. Olson
1995a   Technology's role in student-centered classrooms. In *New Directions for Research on Teaching*, H. Walberg and H. Waxman, eds. Berkeley, CA: McCutchan.

1995b   *Technology's Role in Education Reform: Findings from a National Study of Innovating Schools.* Menlo Park, CA: SRI International.

Means, B., K. Olson, and R. Singh
1995   Beyond the classroom: Restructuring schools with technology. *Phi Delta Kappan* (September):69-72.

Merrill, D.C., B.J. Reiser, M. Ranney, and J.G. Trafton
1992   Effective tutoring techniques: A comparison of human tutors and intelligent tutoring systems. *Journal of the Learning Sciences* 2(3):277-305.

Mestre, J.P., W.J. Gerace, R.J. Dufresne, and W.J. Leonard
1997   Promoting active learning in large classes using a classroom communication system. Pp. 1019-1036 in *The Changing Role of Physics Departments in Modern Universities: Proceedings of the International Conference on Undergraduate Physics Education.* Woodbury, NY: American Institute of Physics.

Miller, A.I.
1986   *Imagery in Scientific Thought.* Cambridge, MA: MIT Press.

Mintz, R.
1993   Computerized simulation as an inquiry tool. *School Science and Mathematics* 93(2):76-80.

Nemirovsky, R., C. Tierney, and T. Wright
1995   Body Motion and Graphing. Paper presented at the 1995 Annual Conference of the American Educational Research Association, San Francisco, California. April.

Neumann, E.K., and P. Horwitz
1997   Linking Models to Data: Hypermodels for Science Education. Association for the Advancement of Computing in Education. Available: http://copernicus.bbn.com/genscope/neumann/link_paper/link.html

O'Neill, D.K., R. Wagner, and L.M. Gomez
1996   Online Mentors: Experiments in Science Class. *Educational Leadership* 54(3):39-42.

O'Neill, K.
1996   Telementoring: One researcher's perspective. The newsletter of the BBN National School Network Project, #12. Electronic document. April.

Paolucci, M., D. Suthers, and A. Weiner
1996   Automated advice-giving strategies for scientific inquiry. In *Intelligent Tutoring Systems: Lecture Notes in Computer Science* #1086:372-381, C. Frasson, G. Gauthier, and A. Lesgold, eds. Berlin: Springer-Verlag.

Pea, R.D.
1985   Beyond amplification: Using computers to reorganize human mental functioning. *Educational Psychologist* 20:167-182.

1993a   Distributed multimedia learning environments: The Collaborative Visualization Project. *Communications of the ACM* 36(5):60-63.

1993b   Learning scientific concepts through material and social activities: Conversational analysis meets conceptual change. *Educational Psychologist* 28(3):265-277.

Pea, R.D., L.M. Gomez, D.C. Edelson, B.J. Fishman, D.N. Gordin, and D.K. O'Neill
1997   Science education as a driver of cyberspace technology development. Pp. 189-220 in *Internet Links for Science Education: Student-Scientist Partnerships*, K.C. Cohen, ed. New York: Plenum.

Pea, R.D., and D.M. Kurland
1987   Cognitive technologies for writing development. Pp. 71-120 in *Review of Research in Education, Vol. 14*. Washington, DC: AERA Press.

Pellegrino, J.W., D. Hickey, A. Heath, K. Rewey, N.J. Vye, and the Cognition and Technology Group at Vanderbilt
1991   Assessing the Outcome of an Innovative Instructional Program: The 1990-91 Implementation of the "Adventures of Jasper Woodbury." Technology Report No. 91-1. Nashville, TN: Vanderbilt Learning Technology Center.

Pollak, H.
1986   The School Mathematics Curriculum: Raising National Expectations: Summary of a Conference. November 7-8, 1986. Paper presented at the conference on the School Mathematics Curriculum, University of California, Los Angeles.

President's Committee on Advisors on Science and Technology
1997   *Report to the President on the use of technology to strengthen K-12 education in the United States*. Washington, DC: U.S. Government Printing Office.

Resnick, L.B.
1987   *Education and Learning to Think*. Committee on Mathematics, Science, and Technology Education, Commission on Behavioral and Social Sciences and Education, National Research Council. Washington, DC: National Academy Press. Available: http://www.nap.edu.

Riel, M.
1992   A functional analysis of educational telecomputing: A case study of Learning Circles. *Interactive Learning Environments* 2(1):15-29.

Riel, M.M., and J.A. Levin
1990   Building global communities: Success and failture in computer networking. *Instructional Science* 19:145-169.

Risko, V.J., and C.K. Kinzer
1998   *Multimedia cases in reading education*. Boston, MA: McGraw-Hill.

Roberts, N., and T. Barclay
1988   Teaching model building to high school students: Theory and reality. *Journal of Computers in Mathematics and Science Teaching* (Fall)13-24.

Roschelle, J., and J. Kaput
1996   Educational software architecture and systemic impact: The promise of component software. *Journal of Educational Computing Research* 14(3):217-228.

Rubin, A.
1992   *The Alaska QUILL Network: Fostering a Teacher Community Through Telecommunication*. Hillsdale, NJ: Erlbaum.

Ruopp, R., S. Gal, B. Drayton, and M. Pfister
1993   *LabNet: Toward a Community of Practice*. Hillsdale, NJ: Erlbaum.

Scardamalia, M., and C. Bereiter

1991   Higher levels of agency for children in knowledge-building: A challenge for the design of new knowledge media. *Journal of the Learning Sciences* 1:37-68.

1993   Technologies for knowledge-building discourse. *Communications of the ACM* 36(5):37-41.

Scardamalia, M., C. Bereiter, and M. Lamon

1994   The SCILE Project: Trying to bring the classroom into World 3. Pp. 201-228 in *Classroom Lessons: Integrating Cognitive Theory and Classroom Practice*, K. McGilly, ed. Cambridge, MA: MIT Press.

Scardamalia, M., C. Bereiter, R.S. McLean, J. Swallow, and E. Woodruff

1989   Computer-supported intentional learning environments. *Journal of Educational Computing Research* 5(1):51-68.

Schlager, M.S., and P.K. Schank

1997   TAPPED IN: A new on-line teacher community concept for the next generation of Internet technology. Proceedings of CSCL '97, The Second International Conference on Computer Support for Collaborative Learning, Toronto, Canada.

Schofield, J.

1995   *Computers and Classroom Culture*. Cambridge, UK: Cambridge University Press.

Schwartz, D.L., X. Lin, S. Brophy, and J.D. Bransford

1999   Toward the development of flexibly adaptive instructional designs. Pp. 183-213 in *Instructional Design Theories and Models: Volume II,* C.M. Reigelut, ed. Hillsdale, NJ: Erlbaum.

Schwartz, J.L.

1994   The role of research in reforming mathematics education: A different approach. In *Mathematical Thinking and Problem Solving*, A.H. Schoenfeld, ed. Hillsdale, NJ: Erlbaum.

Skovsmose, O.

1985   Mathematical education versus critical education. *Educational Studies in Mathematics* 16:337-354.

Songer, N.B.

1993   Learning science with a child-focused resource: A case study of kids as global scientists. Pp. 935-940 in *Proceedings of the Fifteenth Annual Meeting of the Cognitive Science Society*. Hillsdale, NJ: Erlbaum.

Steed, M.

1992   STELLA, a simulation construction kit: Cognitive process and educational implications. *Journal of Computers in Mathematics and Science Teaching* 11:39-52.

Suppes, P., and M. Morningstar

1968   Computer-assisted instruction. *Science* 166:343-350.

Suthers, D., A. Weiner, J. Connelly, and M. Paolucci

1995   Belvedere: Engaging students in critical discussion of science and public policy issues. II-Ed 95, the 7th World Conference on Artificial Intelligence in Education, Washington, DC, August 16-19.

Thornton, R.K., and D.R. Sokoloff
  1998   Assessing student learning of Newton's laws: The force and motion conceptual evaluation and the evaluation of active learning laboratory and lecture curricula. *American Journal of Physics* 64:338-352.
Tinker, B., and B. Berenfeld
  1993   A Global Lab Story: A Moment of Glory in San Antonio. *Hands On!* 16(3)(Fall).
  1994   Patterns of US Global Lab Adaptations. *Hands On!* Available: http://hou.lbl.gov
University of California Regents
  1997   Hands-On Universe. Available: http://hou.lbl.gov/
University of Illinois, Urbana-Champaign (UIUC)
  1997   University of Illinois WW2010: The WeatherWorld2010 Project. Available: http://ww2010.atmos.uiuc.edu
U.S. Congress, Office of Technology Assessment
  1995   *Teachers and Technology: Making the Connection.* OTA-EHR-6i16. April. Washington, DC: U.S. Government Printing Office. Available: ftp://gandalf.isu.edu/pub/ota/teachers.tech/
U.S. Department of Education
  1994   National Assessment of Educational Progress (NAEP), 1994 Long-Term Assessment. Office of Educational Research and Improvement, U.S. Department of Education, Washington, D.C.
Vosniadou, N.J., E. DeCorte, R. Glaser, and H. Mandl, eds.
  1996   *International Perspectives on the Design of Technology-supported Learning Environments.* Mahwah, NJ: Erlbaum.
Vye, N.J., D.L. Schwartz, J.D. Bransford, B.J. Barron, L. Zech, and Cognition and Technology Group at Vanderbilt
  1998   SMART environments that support monitoring, reflection, and revision. In *Metacognition in Educational Theory and Practice*, D. Hacker, J. Dunlosky, and A. Graesser, eds. Mahwah, NJ: Erlbaum.
Wagner, R.
  1996   Expeditions to Mount Everest. In *Tales from the Electronic Frontier: First-Hand Experiences of Teachers and Students Using the Internet in K-12 Math and Science*, R.W.M. Shinohara and A. Sussman, eds. San Francisco: WestEd.
Watts, E.
  1985   How Teachers Learn: Teachers' Views on Professional Development. Paper presented at the annual meeting of the American Educational Research Association, Chicago. April.
Wertheimer, R.
  1990   The geometry proof tutor: An "intelligent" computer-based tutor in the classroom. *Mathematics Teacher* 83:308-317.
White, B.Y.
  1993   ThinkerTools: Causal models, conceptual change, and science education. *Cognition and Instruction* 10(1):1-100.
White, B.Y., and J.R. Fredericksen
  1994   Using assessment to foster a classroom research community. *Educator* Fall:19-24.

1998   Inquiry, modeling, and metacognition: Making science accessible to all students. *Cognition and Instruction* 16(1):3-118.

CHAPTER 11

Elmore, R.F.
1995   Getting to Scale with Successful Education Practices: Four Principles and Some Recommended Actions. Paper commissioned by the Office of Reform Assistance and Dissemination, U.S. Department of Education.

Elmore, R.F., Consortium for Policy Research in Education, and D. Burney
1996   Staff Development and Instructional Improvement Community District 2, New York City. Paper prepared for the National Commission on Teaching and America's Future.

Evans, J. St. B. T.
1989   *Bias in Human Reasoning*. Hillsdale, NJ: Erlbaum.

Goldman, A.I.
1994   Argument and social epistemology. *Journal of Philosophy* 91:27-49.

Habermas, J.
1990   *Moral Consciousness and Communicative Action*. Cambridge, MA: MIT Press.

Hendrickson, G., and W.H. Schroeder
1941   Transfer of training in learning to hit a submerged target. *Journal of Education Psychology* 32:205-213.

Judd, C.H.
1908   The relation of special training to general intelligence. *Education Review* 36:28-42.

Kobayashi, Y.
1994   Conceptual acquisition and change through social interaction. *Human Development* 37:233-241.

Kuhn, D.
1991   *The Skills of Argument*. Cambridge, England: Cambridge University Press.

Lin, X.D., and J. Lehman
1999   Supporting learning of variable control in a computer-based biology environment: Effects of prompting college students to reflect on their own thinking. *Journal of Research in Science Teaching*.

Moshman, D.
1995a   Reasoning as self-constrained thinking. *Human Development* 38:53-64.
1995b   The construction of moral rationality. *Human Development* 38:265-281.

National Research Council
1999   *Improving Student Learning: A Strategic Plan for Education Research and Its Utilization*. Committee on Feasibility Study for a Strategic Education Research Program. Washington, DC: National Academy Press.

Newstead, S.E., and J. St. B.T. Evans, eds.
1995   *Perspectives on Thinking and Reasoning: Essays in Honour of Peter Wason*. Hillsdale, NJ: Erlbaum.

Pea, R.D.
  1999   New media communication forums for improving education research and practice. In *Issues in Education Research: Problems and Possibilities*, E.C. Lagemann and L.S. Shulman, eds. San Francisco: Jossey Bass.
Salmon, M.H., and C.M. Zeitz
  1995   Analyzing conversational reasoning. *Informal Logic* 17:1-23.
Stokes, D.E.
  1997   *Pasteur's Quadrant: Basic Science and Technological Innovation.* Washington, DC: Brookings Institution Press.
Vye, N.J.., S.R. Goldman, C. Hmelo, J.F. Voss, S. Williams, and Cognition and Technology Group at Vanderbilt
  1998   Complex mathematical problem solving by individuals and dyads. *Cognition and Instruction* 15(4).
Youniss, J., and W. Damon.
  1992   Social construction in Piaget's theory. Pp. 267-286 in *Piaget's Theory: Prospects and Possibilities*, H. Berlin and P.B. Pufal, eds. Hillsdale, NJ: Erlbaum.

Biographical Sketches of Committees' Members and Staff

COMMITTEE ON DEVELOPMENTS IN THE SCIENCE OF LEARNING

JOHN D. BRANSFORD (*Cochair*) is Centennial professor of psychology and codirector of the Learning Technology Center at George Peabody College, Vanderbilt University. He is also a senior research scientist at the University's John F. Kennedy Center and senior fellow at the Institute of Public Policy Studies. His research has focused primarily on the nature of thinking and learning and their facilitation, with special emphasis on the importance of using technology to enhance learning. His projects have included the videodisc-based Jasper Woodbury Jasper Problem Solving Series, the Little Planet Literacy Series, and other projects that involve uses of technology to enhance thinking and learning in literature, science, history, and other areas. Bransford serves on the editorial board of several journals and has written numerous books and articles in the fields of psychology and education. He is a member of the National Academy of Education. He received a Ph.D. in cognitive psychology from the University of Minnesota.

ANN L. BROWN (*Cochair*) was the Evelyn Lois Corey Chair at the University of California, Berkeley. She had long-term interests in learning and understanding in children at risk for academic failure and is presently focusing her research on students as researchers and teachers within a wider community of learners. She received many honors and awards in both the United States and England for distinguished contributions to educational research, including a Guggenheim Fellowship, a Spencer Senior Fellowship, the Lifetime Achievement Award from the American Educational Research Association, the 1995 American Psychological Association Distinguished Scientific Award for the Applications of Psychology, and the 1997 American Psychological Society James McKeen Catell Fellow Award for Distinguished Service to

Applied Psychology. She was a member of the National Academy of Education and has served as president of the American Educational Research Association. She has been published widely on such topics as memory strategies, reading comprehension, analogical thinking, and metacognition. She received both her B.A. and Ph.D. in psychology at the University of London, England.

JOHN R. ANDERSON is a professor of psychology and computer science at Carnegie Mellon University. His current research involves the acquisition of cognitive skills and the understanding of how human cognition is adapted to the information processing demands of the environment. He has developed the ACT-R production system and applied it to various domains of memory, problem solving, and visual information processing. He has published widely on human associative memory, language, memory, cognition, and the adaptive character of thought. He received a Ph.D. from Stanford University.

RODNEY R. COCKING is a senior program officer at the National Research Council and director of the Board on Behavioral, Cognitive, and Sensory Sciences. He was previously a social science analyst in the Office of Special Populations at the National Institute of Mental Health. His research focuses on cognition and cross-cultural issues in memory and learning and the higher order cognitive processes of planful behavior. He is cofounder and coeditor, with Irving E. Sigel, of the *Journal of Applied Developmental Psychology*. Cocking is a fellow of the American Psychological Association (developmental psychology). He received a Ph.D. in developmental psychology and cognition from Cornell University.

ROCHEL GELMAN is a professor of psychology at the University of California, Los Angeles. She has been a fellow at the Center for Advanced Study in the Behavioral Sciences and associate dean in the University of Pennsylvania graduate office of the faculty of arts and sciences. She serves on the editorial boards of several journals and has published widely on learning, from theory to classroom applications. She has been a Guggenheim Fellow, an American Psychological Association (APA) William James Fellow, and a recipient of the APA award for distinguished scientific contribution. She has also served on the National Research Council's U.S. National Committee for the International Union of Psychological Science, Committee on Basic Research in the Behavioral and Social Sciences, and Board on Behavioral, Cognitive, and Sensory Sciences. She received a Ph.D. from the University of California, Los Angeles.

HERBERT P. GINSBURG is the Jacob H. Schiff foundation professor of psychology and education at Teachers College, Columbia University. His work focuses on the intellectual development and education of young children, particularly poor and minority children. He has conducted research on the development of mathematical thinking and cognition in children, examining the implications for instruction and assessment in early education. His many publications include *The Development of Mathematical Thinking* (1983), *Piaget's Theory of Intellectual Development* (1988), *Children's Arithmetic* (1989), *Entering the Child's Mind: The Clinical Interview in Psychological Research and Practice* (1997), and *The Teacher's Guide to Flexible Interviewing in the Classroom* (1998). Dr. Ginsburg currently serves on the National Research Council's Committee on Early Childhood Pedagogy and on the Committee on Strategic Education Research Program Feasibility Study. He has a Ph.D. in developmental psychology from the University of North Carolina, Chapel Hill, and has taught at Cornell University, the University of Maryland, and the University of Rochester.

ROBERT GLASER is a Distinguished University professor and the founder of the Learning Research and Development Center at the University of Pittsburgh. He is a member of the James S. McDonnell Foundation's Advisory Panel of Cognitive Studies for Educational Practice and is currently serving as a cochair of the National Research Council's Committee on the Foundations of Assessment. Other National Research Council service includes: Committee on Science Education Standards and Assessment and the Committee on Research in Mathematics, Science, and Technology Education. He is also the editor of the series *Advances in Instructional Psychology*. He received his Ph.D. in psychological measurement and learning theory from Indiana University.

WILLIAM T. GREENOUGH is Swanlund and Center for Advanced Study professor of psychology, psychiatry, and cell and structural biology in the Beckman Institute at the University of Illinois at Urbana-Champaign. He is currently director of the University's interdisciplinary neuroscience Ph.D. program. He is a member of the National Academy of Sciences. He received a Ph.D. from the University of California, Los Angeles.

GLORIA LADSON-BILLINGS is a professor in the Department of Curriculum and Instruction at the University of Wisconsin-Madison and a senior fellow for urban education at the Annenberg Institute for School Reform at Brown University. Her research interests concern the relationship between culture and schooling, particularly successful teaching and learning for African American students. Her publications include both books and numerous journal articles and book chapters. She is currently the editor of the Teaching, Learning, and Human Development section of the *American Educational*

Research Journal. She received a Ph.D. in curriculum and teacher education from Stanford University.

BARBARA M. MEANS is vice president of the Policy Division of SRI International. Her research activities at SRI have focused on the impact of technology on classroom teaching and learning. She directs the evaluation research component of the Global Learning and Observations to Benefit the Environment (GLOBE) program and Silicon Valley Challenge 2000, a public-private partnership to reform schools and promote student learning through active use of multimedia technology. She is also coprincipal investigator of the National Science Foundation-funded Center for Innovative Learning Technologies. Her earlier work included the National Study of Technology and Education Reform. Means has been a visiting researcher at the Rockefeller University Laboratory of Comparative Human Cognition. She received a Ph.D. in educational psychology from the University of California, Berkeley.

JOSÉ P. MESTRE is a professor of physics and astronmy in the University of Massachusetts, Amherst. His research interests include cognitive studies of problem solving in physics with a focus on the acquisition and use of knowledge by experts and novices. Most recently, his work has focused on applying research findings to the design of instructional strategies that promote active learning in large physics classes and on developing physics curricula that promote conceptual development through problem solving. He has served as a member of the National Research Council's Mathematical Sciences Education Board; the College Board's Sciences Advisory Committee, SAT Committee, and Council on Academic Affairs; the Educational Testing Service's Visiting Committee; the American Association of Physics Teacher's Research in Physics Education Committee and of the editorial board of *The Physics Teacher*; and the Federal Coordinating Council for Science, Engineering and Technology's Expert Panel. He earned a Ph.D. in physics from the University of Massachusetts, Amherst.

LINDA NATHAN is the headmaster of newly formed Boston Public School-Boston Arts Academy for the Visual and Performing Arts. Formerly, she served as a codirector and teacher at the Fenway Middle College High School in Boston, Massachusetts, a school recognized for its innovative curriculum that stresses academic preparation and its nationally recognized school-to-career program. She began teaching in Boston as a bilingual mathematics and theater teacher and helped found Boston's first performing arts school. She also cofounded the Center for Collaborative Education and is a senior associate of that organization. Her research interests include new conceptions of curriculum assessment. She received an M.A. in theater arts from Emerson College and an Ed.D. in education from Harvard University.

ROY D. PEA is director of the Center for Technology in Learning at SRI International, in Menlo Park, California, and consulting professor in the School of Education at Stanford University. He also directs the multi-institutional Center for Innovative Learning Technologies, which aims to create a national knowledge network for catalyzing best practices and new designs for improving learning with technologies among researchers, schools, and industries.. Previously, he was a John Evans professor of education and the learning sciences at Northwestern University, where he founded and chaired the learning sciences Ph.D. program and served as dean of the School of Education and Social Policy. He works as a cognitive scientist to integrate theory, research, and the design of effective learning environments using advanced technologies, with particular focus on science, mathematics, and technology. He has been a fellow of the Center for Advanced Study in the Behavioral Sciences and is a fellow of the American Psychological Society. He received his doctorate in developmental psychology from the University of Oxford, England, where he was a Rhodes Scholar.

PENELOPE L. PETERSON is John Evans professor of education and dean of the School of Education and Social Policy at Northwestern University. Previously, she served as University Distinguished professor of education at Michigan State University and Sears-Bascom professor of education at the University of Wisconsin, Madison. She is a past president of the American Educational Research Association. Her recent books focus on classroom structure and school organization. She received a Ph.D. degree in psychological studies in education from Stanford University.

BARBARA ROGOFF is currently UCSC Foundation professor of psychology and professor of education at the University of California, Santa Cruz. She has been a professor at the University of Utah, Osher Fellow of the Exploratorium in San Francisco, a fellow of the Center for Advanced Study in the Behavioral Sciences, a Kellogg Fellow, and a Spencer Fellow. She is editor of *Human Development* and received the Scribner Award from the American Educational Research Association for her book *Apprenticeship in Thinking* (1990, Oxford). She is a fellow of the American Psychological Society, the American Anthropological Association, and the American Psychological Association. She received a Ph.D. in developmental psychology from Harvard University.

THOMAS A. ROMBERG is the Sears Roebuck Foundation-Bascom professor of education at the University of Wisconsin, Madison, and he directs the National Center for Improving Student Learning and Achievement in Mathematics and Science for the U.S. Department of Education. He is an editorial reviewer for many education and cognition journals and has written extensively on cognitive aspects of learning, assessment, and evaluation. His National Research Council service has included membership in the Mathematical Sciences Education Board and the steering committee for the National Summit on Mathematics Assessment. He received his Ph.D. in mathematics education from Stanford University.

SAMUEL S. WINEBURG is an associate professor of educational psychology and adjunct associate professor of history at the University of Washington. He has been a Spencer Foundation Predoctoral Fellow and a National Academy of Education Spencer Fellow. His publications cover the psychology of learning and teaching history, contextualized thinking in history, historical problem solving, and models of wisdom in the teaching of history. His most recent research is on the nature of expertise in historical interpretation. He received a Ph.D. in educational psychology from Stanford University.

COMMITTEE ON LEARNING RESEARCH AND EDUCATIONAL PRACTICE

JOHN D. BRANSFORD (*Cochair*) is Centennial professor of psychology and codirector of the Learning Technology Center at George Peabody College, Vanderbilt University. He is also a senior research scientist at the University's John F. Kennedy Center and senior fellow at the Institute of Public Policy Studies. His research has focused primarily on the nature of thinking and learning and their facilitation, with special emphasis on the importance of using technology to enhance learning. His projects have included the videodisc-based Jasper Woodbury Jasper Problem Solving Series, the Little Planet Literacy Series, and other projects that involve uses of technology to enhance thinking and learning in literature, science, history, and other areas. Bransford serves on the editorial board of several journals and has written numerous books and articles in the fields of psychology and education. He is a member of the National Academy of Education. He received a Ph.D. in cognitive psychology from the University of Minnesota.

JAMES W. PELLEGRINO (*Cochair*) is the Frank W. Mayborn professor of cognitive studies at the Peabody College of Education and Human Development at Vanderbilt University. His research focuses on the application of cognitive research and technology to instructional problems on human cognition and cognitive development. Dr. Pellegrino currently serves on the National Research Council's Committee on Foundations of Educational and Psychological Assessment. He has been a faculty member at the University of Pittsburgh and at the University of California, Santa Barbara. He has a B.A. in psychology from Colgate University and M.A. and Ph.D. degrees from the University of Colorado, both in experimental, quantitative psychology.

DAVID BERLINER is professor of educational leadership and policy studies, professor of curriculum and instruction, and professor of psychology in education at Arizona State University. His recent research has focused on the study of teaching, teacher education, and education policy. His publications include *Putting Research to Work in Your Schools* (1993, with U. Casanova) and *A Future for Teacher Education* (1996). Dr. Berliner currently serves on the National Research Council's Board on Testing and Assessment. Among his many awards are the research into practice award of the American Educational Research Association, and the Distinguished Service Award of the National Association of Secondary School Principals. He has served as president of the American Psychology Association's division of educational psychology and the American Educational Research Association. He has a Ph.D. in educational psychology from Stanford University and has taught at California State University at San Jose, the University of Massachusetts, and the University of Arizona.

MYRNA S. COONEY is a teacher with over 35 years of classroom experience. She currently teaches grades 6 and 7 at the Taft Middle School in Cedar Rapids, Iowa, and serves on curriculum committees for language arts and social studies. She has previously taught grades 4, 5, and 6 at Cleveland Elementary School in Cedar Rapids. Ms. Cooney has a B.A. in education from Coe College and an M.A. in education from the University of Iowa. She has been an instructor in a teacher-in-service program at the University of Iowa and a teacher-in-residence at Vanderbilt University.

M. SUZANNE DONOVAN (*Study Director*) is a senior program officer at the National Research Council's Commission on Behavioral and Social Sciences and Education and study director for the Committee on Minority Representation in Special Education. Her interests span issues of education and public policy. She has a Ph.D. from the University of California, Berkeley, School of Public Policy and was previously on the faculty of Columbia University's School of Public and International Affairs.

ARTHUR EISENKRAFT is the science coordinatory (grades 6-12) and physics teacher in the Bedford Public Schools in Bedford, New York. He has taught high school physics in a variety of schools for 24 years. Dr. Eisenkraft is currently on the Interstate New Teacher Assessment and Support Consortium Science Standards Drafting Committee, and on the National Research Council's Advisory Panel to the Center for Science, Mathematics and Engineering Education. He is the editor and project manager of the National

Science Foundation-supported Active Physics Curriculum Project of the American Institute of Physics and the American Association of Physics Teachers. His many publications include a lab text on laser applications, an audiotape history of the discovery of nuclear fission, middle school and high school curriculum materials, and numerous audiovisual productions. He holds a U.S. patent for a laser vision testing system. Dr. Eisenkraft serves on several science award committees and has served as executive director for the International Physics Olympiad. He has a Ph.D. in science education from New York University and received the Presidential Award for Excellence in Science Teaching in 1986.

HERBERT P. GINSBURG is the Jacob H. Schiff foundation professor of psychology and education at Teachers College, Columbia University. His work focuses on the intellectual development and education of young children, particularly poor and minority children. He has conducted research on the development of mathematical thinking and cognition in children, examining the implications for instruction and assessment in early education. His many publications include *The Development of Mathematical Thinking* (1983), *Piaget's Theory of Intellectual Development* (1988), *Children's Arithmetic* (1989), *Entering the Child's Mind: The Clinical Interview in Psychological Research and Practice* (1997), and *The Teacher's Guide to Flexible Interviewing in the Classroom* (1998). Dr. Ginsburg currently serves on the National Research Council's Committee on Early Childhood Pedagogy and on the Committee on Strategic Education Research Program Feasibility Study. He has a Ph.D. in developmental psychology from the University of North Carolina, Chapel Hill, and has taught at Cornell University, the University of Maryland, and the University of Rochester.

PAUL D. GOREN is the director of Child and Youth Development, Program on Human and Community Development, at the John D. and Catherine T. MacArthur Foundation. Previously, he was the executive director of policy and strategic services for the Minneapolis Public Schools and spent two years teaching middle school history and mathematics. He also worked as the director of the Education Policy Studies Division of the National Governors' Association, and as the coordinator of planning and research for the Stanford Teacher Education Program. He has a Ph.D. from the Stanford University School of Education (1991) and an M.P.A. from the Lyndon B. Johnson School of Public Affairs at the University of Texas (1984).

JOSÉ P. MESTRE is a professor of physics and astronmy in the University of Massachusetts, Amherst. His research interests include cognitive studies of problem solving in physics with a focus on the acquisition and use of knowledge by experts and novices. Most recently, his work has focused on applying research findings to the design of instructional strategies that promote active learning in large physics classes and on developing physics curricula that promote conceptual development through problem solving. He has served as a member of the National Research Council's Mathematical Sciences Education Board; the College Board's Sciences Advisory Committee, SAT Committee, and Council on Academic Affairs; the Educational Testing Service's Visiting Committee; the American Association of Physics Teacher's Research in Physics Education Committee and of the editorial board of *The Physics Teacher*; and the Federal Coordinating Council for Science, Engineering and Technology's Expert Panel. He earned a Ph.D. in physics from the University of Massachusetts, Amherst.

ANNEMARIE SULLIVAN PALINCSAR holds a chair in the University of Michigan's School of Education, where she prepares teachers, teacher educators, and researchers to work in heterogeneous classrooms. She has conducted extensive research on peer collaboration in problem-solving activity, instruction to promote self-regulation, the development of literacy among learners with special needs, and the use of literacy across the school day. She is an editor of the books, *Strategic Teaching and Learning* and *Teaching Reading as Thinking*. Her cognition and instruction article on reciprocal teaching (co-authored with Ann Brown in 1984) is a classic. Dr. Palincsar currently serves on the National Research Council's Committee on the Prevention of Reading Difficulties in Young Children. She received an early contribution award from the American Psychological Association in 1988 and one from the American Educational Research Association in 1991. In 1992 she was elected a fellow by the International Academy for Research in Learning Disabilities. She has M.A. and Ph.D. degrees in special education from the University of Illinois at Urbana-Champaign.

ROY D. PEA is director of the Center for Technology in Learning at SRI International, in Menlo Park, California, and consulting professor in the School of Education at Stanford University. He also directs the multi-institutional Center for Innovative Learning Technologies, which aims to create a national knowledge network for catalyzing best practices and new designs for improving learning with technologies among researchers, schools, and industries.. Previously, he was a John Evans professor of education and the learning sciences at Northwestern University, where he founded and chaired the learning sciences Ph.D. program and served as dean of the School of Education and Social Policy. He works as a cognitive scientist to integrate theory, research, and the design of effective learning environments using advanced technologies, with particular focus on science, mathematics, and technology. He has been a fellow of the Center for Advanced Study in the Behavioral Sciences and is a fellow of the American Psychological Society. He received his doctorate in developmental psychology from the University of Oxford, England, where he was a Rhodes Scholar.

Acknowledgments

A good deal of the excitement surrounding the project that resulted in the original version of this volume was due to people's seeing the relevance of basic science to education. In light of that connection, the committee held a workshop in fall 1996—"The Science of Science Learning"—to broaden its understanding of the influences that cognitive science has had on science and mathematics learning and teaching. We benefited greatly from the stimulating papers and discussions that grew out of that meeting, as have others who since have used the model of the workshop. We extend our thanks especially to the following people who presented papers and led discussions during the workshop: Susan Carey, Department of Psychology, New York University; Orville L. Chapman, Department of Chemistry, University of California, Los Angeles; Kevin Dunbar, Psychology Department, McGill University; Jill H. Larkin, Department of Psychology, Carnegie-Mellon University; Kevin Miller, Beckman Institute, University of Illinois; Edward F. Redish, Department of Physics and Astronomy, University of Maryland; Leona Schauble, Department of Educational Psychology, University of Wisconsin, Madison; Lee S. Shulman, Stanford University School of Education; Herbert A. Simon, Department of Psychology, Carnegie-Mellon University; and Philip Uri Treisman, Dana Center for Mathematics and Science Education, University of Texas, Austin.

Individually and collectively, members of the Committee on Developments in the Science of Learning had discussions with experts on many issues and topics. We wish to acknowledge especially the people who offered suggestions for ways to expand or otherwise improve our collective thinking. In particular, we appreciate the assistance that Ann Rosebery and Beth Warren, both at TERC, Cambridge, MA, provided on issues of science learning and teaching. Catherine A. Brown, Associate Dean for Research and Development at Indiana University's School of Education, was helpful in sharpening the discussion on mathematics learning and teaching. We also had helpful assistance from Robbie Case, Institute of Child Study, University of Toronto, on issues of children's thinking and from Robert Siegler, Department of Psychology, Carnegie-Mellon University, on children's strategies for learning. Our work on teacher learning and professional development benefited from suggestions provided by Allan Feldman, School of Education, University of Massachusetts.

Although the project was an intellectually exciting undertaking for the committee, we were also mindful of the important role of our sponsor. The Office of Educational Research and Improvement (OERI) of the U.S. Department of Education established the committee's charge to review the nation's investment in research and the challenge of determining how that investment can pay high returns. We thank Joseph Conaty, Judith Segal, and C. Kent McGuire for the support they provided to this committee in their individual and official capacities.

Finally, there are several NRC staff and others who made significant contributions to the work of the Committee on Developments in the Science of Learning. Alexandra Wigdor, director of the Division of Education, Labor, and Human Performance of the NRC's Commission on Behavioral and Social Sciences and Education (CBASSE), provided the initial impetus for the project and nurtured it in many different ways that were indispensable to its completion. Eugenia Grohman, associate director for reports of CBASSE, patiently worked with us through several drafts of the volume and significantly improved the text. Key support in facilitating our work came from Jane Phillips, senior project assistant in CBASSE, with assistance from Neale Baxter; Susan M. Coke, division administrative associate; Faapio Poe, administrative assistant, Vanderbilt University; and Carol Cannon, administrative assistant, University of California, Berkeley. All of these "behind the scenes" people played critical roles, and to each of them we are very grateful.

Alexandra Wigdor also was the inspiration for the project that resulted in *How People Learn: Bridging Research and Practice.* Her leadership in guiding the formation and work of the Committee on Learning Research and Educational Practice was central to its success. The vision of focusing the efforts of the research community on classroom practice is that of C. Kent McGuire, assistant secretary for educational research and improvement at the U.S. Department of Education. Rodney Cocking, study director of the Committee on Developments in the Science of Learning, provided support for the efforts of the Committee on Learning Research and Educational Practice. Wendell Grant, project assistant, worked long hours managing the logistics of the latter committee's meetings and events and providing the administrative support for production of the committee's report and its drafts. Christine McShane improved that report with her skilled editing. We also thank Carolyn Stalcup for design support and Sandra Yurchak for secretarial support.

The Committee on Learning Research and Educational Practice held a conference in December 1998 to present the original version of *How People Learn* to an audience of educators, policy makers, and researchers and to elicit their feedback on the promise of, and obstacles to, bridging educational research and practice. The NRC and the OERI cosponsored the conference, and the participation of Bruce Alberts, NRC chair, and C. Kent McGuire, assistant secretary for OERI, contributed to its success. Joseph Conaty and Luna Levinson of OERI assisted with conference planning. Karen Fuson, committee member Annemarie Palincsar, and Robert Bain demonstrated approaches to teaching that use the principles highlighted in this volume. Members of the two panels provided insightful perspectives on the challenge of bridging research and classroom practice. On the panel providing teacher perspectives were David Berliner, Deanna Burney, Janice Jackson, Jean Krusi, Lucy (Mahon) West, and Robert Morse. On the panel providing policy perspectives were Ron Cowell, Louis Gomez, Paul Goren, Jack Jennings, Kerri Mazzoni, and Carol Stewart.

The committee also held a workshop to focus more sharply on the research that would help construct the bridge between research and practice. The workshop was an intensive 2-day effort to work in both large and small groups to cover the areas of research discussed in this volume. We thank each of the participants who joined the committee in this effort: Amy Alvarado, Karen Bachofer, Robert Bain, Cathy Cerveny, Cathy Colglazier, Rodney Cocking, Ron Cowell, Jean Krusi, Luna Levinson, Robert Morse, Barbara Scott Nelson, Iris Rotberg, Leona Schauble, Carol Stewart, and Lucy West.

Both the original version of *How People Learn: Brain, Mind, Experiences, and School* and *How People Learn: Bridging Research and Practice* were reviewed by individuals chosen for their diverse perspectives and technical expertise, in accordance with procedures approved by the Report Review Committee of the National Research Council (NRC). The purpose of this independent review is to provide candid and critical comments that will assist the authors and the NRC in making the published report as sound as possible and to ensure that the report meets institutional standards for objectivity, evidence, and responsiveness to the study charge. The content of the review comments and draft manuscript remain confidential to protect the integrity of the deliberative process.

We wish to thank the following individuals, who are neither officials nor employees of the NRC, for their participation in the review of the original *How People Learn*: Kenji Hakuta, School of Education, Stanford University; Donald Kennedy, Institute for International Studies, Stanford University; R. Duncan Luce, Institute for Mathematical Behavioral Science, University of California, Irvine; Michael Martinez, Department of Education, University of California, Irvine; Kevin Miller, Department of Psychology, University of Illinois; Michael I. Posner, Department of Psychology, University of Oregon; Leona Schauble, School of Education, University of Wisconsin, Madison; Herbert A. Simon, Department of Psychology, Carnegie Mellon University; Patrick Suppes, Professor of Philosophy (emeritus), Stanford University; and Richard F. Thompson, Neurosciences Program, University of Southern California.

We thank the following individuals for their participation in the review of *How People Learn: Bridging Research and Practice:* Dorothy Fowler, Lacey Instructional Center, Annandale, VA; Ramesh Gangolli, Department of Mathematics, University of Washington; Richard Lehrer, Department of Educational Psychology, University of Wisconsin-Madison; Michael Martinez, Education Department, University of California, Irvine; K. Ann Renninger, Program in Education, Swarthmore College; Thomas A. Romberg, National Center for Research in Mathematical Sciences Education, University of Wisconsin-Madison; and Patrick Suppes, Center for the Study of Language and Information, Stanford University.

Although the individuals listed above provided constructive comments and suggestions, it must be emphasized that responsibility for the final content of this volume rests entirely with the authoring committees and the institution.

John D. Bransford, James Pellegrino,
Rod Cocking, and Suzanne Donovan